W9-CKM-216

Gods, Goddesses, and Mythology

VOLUME 11

Index

Marshall Cavendish
New York • London • Singapore

Marshall Cavendish
99 White Plains Road
Tarrytown, New York 10591

www.marshallcavendish.us

Library of Congress Cataloging-in-Publication Data

Gods, goddesses, and mythology/editor, C. Scott Littleton.
      p. cm.
   Includes bibliographical references and index.
   ISBN 0-7614-7559-1 (set : alk. paper)
1. Mythology--Encyclopedias. I. Littleton, C. Scott. II. Marshall
Cavendish Corporation. III. Title.

   BL312.G64 2005
   201'.3'03--dc22

2004040758

ISBN 0-7614-7559-1 (set)
ISBN 0-7614-7570-2 (vol. 11)

Printed and bound in China

09 08 07 06 05   6 5 4 3 2

General Editor
C. Scott Littleton, Occidental College, Los Angeles

Marshall Cavendish
Project Editor: Marian Armstrong
Editorial Director: Paul Bernabeo
Production Manager: Alan Tsai

Brown Reference Group
Project Editor: Chris King
Editor: Tom Webber
Designer: Steve Wilson
Picture Researcher: Helen Simm
Cartographer: Mark Walker
Indexer: Kay Ollerenshaw
Managing Editor: Tim Cooke

CONTENTS

Pronunciation Guide   1444

Major Pantheons   1447

   Aztecs   1447

   Celts   1448

   China   1448

   Egypt   1449

   Greece   1450

   Inca   1457

   India   1457

   Ireland   1459

   Maya   1459

   Mesopotamia   1460

   Rome   1461

   Scandinavia   1462

Glossary   1466

Further Reading   1478

Internet Resources   1487

Resources for Younger Readers   1490

Indexes   1494

   Index of Deities and Mythological   1494
     Beings

   Index of Art and Culture   1514

   Index of Places   1524

   Index of Peoples and Society   1529

   Index of History and Legend   1536

   Index of Worship and Ritual   1537

Comprehensive Index   1541

PRONUNCIATION GUIDE

Using the Pronunciation Guide

A syllable rendered in large capital letters indicates that the syllable should be stressed. Where two syllables are stressed in a single word, large capital letters indicate where the main emphasis should fall, while small capital letters indicate the position of the secondary emphasis.

CENTRAL AMERICA

Chac Mool	chahc MOL
Coatlicue	coh-ah-TLEE-coo-eh
Hunab-ku	hoo-NAHB-koo
Itzamna	eat-zam-NAH
Ixchel	eesh-CHEL
Kukulkan	KOO-KOOL-kan
Quetzalcoatl	ket-SAL-ko-AH-tul
Tlaloc	tlah-LOK
Xib Chac	SHEEB CHAHC
Yum Kaax	Yum KOSH

EGYPT

Anubis	a-NOO-bis
Atum	AH-toom
Geb	GEB
Hapi	HAH-pee
Hathor	HAH-thor
Horus	HOR-us
Isis	EYE-sis
Maat	MAHT
Nepthys	NEP-this
Nut	NOOT
Osiris	o-SIGH-ris
Ptah	FAH
Re	RAY
Sekhmet	SEK-met
Sphinx	SFINKS
Thoth	THOTH
Wadjet	WAHD-jet

GREECE AND ROME

Achelous	AK-e-LOW-us
Achilles	a-KIL-eez
Actaeon	ak-TEE-on
Adonis	a-DON-nis
Aegir	A-jeer
Aeneas	ee-NEE-ass
Agamemnon	ag-uh-MEM-non
Ajax	AY-jaks
Alcestis	al-SES-tis
Andromeda	AN-DROM-eh-da
Anemoi	a-NEE-moy
Antigone	an-TIG-o-nee
Aphrodite	af-ro-DIE-tee
Apollo	a-POL-o
Arachne	a-RAK-nee
Ares	AIR-eez
Ariadne	ar-i-AD-nee
Artemis	AHR-te-mis
Asclepius	as-KLEP-ee-us
Astarte	as-TAR-tay
Atalanta	at-a-LAN-tuh
Ate	AY-tee
Athena	a-THEE-na
Atlas	AT-las
Atreus	AY-tree-us
Attis	AT-is
Bacchus	BAK-us
Bellerophon	bell-AIR-o-fon
Britomartis	brit-O-mar-tis
Cadmus	KAD-mus
Callisto	ka-LIS-toe
Calypso	ka-LIP-so
Cassandra	ka-SAN-dra
Castor	KAS-ter
Circe	SIR-see
Clytemnestra	kly-tem-NES-tra
Cronus	KRO-nus
Cupid	KEW-pid
Cyclops	SI-klops
Daedalus	DED-a-lus
Danae	DAY-nigh

Daphne	DAF-nee	Memnon	MEM-non
Demeter	dem-MEE-ter	Menelaus	MEN-ay-lay-us
Deucalion	dew-KAY-lee-on	Mercury	MUR-cure-ee
Diana	die-AN-a	Midas	MY-das
Diomedes	die-oh-MEE-deez	Minerva	min-ER-ver
Dionysus	die-oh-NIGH-sus	Minos	MY-nos
Dis	DIS	Mnemosyne	nem-OS-i-nee
Dryads	DRY-adz	Momos	MO-mus
Electra	ee-LEK-tra	Morpheus	MOR-fee-us
Endymion	en-DIM-ay-on	Muses	MYOU-ses
Eos	EE-os	Myrmidons	MUR-me-donz
Erichthonius	er-IK-tho-nee-us	Myrrha	MER-ra
Eros	EER-os	Narcissus	nar-SIS-us
Europa	you-RO-pa	Nemesis	NEM-e-sis
Faunus	FAW-nus	Neptune	NEP-tune
Gaia	GUY-er	Nereus	NER-ee-ous
Galatea	gal-a-TEE-a	Nestor	NES-tor
Ganymede	GAN-ee-meed	Nike	NY-kee
Hades	HAY-deez	Nyx	NIKS
Hebe	HEE-bee	Oceanus	o-SEE-a-nus
Hecate	HEK-a-tee	Odysseus	o-DISS-ee-us
Hecuba	HEK-u-ba	Oedipus	E-di-pus
Helios	HE-lee-os	Orestes	o-RES-teez
Hephaestus	hef-EYE-stus	Orion	o-RI-on
Hera	HER-a	Orpheus	OR-fee-us
Heracles	HER-a-kleez	Paeon	PEE-on
Hermaphroditus	her-maf-ro-DI-tus	Pan	PAN
Hermes	HUR-meez	Pandora	pan-DOOR-uh
Hero	HE-ro	Paris	PA-ris
Hesperides	hes-PER-e-deez	Pasiphae	pa-SIF-aye
Hestia	HES-ti-a	Patroclus	pah-TROW-klus
Hippolyte	hip-POL-i-tee	Peleus	PE-lee-us
Hippolytus	hip-POL-i-tus	Pelops	PEE-lops
Hypnos	HIP-nos	Penates	pe-NAY-teez
Icarus	IK-a-rus	Penelope	pen-EL-o-pee
Idomeneus	i-DOM-en-ay-us	Persephone	pur-SEF-o-nee
Iphigeneia	IF-i-jay-NEE-uh	Perseus	PUR-see-us
Janus	JAY-nus	Phaethon	FAY-thon
Jason	JAY-son	Philoctetes	fil-ok-TEE-teez
Juno	JOO-no	Phobos	FO-bos
Jupiter	JOO-pi-ter	Pleiades	PLEE-uh-deez
Laocoon	lay-O-koon	Plutus	PLOO-tus
Laomedon	lay-O-may-don	Pollux	POL-luks
Lares	LAIR-eez	Pomona	po-MO-na
Leda	LEE-da	Poseidon	po-SY-don
Leto	LEE-tow	Priam	PRY-am
Lycaon	lie-KAY-on	Priapus	PRY-a-pus
Maenads	may-NADS	Prometheus	pro-MEE-thee-us
Medea	me-DEE-a	Proteus	PRO-tee-us

Psyche	SY-kee			
Pygmalion	pig-MAY-lee-on			
Remus	REE-mus			
Rhea Silvia	REE-uh sil-VEE-uh			
Romulus	ROM-you-lus			
Satyrs	SAY-ters			
Selene	sel-EE-nee			
Sibyl	SIB-il			
Silenus	si-LEE-nus			
Sisyphus	SIS-e-fuss			
Tantalus	TAN-ter-lus			
Tiresias	tie-REE-see-us			
Theseus	THEE-see-us			
Thetis	THEE-tis			
Tithonus	ti-THO-nus			
Triton	TRY-ton			
Troilus	TROY-lus			
Tyche	TY-kee			
Typhon	TY-fon			
Uranus	YOOR-un-us			
Venus	VEE-nus			
Vesta	VES-ta			
Zeus	ZOOS			

MESOPOTAMIA

An	AN
Baal	BAL
Dumuzi	DOO-moo-zee
Enki	EN-kee
Enlil	EN-lil
Gilgamesh	GIL-GUH-mesh
Inanna	eye-NAN-nuh
Ishtar	ISH-tar
Marduk	MAHR-dook
Ninurta	nin-ER-tuh
Tiamat	TY-uh-mat

SCANDINAVIA

Aegir	AY-jeer
Aesir	AY-zir
Alfar	AL-far
Balder	BALL-der
Bergelmir	BARE-ghel-mere
Bor	BORE
Búri	BOO-ree
Frey	FRAY
Freya	FRAY-UH
Frigga	FRIG-UH
Gefjon	GEF-yon
Gerd	GERD
Heimdall	HIME-dal
Hel	HEL
Hermód	her-MUD
Kvasir	KVAH-seer
Loki	LOW-kee
Nibelungs	NIGH-bel-lungz
Njörd	NYORD
Norns	NAWNS
Odin	O-din
Sigurd	ZEE-gurt
Thor	THAWR
Thrym	THRIM
Valkyries	val-KUH-reez
Vanir	VAH-neer
Ymir	EE-mur

MAJOR PANTHEONS

Reader's Guide

It is very difficult to produce a definitive family tree for the gods and goddesses of any ancient culture. In most cases the deities concerned were worshiped over a prolonged period of time and across a wide geographical area. Beliefs changed over time and varied from place to place. Thus, ancient Egyptians who worshiped a particular god in Memphis in 2500 BCE may have believed him to be the son of a different pair of deities from those assigned to him by worshipers in Thebes 1,000 years later. The following descriptions and family trees use the most widely accepted genealogies.

AZTECS

Chalchiuhtlicue: "She of the Jade Skirt"; goddess of springs, rivers, lakes, and the sea.

Coatlicue: mother of Huitzilopochtli, Coyolxauhqui, and 400 other male deities. She was associated with both birth and death and was commonly depicted with a skirt of snakes.

Coyolxauhqui: earth and moon goddess with great and often dangerous magical power. Warrior sister of Huitzilopochtli.

Huehueteotl: "Old Deity"; god of fire. At the end of each Aztec century (52 years) people were sacrificed so that he would bless the relationship between humans and gods.

Huitzilopochtli: god of war, the sun, and storms; represented as a hummingbird. His birth has similarities with that of the Greek goddess of war, Athena.

Metztli: formerly Tecciztecatl; goddess of the moon, farmers, and the night.

Mictlantecuhtli: god of the underworld; represented as a skeleton or a figure with a skull instead of a head. He was associated with the spider, the owl, and the bat.

Mixcoatl: god of the hunt and war and lord of the North Star. He made the first fire by revolving the heavens around its axis.

Ometeotl: supreme being, creator of the gods, and god of fire; also known as Tonacatecuhtli and Tonacacihuatl.

Popocatépetl: god of sacred mountains. Originally a young Aztec warrior, he was turned into a mountain after he died from grief at the death of his lover, the Aztec princess Iztaccíhuatl.

Quetzalcoatl: one of the chief Aztec deities; god of wisdom, learning, writing, and books, as well as the symbol of death and resurrection. He was represented as a feathered serpent.

Tezcatlipoca: god of the night, beauty, and war. Often characterized as the most powerful deity, he tested people's morality by tempting them to evil. His major emblem was an obsidian mirror.

Tlaloc: god of rain, agriculture, and fire who was the consort of Chalchiuhtlicue. Children were drowned in his honor.

Tonatiuh: sun god, formerly Nanauatzin. His emblem was a solar disk, often worn on the back of the priests who impersonated him during rituals.

Xipetotec: god of agriculture, the seasons, and especially crop seeds. He skinned himself each year, representing maize losing its leaves, to provide food for humans.

Xiuhtecuhtli: fire god who was the personification of light, warmth, life, and hope. He was usually depicted with either a red or yellow face.

Xochipilli: god of music, dance, and flowers; comparable to the Greek deity of wine, Dionysus.

MAJOR PANTHEONS

CELTS

Belenus: god of brightness and the sun, sometimes identified with the Roman Apollo. Belenus was associated with the Celtic festival of Beltane, celebrated at the beginning of May.

Boann: fertility goddess associated with the Boyne River, Ireland. Boann's symbol was the white cow.

Cernunnos: god of fertility, animals, hunting, and the underworld. Cernunnos was depicted as a man with the antlers of a stag. The Celts believed that he was born on the summer solstice and died on the winter solstice.

Dana: also Danu; spirit of the Danube.

Epona: goddess associated with fertility and horses. She accompanied the soul on its final journey to the underworld. Celtic in origin, Epona was later adopted by Roman soldiers.

Esus: agricultural deity worshiped in northwestern France. Esus was associated with a three-headed bull.

Govannon: a smith and metalworker; the Celtic equivalent of the Greek Hephaestus. He accidentally killed his nephew Dylan, a sea deity.

Grannus: god of healing, later associated with the sun. Grannus was sometimes identified with the Roman Apollo.

Lugh: god of the sun, crafts, and travel. Although Lugh was famous for being equally skilled in all crafts, he was especially associated with shoemaking. His festival was Lughnasadh, held at the beginning of fall.

Sabrina: goddess of the Severn River, Wales.

Sequana: goddess of the Seine River, France.

Sucellus: Gaulish god usually depicted with a hammer. Either a fertility deity or a god of thunder.

Sulis: goddess associated with the healing springs at Bath, England; sometimes identified with the Roman Minerva.

Teutates: a war god, identified with the Roman Mars. Human sacrifices were performed to appease him.

CHINA

Ch'ang O: moon goddess. She took refuge in the moon after she stole a potion of immortality from her husband, Hou-I, the Lord Archer. Ch'ang O was famous for her great beauty.

Ch'eng Huang: protective deities that guarded cities and towns. They provided rain during periods of drought and also guided souls in the afterlife.

Chen Hsu: sixth of the 10 mythical emperors of the Golden Age.

Fu Hsi: first emperor of the Golden Age. He taught humankind how to fish and tame wild animals. He is depicted as a human being with the body of a snake.

Fu Hsing: the Chinese god of happiness. Traditionally depicted in the clothes of a government official, Fu Hsing was believed to have been a human civil servant who was later deified.

Fu Shen: a god of the Fu–Shou–Lu trinity.

Hou-I: the Lord Archer; also known as Shen Yi. When the Earth was threatened by a drought caused by the appearance of 10 suns in the sky, Hou-I shot down nine of them with his bow. He then became god of the one remaining sun.

Huang Ti: fourth mythical emperor of the Golden Age, otherwise known as the Yellow Emperor. Huang Ti is credited with inventing writing and the potter's wheel.

K'u: seventh mythical emperor of the Golden Age.

K'uei Hsing: dwarf god of examinations.

Panku: primordial giant who was born from a cosmic egg. The top of the egg shell formed the heavens, while the bottom formed the earth. As Panku grew, the heavens and the earth were pushed farther and farther apart.

Shao Hao: fifth of the 10 mythical emperors of the Golden Age.

Shen Nong: second of the 10 mythical emperors, depicted with the head of a bull and the body of a man.

He invented the plow and introduced agriculture to humankind.

Shou Hsing: god of longevity, depicted with a high, bald head. In his hand he held the peach of immortality.

Shun: ninth mythical emperor of the Golden Age.

Ta Yü: last emperor of Golden Age; the Tamer of the Flood.

Ts'ai Shen: Taoist god of wealth, who also had the power to ward off thunder and lightning. He was often depicted riding a black tiger.

Tsao Shen: domestic hearth god.

T'u-ti: any of the gods of small places.

Yao: eighth mythical emperor of the Golden Age. Yao's reign was characterized by peace and prosperity.

Yü Ti: the Jade Emperor; supreme Taoist deity. Yü Ti presided over a celestial court that mirrored the government of China. He was usually depicted sitting on a throne wearing the ceremonial clothes of an emperor.

Wang Mu: the Queen Mother of the West; wife of Yü Ti. She was the keeper of the peaches of immortality. Yü Ti and Wang Mu had nine daughters, each of whom lived in one of the nine heavens.

Wen Ti: god of literature. His help was sought by those taking entrance examinations. Wen Ti was believed to be the author of various literary works that had been passed down to humankind.

EGYPT

Amun: sun god and principal deity of Egypt; later known as Re-Amun. He was originally god of wind and ruler of the air. He was father of the moon god Khonsu.

Anubis: escorted the dead to judgment. The son of Seth, Anubis was often depicted as a jackal-headed man. He was also worshiped as an embalmer responsible for preserving the bodies of the dead.

Aten: the sun's disk; worshiped during the reign of Akhenaton (ruled 1379–1362 BCE).

Atum: sun god sometimes said to have created the universe; usually portrayed as a ram-headed man or ram-headed bird. He was considered the father of new pharaohs and played an important part in coronation ceremonies. Among his many forms were an old man, a snake, and a scarab beetle.

Bastet: goddess of music; depicted as a cat or a cat-headed woman. She was originally associated with wild cats such as lions but was later identified with domestic cats. The Greeks projected many of her attributes onto Artemis, their goddess of the hunt.

Bes: god of music, childbirth, and guardian of the bed chamber. He used weapons and musical instruments to keep away evil spirits.

Geb: earth god; husband and brother of Nut and father of Osiris, Isis, Nepthys, and Seth. He was usually depicted with green or black skin and was associated with geese.

Hathor: goddess of love, music, and foreign lands; her alter ego was Sekhmet. In ancient Egypt she was associated with queens; her many forms included a falcon, a cobra, and a lioness.

Horus: the son of Isis and Osiris, Horus was identified with the living king of Egypt. Horus had many forms, but was most commonly depicted as a falcon-headed man.

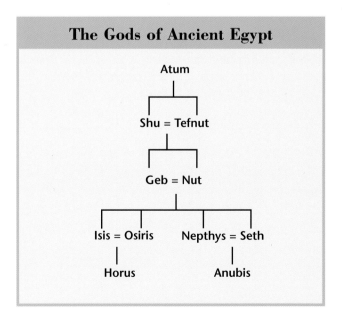

The Gods of Ancient Egypt

Atum

Shu = Tefnut

Geb = Nut

Isis = Osiris   Nepthys = Seth

Horus   Anubis

MAJOR PANTHEONS

Isis: sister and wife of Osiris and mother of Horus. She was the daughter of the earth god Geb and the sky goddess Nut. Her name is said to mean "knowledge."

Khmun: potter god and creator of human souls. He was usually depicted with the head of a ram. Khmun was associated with Heqet, goddess of childbirth and protector of the dead.

Khonsu: moon god and "master of time"; son of Amun and Mut. Greeks later identified him with Thoth, god of wisdom.

Maat: personification of Cosmic Order; sometimes described as the daughter of Re or as one of his eyes. She was invoked by pharaohs who viewed themselves as upholders of universal order.

Min: god of fertility and patron of desert travelers and caravans. Min was celebrated during coronation ceremonies because pharaohs associated him with sexual prowess.

Mut: consort of Amun and patron of the city of Thebes. She was also a sky and mother goddess.

Neith: creator goddess associated with the city of Sais. She emerged from the primeval water and traveled along the Nile to the delta, where she founded the city.

Nekhbet: vulture goddess of Upper Egypt who became the protectress of kings and attended the births of gods and pharaohs. She was also a goddess of childbirth, the sun, and the moon.

Osiris: son of Nut and Geb and the first king of Egypt. He was killed by his brother Seth, but then he was revived by his sister and wife Isis. Osiris symbolized the fertility of the land and its rebirth each year after the Nile flood. He was also a sky god and protector of the dead.

Ptah: god of craftspeople who was closely associated with stoneworking. Ptah was also sometimes believed to be the creator of the universe.

Re: also known as Ra. Sun god who merged with Amun in the New Kingdom. He created himself from the primeval waters or from a primordial lotus flower, which became one of his symbols. He created the sky and moisture from which were born the earth god Geb and the sky goddess Nut.

Sekhmet: lion-headed goddess of violence and plague; consort of Ptah and alter ego of Hathor.

Seth: son of Geb and Nut and murderer of his brother, Osiris. Seth represented chaos and the desert. He was god of war and foreign lands and fought and lost an 80-year battle with Horus. He protected Re's sun-boat during its nightly journey through the underworld.

Taweret: hippopotamus goddess of childbirth. She was often associated with another goddess of childbirth, Bes.

Thoth: Greek name for the Egyptian deity Djeheuty, god of wisdom, history, and writing. He was usually depicted as an ibis-headed man. He was either the son of Re or was born from the head of Seth.

Wadjet: snake goddess of Lower Egypt and protector of the king. She later became associated with fire and heat. Wadjet was also often associated with the vulture goddess Nekhbet.

GREECE

OLYMPIAN DEITIES

Aphrodite: goddess of love and beauty. She was married to the smith god Hephaestus, although she took numerous lovers, including Adonis and Ares.

Apollo: god of prophecy and divination, and patron of music and the arts. Apollo provided humans with laws and a sense of community.

Ares: son of Zeus and Hera; god of war. During battles he rode in a chariot wielding a sword and was accompanied by his sons Phobos and Deimos.

Artemis: virgin goddess of hunting and protector of the wilderness and unmarried women. She was also worshiped as the goddess of childbirth. Her parents were Zeus and Leto.

Athena: goddess of wisdom, crafts, and war. She taught mortals to use the plow and invented the trumpet.

Demeter: goddess of corn and cultivation. Hades stole

Partial Family Tree of Ancient Greek Deities

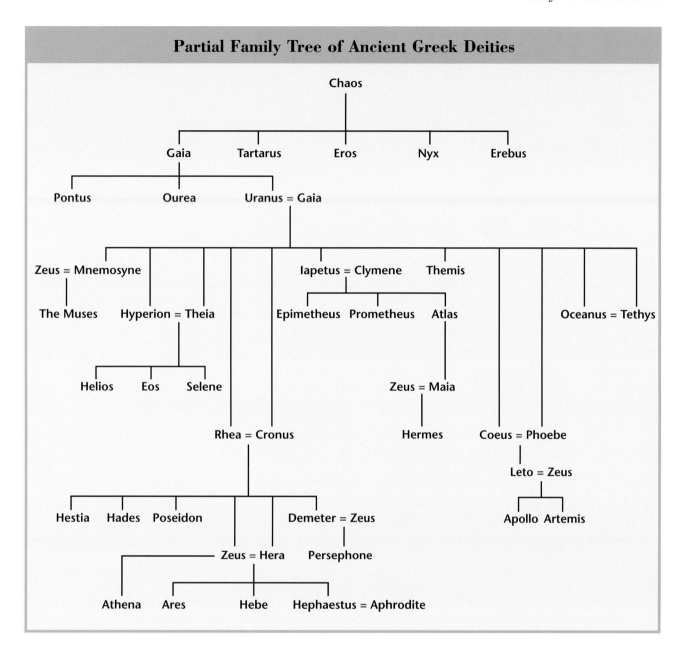

her daughter Persephone and held her in the underworld for four months of the year.

Dionysus: son of Zeus and Semele; he was the god of wine, vegetation, and human emotion. He was rescued unborn from the ashes of his incinerated mother and was sewn into Zeus's thigh, from which he eventually was born.

Hades: god of the underworld and lord of the dead. Hades was married to Persephone, whom he abducted and tricked into living with him for four months of the year.

Hephaestus: god of fire and metalworking who fashioned armor for the gods. He was born lame and was mocked by

the other gods for his disability. Hephaestus was the husband of Aphrodite.

Hera: queen of the gods and goddess of women and marriage. She was married to Zeus and occupied herself restricting his extramarital exploits.

Hermes: messenger god and god of boundaries. He was one of the youngest gods, and was worshiped by those who had to cross a boundary, such as shepherds and heralds. He escorted the dead to the underworld.

Hestia: virgin goddess of the hearth. Hestia was responsible for maintaining harmony in the home and in cities.

Persephone: goddess of agriculture and the underworld. The daughter of Zeus and Demeter, she was taken to the underworld by her uncle, Hades, and forced to stay there for four months of the year.

Poseidon: god of the sea, known for his fearsome temper. He was capable of creating violent storms. Poseidon was often depicted holding a trident.

Zeus: supreme god of the cosmos and of justice. He was married to Hera, but his sexual appetite was unequalled; he took many lovers and fathered many children.

TITANS

Atlas: uncle to the parents of the human race. He was father of the Pleiades, and the Hyades, and according to some sources, the Hesperides. He is famous for the punishment inflicted upon him by Zeus—to hold the heavens on his shoulders.

Coeus: husband of Phoebe and father of Leto; often associated with intelligence.

Crius: grandfather of the four winds and all the stars. He married Eurybia, and was the father of Astraeus, Pallas, and Perses.

Cronus: youngest of the first generation of Titans. He castrated his father, Uranus, and saved his mother, Gaia, from agony by releasing his brothers and sisters from her womb. Cronus married his sister Rhea, and was the father of the Olympian deities Hestia, Demeter, Hera, Hades, Poseidon, and Zeus.

Helios: god of the sun who brought light to the world by driving his chariot across the sky.

Hyperion: husband and brother of Theia and father of Helios, Selene, and Eos.

Iapetus: father of Atlas, Epimetheus, and Prometheus.

Leto: by Zeus, the mother of Apollo and Artemis. She gave birth to the two deities on the floating island of Delos. She had traveled there to escape the wrath of Zeus's jealous wife, Hera.

Mnemosyne: Titan who was widely associated with the

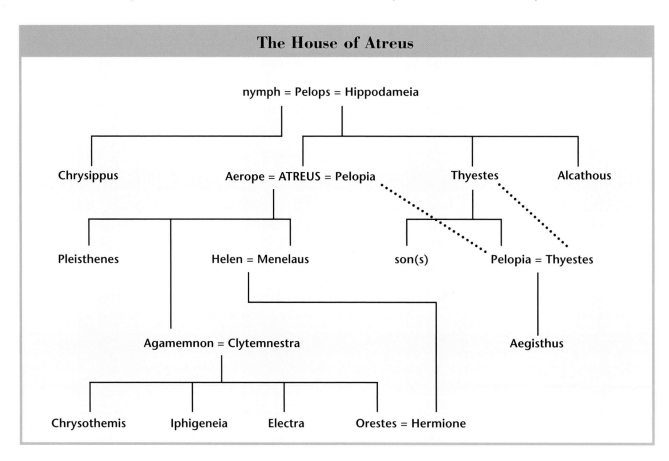

The House of Atreus

power of memory. By Zeus, she was the mother of the Muses, goddesses who provided inspiration to artists.

Oceanus: eldest of the Titans, and god of the river that Greeks believed surrounded the earth. He married his sister Tethys and by her was the father of the Oceanids, three thousand water nymphs.

Phoebe: mother of Leto and Asteria by her brother Coeus. She was the grandmother of Apollo, who took the name Phoebus Apollo in her honor.

Prometheus: either the creator of humankind or its champion. Prometheus stole fire from the gods and gave it to humans. His punishment, inflicted by Zeus, was to endure daily an eagle eating his liver while he was chained to a rock.

Rhea: mother of the Olympian gods Hestia, Demeter, Hera, Hades, Poseidon and Zeus. Rhea married her brother Cronus.

Tethys: Titan who married her brother Oceanus. By him, she was the mother of the Oceanids—the three thousand nymphs of the waters and land.

Theia: mother of Helios, Selene, and Eos. Theia married her brother Hyperion.

Themis: goddess of justice, law, and order. By Zeus, she was the mother of the Horae (seasons) and the three Fates. She presided over the assemblies of the gods.

NYMPHS

Aegle: Naiad who was the mother of the Charites, or Graces, by Helios, the sun god.

Arethusa: one of the Hesperides. She was pursued to Sicily by the river god Alpheus, who was in love with her. Artemis changed Arethusa into a fountain (the Fonte

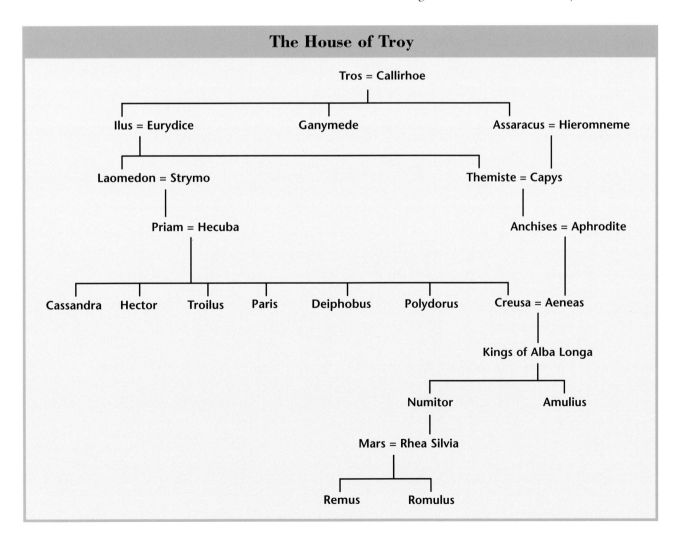

The House of Troy

Tros = Callirhoe

Ilus = Eurydice   Ganymede   Assaracus = Hieromneme

Laomedon = Strymo   Themiste = Capys

Priam = Hecuba   Anchises = Aphrodite

Cassandra   Hector   Troilus   Paris   Deiphobus   Polydorus   Creusa = Aeneas

Kings of Alba Longa

Numitor   Amulius

Mars = Rhea Silvia

Remus   Romulus

Aretusa in Syracuse), but Alpheus went beneath the sea and merged his waters with hers.

Asia: Oceanid for whom the continent of Asia was named. She was sometimes said to be the mother of Prometheus.

Byblis: a granddaughter of Apollo who fell in love with her brother, Caunus. He did not return her feelings, and she wept so much that other nymphs took pity and decided to turn her into a spring.

Callisto: mountain nymph who was raped by Zeus. Hera turned her into a bear when she discovered her husband's infidelity. Callisto's son, Arcas, was ignorant of her identity and nearly hunted her down. However, Zeus took pity on Callisto and transformed her into a constellation called Ursa Major (great bear).

Calypso: daughter of the Oceanid Perse. Her powers of seduction were enough to keep Odysseus on her island and away from his home for seven years.

Chelone: nymph who refused to attend the wedding of Zeus and Hera, and so was turned into a turtle.

Clytie: beautiful water nymph who fell in love with the sun god, Helios. He refused to love her, and so she could only watch him rise and set on the horizon. After years of pining, Clytie sprouted roots and became a sunflower.

Cyrene: huntress and daughter of Creusa and Hypseus, king of Lapith. The god Apollo fell in love with Cyrene when he saw her wrestling a lion.

Daphne: mountain nymph who was pursued by the god Apollo after he had been struck by one of Eros's arrows. Daphne rejected his advances and was transformed into a laurel tree by her father, the river-god Peneius.

Echo: mountain nymph and a servant of Hera. She agreed to Zeus's plea for her to distract Hera, but was discovered and punished. She lost her ability to speak her thoughts and was only able to repeat what others had already said. Unable to articulate her love for the beautiful Narcissus, she pined away until only her voice remained.

Erytheia: one of the Hesperides. She lived in a beautiful garden in which grew the golden apples that Heracles retrieved for his 11th labor.

Eurydice: wife of the singer and musician Orpheus. She died twice, first from a snake bite and later when her husband narrowly failed in his attempt to rescue her from the underworld.

Harmonia: mother by the war god Ares of a race of warrior women called the Amazons.

Hesperides: four Naiads named Aegle, Arethusa, Erytheia, and Hesperia who lived in a garden at the edge of the world. There they guarded the golden apple tree that Gaia had given to Hera.

Lara: Naiad daughter of the river god Almo. She reported to Hera that Zeus loved a nymph named Juturna, and had her tongue torn out as a punishment. She was then sent to Hades. Lara was also the mother of the Lares—twin brothers who guarded crossroads and cities. The Lares were widely worshiped by the Romans.

Liriope: lover of the river god Cephissus and mother of the beautiful but conceited Narcissus.

Melite: water nymph who had a liaison with Heracles and gave birth to Hyllus. Hyllus avenged Heracles' death on his father's old enemy Eurystheus.

Perse: Oceanid who was mother of four famous mythological characters: Calypso, who fell in love with Odysseus and kept him on her island for seven years; Aeetes, a fierce king who set a dragon to guard the Golden Fleece; Circe, who detained Odysseus for a year on her island; and Pasiphae, mother of the monstrous Minotaur.

Pleione: Oceanid who was mother of the seven Pleiades. They were immortalized in the night sky as a cluster of seven stars.

Pomona: Dryad who, despite her efforts to remain chaste, was seduced by Vertumnus, the Roman god of the changing seasons.

Rhode: Oceanid for whom the Greek island of Rhodes was named.

Salmacis: Naiad who fell in love with Hermaphroditus, the son of Aphrodite and Hermes. The gods honored her wish to be with him by fusing the two in one body. The Salmacis spring was named for her.

Syrinx: river nymph who was pursued by the god of shepherds, Pan. The gods took pity on Syrinx and changed her into a reed, but Pan cut the reed into pieces and fashioned pipes from it.

Telesto: Oceanid for whom one of the moons of Jupiter is named.

HEROES OF THE TROJAN WAR

Achilles: Greek champion who was the son of Peleus and the Nereid Thetis. A prophecy told that Troy would not fall without his help. Achilles died at the hands of Trojan prince Paris, whose arrow hit the one part of Achilles's body that was vulnerable—his heel.

Aeneas: son of Aphrodite and a Trojan prince called Anchises. Aeneas was an ally of King Priam and fought bravely against Diomedes and Achilles. His heroics at Troy are described by Homer, while his escape from Troy and founding of the Roman civilization are recorded by Virgil (70–19 BCE) in the *Aeneid*.

Agamemnon: son of Atreus and Aerope and brother of Menelaus. He was king of Mycenae and commander of the Greek army. Agamemnon was a brave and efficient fighter but a poor leader who needed encouragement from his men. He was murdered on his return from the war by his wife Clytemnestra and her lover Aegisthus.

Ajax: son of Telamon, king of Salamis, and Eriboea. He took 12 ships to Troy to honor the oath taken by all Helen's suitors to protect her marriage vows. Ajax was famous for his great size and strength and was considered to be one of the greatest Greek fighters. He dueled with Hector twice and came close to victory on both occasions.

Diomedes: son of Tydeus and Deipyle. In the *Iliad* Homer describes him as one of the greatest Greek warriors who ever fought—he even wounded the war god Ares. Diomedes was one of the soldiers concealed in the wooden horse that the Greeks deceitfully gave to the Trojans.

Hector: leader of the Trojan army and Troy's greatest warrior. Hector's bravery ultimately proved to be his undoing. Advised not to fight Achilles, he did so anyway and was killed.

Menelaus: son of Atreus and Aerope and brother of Agamemnon. He was married to Helen of Sparta, who was considered to be the most beautiful woman in the world. Menelaus fought her abductor, Paris, in a duel and the latter was only saved by the intervention of Aphrodite.

Neoptolemus: son of Achilles who was considered to be a ruthless fighter. He was among the Greek soldiers who hid in the wooden horse. He killed Priam, king of Troy.

Odysseus: king of Ithaca whose great cunning was a key factor in the Greeks' success. The 10-year journey home that he endured after the war was the subject of the *Odyssey* by Homer (c. ninth–eighth century BCE).

Paris: son of Priam and Hecuba. His abduction of Helen, queen of Sparta, was the catalyst for the Trojan War. A great archer, Paris killed Achilles with an arrow that hit the Greek warrior's one weak spot—his heel.

Patroclus: son of Menoetius and the comrade of Achilles. When Achilles refused to fight, Patroclus dressed in his friend's armor and took to the battlefield in his place. Many Trojans died at Patroclus's hands, but he was finally killed by Hector.

Philoctetes: son of Poeas and holder of Heracles' great bow, the arrows of which never missed their target. He killed Paris and returned safely after the war to either Greece or Italy.

OTHER MORTALS

Arachne: daughter of Idmon of Colophon. She was renowned for her talent for weaving, but was turned into a spider after beating the goddess Athena in a contest to see who could weave the best tapestry.

Cassandra: seer daughter of King Priam and Hecuba who was cursed so that no one would believe her prophesies. After the end of the Trojan War she was taken as a concubine by Agamemnon. She was killed by his wife Clytemnestra on the couple's return to Mycenae.

Clytemnestra: daughter of Tyndareos and Leda; sister of Castor, Helen, and Pollux; and wife of Agamemnon. She was angered by Agamemnon's sacrifice of their daughter

Iphigeneia, and jealous of the relationship between Agamemnon and Cassandra. She murdered the lovers when they returned from the Trojan War.

Heracles: the greatest Greek hero. He was the son of Zeus and Alcmene. Heracles was most famous for the 12 labors he was set by Eurystheus as purification for killing his wife, Megara, and their two children. He aided the gods in their successful battle against the Giants, and for his deeds and heroics was immortalized among the gods and had a constellation named for him by Zeus.

Iole: beautiful daughter of Eurytus, king of Oechalia. She was offered in marriage by her father to the winner of an archery contest. It was won by Heracles, but Eurytus did not keep his word. Iole was later taken as a concubine by Heracles. On his death she married Hyllus.

Iphigeneia: daughter of Agamemnon and Clytemnestra and the sister of Electra, Orestes, and Chrysothemis. She was sacrificed by Agamemnon in order to summon a wind that would take the Greek fleet to Troy.

Leda: daughter of the Aetolian king Thestius, and wife of Tyndareos. She was seduced by Zeus in the shape of a swan. Leda subsequently gave birth to two sets of twins—Castor and Pollux, and Helen and Clytemnestra.

Narcissus: beautiful son of the river god Cephissus and the nymph Liriope. Known for his vanity, Narcissus fell in love with his own reflection while gazing into a pool of water.

Niobe: daughter of Tantalus, and wife of Amphion, king of Thebes, by whom she had many children. Niobe's boasts about her fertility angered the goddess Leto, who sent her son Apollo and daughter Artemis to kill Niobe's children. In her grief Niobe was turned into a rock on Mount Sipylus, where water ran down her face like tears.

Oedipus: son of Laius, king of Thebes, and Jocasta. He unwittingly killed his father and married his mother. By Jocasta he had four children: Antigone, Eteocles, Ismene, and Polyneices.

Orestes: son of Agamemnon and Clytemnestra, and the brother of Electra, Iphigeneia, and Chrysothemis. Orestes killed his mother and her lover, Aegisthus, after they murdered Agamemnon. Orestes was then pursued by the Furies, who wanted to punish him. However, he was saved by the intervention of Apollo.

Orpheus: the most gifted singer and musician in the Greek world, he outsang the sirens while traveling with the Argonauts. Orpheus visited the underworld in a failed attempt to retrieve his dead wife, Eurydice. He then wandered the land mourning her until he was torn to pieces by Thracian women.

Peleus: son of Aeacus, king of Aegina, and Endeis, and brother of Telamon. He was a great warrior and was rewarded with a rare opportunity to marry a goddess, Thetis, by whom he fathered Achilles.

Pelops: son of Tantalus, king of Lydia. He was killed as a child then cooked and served by his father to the gods, who brought him back to life. Pelops eventually became ruler of most of southern Greece. He married Hippodameia, with whom he had many children.

Penelope: daughter of Icarius and the nymph Periboea; wife of Odysseus and mother of Telemachus. For 10 years Penelope waited patiently for Odysseus to return from the Trojan War.

Perseus: son of Zeus and Danae. He killed the Gorgon, Medusa; rescued Andromeda from a sea monster; and founded the city of Mycenae. He and Andromeda married and had a son, Perses.

Psyche: lover of Cupid. With Zeus's permission they were married and Psyche became immortal.

Semele: daughter of Cadmus and Harmonia, and by Zeus the mother of Dionysus. Semele demanded that Zeus appear to her in all his splendor, which he did, burning her to death. Zeus snatched her unborn baby and sewed it into his thigh, from which Dionysus was born.

Sisyphus: wily son of Aeolus, king of Thessaly, and Enarete. He founded Ephyra, which was later called Corinth. He cheated death twice, and when he finally died of old age he was condemned in the underworld to perpetually roll a boulder up a hill only for it to roll back down again.

Tantalus: father of Pelops, Broteas, and Niobe. He was punished by the gods for serving them the flesh of his son,

Pelops. His sentence was to stand in water that disappeared when he was thirsty, and within arm's reach of plentiful fruit that moved away from each of his hungry lunges.

Theseus: son of either Poseidon or Aegeus, king of Athens, and Aethra. By the Amazon Antiope, he fathered Hippolytus; later he married Phaedra. Theseus accomplished many heroic deeds, including slaying the Minotaur, a monster with the body of a man and the head of a bull. Theseus was eventually killed by Lycomedes, king of Scyros.

Tyndareos: king of Sparta, husband of Leda, and the father of Castor, Clytemnestra, Pollux, and Helen. On the advice of Odysseus, Tyndareos proposed an oath be taken by Helen's many suitors that bound them to protect her choice of husband. The oath led to the Trojan War.

INCA

Apocatequil: god of lightning; also the name for the chief priest of the Inca moon god.

Chasca: goddess of dawn and dusk and the planet Venus. Chasca was the protector of virgins and the servant of the sun.

Chasca Coyllur: god of flowers and protector of maidens. It was also a name for the planet Venus.

Cochamama: goddess of the sea, protector of mariners and fishers. She was the wife of Viracocha and the mother of Inti.

Cocomama: goddess of health, prosperity, and happiness. She was represented as the coco plant, the intoxicating effects of which were ascribed to her power.

Copacati: goddess associated with Lake Titicaca.

Illapa: god of weather, especially thunder, lightning, and rainstorms. He was often depicted as a man in shining clothes, or carrying a club and rocks.

Inti: god of the sun and father of the first Inca emperor, Manco Capac. He was the son of creator god Viracocha. Inca emperors were believed to be incarnations of Inti.

Kilyamama: goddess of the moon who was the daughter of Viracocha, wife of Inti, and mother of Manco Capac. She oversaw marriages and the calendar.

Manco Capac: god of fire, forefather of the Incas, and the brother of Pachacamac.

Pachacamac: creator god and god of the earth. His consort was Pachamama and his brothers were Viracocha and Manco Capac. His human creations were beset by problems and were turned into rocks and islands by his half-bother Vichama.

Pachamama: goddess of the earth and overseer of harvests. She was the mother and consort of Pachacamac. Pachamama was sometimes depicted as a dragon.

Saramama: goddess of maize who was represented as an ear of maize or as a doll.

Supay: god of the underworld and the name for evil spirits.

Urcaguary: god of underground treasures who had a snake's body and a deer's head.

Vichama: god of death and the son of Inti. His mother was murdered by his half-brother Pachacamac, so he turned humans created by Pachacamac into rocks and islands. Vichama hatched three eggs from which was born a new human race.

Viracocha: creator of the world with aspects of a storm and sun god. Father, by Cochamama, of Inti. Viracocha appeared on Earth in the form of a bearded man dressed in a long tunic.

Yakumama: goddess of the rivers and streams who nourished the Earth with water.

INDIA

Aditi: mother goddess and personification of the earth and sky. Aditi was the mother of the Adityas, the 12 gods of the sun.

Agni: fire deity and messenger of the gods. One of the

three main gods of the Rig Veda, Agni cleansed human beings from sin after death. He is usually depicted with two heads and seven tongues.

Brahma: creator god; part of the supreme trinity with Siva and Vishnu. Brahma was believed to have been born either from a cosmic egg or from the navel of Vishnu. Brahma is usually depicted with four heads.

Ganesa: god of wisdom and literature, depicted with the head of an elephant and the body of a man. Ganesa is also associated with the rat, on which he rides. Prayers are made to Ganesa at the beginning of any important undertaking.

Ganga: the personification of the Ganges River, usually depicted as a beautiful woman with the tail of a fish. The Ganges River is sacred to Hindus, who believe that its waters can wash away their sins.

Hanuman: monkey god and patron of learning. Hanuman was the son of the wind god Vayu, from whom he inherited the ability to fly. Hanuman was an ally of the hero Rama. In the epic poem the *Ramayana*, Hanuman helps Rama in his battles against the demon king Ravana.

Indra: god of storms and war and the king of the gods in the Rig Veda. Indra slayed the serpent Vritra, which had swallowed the cosmic waters, by splitting its stomach open with a thunderbolt.

Kali: goddess of death and destruction. A malevolent aspect of Devi, the wife of Siva, Kali is depicted with four arms; one carries a bloody sword, while another holds aloft a severed head. Around her neck hangs a necklace of skulls.

Krishna: divine hero who was the eighth avatar, or earthly incarnation, of the god Vishnu. In the epic poem the *Mahabharata*, Krinshna takes part in a war between two rival families, the Pandavas and the Kuravas.

Lakshmi: goddess of wealth, good fortune, and agriculture. She was associated with the lotus, a sacred aquatic flower with white petals. She was the wife of Vishnu and symbolized his creative energy.

Mithra: god personifying social order, and the twin brother of Varuna. Mithra was later adopted by the Persians. His worship then spread to the Roman empire, where he became known as Mithras.

Parvati: a consort of Siva associated with the Himalaya mountains. She was mother of both the elephant god Ganesa and the warrior Karttikeya.

Rama: divine hero and one incarnation of the god Vishnu. Rama is the hero of the epic poem the *Ramayana*. The work tells the story of Rama's battle against Ravana, the demon king of Sri Lanka.

Ravana: the 10-headed demon king of Sri Lanka. In the epic poem the *Ramayana*, Ravana kidnaps Sita, the wife of the hero Rama. Rama eventually rescues his wife and kills Ravana.

Siva: part of supreme trinity with Brahma and Vishnu. Siva embodied the forces of destruction, although he was also associated with fertility and regeneration. He is depicted as a naked man with a third eye in the center of his forehead and a necklace of skulls.

Soma: god of the moon and personification of the drug Soma. The Vedic gods drank the intoxicating beverage in order to preserve their immortality.

Surya: the embodiment of the sun. Like his Greek counterpart Helios, he rode through the sky in a chariot drawn by horses. The chariot was driven by his wife Aruna, goddess of the dawn.

Varuna: a pre-Vedic deity who, like his brother Mithra, was associated with cosmic order. Varuna was the god of the cosmic waters and was depicted as a man in golden armor riding a sea monster.

Vayu: god of winds, often linked with the sky god Indra. He was often accompanied by storm demons. Vayu was also the father of the monkey god Hanuman.

Vishnu: part of supreme trinity with Brahma and Siva. While Brahma and Siva were the creator and destroyer of the universe, respectively, Vishnu was its preserver. Vishnu descended to earth in a number of avatars, or incarnations. The most famous were Krishna and Rama. Hindus believe that the 10th avatar of Vishnu has yet to appear on Earth.

Yama: god of the dead and guardian of hell. Yama acted as the judge of the dead and the punisher of human sins. Yama was armed with a noose and a club and was depicted sitting on a buffalo.

IRELAND

Bresal: king of the Fomorians. He battled with the Tuatha de Danann but lost; his life was spared because he was a skilled teacher of agriculture.

Brigid: daughter of Eochaid, wife of Bresal, and protectress of fairs at Carman and Tailtiu. She was patroness of poetry, healing, and smith work.

Cathbad: Conchobar's druid; sometimes also credited as his father. He was known for his powers of divination and prophecy.

Conchobar: legendary king and warrior of Ulster; son of Nessa. He possessed a magical shield that shrieked to warn him of danger.

Cú Chulainn: leading hero of the Ulster cycle. He was renowned for his sexual prowess, as a great warrior, and for his invulnerability to magic.

Dian Cécht: god of healing and physician of the gods. He blessed a well named Slane in which wounded warriors bathed so that they could return to battle.

Eochaid: chief god who possessed a club that killed with one end and resurrected with the other. He was a warrior, magician, and craftsman.

Fedelm: the daughter of Conchobar; called "lawgiver." She was a beautiful prophetess and a great warrior.

Fergus: hero, king, and messenger between Connacht and Ulster. He was associated with sexual prowess.

Fionn: warrior son of Cumhall, hero of the Fenian cycle and leader of the Fianna. He was known for his wisdom, honesty, and generosity.

Macha: goddess of Ulster and of war who fed on the heads of her dead enemies. She had the ability to assume the form of a raven.

Manannan: god of the sea, over which he traveled in a chariot. He was the first king of the Isle of Man.

Medb: daughter of Eochaid, lover of Fergus, and goddess of Connacht. She was known for her sexual promiscuity—she took 30 lovers a day—and for her ability to wreak destruction

Midir: foster father of Oengus; sometimes identified with Eochaid.

Morrigan: goddess associated with war and cattle. She appeared as a crow or raven and hovered over battlefields.

Oengus: god of the sun; son of Eochaid. His many forms included that of a swan with a gold chain around its neck.

MAYA

Ah Ciliz: god of eclipses. Between eclipses he served the sun at a table and during an eclipse he devoured the sun.

Ah Cuxtal: god of childbirth who ensured the safe passage of a baby into the world.

Ah Peku: god of thunder who lived on the tops of mountains; when there was a storm he climbed into the clouds and produced thunder.

Ah Puch: god of death and ruler of the worst part of the underworld. He was represented as an owl-headed man, a skeleton, or a bloated corpse.

Alaghom Naom: mother goddess, and goddess of wisdom, consciousness, education, and the intellect.

Camaxtli: creator god and god of hunting, war, fate, and fire.

Ek Chuah: god of warriors and merchants who was represented as a swarthy man with a scorpion's tail, carrying a bag of merchandise over his shoulder.

Heart of Heaven: creator god formed by the merging of two deities, Kukulkan and Tepeu.

Hunab Ku: chief Mayan deity and creator god who rebuilt the world after a series of floods.

Hunahpu: twin brother of Xbalanque. The two heroes descended to the underworld and defeated its rulers in a ball game. Hunahpu then became a sun god.

Hun Cam: one of the two lords of Xibalba, the Mayan underworld, the other being Vucub Cam. Hun Cam was killed by the hero twins Hunahpu and Xbalanque in revenge for his murder of their father.

Huracan: god of wind, storm, and primeval mists. A manifestation of Heart of Heaven. Huracan unleashed the flood that destroyed the first race of humans. The word *hurricane* is derived from his name.

Itzamna: lord of knowledge, believed to be the founder of Mayan culture. From his teaching Mayans received knowledge of writing, medicine, and the calendar.

Ixchel: earth and moon goddess; goddess of pregnancy and weaving.

Ixtab: goddess of gallows and suicide. She was represented as a woman hanging from a tree by a noose around her neck. Ixtab gathered together those who had committed suicide and led them to heaven.

Kinich Ahau: sun god who took the form of a firebird; occasionally identified with Itzamna.

Kukulkan: supreme god; god of resurrection, reincarnation, and the four elements. The Mayan counterpart of the Aztec god Quetzalcoatl, Kukulkan was usually depicted as a feathered serpent.

Votan: god of the drum; deified hero who became the husband of Ixchel.

Vucub Cam: one of the twin rulers of the underworld, the other being Hun Cam. The pair were killed by the hero twins Hunahpu and Xbalanque. Vucub Cam was often depicted as a macaw.

Xbalanque: twin brother of Hunahpu. The two heroes defeated the gods of the underworld in a ball game and then killed them. Xbalanque then switched genders to become a moon goddess.

Xib Chac: god of rain who was usually represented as part man, part amphibian, and was associated with the frog.

Yum Kaax: god of agriculture and maize who was the personification of beauty.

MESOPOTAMIA

An: Sumerian sky god, known to the Babylonians as Anu. Among his numerous consorts were Ki (the earth) and various manifestations of the mother goddess.

Assur: chief deity of the Assyrians. He was often depicted as a winged sun disk containing a bearded god holding a bow.

Ea: Akkadian deity who was a later form of the Sumerian Enki. Ea was a water god, a creator god, and a god of wisdom and magic.

Enki: Sumerian earth god who was also god of wisdom, arts, crafts, fate, and magic. He was later identified with Ea. Enki created order in the universe and developed key tools for humans, including the plow.

Enlil: god of air, wind, and storms. He was born to the sky god An and the Earth goddess Ki. Enlil possessed the Tablets of Destiny, which gave him power over the universe.

Ereshkigal: Sumerian goddess of death and the underworld; sister of Inanna and wife of Gugulanna. Later Ereshkigal became the consort of Nergal and lost much of her power to him.

Inanna: goddess of love, fertility, and war; consort of Dumuzi, god of fertility. She was sister of Ereshkigal and was the daughter of either the sky god An or the moon god Nanna. She was the personification of the planet Venus, and was sometimes the queen of the sky.

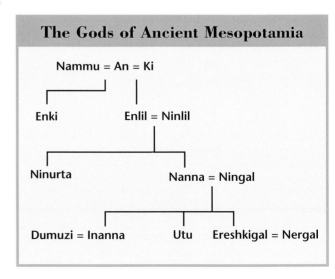

The Gods of Ancient Mesopotamia

Nammu = An = Ki

Enki   Enlil = Ninlil

Ninurta   Nanna = Ningal

Dumuzi = Inanna   Utu   Ereshkigal = Nergal

Ishtar: goddess of love and sexuality; also associated with war. Ishtar was the Babylonian equivalent of the Sumerian goddess Inanna.

Marduk: chief god of Babylon; credited with the organization of the universe. He was originally a god of thunderstorms, but later became a fertility god. Marduk gained his power by slaying the monsters of chaos, Tiamat and Kingu.

Nanna: Sumerian moon god. The son of Enlil and Ninlil; he traveled across the sky in a small boat made of woven twigs and tar, accompanied by the planets.

Nergal: god of the underworld; an evil god associated with war and devastation.

Ninhursaga: one of the many manifestations of the mother goddess. She was goddess of vegetation and fertility and the partner of the supreme god Enki.

Ninlil: Sumerian goddess whose name means "Lady Air"; also known as Ninmah; consort of Enlil and mother of Ninurta and Nanna.

Ninmah: means "great lady" in Sumerian; one of the many manifestations of the mother goddess; also a title given to Ninlil and Ninhursaga.

Ninurta: Sumerian warrior god who was also a god of rain and fertility. He was the son of Enlil and was married to the goddess of healing, Gula.

Shamash: Babylonian sun deity and god of justice; known to the Sumerians as Utu. Shamash was the husband and brother of the goddess of love and fertility, Ishtar. He was a celebrated warrior and god of wisdom.

ROME

Apollo: god of prophecy and patron of the arts who shared his name with his Greek equivalent. He was the guardian of shepherds and the god of healing. He came to be associated with the sun.

Bacchus: god of wine whose Greek equivalent was Dionysus. He was later known to Romans as Liber, the god of vegetation, fertility, theater, and of all wild nature. His worshipers included the satyrs.

Ceres: earth goddess whose Greek equivalent was Demeter. She was patroness of agriculture, especially of fruit and grain. When she shut herself away in grief at the abduction of her daughter Proserpina, the world became barren until Proserpina returned.

Consus: god of grain storage; husband of Ops, goddess of plenty. Because grain was stored in holes underneath the earth, so was Consus's altar. He was later worshiped as god of secret counsels.

Cupid: god of love and the son of Venus; closely identified with Amor. He was the equivalent of the Greek Cupid and was the lover of Psyche. He carried a bow that shot love-inducing arrows.

Cybele: earth goddess and mother of the gods; goddess of fertility and wild nature. Her consort was the god of vegetation, Attis. Cybele was identified with the Greek mother of the gods, Rhea.

Diana: goddess of women and childbirth, hunting, and the moon. She was identified with Artemis and later worshiped by slaves who sought refuge in her temples.

Dis: god of the underworld; another title for Pluto. Dis was the equivalent of the Greek Hades.

Flora: goddess of flowers, fertility, and spring. One myth recounted that she was originally a nymph called Chloris, but was transformed into a goddess when she was kissed by the West Wind, Zephyrus.

Fortuna: goddess of fortune and good luck; she was originally a goddess of fertility and blessing worshiped largely by mothers. Her Greek equivalent was Tyche.

Furiae: the Furies; avenging goddesses who pursued criminals through life and beyond death. They were born from the drops of blood shed on the Earth, Gaia, when Cronus castrated his father Uranus.

Juno: chief goddess whose Greek equivalent was Hera; sister and wife of Jupiter. One of the Capitoline Triad, Juno was goddess of marriage and childbirth. She was the mother of Mars and Minerva.

MAJOR PANTHEONS

Jupiter: chief god, known as Optimus Maximus ("best and greatest"); the equivalent of the Greek Zeus. Originally Jupiter was worshiped as a sky and weather god. He was the husband of Juno and the father of Minerva.

Lares: guardian spirits that protected houses, fields and crossroads. They were usually portrayed as dancing youths carrying drinking cups.

Mars: god of war whose Greek equivalent was Ares. He may originally have been a guardian of crops. He was the father by Rhea Silvia of the twins Romulus and Remus, the founders of Rome.

Mercury: messenger of the gods; god of commerce and guardian of merchants and travelers. He shared many attributes with his Greek equivalent Hermes, except that Mercury was also father by the nymph Lara of the guardian spirits called the Lares.

Minerva: goddess of wisdom, arts and crafts, and war. She was daughter of Jupiter and Juno and one of the Capitoline Triad. Her Greek equivalent was Athena, whose attributes she shared.

Neptune: god of the sea; originally an Italian god of fresh water. He was identified with the Greek god Poseidon. The Romans also worshiped him as Neptune Equester, god and patron of horse racing.

Ops: goddess of plenty; wife of Consus. She was identified with the Greek goddess Rhea and was also said to be the wife and sister of Saturn. She was worshiped with Ceres as the protector of harvests.

Quirinus: god associated with the fruitfulness of the harvest; later identified with the deified Romulus. One of the Roman hills, the Quirinalis, was named for him.

Saturn: god of agriculture who taught humans the benefits of civilization. He was identified with the Greek god Cronus and was the husband of Ops. From his name came the word *Saturday*.

Tellus: ancient earth goddess, later identified with Cybele. Her Greek equivalents were Gaia and Ceres and she was mother of the personification of rumor, Fama.

Venus: goddess of love, beauty, grace, and fertility. She was the equivalent of the Greek goddess Aphrodite and was the daughter of Jupiter. Her lovers included Mars, Vulcan, and Adonis.

Vesta: virgin goddess of the hearth and its fire who was the equivalent of the Greek goddess Hestia. Her cult was at first followed in private homes but became a state cult; vestal virgins maintained a fire in her temple on the Palatine Hill in Rome.

Vulcan: god of fire, especially the destructive fire of volcanoes; invoked to prevent fires. He was the equivalent of the Greek smith god Hephaestus. Vulcan was patron of smiths and craftspeople who worked with fire. He was the father of Caeculus and the fire-breathing monster killed by Hercules, Cacus.

SCANDINAVIA

DEITIES

Balder: son of Odin and Frigga and god of light, beauty, and innocence. Balder was shot dead by a mistletoe dart fired by his brother, Höd. Balder's wife was Nanna, with whom he had a son, Forseti.

Frey: fertility god; beautiful brother of Freya. He was invoked to make a marriage fertile.

Freya: chief goddess of the Ásynjur, or female Aesir; lover of many men. Sister of Frey and daughter of Njörd. Dead warriors were sent to her hall to wait on her and the other Ásynjur.

Frigga: wife of Odin and the mother of Balder and the queen of the Ásynjur. She was goddess of love, fertility, marriage, and motherhood. She had the power of foresight but could not change the future.

Gefjon: one of the goddesses of the Ásynjur who was associated with good fortune, virgins, and the plow. She was either a virgin goddess or the wife of Odin's son Skjöld.

Heimdall: son of nine mothers and watchman of the gods. His senses were so good that he could hear grass grow and see more than than 100 miles (150 km). During Ragnarok he killed Loki but later died from his wounds.

Partial Family Tree of Scandinavian Deities

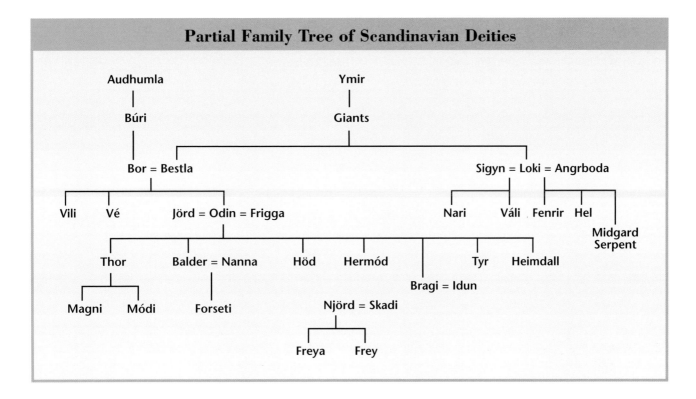

Hel: the underworld and the goddess who ruled it. She was the daughter of Loki and the giantess Angrboda, and the sister of the Midgard Serpent and Fenrir.

Hermód: son of Odin and Frigga and the brother of Balder. Hermód volunteered to travel to Hel to free Balder but returned without him.

Höd: god of darkness and winter; the blind son of Odin and Frigga, Höd killed his brother Balder, for which he was killed in turn by Odin's youngest son, Váli. Höd was destined to return to life after Ragnarok.

Hoenir: one of Odin's companions, he helped to fashion the first humans from ash trees.

Idun: goddess of fertility, youth, and death who belonged to the Ásynjur; custodian of the apples the Aesir ate to stay young. She was married to Bragi.

Lodur: one of Odin's companions who helped to create the first humans from ash trees.

Loki: trickster god and problem solver; father of Fenrir, Hel, and the Midgard Serpent. He was associated with fire and magic, and was a shape-shifter. Loki was indirectly responsible for the death of Balder and was chained to a rock by the rest of the gods as punishment.

Njörd: fertility god who was the father of Frey and Freya and the husband of the giantess Skadi. Njörd was also the god of wind, sea, and fire.

Odin: chief god of the Aesir and son of Bor and Bestla. He was father of humankind and, by the goddess Jörd, father of Thor. By Frigga he fathered Balder, Höd, and Hermód. Odin was god of wisdom and poetry. He had only one eye—he traded the other for a drink from the well of wisdom.

Thor: god of thunder and son of Odin; chief giant-killer. He was married to the fertility goddess Sif. During Ragnarok Thor killed the Midgard Serpent but later died from its poison.

Tyr: member of the Aesir associated with battle; his hand was bitten off by the wolf Fenrir. Tyr was the god of war and justice. During Ragnarok he fought and defeated the guardian hound of the underworld, but later died from wounds he suffered in the battle.

Vé: brother of Odin and Vili and the son of Bor and Bestla. Together with his brothers he created heaven and earth from the dead body of the frost giant Ymir.

Vili: brother of Odin and Vé. He and his two brothers created the world from the dead body of Ymir.

OTHER NORSE FIGURES

Angrboda: giantess who was the mother by Loki of Fenrir, the Midgard Serpent, and Hel. Her children were taken from her when the gods discovered their power.

Ask: the first man, created from an ash tree by Odin and his companions Hoenir and Lodur.

Atli Budlason: powerful legendary leader who was identified with the historical figure Attila the Hun. Atli was the son of Budli.

Audhumla: great primeval cow who licked Búri free from primordial ice and who provided four streams of milk to nourish Ymir, the first giant.

Bergelmir: grandson of the giant Ymir and a giant himself. He escaped a flood caused by the letting of Ymir's blood and re-established the race of giants.

Bestla: giantess who was wife of Bor and mother of Odin, Vili, and Vé.

Brynhild: Valkyrie who was the daughter of Budli and the sister of Atli Budlason. She threw herself onto Sigurd's funeral pyre from love for the dead hero.

Bor: giant who was the son of Búri and father by the giantess Bestla of Odin, Vili, and Ve.

Budli: powerful father of Brynhild and Atli Budlason.

Búri: giant who was licked free from primordial ice by the primeval cow Audhumla. He had a son called Bor and was the grandfather of Odin, Vili, and Vé.

Embla: the first woman, created from an ash tree by Odin and his two companions Hoenir and Lodur.

Fenrir: mighty wolf that bit off the hand of Tyr—the only god who dared to feed him. Fenrir eventually swallowed Odin at Ragnarok. He was the offspring of Loki and the giantess Angrboda.

Gerd: giantess wife of the fertility god Frey who was famous for her great beauty. Gerd was also the personification of fertile soil, and was often considered an earth goddess.

Gjúki: powerful king who was the husband of Grímhild. He was the father of Gunnar, Högni Gjúkason, Gudrún, and Gutthorm.

Grendel: a monster that had the shape of a man but the strength of 30 men. It battled and lost to Beowulf.

Gudrún: daughter of Gjúki and the sister of Gunnar, Gutthorm, and Högni Gjúkason. Her tragic life was characterized by the death of many people who were close to her.

Gunnar: eldest son of Gjúki and Grímhild and the brother of Gudrún and Högni Gjúkason. He was a great warrior and married Brynhild.

Gutthorm: warrior son of Gjúki and Grímhild. He was the brother of Gunnar, Högni Gjúkason, and Gudrún. He died by the same sword with which he fatally stabbed Sigurd.

Hrungnir: giant with a stone head and heart who challenged Odin and was defeated by Thor.

Jónakr: powerful king who married Gudrún. They had three children: Hamdir, Sörli, and Erp Jónakrsson.

Jörd: giantess daughter of Nótt, the night, and by Odin the mother of Thor. She was also a personification of the primitive earth.

Kvasir: man created from the saliva of the Aesir and the Vanir. He was murdered by the dwarfs Fjalar and Galar; his blood became the mead of poetry. When drunk, it stimulated wisdom and scholarship.

Leifthrasir: mortal who survived Ragnarok by hiding in Yggdrasil. He and Líf created the new race of humans.

Líf: mortal who survived Ragnarok. She and her husband Leifthrasir created the new race of humans.

Magni: son of Thor; renowned for his strength. Magni was destined to survive Ragnarok and, along with his brother Módi, to inherit his father's hammer, Mjöllnir.

Módi: son of Thor who was destined to survive Ragnarok and to inherit his father's hammer Mjöllnir. He was known for his ferocity on the battlefield.

Regin: skillful dwarf who fostered and educated Sigurd and forged for him the sword Gram. He was eventually killed by Sigurd for planning his harm.

Sigmund: son of Völsung, brother and lover of Signy, and father of Sigurd. He drew the sword Gram from a log into which Odin had thrust it. When he died he passed the sword onto his son.

Signy: daughter of Völsung who was the sister and lover of Sigmund.

Sigurd: famous dragon slayer who was the son of Sigmund. He loved Brynhild but married Gudrún. He was stabbed by Gutthorm and died from the wound.

Skadi: giantess daughter of the giant, Thjazi; the wife of Njörd and later of the god of justice, Ull.

Surt: mighty fire demon or giant who stood sentry at the entrance to the realm of fire. He killed many of the Aesir at Ragnarok.

Suttung: giant who sometimes was the owner of the mead of poetry.

Thjazi: giant who was the father of Skadi. He held the goddess Idun captive and was eventually killed by Thor.

Thrym: giant who stole Thor's hammer Mjöllnir as part of a plan to marry Freya; he was killed for the theft.

Váli: son of Odin who killed Höd. He was destined to survive Ragnarok.

Völsung: father of Sigmund and Signy and grandfather of Sigurd.

Ymir: primordial giant from whom the world was created. He was nourished by the milk of the primeval cow, Audhumla. He was slain by Odin, Vili, and Vé. His body became the Earth, while his blood formed the world's lakes, rivers, and seas.

GLOSSARY

acropolis: a raised fortified part of an ancient Greek city. The most famous acropolis is in Athens; it is home to various large temples, including the Parthenon.

Aesir: in Norse mythology the supreme gods who were associated with war and death. Traditionally there were 13 members of the Aesir: Odin, Thor, Njörd, Frey, Tyr, Heimdall, Bragi, Váli, Vídar, Ull, Hoenir, Forseti, and Loki.

acculturation: the process of change and adaptation that occurs when one culture merges with another.

aetiology: the study of causes and origins. Mythographers sometimes analyze myths for their ability to explain the origins of a ceremony, ritual, or historical event such as the Trojan War.

afterlife: an existence that follows death. A belief in life after death is a feature of numerous ancient religions.

Age of Reason: a name given to a period during the 17th and 18th centuries when many European thinkers believed that the universe and human existence could be scientifically studied and explained by reason, observation, and experiment. Also known as the Enlightenment.

agora: the public square that was the political, cultural, and commercial center of an ancient Greek city.

alchemy: a medieval science that aimed to transform metals into gold, to discover a universal cure to all illnesses, and to find a source of immortality.

allegory: a work that uses fictional characters to convey a moral message or to comment on human existence.

altar: any place where a sacrifice or offering is made to a god or gods.

ambrosia: the food of the Greek and Roman gods.

amphora: a Roman unit of capacity that was approximately equal to 25.5 liters (6.7 gallons). The

Romans took the word from the Greeks, whose *amphora* was equal to 34 liters (9 gallons).

amulet: a charm that protects the wearer against harm.

ancestor worship: a system of belief marked by ceremonies, rituals, prayers, and sacrifices performed to honor the spirits of ancestors, and to ensure their blessing for the living. Ancestor worship is especially popular in religions in Africa and Asia.

animism: a belief that everything in nature has a spirit, including trees, rocks, rivers, and clouds.

ankh: an ancient Egyptian symbol that represented both physical and eternal life.

anthropology: the study of human beings in their environment.

Apocalypse: in Judeo-Christian teachings, the end of the world. Jews and Christians believe that the Earth will be destroyed and the righteous taken to a kingdom ruled by God.

apocrypha: in Christian teaching, books of the Bible excluded from the Jewish and Protestant canons. Specifically the term refers to early Christian texts not included in the New Testament.

apparition: a ghostly figure.

Archaic period: a period in Greek history from about 750 BCE to 500 BCE that was characterized by highly detailed naturalistic artworks.

artifact: any object created by humans, usually for a specific, practical purpose.

asceticism: a form of spiritual discipline that emphasizes self-control and the denial of physical and psychological desires. Many religions feature elements of asceticism, but it is most commonly associated with Hinduism.

assimilation: the process that occurs when something is absorbed and used. Cultural assimilation involves one culture replacing another culture and adopting its traditions and characteristics.

astrology: the study and forecast of the apparent influence of the heavenly bodies on events on earth. A belief in astrology was a feature of many ancient civilizations.

astronomy: the scientific study of the planets and the stars, the movements of which formed the basis of the calendar in many early societies.

atonement: reconciliation with a deity through sacrifice.

augury: a form of fortune-telling based on the observation of omens, such as lightning and thunder or the flight and feeding patterns of birds. In ancient Rome augurs interpreted the will of the gods in such signs before Roman leaders embarked on new civil projects or went to war.

autochthonous: indigenous.

avatar: in Hinduism an earthly incarnation of a deity.

Axis Mundi: in ancient thought a notional line through the center of the Earth, around which the sky revolved.

bacchant: a female partaker in ancient rites in honor of Bacchus, Roman god of wine. These included drinking, dancing, and singing.

bard: a poet-singer whose compositions often celebrated his people's history or the deeds of its heroes.

berserk: an ancient Scandinavian warrior who was considered to be invincible in battle. Berserks fought in such a frenzy that the word *berserk* has come to describe any crazed behavior.

bestiary: a literary work from the Middle Ages that uses real or imaginary animals as the basis for an allegorical or moral message; also a collection of descriptions of real or imaginary animals.

bewitchment: the act of influencing someone or something using witchcraft.

book of the dead: in ancient Egypt, a collection of spells and instructions that was buried with the dead to guide them in the afterlife.

Brahman: a Hindu priest. Such priests form the highest level of the Indian caste system.

Bronze Age: a name given to the historical period beginning between 4000 and 3000 BCE, during which human culture began to use bronze. The Bronze Age ended when the Iron Age began between 1200 and 600 BCE.

Buddhism: the religion founded by Siddhartha Gautama (c. 563–c. 483 BCE), commonly known as the Buddha. Buddhism's central beliefs are that suffering is inherent in life and that mental and moral purification can liberate people from desire and the cycle of life, death, and rebirth. The perfect state of purification is called *nirvana*. The major schools of Buddhism are Theraveda (the greater way) and Mahayana (the lesser way).

caesar: a title taken by Roman emperors succeeding Augustus Caesar (ruled 27 BCE–14 CE).

caliph: the religious and political head of Islam. He is considered to be a successor to Muhammad, the founder of Islam.

Campus Martius: an area on the banks of the Tiber River in ancient Rome, dedicated to Mars, where military exercises, sports, games, and public meetings were held. It was home to many temples and monuments.

canopic jar: a jar in which ancient Egyptians buried a dead person's organs with the corpse.

cannibalism: human consumption of human flesh, which in the past sometimes formed part of a religious ritual.

carnival: a festival that often includes feasting, dancing, singing, and masquerading. Historians believe that the origins of carnival date from ancient Greece, when the spring festival was held in honor of Dionysus, god of wine.

caryatids: in architecture, statues of draped female figures used as supports instead of columns. They were named for women of an ancient Greek town called Caryae, which sided with the invading Persian forces. As a punishment the women were sentenced to hard labor.

caste system: a social system in India and other parts of Asia that divides society into four hereditary categories based on occupation, each with its own rights and obligations: Brahmans (priests), Kshatriyas (warriors and kings), Vaishyas (landowners), and Shudras (servants). Members of the rest of society are classed as "Untouchables." Contact among or between the castes is severely restricted.

celibacy: abstinence from sexual intercourse or marriage. The concept of celibacy featured in a number of classical myths; for example, the Greek Hippolytus died as a result of his celibacy.

Celts: the name given to a group of people who lived in central and western Europe, from the British Isles to Hungary, from around 1000 BCE. They entered Spain and northern Italy around 400 BCE, and sacked Rome. The Roman general Julius Caesar later subjugated them, and those living in Gaul were Romanized.

centaur: a member of a mythological race of creatures that were part man, part horse. They were believed to live in the mountains of Thessaly in ancient Greece.

chac mool: a statue of a reclining figure representing the Mayan messenger god of the same name. The statues featured a receptacle, into which offerings were put. These statues were found in many Mayan cities.

chaos: in many religions, the state of the universe before life existed.

charm: a spell or an object such as an amulet that is usually believed to protect the bearer from harm.

chastity: abstention from sexual intercourse.

chorus: in literature and drama a group of characters that comments on the action or plot of the story, often repeating themselves for emphasis.

Christianity: the monotheistic religion that was founded by followers of Jesus Christ, who consider him the son of God, sent to earth to bear the sins of humankind through his death and resurrection. Christianity became the state religion of Rome during the reign of Emperor Constantine (reigned 306–337). The central texts included in the Judeo-Christian Bible are the Old and New Testaments.

chronicler: a person who records historical information.

chthonic: an adjective describing anything related to the earth or the underworld.

city-state: in ancient Greece an area governed by one central city. Athens and Sparta were two of the most important city-states.

clairvoyance: an ability to detect objects, figures, events, or any other phenomena that are not apparent to the senses of normal human beings.

classical: a broad term used to describe anything from ancient Greece and Rome, including art, politics, religion, and mythology.

Classical period: a period in Greek history (c. 500–334 BCE) marked by the Persian Wars (492–479 BCE), during which Athenians revolted against Persian rule, and the Peloponnesian War (431–404 BCE), when Athens fought with Sparta for territory on mainland Greece.

codex (plural codices): a manuscript book that usually contains scriptures, mythology, historical annals, or other records of a culture. Among the most famous codices are those that record Aztec and Mayan culture.

Colosseum: a great amphitheater built in Rome in the first century CE to stage circus games and gladitorial combat. It was named for the Colossus, a huge sculpture of Roman emperor Nero.

comparative mythology: a form of study that considers the common factors of myths and legends from different cultures.

Confucianism: the Chinese philosophy founded by Confucius (Kong-fu-tse) in the fifth–sixth century BCE that focused on human ethics and regularly observed rituals within an ordered society. During the Han dynasty (206 BCE–8 CE) it was the state ideology, and it eventually spread by Chinese literate culture to much of eastern Asia, including Korea, Japan, and Vietnam.

constellation: a configuration of stars believed to take the form of an animal, an object, or a person. Many constellations are named for figures from Greek and Roman mythology.

cosmogony: a theory for the origins or creation of the universe.

cosmos: the universe and everything within it.

cult: an organization of religious beliefs, rituals, and practice dedicated usually to an unorthodox deity or an unorthodox interpretation of a mainstream deity. The cult of Mithras, for example, was largely followed by Roman soldiers who related to the cult's value of brotherhood.

cuneiform: the earliest form of writing in Mesopotamia. It consisted of characters pressed into clay with the use of wedge-shaped styluses. It was created by the native Mesopotamians, and used by the Sumerians and the Semites. Cuneiform began as a pictorial system but evolved into a syllabic script.

cupbearer: a person whose duty it is to fill and hand out vessels of wine.

curse: a prayer or invocation for the gods to inflict misfortune on someone. The idea of the curse featured widely in classical mythology.

Cyclopes: in classical mythology, a race of giants, each with one eye in the middle of his forehead. The Cyclops Polyphemus captured Greek hero Odysseus and his men and held them in his cave.

Dalai Lama: the spiritual head of Tibetan Buddhism.

Darwinism: a theory of evolution based on the theory of English naturalist Charles Darwin (1809–1882) that natural selection favors the survival of better-adapted species.

deity: a god or goddess.

demigod: a semi-divine figure from mythology who is more powerful than a mortal but does not have all the power of a god. Demigods usually had one mortal and one divine parent.

democracy: a system of government that emerged at the end of the sixth century BCE in Athens. A leader and a council is chosen by a majority of people, either directly or through elected representatives.

demon: an evil spirit.

divination: the prediction of future events or learning of hidden knowledge through the interpretation of omens or the harnessing of supernatural powers.

dragon: a mythological monster that resembled a giant lizard or serpent. Dragons often terrorized people and guarded treasure.

druid: a priest of various Celtic peoples; druids had significant power due to their religious and medical knowledge and led resistance against the Roman conquerors of northern Europe.

Dryad: in classical mythology, a nymph that lived in a tree, especially an oak tree.

dualism: the belief that the universe is characterized by a struggle between the opposing forces of good and evil, which are personified by deities. An ancient Persian religion, called Zoroastrianism, is believed to be the root of dualism. It taught that there was one god of goodness, and another, his evil brother, who was the god of darkness.

dwarf: a humanlike, mythological creature characterized by his small stature. Dwarves were often skilled craftsmen.

dynasty: a succession of rulers from the same line of descent.

Edda: one of two bodies of Icelandic literature describing Germanic mythology—the *Poetic Edda* and the *Prose Edda*. The *Prose Edda* was composed by Snorri Sturluson (1179–1241); the authorship of the *Poetic Edda* is unknown, but it is believed to date to between 800 and 1100 CE.

Earth mother: the name used to describe a female agricultural deity who was also a personification of the Earth.

eclipse: a total or partial obscuring of one heavenly body by another.

Eleusinian mysteries: a famous secret initiation ceremony that originated from the myth of the Greek goddess of agriculture Demeter. Rites were performed that invoked the separation and reunion of Demeter and her daughter Persephone and Demeter's failure to immortalize the son of the queen of Eleusis.

embalming: a method of preserving a dead body that was practiced by some ancient civilizations. In most cases it involved treating the body to prevent decay. Embalming was common among ancient Egyptians, who believed that after death the body had to reattract the soul.

Enlightenment: a philosophical movement that flourished in 18th-century Europe. It rejected traditional religious and political ideas in favor of principles based on observation and reason.

epic: a long narrative poem, usually about mythological heroes and events. Well-known examples of epics include the *Iliad* and *Odyssey* by Greek poet Homer (ninth–eighth century BCE) and the *Aeneid* by Roman poet Virgil (70–19 BCE).

equinox: the two times in the year when the sun is directly above the equator, meaning that day and night are of the same length.

ethnography: the study and recording of human society with particular attention to the everyday life of its members. Fifth-century-BCE Greek historian Herodotus is believed to have been one of the first people to study and record cultures in this way.

etymology: the history of a word, including its roots and the changes in its meaning over time.

euhemerism: a method of interpreting myths that assumes that they are accounts of historical people and events that have been embellished over time.

exodus: a mass departure of people from a particular place, often stimulated by dramatic political change.

exposure: an ancient method of dealing with unwanted children by abandoning them in the open. In Greek society exposure was common, as was the adoption of exposed babies.

extispicy: a form of divination carried out in ancient Rome whereby an augur (priest) examined animal entrails to determine the will of the gods.

faience: tin-glazed earthenware that is often adorned by intricate designs and made in France, Germany, Spain, and Scandinavia.

fairy: a magical mythical being mainly associated with the folklore of Cornwall, Ireland, Scotland, and Wales. Fairies were often very small but had human form. Some accounts portrayed fairies as benevolent creatures; others reported that they were mischievous.

Fates: in Greek mythology, figures who determined people's lifespans. Traditionally they were called Clotho, Lachesis, and Atropos.

fauns: creatures in Roman mythology that were part human and part goat. They were similar to satyrs, but had a gentler nature. They were named for Faunus, Italian god of the wild forests.

fertility: the quality of being productive. Ancient civilizations associated fertility gods and goddesses with events such as birth or a successful harvest.

festival: a celebration held in honor of an important figure, event, or occasion. Many ancient civilizations included festivals in their calendars.

fetish: an object that is thought to possess magical power or to protect its owner.

flamen (plural: flamines): a Roman priest. During the republic there were fifteen flamines, the three most important of which served Jupiter, Mars, and Quirinus.

fraternity: a brotherhood of like-minded men united by a common purpose and common values.

fratricide: the murder of a brother or sister.

freemasons: a fraternal society dating from ancient times, whose principles include a belief in a supreme god and the importance of mutual assistance. Processes of initiation and the practice of rituals are known to exist within freemasonry, and until recently the details were kept secret.

fresco: a wall painting, usually made directly onto wet plaster. Sometimes the paint is applied to dry plaster, in which case the technique is known as secco fresco.

frieze: a long horizontal decorated panel that appears above the columns of Roman temples, and sometimes as a form of decoration on walls. Historical and mythological events were depicted in relief on many Roman friezes.

funerary: associated with burial.

Furies: in Greek mythology, goddesses of retribution who administered punishment to those who committed serious crimes such as the murder of a family member. The Furies were also known as the Eumenides.

geology: the study of the Earth, including its physical properties and history.

genealogy: the study of family origins and history.

genius: a Roman guardian spirit closely associated with a specific place.

ghost: the invisible soul of a dead person. Belief in ghosts is founded on the ancient belief that a person's soul is separated at death from the body, and from then on exists in another world.

giant: a mythical being marked by its large size and unusual strength. In Greek mythology, the Giants were a race of monstrous creatures who warred with the Olympian gods. In Scandinavian mythology, the Frost Giants battled with the gods of the Aesir.

golden age: any period in the history of a civilization that is marked by outstanding cultural achievements and civic happiness.

glyph: a figure, character, or symbol carved in relief.

Graces: Greek goddesses who lived on Mount Olympus and were personifications of beauty, charm, and grace. According to one account they were daughters of Zeus and the Oceanid Eurynome and were named Aglaea, Euphrosyne, and Thalia.

grave goods: objects placed with the deceased on burial. In Scandinavian history vikings buried their dead leaders in ships with weapons and treasure so that they would be protected and wealthy in their next existence.

great spirit: in native American folklore the omnipresent lifegiving deity that has no definite form but is often worshiped as the sun.

hallucination: a false perception of an object or person created by the mind.

harpies: in Greek mythology, a race of winged female monsters who snatched away their victims and delivered them to the underworld.

haruspicy: a form of divination practiced by the Etruscans and Romans that involved determining divine will by examining animal entrails.

hearth: an ever-burning fire at the center of Roman houses and public spaces that not only served as a source of heat in cold periods, but also symbolized the spiritual heart of the home or city.

hegemony: authority over people achieved by means of controlling the cultural, ideological, and economic foundations of society.

herm: a square stone pillar usually topped by a bust of Hermes or another deity.

hero: in general terms, a legendary figure with great strength and courage and renowned for his deeds. More specifically, in ancient Greece, heroes were mortals who lived on after their deaths.

hieroglyphs: the oldest form of Egyptian script. The system was originally based on images but later developed into a combination of ideograms, letters, and signs representing syllables.

Hinduism: the predominant religion in modern India. It originated from Brahmanism and is characterized by a belief in many gods, the most important of whom are Brahma, Shiva, and Vishnu.

hubris: excessive pride or self-confidence.

ichor: in Greek mythology, the colorless blood of the Olympian gods.

iconography: the traditional images or motifs that play a significant part in a cult or a religion. The crucifix, for example, is an important part of Christian iconography.

idolatry: the worship of any human being or physical object as a god.

immortality: everlasting life. Most deities are considered immortal; many religions promise immortality to the soul.

incantation: the recital of spells or charms as part of a magic ritual.

incest: sexual intercourse between members of the same family, a common theme in ancient myths.

Indo-European: an ancient language from which many modern languages are derived. The languages of a number of ancient civilizations, including ancient Greece, Rome, and northern India, were Indo-European in origin, and there were many similarities between the mythologies of these cultures.

initiation: a process including rites, ceremonies, and ordeals, through which a person must pass in order to join a religious group.

initiation ceremony: a ritual that marks induction into a cult or the transition from one lifestage to another, such as the passage from childhood into adulthood.

Iron Age: a broad term relating to the stage of human cultural development that followed the Stone Age and Bronze Age. It was characterized by the use of iron for weapons and tools and is thought to have begun in Asia and Egypt around 1000 BCE.

Judaism: a monotheistic religion that emerged before 1000 BCE in present-day Israel. It was developed by ancient Hebrews and is now practiced by Jews. The patriarch Abraham is considered to be its founding father.

kabbalah: a Jewish mystical tradition, dating from the 12th century, that claims to possess a secret unwritten record of a revelation that God communicated to Moses and Adam. Some Jewish worshipers believe that they communicate with God more directly through the kabbalah.

karma: in Hinduism and Buddhism, the force generated by a person's actions that determines a person's next existence.

Ker (plural: Keres): in Greek mythology, either a female spirit of death or doom or a concept similar to fate.

Koran: the holy book of Islam. Muslims believe that the book contains the word of God as told to the prophet Muhammad.

labor: a task. In Greek mythology Heracles had to complete 12 labors before his crime of murdering his family was forgiven.

labyrinth: a mazelike arrangement of intricate passageways and dead ends. In Greek mythology, the most famous labyrinth was on the island of Crete; it was home to a fearsome monster called the Minotaur.

Lar (plural Lares): in Roman myth a protective guardian spirit of the household and other locations. A *lararium* was a room containing statues of Lares.

legend: a story passed down over time that is popularly regarded as historical but which often contains numerous unreliable elements.

linear A: an ancient form of script composed of symbols similar to hieroglyphs that was used in Crete from between the 18th and 15th centuries BCE.

linear B: an ancient form of syllabic script employed on Crete and on the Greek mainland from the 15th to the 12th centuries BCE.

lycanthropy: the transformation of a human into a wolf, either through magic or self-delusion.

lyre: a stringed musical instrument resembling a hand-held harp that was commonly carried by ancient bards and other musicians.

maat: the ancient Egyptian principle of universal order, which was maintained by the pharaoh's role as appeaser of the gods. The concept of maat was personified by the goddess of the same name.

magi: priests of the ancient tribes of Medes and Persians; also used to describe the wise men described in the Bible as visiting Jesus' birth.

magic: a form of power in which apparently supernatural forces are used to overcome the laws of nature. Today the term has come to describe any illusions that are achieved by secret means.

matriarchal: a term describing a society or family led by women in which descent is traced through the mother's line rather than the father's.

meditation: a deep and sustained form of contemplation that is used in mystical religions to focus reflection on divine truth by unifying the body and the mind.

messianic: relating to a messiah or the leader of a cause.

metaphor: a literal example used instead of another to make or emphasize a comparison.

metaphysical: relating to a reality that cannot be perceived by the physical senses.

Milky Way: the historical and popular name for the band of light containing thousands of indistinct stars that surround the Earth and belong to its galaxy.

miracle: an extraordinary occurrence that is attributed to divine power.

monotheism: a belief in one god. Christianity, Islam, and Judaism are monotheistic religions.

Morning Star: the historical and popular name for the planet Venus, which appears as a bright light in the sky shortly before or during sunrise.

mortality: the condition of being subject to death.

mosaic: an often pictorial decoration created by arranging many small pieces of material of various colors. Roman mosaics were frequently composed of small clay tiles and arranged in patterns on floors, walls, and ceilings.

motif: in art, music, or literature, a color, theme, or symbol that is continually repeated.

mummification: The process of preserving a body after death by embalming it and wrapping it in linen. Mummification is associated largely with ancient Egypt, although other cultures also practiced it.

Muse: any of the nine goddess daughters of Zeus and Mnemosyne. Artists worshiped them and depended upon them for inspiration. The Muses were usually said to be Calliope, Clio, Euterpe, Thalia, Melpomene, Terpsichore, Erato, Polymnia, and Urania.

mystery cult: a religion that uses secret rites to offer spiritual support to its initiates.

mysticism: a spiritual quest for enlightenment, the ultimate goal of which is access to a divine or sacred realm.

myth: a symbolic story that conveys the views and traditions of a culture.

mythographer: a writer who produces critical compilations of myths.

Neanderthal: an early hominid, or human-like creature. The Neanderthals lived between 30,000 and 200,000 years ago.

necromancy: a form of magic that involves communicating with the dead in an attempt to reveal or influence the future.

nemesis: an agent of retribution or vengeance named for the Greek goddess of retribution.

Nereid: in Greek mythology any one of a number of nymphs who lived in the sea and whose father was the sea god Nereus.

nirvana: in Buddhism a blissful condition free from suffering, which a person achieves through denial of desire and individual consciousness.

numerology: the study of the magical significance of numbers, sometimes used to predict the future.

nymph: in Greek mythology a female nature spirit. Among the different kinds of nymphs were Naiads, Dryads, Hamadryads, and Oceanids. They were distinguished by their parentage and the natural feature they inhabited.

Oceanid: in Greek mythology, a water nymph associated with the seas, oceans, and rivers. The Oceanids were born to the Titans Oceanus and Tethys. Their main task was to protect children.

Olympian gods: the chief gods of Greek mythology, named for their home on Mount Olympus in Thessaly. Accounts vary as to which gods belonged to the group, but it was usually said to include Aphrodite, Apollo, Ares, Artemis, Athena, Demeter, Dionysus, Hades, Hephaestus, Hera, Hermes, Hestia, Persephone, Poseidon, and Zeus.

Olympic Games: an athletic festival held in honor of

Zeus that originated in ancient Greece before 700 BCE. Events included horse racing, running, wrestling, javelin and discus throwing, the long jump, and boxing. The games were abolished during the reign of Roman Emperor Theodosius (379–395). They were revived in 1894.

omen: a sign that can be interpreted as signifying a future event.

Omphalos: a carved oval-shaped stone held at Delphi. The ancient Greeks believed that it represented the center of the Earth. According to myth, two eagles sent by Zeus to determine this point flew from each side of the Earth and met at Delphi.

oracle: in ancient religion, a person such as a priest or priestess through whom a deity communicated with humans. *Oracle* has come to mean an adviser who is considered to be an authority on predicting future events.

pagan: a person who practices an unorthodox religion. Pagan religions are usually polytheistic. The term was originally used by ancient Romans to describe the beliefs of those who dwelt in the countryside.

pantheism: a religious doctrine that states that god is present within everything in the universe.

pantheon: the complete group of gods worshiped by a polytheistic culture. It was named for the Pantheon, a round temple that was dedicated to all the gods of the Roman empire.

papyrus: a scroll made from pressed strips of the papyrus plant, which grows in abundance in the Nile River valley.

parthenogenesis: reproduction without fertilization.

Parthenon: a temple on the acropolis at Athens that was built between 447 and 438 BCE and dedicated to the goddess Athena.

pastoral: a literary work that describes rural life in an idealized way and seeks to contrast its innocent pleasures with the tough nature of urban life.

patriarchal: a term describing a society or family that is dominated by men and in which descent is traced through the male line.

patricide: the murder of a father by his child or children. In Greek mythology, Oedipus unwittingly killed his father following an argument on a road.

penance: an act usually involving a form of sacrifice or suffering committed to repent for a sin.

Penates: Roman household gods who were worshiped along with the Lares and Vesta, goddess of the hearth. They were believed to protect domestic spaces, and sometimes the Roman state.

pharaoh: an Egyptian king who was believed to be the earthly incarnation of the supreme creator god. The pharaoh was considered to be the son of Re, the personification of the sun, and an incarnation of the falcon-headed Horus.

pharaonic: an adjective describing anything that is characteristic of the pharaohs, especially in reference to work on a great scale.

plutocracy: a government composed of the wealthy members of society.

polis **(plural:** *poleis*): Greek for "city," referring to an ancient Greek city-state.

polytheism: the belief in more than one god. Polytheistic religions include Hinduism, Voodoo, and the ancient religions of Greece, Egypt, and Rome.

Pontifex Maximus: the most senior priest in the council of priests in ancient Rome.

predestination: the idea that a person's fate is decided by divine will before they are born.

premonition: an awareness of an event before it happens.

priests and priestesses: religious figures chosen for their devotion to a faith who perform rituals and ceremonies and lead communal worship.

primeval: a word referring to the earliest stages of creation.

primitive: a word describing something relating to a very early period of history.

prophecy: a divine revelation of future events. Famous prophecies in Greek mythology include those made by Tiresias, the seer, which saved Thebes from a plague and helped Odysseus to return home.

Puranas: a collection of ancient Hindu sacred writings dating from 300 to 750 CE. They included traditional myths, legends, and folklore.

purification: a set of rituals performed to cleanse or protect someone from an unwanted presence in his or her body or soul.

pyramid: a monumental Egyptian royal tomb having a square base and four triangular sides that meet at a single point. The slopes symbolized the primeval mound of creation. Pyramid building reached its height during the Fourth Dynasty (2575–2450 BCE). The most famous pyramids are found at Giza.

Reformation: the religious schism that occurred in the Christian church during the 16th century, when the Protestant church split from Catholicism.

reincarnation: the rebirth of a soul after death in another animal, human being, or plant. Belief in reincarnation is most common in Asian religions but was also present in Greek mythology.

regicide: the murder of a king.

relief: a style of sculpture in which the subject is raised from the surface of a background medium. Types of relief include bas-relief where the design projects slightly from the background; and high relief, where half or more of the subject's natural circumference projects from the background.

resurrection: a return from death to a previous existence.

revelation: a communication of divine truth from God to a human. It has also come to mean a disclosure of something that was previously unknown.

rite of passage: a ceremony marking the passage from one social category or group to another, such as the transition from youth to adulthood, marriage, or becoming a parent. Many cultures celebrate rites of passage with rituals and festivals.

ritual: the performance of traditional ceremonial acts.

rune: a character in any Germanic alphabet dating from between the third and thirteenth century.

sacrifice: a ritual act in which an object is offered to a deity in order to earn that deity's good will. In many cultures sacrifice involved the killing of an animal or a human being.

sacrilege: in religious or civil law the theft of or damage to anything sacred.

sanctuary: a sacred refuge for people fleeing persecution or who are in search of a peaceful environment. In classical mythology sanctuaries were protected by various deities.

sarcophagus: a stone coffin usually made from limestone. The pharaohs of ancient Egypt were buried in particularly ornate sarcophagi.

satyr: in Greek and Roman mythology a wild creature, part man and part horse or goat, that passed its time in revelry and debauchery. The most famous Greek satyr was the drunken Silenus, companion of Dionysus, god of wine.

scripture: an important body of writing that is considered to be sacred or authoritative.

shaman: a priest or priestess who uses magic to summon natural forces or to cure the sick. Although shamanism is an ancient form of mysticism, shamans can still be found in Siberia, North America, and Scandinavia.

shape-shifting: the act of changing between physical forms. In Greek mythology, the god Zeus often shape-shifted in order to seduce women.

shrine: a place where worshipers show their devotion to a religious figure such as a saint or god. The shrine often houses relics, idols, or other representations of religious figures that are worshiped.

Sibyl: in Greek legend a prophetess, traditionally an old woman.

sin: an immoral act against divine law.

skald: a poet in ancient Scandinavia.

Solar system: the astronomical term for the planets and other bodies that orbit the Earth's sun.

sorcery: traditionally, a form of usually harmful magic.

specter: a visible disembodied spirit, much like a ghost.

spell: a spoken set of words that has magical power.

spirit: the supernatural essence of a being that is sometimes believed to live on after the body dies.

superstition: misconceived views of natural occurrences explained in terms of the supernatural, magic, and chance.

sympathetic magic: a form of magical power that influences someone by naming them or by directing magic at a representation of the person, such as a doll.

syncretism: the combination of different religious beliefs and practices that occurs when two cultures mix, or when one culture absorbs another.

taboo: an adjective used to describe an action that breaks sacred laws.

temple: a building where religious rituals are practiced.

terra-cotta: baked clay that is made into statues, vases, and architectural features. Terra-cotta was popular in the classical world and was often used for ornamental purposes.

Titans: in Greek mythology, the exceptionally large and strong firstborn children of Uranus and Gaia. Traditionally 12 in number, they fought and lost a great battle against Zeus and his fellow Olympians.

totem: a symbol of personal historical significance associated with the ancestors of a group or an individual. Totems are often animals or plants.

tragedy: a drama in which the central protagonists encounter great personal misfortune. Tragedies originated in ancient Greece and were traditionally performed at religious festivals.

trance: a dreamlike state in which the person concerned is awake but partially loses control of his or her senses. In the ancient world, priests, shamans, and oracles all entered trances, during which they were believed to be able to contact the gods.

transgression: the violation of a divine code or law.

trickster: a god characterized by deception and mischievousness. Trickster deities are common in Native American mythologies.

Trojan War: a legendary conflict between the Greeks and the inhabitants of the city of Troy in Asia Minor, possibly based on a real war that occurred in the 12th or 13th century BCE. The war, which lasted for 10 years, is central to several classical works, most notably the *Iliad* by Homer (ninth–eighth century BCE).

tutelary: describes protection, usually from a god, goddess, or other guardian spirit.

underworld: in most cultures the land of the dead, usually ruled by a deity. The lord of the Egyptian underworld was Osiris; Greeks and Romans believed it was Hades; and the Norse believed it was the goddess Hel.

ushabti: a small figurine that ancient Egyptians buried with their dead in the belief that it would act as a servant in the afterlife. Ushabtis were often inscribed with passages from the Book of the Dead.

vampire: a dead person who rises from the grave to feed on human blood. Myths about vampires exist in many cultures. The most famous vampire is Count Dracula, created by writer Bram Stoker (1847–1912).

Vanir: in Norse mythology, fertility deities who warred with a rival group of gods known as the Aesir.

Vedas: Hindu sacred scriptures. From the fifth century BCE, Hindus considered them to be the record of the eternal truth revealed to ancient seers, which is written in the perfect language. The four most important texts are the Rig Veda, Yajur Veda, Sama Veda, and Atharva Veda.

vestal virgins: Roman priestesses who served Vesta, the symbol of the Roman state, and goddess of the hearth. They took vows of chastity and were charged with maintaining the fire in the Temple of Vesta.

virginity: a state of sexual purity.

vision: the sight or appearance of an omen.

Voodoo: a polytheistic religion practiced in Haiti that mixes Catholic elements with traditional African beliefs brought to the island by slaves.

votive: an adjective describing anything that includes a vow or wish. Marriage, for example, is a votive ceremony.

wergild: in Germanic and Scandinavian history, the compensation paid by a murderer to his victim's family.

witchcraft: the use of sorcery or magic to influence and control people or events.

woodcut: a print made by an inked woodblock with a design in relief cut into its surface.

world tree: a tree that represents the center of the world and links different mythological realms. The most famous example is Yggdrasil, the world tree of Norse mythology. It linked Asgard (home of the Aesir), Jotunheim (home of the giants), Midgard (home of the human race), and Niflheim (home to evil-doers).

ziggurat: a stepped temple tower built from mud bricks and sometimes covered with mosaic tiles or landscaped with trees and shrubbery. Ziggurats were characteristic of Sumerian, Babylonian, and Assyrian civilizations in ancient Mesopotamia.

zodiac: a belt of space seen from the Earth that extends 9° either side of the sun's annual path among the constellations.

Zoroastrianism: the Persian religion founded by Iranian prophet Zoroaster in the sixth-century BCE. It contains elements of monotheism and dualism, and was largely replaced by Islam.

FURTHER READING

AFRICA

Altman, Linda Jacobs. *African Mythology*. Berkeley Heights, NJ: Enslow Publishers, 2003.

Herbert, Eugenia W. *Iron, Gender, and Power: Rituals of Transformation in African Societies*. Bloomington, IN: Indiana University Press, 1993.

Mutwa, Vusamazulu Credo. *Indaba, My Children*. New York: Grove Press, 1999.

Parrinder, Geoffrey. *African Mythology*. New York: Peter Bedrick Books, 1991.

Scheub, Harold. *A Dictionary of African Mythology*. New York: Oxford University Press, 2000.

Some, Malidoma Patrice. *Of Water and the Spirit: Ritual, Magic, and Initiation in the Life of an African Shaman*. New York: Penguin, 1995.

AUSTRALIA AND OCEANIA

Alpers, Anthony. *Legends of the South Sea*. New York: Crowell, 1970.

Berndt, R. M., and C. H. Berndt. *The Speaking Land: Myth and Story in Aboriginal Australia*. Rochester, VT: Inner Traditions, 1994.

Boutilier, James A., Daniel T. Hughes, and Sharon W. Tiffany. *Mission, Church and Sect in Oceania*. Ann Arbor, MI: University of Michigan Press, 1992.

Campbell, I. C. *Island Kingdom: Tonga Ancient and Modern*. Christchurch, New Zealand: Canterbury University Press, 1992.

Nganjmirra, Nawakadj. *Kunwinjku Spirit*. Melbourne: Melbourne University Press, 1997.

CELTS

Davidson, H. R. Ellis. *Myths and Symbols in Pagan Europe: Early Scandinavian and Celtic Religions*. Syracuse, NY: Syracuse University Press, 1989.

Ellis, Peter Berresford. *A Brief History of the Druids*. New York: Carroll and Graf, 2002.

Ellis, Peter Berresford. *Celtic Myths and Legends*. New York: Carroll and Graf, 2002.

Ellis, Peter Berresford. *The Druids*. Grand Rapids, MI: William B. Eerdmans Publishing Company, 1995.

Green, Miranda J., ed. *The Celtic World*. London: Routledge, 1995.

Gregory, Augusta. *Irish Myths and Legends*. Philadelphia: Running Press, 1999.

Heinz, Sabine. *Symbols of the Celts*. New York: Sterling Publications, 1999.

MacKillop, James. *A Dictionary of Celtic Mythology*. New York: Oxford University Press, 1998.

Markale, John, and Jon Graham, trans. *The Druids*. Rochester, VT: Inner Traditions International, 1999.

Synge, Ursula. *Weland, Smith of the Gods*. London: The Bodley Head, 1972.

CENTRAL ASIA, CHINA, KOREA, AND JAPAN

Allan, Sarah. *The Shape of the Turtle: Myth, Art, and Culture in Early China*. New York: State University of New York Press, 1991.

Bates, Roy. *Chinese Dragons*. New York: Oxford University Press, 2002.

Chun Shin-Yong, ed., Lee Tae-Dong, and Dolores C. Geier, trans. *Korean Folk-tales.* Seoul, Korea: International Cultural Foundation, 1979.

Feuerstein, Georg, Subhash Kak, and David Frawley. *The Search of the Cradle of Civilization.* Wheaton, IL: Quest Books, 2001.

Hadland, Davis F. *Myths and Legends of Japan.* New York: Dover Publications, 1992.

Janelli, Roger, and Dawnhee Yim Janelli. *Ancestor Worship and Korean Society.* Stanford, CA: Stanford University Press, 1992.

Kister, Daniel A. *Korean Shamanist Ritual: Symbols and Dramas of Transformation.* Budapest: Akadémiai Kiadó, 1997.

Knappert, Jan. *Mythology and Folklore in South-East Asia.* New York: Oxford University Press, 1999.

Kriwaczek, Paul. *In Search of Zarathustra: The First Prophet and the Ideas that Changed the World.* New York: Knopf, 2003.

Lee, Peter H. *Sourcebook of Korean Civilization: From Early Times to the Sixteenth Century.* New York: Columbia University Press, 1996.

Metternich, Hilary Roe, ed. *Mongolian Folktales.* Boulder, CO: Avery Press, 1996.

Nigosian, S. A. *The Zoroastrian Faith: Tradition and Modern Research.* Montreal: McGill-Queen's University Press, 1993.

Odigan, Sarangerel, and Julie Ann Stewart. *Riding Windhorses: A Journey into the Heart of Mongolian Shamanism.* Rochester, VT: Destiny Books, 2000.

Riordan, James. *Korean Folk-tales.* New York: Oxford University Press, 1994.

Sermier, Claire, and Helen Loveday, trans. *Mongolia: Empire of the Steppes.* Union Lake, MI: Odyssey Publications, 2002.

Storm, Rachel. *Asian Mythology: Myths and Legends of China, Japan, Thailand, Malaysia and Indonesia.* London: Lorenz Books, 2000.

Storm, Rachel. *The Encyclopaedia of Eastern Mythology.* London: Lorenz Books, 1999.

Walls, Neal H. *Desire, Discord, and Death: Approaches to Ancient Near Eastern Myth.* Boston: American Schools of Oriental Research, 2001.

Werner, E. T. C. *Myths and Legends of China.* New York: Dover Publications, 1994.

Wilson, Epiphanius. *Sacred Books of the East (Including Selections from . . . the Zend Avesta . . .).* Columbia, MO: South Asia Books, 1999.

EGYPT

Faulkner, Raymond, trans. *The Egyptian Book of the Dead: The Book of Going Forth by Day.* San Francisco, CA: Chronicle Books, 2000.

Hayes, Michael. *The Egyptians.* New York: Rizzoli International Publications, 1996.

Hobson, Christine. *The World of the Pharaohs.* New York: Thames and Hudson, 1990.

Lehner, Mark. *The Complete Pyramids.* New York: Thames and Hudson, 1997.

Mercatante, Anthony S. *Who's Who in Egyptian Mythology.* New York: Metro Books, 2002.

Nakhai, Beth Alpert. *Archaeology and the Religions of Canaan and Israel.* Atlanta, GA: American Schools of Oriental Research, 2001.

Nelson, Richard. *Make Prayers to the Raven.* Chicago: University of Chicago Press, 1983.

Oakes, Lorna, and Lucia Gahlin. *Ancient Egypt.* New York: Anness Publishing Limited, 2002.

Redford, Donald B. *Egypt, Canaan, and Israel in Ancient Times.* New Jersey: Princeton University Press, 1992.

Redford, Donald B. *The Ancient Gods Speak.* New York: Oxford University Press, Inc., 2002.

FURTHER READING

Redford, Donald B. *The Oxford Essential Guide to Egyptian Mythology.* New York: Oxford University Press, 2003.

Sauneron, Serge, and David Lorton, trans. *The Priests of Ancient Egypt.* Ithaca, NY: Cornell University Press, 2000.

Seton-Williams, M.V. *Egyptian Legends and Stories.* New York: Barnes and Noble, Inc., 1999.

Shaw, Ian, ed. *The Oxford History of Ancient Egypt.* New York: Oxford University Press, 2000.

Shuter, Jane. *Pharaohs and Priests.* Oxford: Heinemann Library, 1998.

Spence, Lewis. *Ancient Egyptian Myths and Legends.* New York: Dover Publications, 1991.

Wilkinson, Richard H. *The Complete Gods and Goddesses of Ancient Egypt.* New York: Thames and Hudson, 2003.

GREECE AND ROME

Aeschylus, and Robert Fagles, trans. *The Oresteia.* New York: Penguin USA, 1984.

Agha-Jaffar, Tamara. *Demeter and Persephone: Lessons from a Myth.* Jefferson, NC: McFarland and Company, 2002.

Alberti, Leon Battista, and Virginia Brown, ed. *Momus.* Cambridge, MA: Harvard University Press, 2003.

Apollodorus, and Robin Hard, trans. *The Library of Greek Mythology.* New York: Oxford University Press, 1999.

Apollonius Rhodius, and R. C. Seaton, trans. *The Argonautica.* Boston, MA: Harvard University Press, 1990.

Apuleius, and E. J. Kenney, ed. *Apuleius: Cupid and Psyche.* New York: Cambridge University Press, 1991.

Apuleius, and E. J. Kenney, trans. *The Golden Ass: Or Metamorphoses.* New York: Penguin USA, 1999.

Barber, Antonia. *Apollo and Daphne: Masterpieces of Greek Mythology.* Los Angeles: Paul Getty Museum Publications, 1999.

Beard, Mary, John North, and Simon Price. *Religions of Rome.* New York: Cambridge University Press, 1998.

Bremmer, J. N., and N. M. Horsfall. *Roman Myth and Mythography.* London: University of London Institute of Classical Studies, 1987.

Bulfinch, Thomas. *Bulfinch's Mythology.* New York: Modern Library, 1998.

Burr, Elizabeth, trans. *The Chiron Dictionary of Greek and Roman Mythology: Gods and Goddesses, Heroes, Places, and Events of Antiquity.* New York: Chiron Publications, 1994.

Calame, Claude, and Daniel W. Berman, trans. *Myth and History in Ancient Greece.* Princeton, NJ: Princeton University Press, 2003.

Camus, Albert, and Justin O'Brien, trans. *The Myth of Sisyphus.* London: Penguin, 2000.

Clauss, Manfred, and Richard Gordon, trans. *The Roman Cult of Mithras.* New York: Routledge, 2001.

Craft, M. Charlotte. *Cupid and Psyche.* New York: William Morrow and Company, 1996.

Crossley-Holland, Kevin. *The Norse Myths.* London: The Folio Society, 1989.

Crudden, Michael, trans. *The Homeric Hymns.* New York: Oxford University Press, 2002.

Dumézil, Georges, and Philip Krapp, trans. *Archaic Roman Religion.* Baltimore, MD: Johns Hopkins University Press, 1996.

Edwards, Ruth B. *Kadmos the Phoenician: A Study in Greek Legends and the Mycenean Age.* Amsterdam: Hakkert, 1979.

Euripides, and Ted Hughes, trans. *Alcestis.* New York: Farrar, Straus, and Giroux, 2000.

Euripides, and Paul Roche, trans. *10 Plays.* New York: Signet Classic, 1998.

Farnaux, Alexandre, and David J. Baker, trans. *Knossos: Searching for the Legendary Palace of King Minos.* New York: Harry N. Abrams, 1996.

Felix Guirand, ed. *Larousse Encyclopedia of Mythology.* London: Batchwood Press, 1959.

Finley, M. I. *The World of Odysseus.* New York: New York Review of Books, 2002.

Fleming, Stuart. *Vinum: The Story of Roman Wine.* Glen Mills, PA: Art Flair, 2001.

Foley, Helene P. *The Homeric Hymn to Demeter.* Princeton, NJ: Princeton University Press, 1993.

Garber, Marjorie, and Nancy J. Vickers, eds. *The Medusa Reader.* New York: Routledge, 2003.

Gardner, Jane F. *Roman Myths.* Austin, TX: University of Texas Press, 1994.

Gibbon, Edward, and David Womersley, ed. *The Decline and Fall of the Roman Empire.* New York: Penguin USA, 1996.

Goldsworthy, Adrian. *The Complete Roman Army.* New York: Thames and Hudson, 2003.

Graves, Robert. *The Greek Myths.* New York: Penguin USA, 1993.

Guerber, H. A. *The Myths of Greece and Rome.* New York: Dover Publications, 1993.

Harding, Anthony. *The Mycenaeans and Europe.* San Diego: Academic Press, 1997.

Hesiod, and M. L. West, trans. *Theogony; and Works and Days.* New York: Oxford University Press, 1999.

Homer, and Robert Fagles, trans. *The Iliad.* New York: Penguin USA, 2003.

Homer, and Robert Fagles, trans. *The Odyssey.* New York: Penguin USA, 1999.

Horace, and David West, trans. *The Complete Odes and Epodes.* New York: Oxford University Press, 2000.

Howatson, M. C., and Ian Chilvers. *Concise Oxford Companion to Classical Literature.* New York: Oxford University Press, 1993.

Hughes, Dennis D. *Human Sacrifice in Ancient Greece.* New York: Routledge, 1991.

Kerenyi, Karl, and Ralph Manheim, trans. *Eleusis.* Princeton, NJ: Princeton University Press, 1991.

Komar, Kathleen L. *Reclaiming Klytemnestra.* Champaign, IL: University of Illinois Press, 2003.

Macgillivray, Joseph Alexander. *Minotaur: Sir Arthur Evans and the Archaeology of the Minoan Myth.* New York: Hill and Wang, 2000.

March, Jenny. *Cassell's Dictionary of Classical Mythology.* London: Cassell, 1998.

Matyszak, Philip. *Chronicle of the Roman Republic.* New York: Thames and Hudson, 2003.

McLaren, Clemence. *Inside the Walls of Troy.* New York: Atheneum, 1996.

O'Neill, Eugene. *Three Plays: Desire under the Elms, Strange Interlude, Mourning Becomes Electra.* New York: Vintage Books, 1995.

Ovid, and A. D. Melville, trans. *Metamorphoses.* New York: Oxford University Press, 1998.

Pausanias, and Peter Levi, trans. *Guide to Greece.* New York: Viking Press, 1984.

Pindar, and Richard Stoneman, trans. *The Odes: And Selected Fragments.* New York: Everyman's Library, 1998.

Pinsent, John. *Greek Mythology.* London: Hamlyn, 1982.

Plato, and G. M. A. Grube, trans. *Republic.* Cambridge, MA: Hackett Publishing, 1992.

Plato, and James H. Nichols, Jr., trans. *Gorgias and Phaedrus.* Ithaca, NY: Cornell University Press, 1998.

Pomeroy, Sarah B. *Goddesses, Whores, Wives, and Slaves: Women in Classical Antiquity.* New York: Schocken Books, 1995.

Race, William H., ed. *Pindar: Olympian Odes, Pythian Odes.* Cambridge, MA: Harvard University Press, 1997.

FURTHER READING

Rose, Carol. *Giants, Monsters, and Dragons*. New York: Norton, 2000.

Scheid, John. *An Introduction to Roman Religion*. Bloomington, IN: Indiana University Press, 2003.

Scullard, H. H. *Festivals and Ceremonies of the Roman Republic*. Ithaca, NY: Cornell University Press, 1981.

Sirracos, Constantine. *History of the Olympic Games*. Long Island City, NY: Seaburn Books, 2000.

Sophocles, and Judith Affleck, and Ian McAuslan, eds. *Oedipus Tyrannus*. Cambridge University Press, 2003.

Turcan, Robert, and Antonia Nevill, trans. *The Gods of Ancient Rome*. New York: Routledge, 2001.

Ulansey, David. *The Origins of the Mithraic Mysteries*. New York: Oxford University Press, 1991.

Virgil, and Robert Fitzgerald, trans. *The Aeneid*. New York: Vintage, 1990.

West, Martin L., ed. *Homeric Myths, Homeric Apocrypha, Lives of Homer*. Cambridge, MA: Loeb Classical Library, 2003.

Wilk, Stephen R. *Medusa: Solving the Mystery of the Gorgon*. New York: Oxford University Press, 2000.

Wiseman, T. P. *Catullus and His World: A Reappraisal*. Cambridge: Cambridge University Press, 1985.

Wiseman, T. P. *Remus: A Roman Myth*. New York: Cambridge University Press, 1995.

INDIA

Daniélou, Alain. *The Gods of India: Hindu Polytheism*. New York: Inner Traditions International, 1985.

Levacy, William R. *Beneath a Vedic Sky: A Beginner's Guide to the Astrology of Ancient India*. Carlsbad, CA: Hay House, 1999.

McIntosh, Jane R. *A Peaceful Realm: The Rise and Fall of the Indus Civilization*. Boulder, CO: Westview Press, 2001.

MESOAMERICA

Arnold, Philip P. *Eating Landscape: Aztec and European Occupation of Tlalocan*. Niwot, CO: University of Colorado Press, 1999.

Cobo, Bernabe, and Roland Hamilton, trans. *Inca Religion and Customs*. Austin, TX: University of Texas Press, 1990.

Coe, Michael, and Rex Koontz. *Mexico: From the Olmecs to the Aztecs*. New York: Thames and Hudson, 2002.

Ferguson, Diana. *Tales of the Plumed Serpent: Aztec, Inca and Mayan Myths*. New York: Sterling, 2000.

Henderson, John S. *The World of the Ancient Maya*. Ithaca, NY: Cornell University Press, 1997.

Luckert, Karl W. *Olmec Religion: A Key to Middle America and Beyond*. Norman, OK: University of Oklahoma Press, 1976.

Martin, Simon, and Nikolai Grube. *Chronicle of the Maya Kings and Queens: Deciphering the Dynasties of the Ancient Maya*. New York: Thames and Hudson, 2000.

Nicholson, H. B., and Gordon Randolph Willey. *Topiltzin Quetzalcoatl: The Once and Future Lord of the Toltecs*. Boulder, CO: University of Texas Press, 2000.

Scarre, Christopher, and Brian M. Fagan. *Ancient Civilizations*. New York: Longman, 1997.

Schele, Linda, and David Freidel. *A Forest of Kings: The Untold Story of the Ancient Maya*. New York: William Morrow and Company, Inc., 1990.

Stuart, Gene S., and George E. Stuart. *Lost Kingdoms of the Maya*. Washington, D.C.: National Geographic Society, 1993.

Taube, Karl. *Aztec and Maya Myths*. Austin, TX: University of Texas Press, 1993.

Urton, Gary. *Inca Myths*. London: British Museum Publications, 1999.

MESOPOTAMIA

Black, Jeremy, and Anthony Green. *Gods, Demons, and Symbols of Ancient Mesopotamia: An Illustrated Dictionary.* Austin, TX: University of Texas Press, 1992.

George, Andrew, trans. *The Epic of Gilgamesh.* New York: Penguin Books, 2003.

Guirand, Félix, ed. *Larousse Encyclopedia of Mythology.* London: Hamlyn, 1983.

Hoffner, Harry, trans. *Hittite Myths.* Atlanta, GA: Scholars Press, 1990.

Hoyland, Robert G. *Arabia and the Arabs: From the Bronze Age to the Coming of Islam.* New York: Routledge, 2001.

Kovotaev, A. V. *Pre-Islamic Yemen.* Wiesbaden, Germany: Harrosowitz, 1996.

Kramer, Samuel Noah. *Sumerian Mythology: A Study of Spiritual and Literary Achievement in the Third Millennium BC.* Philadelphia: University of Pennsylvania Press, 1998.

MacQueen, J. G. *The Hittites.* London: Thames and Hudson, 1996.

Mason, Herbert. *Gilgamesh: A Verse Narrative.* Boston, MA: Houghton Mifflin, 2003.

McCall, Henrietta. *Mesopotamian Myths.* Austin, TX: University of Texas Press, 1991.

Oates, Joan. *Babylon.* New York: Thames and Hudson, 1986.

Roaf, Michael. *The Cultural Atlas of Mesopotamia and the Ancient Near East.* New York: Checkmark Books, 1990.

Stetkevych, Jaroslav. *Muhammad and the Golden Bough: Reconstructing Arab Myth.* Bloomington, IN: Indiana University Press, 1996.

Willis, Roy, ed. *World Mythology: The Illustrated Guide.* New York: Simon and Schuster, 1993.

NATIVE AMERICANS

Anderson, Bernice G. *Indian Sleep Man Tales.* Caldwell, ID: Caxton Printers, Ltd., 1940.

Cooper, J. C. *Symbolic and Mythological Animals.* New York: HarperCollins, 1992.

Grinnell, George Bird. *Blackfoot Lodge Tales, The Story of a Prairie People.* Lincoln, NE: University of Nebraska Press, 1962.

Hirschfelder, Arlene, and Paulette Molin. *Encyclopedia of Native American Religions.* New York: Checkmark Books, 2000.

Jaimes, M. Annette, ed. *The State of Native America.* Boston: South End Press, 1992.

Nesper, Larry. *The Walleye War.* Lincoln, NE: University of Nebraska Press, 2002.

Reichard, Gladys A. *Navaho Religion: A Study of Symbolism.* Tucson, AZ: University of Arizona Press, 1983.

Sullivan, Lawrence E., ed. *Native Religions and Cultures of North America, Anthropology of the Sacred.* New York: Continuum, 2000.

Wyman, Leland Clifton. *The Windways of the Navaho.* Colorado Springs: Taylor Museum of the Colorado Springs Fine Arts Center, 1962.

SCANDINAVIA

Byock, Jesse L., trans. *The Saga of the Völsungs: The Norse Epic of Sigurd the Dragon Slayer.* Berkeley, CA: University of California Press, 2002.

Colum, Padraic. *Nordic Gods and Heroes.* New York: Dover Publications, 1996.

Davidson, H. R. Ellis. *Gods and Myths of Northern Europe.* New York: Viking Press, 1990.

Davidson, H. R. Ellis. *Scandinavian Mythology.* New York: Peter Bedrick Books, 1982.

DuBois, Thomas A. *Nordic Religions in the Viking Age.* Philadelphia: University of Pennsylvania Press, 1999.

Heaney, Seamus, trans. *Beowulf.* New York: W. W. Norton, 2001.

Larrington, Carolyne, trans. *The Poetic Edda.* New York: Oxford University Press, 1996.

Lindow, John. *Norse Mythology.* New York: Oxford University Press, 2002.

McKinnell, John. *Both One and Many: Essays on Change and Variety in Late Norse Heathenism.* Rome: Il Calamo, 1994.

Orchard, Andy. *Cassell's Dictionary of Norse Myth and Legend.* London: Cassell, 2002.

Page, R. I. *Norse Myths.* Austin, TX: University of Texas Press, 1991.

Sawyer, Peter, ed. *The Oxford Illustrated History of the Vikings.* New York: Oxford University Press, 1997.

Simek, Rudolf, and Angela Hall, trans. *A Dictionary of Northern Mythology.* Rochester, NY: Boydell and Brewer, 1993.

Snorri Sturluson, and Anthony Faulkes, trans. *Edda.* New York: Oxford University Press, 1991.

Turville-Petre, E.O.G. *Myth and Religion of the North.* Westport, CT: Greenwood, 1975.

Wagner, Richard, and Andrew Porter, trans. *Ring of the Nibelung.* New York: W. W. Norton, 1983.

Wagner, Richard, and Nicholas John, ed., and Andrew Porter, trans. *The Valkyrie.* New York: Riverrun Press, 1988.

GENERAL

Agrawal, M. M. *Individuality and Reincarnation.* New Delhi, India: Sunrise International, 1978.

Armstrong, Karen. *A History of God.* New York: Knopf, 1993.

Beard, Mary, and John North, eds. *Pagan Priests: Religion and Power in the Ancient World.* Ithaca, NY: Cornell University Press, 1990.

Bowker, John Westerdale. *World Religions.* New York: Dorling Kindersley Publishing, 1997.

Cashford, Jules. *The Moon: Myth and Image.* New York: Four Walls Eight Windows, 2003.

Cavendish, Richard, ed. *Man, Myth, and Magic.* New York: Marshall Cavendish, 1995.

Chaucer, and Nevill Coghill, trans. *Troilus and Criseyde.* London: Penguin, 1971.

Cotterell, Arthur. *Oxford Dictionary of World Mythology.* Oxford: Oxford University Press, 1986.

Davies, Jon. *Death, Burial, and Rebirth in the Religions of Antiquity.* New York: Routledge, 1999.

Davies, Nigel. *Human Sacrifice in History and Today.* New York: Morrow, 1981.

Davis-Kimball, Jeannine, with Mona Behan. *Warrior Women: An Archaeologist's Search for History's Hidden Heroines.* New York: Warner Books, 2003.

Delacampagne, Ariane, and Christian Delacampagne. *Here Be Dragons: A Fantastic Bestiary.* Princeton, NJ: Princeton University Press, 2003.

De Silva, Lynn A. *Reincarnation in Buddhist and Christian Thought.* Colombo, Sri Lanka: Christian Literature Society of Ceylon, 1968.

Dietrich, Wendell S. *Ethical Monotheistic Religion and Theory of Culture.* Atlanta, GA: Scholars Press, 1986.

Eliade, Mircea, and Willard R. Trask, trans. *Birth and Rebirth: The Religious Meanings of Initiation in Human Culture.* New York: Harper, 1958.

Eliade, Mircea, and Willard R. Trask, trans. *Shamanism.* Princeton, NJ: Princeton University Press, 1972.

Ferguson, Diana. *The Magickal Year.* York Beach, ME: Red Wheel, 2002.

Finn, Thomas M. *From Death to Rebirth: Ritual and Conversion in Antiquity*. Mahwah, NJ: Paulist Press, 1997.

Forsyth, Neil. *The Old Enemy*. Princeton, NJ: Princeton University Press, 1989.

Franklin, Anna. *The Illustrated Encyclopaedia of Fairies*. London: Vega, 2002.

Frazer, James George. *The Golden Bough*. New York: Simon and Schuster, 1996.

Gardell, Mattias. *Gods of the Blood*. Durham, NC: Duke University Press, 2003.

Gayley, Charles Mills. *The Classic Myths in English Literature and Art*. Boston: Ginn and Company, 1893.

Gennep, Arnold van, Monika B. Vizedom, and Gabrielle L. Caffe, trans. *The Rites of Passage*. London: Routledge and Paul, 1960.

Gikatilla, Rabbi Joseph. *Gates of Light (Sha'are Orah)*. San Francisco: HarperCollins Publishers, 1994.

Gimbutas, Marija. *The Goddesses and Gods of Old Europe*. Berkeley, CA: University of California Press, 1982.

Goodenough, Ursula. *The Sacred Depths of Nature*. New York: Oxford University Press, 1998.

Goodman, Lenn. *Monotheism*. Totowa, NJ: Allanheld, Osmun, 1981.

Gottlieb, Roger, ed. *This Sacred Earth: Religion, Nature, Environment*. New York: Routledge, 2000.

Greaves, Richard, et al. *Civilizations of the World*. New York: Longman, 1997.

Green, Miranda. *Dying for the Gods: Human Sacrifice in Iron Age and Roman Europe*. London: Tempus Publishing, 2002.

Greimas, Algirdas, and Milda Newman, trans. *Of Gods and Men: Studies in Lithuanian Mythology*. Bloomington, IN: Indiana University Press, 1992.

Hamilton, Edith. *Mythology: Timeless Tales of Gods and Heroes*. New York: Warner Books, 1999.

Hamilton, Virginia. *In the Beginning: Creation Stories from Around the World*. San Diego, CA: Harcourt, 1991.

Hawke, Elen. *Praise to the Moon: Magic and Myth of the Lunar Cycle*. St. Paul, MN: Llewellyn Publications, 2002.

Hudec, Ivan, and Dusan Caplovic. *Tales from Slavic Myths*. Wauconda, IL: Bolchazy Carducci, 2001

Insoll, Timothy, ed. *Archaeology and World Religion*. New York: Routledge, 2001.

Jacobson, Thorkild, and Mircea Eliade, ed. *The Encyclopedia of Religion*. New York: Macmillian Publishers, 1987.

James, E. O. *Prehistoric Religion: A Study in Prehistoric Archaeology*. New York: Barnes and Noble, 1961.

Joyce, James, and Seamus Deane, ed. *Portrait of the Artist as a Young Man*. New York: Penguin Books, 2003.

Kakar, Sudhir. *Shamans, Mystics, and Doctors*. Chicago: University of Chicago Press, 1991.

Kaplan, Steven J., ed. *Concepts of Transmigration: Perspectives on Reincarnation*. Lewiston, NY: Mellen Press, 1996.

Kirsch, Jonathan. *God against the Gods: The History of the War between Monotheism and Polytheism*. New York: Viking, 2004.

Leeming, David Adams, and Margaret Adams Leeming. *A Dictionary of Creation Myths*. New York, NY: Oxford University Press, 1996.

Lehner, Ernst, and Johanna Lehner. *Folklore and Symbolism of Flowers, Plants and Trees*. London: Marshall Cavendish, 1995.

Littleton, C. Scott, ed. *Mythology: The Illustrated Anthology of World Myth and Storytelling*. San Diego, CA: Thunder Bay Press, 2002.

Lovelock, James. *Gaia: A New Look at Life on Earth*. New York: Oxford University Press, 2000.

Mackenzie, Dana. *The Big Splat, or How Our Moon Came to Be*. New York: John Wiley and Sons, 2003.

McVicker Edwards, Carolyn. *In the Light of the Moon:*

Thirteen Lunar Tales from Around the World Illuminating Life's Mysteries. New York: Marlowe and Company, 2003.

Mercatante, Anthony S. *Zoo of the Gods: The World of Animals in Myth and Legend*. Berkeley, CA: Seastone, 1999.

Mersey, Daniel. *Legendary Warriors: Folklore's Greatest Heroes in Myth and Reality*. Dulles, VA: Brassey's Inc., 2003.

Mills, Philo Laos. *Prehistoric Religion: A Study in PreChristian Antiquity*. Washington: Capital Publishers, Inc., 1918.

Narayan, R. K. *Gods, Demons, and Others*. Chicago: University of Chicago Press, 1993.

Nyenhuis, Jacob E. *Myth and the Creative Process: Michael Ayrton and the Myth of Daedalus*. Detroit, MI: Wayne State University Press, 2003.

Pagels, Elaine. *The Origin of Satan*. New York: Vintage Books, 1996.

Pennick, Nigel. *The Pagan Book of Days: A Guide to the Festivals, Traditions, and Sacred Days of the Year*. Rochester, VT: Inner Traditions Intl. Ltd., 1999.

Phillips, Charles, and Michael Kerrigan. *Forests of the Vampires: Slavic Myth (Myth and Mankind)*. New York: Time-Life Books, 2000.

Pizzato, Mark. *Theatres of Human Sacrifice from Ancient Ritual to Screen Violence*. Albany NY: State University of New York Press, 2004.

Pollock, Robert. *The Everything World's Religions Book: Discover the Beliefs, Traditions, and Cultures of Ancient and Modern Religions*. Avon, MA: Adams Media Corporation, 2002.

Ridpath, Ian. *Smithsonian Handbooks: Stars and Planets*. New York: Dorling Kindersley, 2002.

Rosenberg, Donna. *World Mythology: An Anthology of the Great Myths and Epics*. New York: McGraw-Hill, 1994.

Russell, Charles Coulter, and Patricia Turner. *Encyclopedia of Ancient Deities*. Jefferson, NC: McFarland and Company, 2000.

Sasaki, Chris. *The Constellations: Stars and Stories*. New York: Sterling Publishing, 2001.

Scarre, Christopher, and Brian M. Fagan. *Ancient Civilizations*. New York: Longman, 1997.

Shakespeare, William. *The History of Troilus and Cressida*. New York: Penguin USA, 2000.

Shuker, Karl P. *Dragons: A Natural History*. New York: Simon and Schuster, 1995.

Simoons, Frederick J. *Plants of Life, Plants of Death*. Mineola, NY: Dover Publications, 2003.

Smyers, Karen A. *The Fox and the Jewel*. Honolulu: University of Hawaii Press, 1998.

Summer, Montague. *The Vampire in Lore and Legend*. New York: Dover Publications, 2001.

Tennyson, Alfred, and Christopher Ricks, ed. *A Collection of Poems by Alfred Tennyson*. Garden City, NY: International Collectors Library, 1972.

Vitebsky, Piers. *The Shaman: Voyages of the Soul Trance, Ecstacy, and Healing from Siberia to the Amazon*. London: Duncan Baird Publishers, 2001.

Warner, Marina, ed. *World of Myths*. London: British Museum Press, 2003.

INTERNET RESOURCES

The Age of Fable: Thomas Bulfinch
Electronic version of the 1913 edition of Bulfinch's compilation of myths. The site contains versions of a number of famous Greek and Roman myths, as well as stories from Arthurian legend and the medieval world.
www.bartleby.com/bulfinch

Ancient China
General site about ancient China that includes sections on Chinese deities, dragons, Confucianism, Buddhism, and Taoism. The site also contains information about many other aspects of ancient Chinese culture. Suitable for younger users.
www.crystalinks.com/china.html

Ancient India
A concise history of ancient India that includes sections on both Vedic and pre-Vedic religious beliefs. It also gives an account of the history of Buddhism in the region.
*http://www.wsu.edu:8080/~dee/ANCINDIA/
CONTENTS.HTM*

Avesta: Zoroastrian Archives
Web site dedicated to the major text in the Zoroastrian faith, the *Avesta*. The site contains a translation of the original text, a history of the religion, and lists of Zoroastrian festivals and rituals.
www.avesta.org

The Children's Literature Web Guide: Folklore, Myth, and Legend
Contains links to electronic versions of a variety of folktales and myths, including Aesop's fables and a number of Native American legends.
http://www.ucalgary.ca/~dkbrown/storfolk.html

Comparative Religion
Comprehensive Web site that examines the major world religions and their roots in ancient mythology. The site contains links to translations of sacred texts, as well as forums in which contemporary religious issues are discussed.
www.comparative-religion.com

Digital Librarian: Mythology
A collection of links to Web sites useful to students of mythology.
www.digital-librarian.com/mythology.html

Encyclopedia Mythica
Encyclopedia of mythology, folklore, and legends from around the world. The Web site is divided geographically, with each section listing the gods and goddesses of a particular culture. Each entry includes a brief summary of the role of the deity. The Web site also features diagrams of family trees. It is fully searchable.
http://www.pantheon.org

Encyclopedia of the Celts
A comprehensive encyclopedia of Celtic mythology that gives detailed biographies of all the major deities and heroes.
*www.celt.net/Celtic/celtopedia/indices/encycintro.
html*

Etymological Dictionary of Classical Mythology
A Web site that lists modern words and terms derived from figures or episodes from classical mythology. One subsection of the site lists examples of the influence of classical mythology on popular culture; another lists stars and constellations that derive their names from characters in Greek mythology.
http://www.kl.oakland.edu/kraemer/edcm/contents.html

Folklore and Mythology: Electronic Texts
Collection of myths and folktales from around the world, with particular emphasis placed on stories from central and northern Europe.
http://www.pitt.edu/~dash/folktexts.html

Forum Romanum
A Web site dedicated to bringing Roman literature to a wider audience. The Web site contains works by a vast number of Roman authors in the form of both original Latin texts and English translations. Authors featured include Ovid and Apuleius.
www.forumromanum.org

INTERNET RESOURCES

Gateways to Babylon

Web site dedicated to ancient Mesopotamia—its history, cultures, religions, and people. The site contains biographies of Mesopotamian deities, descriptions of festivals, and translations of ancient texts.

www.gatewaystobabylon.com

God Checker

Humorous Web site aimed largely at younger users. The Web site contains descriptions of the gods of a variety of ancient civilizations.

www.godchecker.com

Gods, Heroes, and Myth

General Web site for world mythology. The site contains particularly comprehensive lists of Native American deities, with separate sections for peoples such as the Cherokee, Iroquois, and Navajo.

www.gods-heros-myth.com

The Golden Bough: A Study in Magic and Religion

Electronic version of the 1922 edition of James Frazer's *The Golden Bough*, a study in comparative mythology. The work identifies the common themes found in myths from different cultures.

www.bartleby.com/196

Greek Mythology Link

Extensive Web site that includes maps, timelines, and biographies of all the major characters in Greek mythology. An introduction gives an overview of the history of the recording of Greek myths. The site also features lists of groups of characters such as the suitors of Penelope and the Greek heroes who hid in the Trojan horse.

www.homepage.mac.com/cparada/GML

Hieroglyphs

Aimed at younger users, this interactive Web site examines the ancient Egyptian system of writing and makes comparisons with modern alphabets.

www.greatscott.com/hiero/index.html

Internet Classics Archive

Collection of electronic versions of ancient texts, all translated into English. The site contains links to works by Greek and Roman authors such as Apollodorus, Pausanias, and Ovid, as well as texts by Chinese writers Confucius and Lao-tzu.

http://classics.mit.edu/index.html

Luminarium

A Web site mainly dedicated to medieval, Renaissance, and 17th-century literature that includes a large section on Irish mythology.

www.luminarium.org/lumina.htm

The Mystica

Web site that provides information on the occult and the paranormal and also contains a section on world mythology. The site features sections on magic and witchcraft, the Druids, Mithraism, and a variety of ancient religious practices.

www.themystica.org

MythHome

Comprehensive Web site that covers all the major pantheons. As well as the more recognizable deities from ancient Greece, Rome, and Egypt, the site also provides extensive lists of gods and goddesses from Africa, Japan, and the Pacific region.

www.mythome.org/mythhome.htm

Mythography

Web site dedicated to Greek, Roman, and Celtic mythology. It contains separate lists of the gods of ancient Ireland, Wales, and Gaul. The site includes links to other relevant resources such as recent books and other Web sites.

www.loggia.com/myth/myth.html

Mythology Gallery Directory

Web site that offers a basic overview of ancient Egyptian mythology. The site lists all of the culture's major gods and goddesses, giving brief biographies of each. Other aspects of ancient Egyptian culture, such as mummification and the building of the pyramids, are also discussed. The site also features a section that allows users to translate hieroglyphs by clicking on relevant symbols.

www.members.aol.com/egyptart/mytho.html

Myth Search

Search engine dedicated to Web sites on mythology.

www.mythsearch.com

Mythweb

Aimed primarily at younger users, this Web site provides a basic introduction to Greek mythology. It gives brief biographies of all the Olympian deities and synopses of the major myths.

www.mythweb.com

Native American Authors

Web site dedicated to Native American culture. Each of the sections of the Web site is dedicated to a particular people. Many of the articles contained within the site contain information about Native American myths and religious beliefs.

www.ipl.org/div/natam

Norse Mythology

Introductory Web site to Scandinavian mythology. It provides brief biographies of all the major Norse deities. Links to source materials allow the user to read Norse myths in their original form.

www.ugcs.caltech.edu/~cherryne/myth.cgi

Oceania Mythology Home Page

Web site that provides information on mythology from Oceania and the islands of the Pacific. Divided into geographical sections, the site allows users to find out about the myths and gods of specific groups of islands. The site also gives a brief cultural history of each island group.

www.janeresture.com/oceania_myths/index.htm

Okana's Web

Site dedicated to Slavic and Polish mythology and culture. It contains traditional Polish folktales and descriptions of traditional customs.

www.okana.org

Olga's Gallery: Ancient Greek and Roman Myths

Catalog of paintings that depict scenes from classical mythology. The site allows the user to select a Greek deity or hero and then view a selection of paintings featuring him or her. The site includes links to works by a wide number of artists, including Caravaggio, Titian, and Poussin.

http://www.abcgallery.com/mythindex.html

Sacred Texts

Contains links to electronic versions of the sacred texts of most of the world's religions, including Christianity, Buddhism, and Hinduism. The Web site also includes translations of classical works such as the *Iliad* and the *Odyssey*, Mesopotamian poems such as the *Enuma Elish*, and ancient Egyptian texts such as the Book of the Dead.

www.sacred-texts.com/index.htm

Theoi Project: A Guide to Greek Gods, Spirits, and Monsters

Comprehensive Web site devoted exclusively to Greek mythology. The Web site is divided into alphabetical sections featuring extensive lists of Greek mythological figures, both major and minor. For each deity, hero, or mythological creature, the Web site gives the subject's parentage, the derivation of his or her name, and the equivalent figure in Roman mythology. It also lists all the major classical sources in which the figure features.

www.theoi.com

Windows to the Universe

Site aimed at younger users that is dedicated to space and the solar system. The Web site includes a large subsection about space and mythology that includes entries on sun, moon, and sky deities from across the world. A section about constellations gives details of the myths associated with them.

www.windows.ucar.edu/windows.html

RESOURCES FOR YOUNGER READERS

AFRICA

Arnott, Kathleen, and Rosamund Fowler, illustrator. *Tales from Africa*. Oxford: Oxford University Press, 2000.

Bennett, Martin. *West African Trickster Tales*. New York: Oxford University Press, 1994.

Giles, Bridget. *Myths of West Africa*. Austin, TX: Raintree Steck-Vaughn, 2002.

Hunter, Bobbi Dooley. *The Legend of the African Bao-Bab Tree*. Trenton, NJ: Africa World Press, 1995.

Knappert, Jan, and Francisca Pelizzoli, illustrator. *Kings, Gods, and Spirits from African Mythology*. New York: Peter Bedrick Books, 1995.

Mandela, Nelson, ed. *Nelson Mandela's Favorite African Folktales*. New York: W. W. Norton, 2002.

Washington, Donna L., and James Ransome, illustrator. *A Pride of African Tales*. New York: HarperCollins, 2004.

AUSTRALIA AND OCEANIA

Dalal, Anita. *Myths of Oceania*. Austin, TX: Raintree Steck-Vaughn, 2002.

CHINA AND JAPAN

Birch, Cyril, and Rosamund Fowler, illustrator. *Tales from China*. New York: Oxford University Press, 2000.

Cotterell, Arthur. *Eyewitness: Ancient China*. New York: Dorling Kindersley Publishing, 2000.

Green, Jen. *Myths of China and Japan*. Austin, TX: Raintree Steck-Vaughn, 2002.

Krasno, Rena, Yeng Fong Chiang, and Kevin J. Smant. *Cloud Weavers: Ancient Chinese Legends*. Berkeley, CA: Pacific View Press, 2002.

Martens, Frederick H. *Chinese Fairy Tales*. New York: Dover Publications, 1998.

Haviland, Virginia, and Carol Inouye. *Favorite Fairy Tales Told in Japan*. New York: Beech Tree Books, 1996.

McAlpine, Helen, William McAlpine, and Rosamund Fowler, illustrator. *Tales from Japan*. New York: Oxford University Press, 2002.

EASTERN EUROPE

Avery, Gillian. *Russian Fairy Tales*. New York: Everyman's Library, 1995.

Dalal, Anita. *Myths of Russia and the Slavs*. Austin, TX: Raintree Steck-Vaughn, 2002.

Mayer, Marianna. *Baba Yaga and Vasilisa the Brave*. New York: William Morrow, 1994.

McNally, R. T. *In Search of Dracula*. Boston, MA: Houghton Mifflin, 1994.

Phillips, Charles, and Michael Kerrigan. *Forests of the Vampire: Slavic Myth and Mankind*. Alexandria, VA: Time Life, 1999.

Warner, Elizabeth, and Alexander Koshkin, illustrator. *Heroes, Monsters, and Other Worlds from Russian Mythology*. New York: Peter Bedrick Books, 1996.

EGYPT

Ardagh, Philip, and Danuta Mayer, illustrator. *Ancient Egyptian Myths and Legends*. Chicago: World Book, 2002.

Ashworth, Leon. *Gods and Goddesses of Ancient Egypt*. North Mankato, MN: Smart Apple Media, 2002.

Fisher, Leonard Everett. *The Gods and Goddesses of Ancient Egypt*. New York: Holiday House, 1997.

Gahlin, Lucia. *Egypt: Gods, Myths, and Religion*. London: Lorenz Books, 2001.

Harris, Geraldine, and David O'Connor and John Sibbick, illustrators. *Gods and Pharaohs from Egyptian Mythology*. New York: Peter Bedrick Books, 1996.

Hart, George. *Eyewitness: Ancient Egypt*. New York: Dorling Kindersley, 2000.

Martell, Hazel Mary. *The Great Pyramid*. Austin, TX: Raintree Steck-Vaughn, 1998.

Millard, Anne, and L. R. Gallante, illustrator. *The World of the Pharaoh*. New York: Peter Bedrick Books, 1998.

Morley, Jacqueline, and Giovanni Caselli, illustrator. *Egyptian Myths*. Lincolnwood, IL: Peter Bedrick, 1999.

GREECE AND ROME

Ashworth, Leon. *Gods and Goddesses of Ancient Egypt*. North Mankato, MN: Smart Apple Media, 2002.

Bolton, Lesley. *The Everything Classical Mythology Book: Greek and Roman Gods, Goddesses, Heroes, and Monsters from Ares to Zeus*. Avon, MA: Adams Media Corporation, 2002.

Colum, Padraic. *The Children's Homer: The Adventures of Odysseus and the Tale of Troy*. Mineola, NY: Dover Books, 2004.

Colum, Padraic. *The Golden Fleece: And the Heroes Who Lived before Achilles*. New York: Collier Books, 1983.

Connolly, P. *Ancient World: The Ancient Greece of Odysseus*. New York: Oxford University Press, 1999.

Day, Nancy. *Passport to History: Your Travel Guide to Ancient Greece*. Minneapolis, MN: Runestone, 2000.

Evslin, Bernard. *Heroes, Gods, and Monsters of the Greek Myths*. Minneapolis, MN: Sagebrush Educational Resources, 1999.

Fleischman, Paul. *Dateline: Troy*. Cambridge, MA: Candlewick Press, 1996.

Green, Jen. *Myths of Ancient Greece*. Austin, TX: Raintree Steck-Vaughn, 2001.

Homer, Geraldine McCaughrean, and Victor G. Ambrus, illustrator. *The Odyssey*. New York: Oxford University Press, 1999.

Hull, Robert E. *World of Ancient Greece: Religion and the Gods*. Danbury, CT: Franklin Watts, 2000.

Innes, Brian. *Myths of Ancient Rome*. Austin, TX: Raintree Steck-Vaughn, 2001.

James, Simon. *Eyewitness: Ancient Rome*. New York: Dorling Kindersley, 2000.

Lively, Penelope, and Ian Andrews, illustrator. *In Search of the Homeland: The Story of the Aeneid*. New York: Delacorte Press, 2001.

Low, Alice, and Arvis L. Stewart, illustrator. *The Macmillan Book of Greek Gods and Heroes*. New York: Maxwell Macmillan International, 1994.

McCaughrean, Geraldine, and Emma Chichester Clark, illustrator. *Greek Myths*. New York: Margaret K. McElderry Books, 1993.

McCaughrean, Geraldine, and Emma Chichester Clark, illustrator. *Roman Myths*. New York: Margaret K. McElderry Books, 2001.

McLaren, Clemence. *Aphrodite's Blessings: Love Stories from the Greek Myths*. New York: Atheneum Books, 2002.

Múten, Burleigh, and Rebecca Guay, illustrator. *Goddesses: A World of Myth and Magic*. Barefoot Books, 2003.

RESOURCES FOR YOUNGER READERS

Osborne, Mary Pope, and Troy Howell, Illustrator. *Favorite Greek Myths*. New York: Scholastic Press, 1991.

Pearson, Anne. *Eyewitness: Ancient Greece*. New York: Dorling Kindersley, 2000.

Ross, Stewart. *Ancient Greece: The Original Olympics*. New York: Peter Bedrick Books, 1999.

Sharman-Burke, Juliet, and Jackie Morris, illustrator. *Stories from the Stars: Greek Myths of the Zodiac*. New York: Abbeville Kids, 1996.

INDIA

Dalal-Clayton, Diksha, and Marilyn Heeger, illustrator. *The Adventures of Young Krishna: The Blue God of India*. Oxford: Oxford University Press, 2000.

Gray, J. E. B., and Rosamund Fowler, illustrator. *Tales from India*. New York: Oxford University Press, 2001.

Guruseva, Dasi. *Churning the Milk Ocean: A Young Reader's Edition of the Classic Story from the Puranas of Ancient India*. LaCrosse, FL: Bhavani Books, 2002.

Marchant, Kerena, Rebecca Gryspeerdt, illustrator, and Frank A. Sloan, ed. *Hindu Festival Tales*. Austin, TX: Raintree Steck–Vaughn, 2001.

Ness, Caroline, and Jaqueline Mair, illustrator. *The Ocean of Story: Fairy Tales from India*. New York: Lothrop Lee and Shephard, 1996.

Uma, Krishnaswami. *The Broken Tusk: Stories of the Hindu God Ganesha*. North Haven, CT: Linnet Books, 1996.

MESOAMERICA

Baquedano, Elizabeth. *Eyewitness: Aztec, Inca, and Maya*. New York: Dorling Kindersley Publishing, 2000.

Dalal, Anita. *Myths of Pre-Columbian America*. Austin, TX: Raintree Steck-Vaughn, 2001.

Gifford, Douglas, and John Sibbick, Heather Dew, and John Sibbeck, illustrators. *Warriors, Gods, and Spirits from Central American Mythology*. New York: Peter Bedrick Books, 2000.

McManus, Kay. *Land of the Five Suns: Looking at Aztec Myths and Legends*. Lincolnwood, IL: NTC Publishing Group, 1997.

MESOPOTAMIA AND WESTERN ASIA

Finkel, Irving. *The Hero King Gilgamesh*. Lincolnwood, IL: NTC Publishing, 1998.

McCaughrean, Geraldine, and David Parkins, illustrator. *The Epic of Gilgamesh*. Grand Rapids, MI: Eerdmans Books for Young Readers, 2003.

Zeman, Ludmila. *The Revenge of Ishtar*. Plattsburgh, NY: Tundra Books, 1993.

NATIVE AMERICANS

Bruchac, Joseph, and John Kahiones Fadden, illustrator. *Native American Stories*. Golden, CO: Fulcrum Publishing, 1991.

Dalal, Anita. *Myths of the Native Americans*. Austin, TX: Raintree Steck–Vaughn, 2001.

Max, Jill. *Spider Spins a Story: Fourteen Legends from Native America*. Flagstaff, AZ: Rising Moon, 1997.

Wood, Marion. *Myths and Civilizations of the Native Americans*. New York: Peter Bedrick Books, 1998.

Yoe, Charlotte, and David Yoe. *The Wigwam and the Longhouse*. Boston, MA: Houghton Mifflin, 2000.

NORTHERN EUROPE

Colum, Padraic. *The Children of Odin: The Book of Northern Myths*. New York: Collier Books, 1984.

Daly, Kathleen N., and Marian Rengel. *Norse Mythology A to Z*. New York: Facts on File, 2003.

Fisher, Leonard Everitt. *Gods and Goddesses of the Ancient Norse*. New York: Holiday House, 2001.

Green, Jen. *Gods and Goddesses in the Daily Life of the Vikings*. Columbus, OH: Peter Bedrick Books, 2003.

Gross, Gwen, and Norman Grant, illustrator. *Knights of the Round Table*. New York: Random House, 2004.

Kerven, Rosalind. *Enchanted Kingdoms*. Lincolnwood, IL: NTC Publishing, 1998.

Macuistin, Liam, and Maria A. Negrin, illustrator. *Celtic Magic Tales*. Chester Spring, PA: O'Brien Press; 1993.

McBratney, Sam, and Stephen Player, illustrator. *Celtic Myths*. New York: Peter Bedrick Books, 2002.

Osborne, Mary Pope, and Troy Howell, illustrator. *Favorite Medieval Tales*. New York: Scholastic Press, 1998.

Osborne, Mary Pope, and Troy Howell, illustrator. *Favorite Norse Myths*. New York: Scholastic, 2001.

Philip, Neil, and Maryclare Foa. *Odin's Family: Myths of the Vikings*. New York: Orchard Books, 1996.

Picard, Barbara Leonie, and Rosamund Fowler, illustrator. *Tales of the Norse Gods*. New York: Oxford University Press, 2001.

Shetterly, Will. *Thor's Hammer*. New York: Random House, 2000.

GENERAL

Colum, Padraic, and Boris Artzybasheff, illustrator. *Myths of the World*. Edinburgh, UK: Floris Books, 2002.

Hamilton, Virginia. *In the Beginning: Creation Stories from around the World*. San Diego, CA: Harcourt Paperbacks, 1991.

January, Brendan. *Amazing Mythology: A Book of Answers for Kids*. New York: Wiley, 2000.

Keenan, Sheila, and Belgin Wedman, illustrator. *Gods, Goddesses, and Monsters*. New York: Scholastic, 2000.

Pollock, Robert. *The Everything World's Religions Book: Discover the Beliefs, Traditions, and Cultures of Ancient and Modern Religions*. Avon, MA: Adams Media Corporation, 2002.

Rose, Carol. *Giants, Monsters, and Dragons: An Encyclopedia of Folklore, Legend, and Myth*. New York: W. W. Norton, 2000.

Waldherr, Kris. *Sacred Animals*. New York: HarperCollins, 2001.

Wilkinson, Philip, and Neil Philip. *Illustrated Dictionary of Mythology*. New York: Dorling Kindersley Publishing, 1998.

INDEX OF DEITIES AND MYTHOLOGICAL BEINGS

Page numbers in **bold** refer to main articles; those in *italics* refer to pictures.

Abena **1**:42
Abzu **6**:830; **7**:868
Acantha **1**:105
Acastus **6**:779; **8**:1096
Acca Larentia **9**:1240
Achaeus **3**:398
Achelous **1**:13; **5**:665
Achilles **1**:**14–19**; **3**:390; **7**:1000; **9**:1181, 1186
  and the Amazon queen **1**:*62*, 64
  comparison with Aeneas **1**:30
  death of Achilles **1**:18, 133; **5**:622; **6**:853; **7**:*928*, 1000; **8**:1088; **10**:1357
  death of Hector **1**:17–*18*; **5**:622–*623*; **8**:1095; **9**:1166
  death of Lycaon **9**:1166
  death of Memnon **6**:853; **10**:1380–1381
  death of the sons of Priam **9**:1164–*1166*
  death of Troilus **9**:1166; **10**:1388
  disguised as a girl **1**:14–15, 16; **3**:*412*; **10**:1357
  dispute with Agamemnon **1**:17, 19; **2**:*169*, 174; **7**:971; **8**:1094–1095
  education by Cheiron **1**:14, *16*; **8**:1097
  immortal horses **1**:*18*, 85, *86*; **5**:612
  marriage to Helen **5**:638
  and the Myrmidons **7**:*928*
  and Patroclus **1**:133; **5**:622, 623; **8**:1094, 1095; **10**:1357
  Thetis and **1**:14, *15*, 17; **6**:853; **7**:1000; **10**:1356–*1357*
  and the Trojan War **1**:15–16, 50; **6**:853

Acis **3**:356, *357*; **4**:546
Acrisius **3**:362, 363; **8**:1110, 1114; **10**:1436
Actaeon **1**:**20–21**
  and Artemis (Diana) **1**:*20*, 21; **2**:*156*, 157, *158*; **3**:*409*
Acusilaus **8**:1032
Adam and Eve **4**:509
Aditi **6**:738
Admete **5**:687
Admetus **1**:*55*, 132; **4**:495; **5**:662
Adonis **1**:**22–25**
  and Aphrodite (Venus) **1**:22–*24*, 25, 116; **7**:936; **10**:1409
  birth **1**:22, 116; **7**:*929*
  a Canaanite and Phoenician god **2**:268, 269–270, 271
  death of **1**:116; **2**:150
  and the seasons **5**:717
Adrasteia **3**:335; **7**:959, 961
Adroa **4**:447
Aeacus **5**:606, 654; **6**:806; **7**:*927–928*; **8**:1096
  a judge in the underworld **7**:888
Aed **6**:757
Aedon **5**:653
Aeetes **3**:426; **6**:777, 848
Aegeus **3**:327, 329; **9**:*1291*; **10**:*1351*, 1352, 1353
Aegina **5**:654; **7**:927
Aegir (Hlér; Gymir) **1**:**26–27**; **9**:1269
  and the apocalypse **1**:126
Aegisthus **1**:50; **2**:183; **3**:313; **8**:1050–*1051*; **10**:1349
Aegle **5**:681
Aello **5**:611, 614
Aeneas **1**:**28–33**; **3**:390, 409; **6**:785, 861
  death **1**:33
  and Dido **1**:*31*, 32; **6**:785
  and the foundation of Rome **9**:1232

and the Harpies **5**:612, *613*
  Juno and **6**:780–781
  and the Penates **8**:1101–*1102*, *1103*
  Romanization of **1**:28
  ship caught in a storm **10**:*1314*
  and the Trojan War **1**:28–30
  in the underworld **1**:32; **9**:1292
  wanderings with the Trojans **3**:313
Aeneas Silvius **9**:1220
Aeode **7**:900
Aeolus **3**:398; **8**:1035–1036
Aerope **2**:183, 184
Aesacus **1**:91; **9**:1164
Aesculapius *see* Asclepius
Aesir **1**:**34–37**; **4**:531, 554
  war with the Vanir **4**:531; **7**:988–989; **10**:1404–1405
Aether **3**:352
Aethlius **4**:473
Aethon **3**:398
Aethra **8**:1130; **10**:*1351*
Aetolus **4**:473, 475
Agamemnon **1**:**48–51**; **6**:855–856
  abduction of Chryseis **9**:1174
  and Artemis **1**:49; **2**:159, 160; **6**:740
  and Ate **2**:*169*
  and Cassandra **1**:50; **2**:273–274; **3**:313; **4**:470; **6**:742; **8**:1051; **10**:1418
  dispute with Achilles **1**:17, 19; **2**:*169*, 174; **7**:971; **8**:1094–1095
  in literature **1**:51
  murdered by Clytemnestra and Aegisthus **1**:50, *51*; **2**:185, 273–274; **3**:*313*; **4**:470; **5**:634
  sacrifice of Iphigeneia **1**:16, 49; **2**:159, 160; **3**:312, 408;

4:470; **6**:740, 856; **8**:1050, 1087
  and the Trojan War **1**:49–50; **7**:920
Aganippe **1**:105
Agas **3**:402
Agave (Aguae) **2**:216, 253; **3**:417
Agdistis **2**:186; **9**:1237
Agenor **1**:76; **2**:251; **8**:1113
Aglaea **5**:582, 584
Aglaurus **2**:150; **4**:486, *487*
Agni **3**:382, 403; **6**:735, 738; **10**:1340
Ahau-Kin **9**:1211
Ah Ciliz **6**:845
Ah Cuxtal **6**:845
Ah Peku **6**:845
Ah Puch **6**:845
Ahriman *see* Angra Mainyu
Ahura **4**:443
Ahura Mazda (Ormazd) **3**:314, *402*; **4**:443, *444*; **6**:744, 746–747, *748*, 749
Ai **3**:296
Aiantis **1**:53
Aidos **7**:959, 961
Aithalides **9**:1214–1215
Ajax **1**:**52–54**
  Ajax of Locris (Little Ajax; Lesser Ajax; Locrian Ajax) **1**:*52*, 53–54; **2**:174, 273, 274
  Telamonian Ajax (Great Ajax) **1**:52, *53*, *54*
Alaghom Naom **6**:845
Alalus **5**:693
Ala Tala **10**:1323, 1326, 1328
Al-Basti (Red Mother) **3**:297
Alberich **7**:*972*, 974
Alcestis **1**:**55–56**, 132; **4**:495; **5**:662
Alcibiades **5**:672
Alcinous **8**:1038
Alcmene **3**:394; **5**:654, 659, 709; **10**:1436

Alcyone **8**:1131

Alcyoneus **4**:566, 568

Alecto **4**:540

Alectryon **1**:114

Alexikakos **1**:130

Alf **10**:1300

Alfar **1:57–59**

Alignak **9**:1271

Al-Karisi (Red Woman) **3**:297

Allah **7**:909

Allat **7**:*909*

Almaqah **1**:137

Alpheus **7**:1002; **10**:*1420*

Althaea **2**:168; **4**:495

Amairgen **1**:105

Amaltheia **1**:105; **3**:326, 335, *338*; **10**:*1433*

  horn of plenty **1**:13

Ama no Uzume **10**:1345–1346

Amaterasu **3**:316; **4**:446; **10**:*1345–1346*, 1347

  Ise-Jingu shrine **10**:*1347*

Amazons **1:60–65**; **2**:231; **8**:1122

  Heracles and **1**:62; **5**:662, 687

  Theseus and **1**:62–63; **5**:*687–688*; **8**:*1122*; **10**:*1354*

  see also Antiope; Hippolyte

Amei Awi **10**:1326

Amemait **1**:*111*

Amenti **3**:373

Ameretat **1**:102; **6**:747, 748

Amesa Spentas **3**:402; **6**:747

Amida Buddha **7**:909

Amma **1**:40

Am-mut **5**:608

Amorgen **6**:757

Amotken **3**:314

Amphiaraus **3**:394, *395*

Amphictyon **3**:398

Amphinomus **8**:1104

Amphion **7**:985

Amphitrite **7**:965, 970; **8**:1144, *1148*

  and Theseus **10**:1352

Amphitryon **5**:654, 709

Amulius **6**:835; **9**:*1221*, 1231–1232, 1240, 1241–1242; **10**:*1414–1415*

Amun (Amen; Amun-Re; Re-Amun) **2**:190; **4**:463, 466; **6**:788; **7**:994; **9**:*1172*, 1206, 1209; **10**:1342

Amycus **6**:777

Amyklas **7**:986

An **1:66–68**; **3**:318; **4**:476, 480; **7**:870, *872*

  see also Anu

Anahita **6**:*747*

Anansi **1**:42

Ananta **3**:*319*

Anat **2**:164, 166, 212, 267, 268; **8**:1056

  and Baal **2**:166, 213, 215, 268

Anaxarete, Iphis and **8**:1141–1142

Anchises **1**:28, *30*, 31, 32; **2**:158

Anchurus **7**:879

Androcles **1**:*84*–85

Androgeos **7**:887; **8**:1092

Andromache **5**:621

Andromeda **1:75–76**; **7**:*970*

  Perseus and **1**:*75–76*; **3**:424–425, *429*; **5**:581; **8**:*1110, 1112*–1113, *1147*

Andvari **10**:1303

Anemoi **1:77**

Angatch **1**:46

angatra **1**:74

angkors **10**:1322

Angra Mainyu (Ahriman) **3**:*402*; **4**:443, *444*; **6**:746–747, 748, 749

Angrboda **6**:818; **10**:1404

animal-headed figures **1:78–83**

  Australian Aboriginal **1**:81

  Buddhist **1**:79–80

  Egyptian **1**:78–*79*, 83; **4**:*465*, *466*; **5**:*702, 708*; **10**:*1393*

  Greek *see* Minotaur

  Hindu **1**:*80*–81

  Judeo-Christian **1**:81

  Mesopotamian **1**:79

Animal Mothers **1**:87

Annunaki (Igigi), the **1**:67; **7**:877

Anshar **10**:1369

Antaeus **4**:568; **5**:*661*, 663; **8**:*1144–1146*

Anteia (Stheneboea) **2**:230, 232

Antenor **10**:1388

Antero Vipunen **4**:566

Anthas **8**:*1130*, 1131

Antheia **5**:582

Anticlia **10**:1307

Anticlus **8**:1034

Antigone (daughter of Eurytion) **7**:928; **8**:1096

Antigone (daughter of Oedipus) **1:106–107**; **8**:*1042, 1045*

Antinous **8**:1104

Antiope **1**:62–63; **5**:*687*, 688; **8**:*1122*; **10**:1354

Antum **1**:67

Anu **5**:693, 696; **10**:1398

  see also An

Anubis **1**:78, **108–111**; **4**:466; **8**:*1065*

  a guide for the dead **5**:703

  a judge of the dead **1**:*111*; **5**:608

  and mummification **1**:88, *109*; **3**:*375*

  representations of **1**:*88*, 109

Anukis **7**:981

Ao **8**:1013

Aoede **7**:924

Aphaea (Aphaia) **2**:247, *248*

Aphrodite **1:112–119**; **2**:148; **5**:656

  and Adonis **1**:22–*24*, 25, 116; **7**:936

  and Aeneas **1**:28

  and Ares **1**:*114*; **2**:150–151; **5**:643, 646–648; **8**:*1121*

  birth **1**:*112*; **10**:1397, *1409*

  creation **3**:318, 334

  and the Graces **5**:*582*

  and Helios **5**:643

  and Hermes **5**:666

  and Hippolytus and Phaedra **1**:116; **10**:1354

  importance to brides **5**:667

  loss of ichor (divine blood) **2**:236

  love affair with Zeus **5**:655

  mother of Eros **4**:488, *491*

  and Myrrha **7**:929

  and Pasiphae **8**:1091

  and Poseidon's "courtship" tidal wave **7**:951

  and Priapus **9**:1168

  and Psyche **4**:491

  and Pygmalion **1**:115; **9**:*1197*, 1198

  rescues Paris **2**:236; **6**:857

  Roman equivalent *see* Venus

  squeaking sandal **7**:*904*

  symbols of **1**:115

  wife of Hephaestus **1**:*113–114*; **5**:643, 646–648; **7**:951

  and the women of Lemnos **1**:117–118

  worship of **1**:119

  see also Paris, Judgment of

Apis (Hapi; Hepu) **1**:93; **5**:610

  Ptah and **9**:1195

Apocatequil **6**:727

Apollo **1:128–135**; **9**:1231

  adopted by the Romans **8**:1136; **9**:*1239*

  Apollo Grannus **2**:279

  Apollo Medicus **1**:133

  Apollo Mithras **6**:746

  battle against Python **1**:128, 129, *131*; **3**:422–424

  birth **1**:128; **2**:157; **6**:815

  Clytie and **7**:1002

  conspiracy against Zeus **1**:131

  and Coronis **1**:134; **2**:161

  cult of **1**:129, 133; **9**:1235–1236

  curse on Cassandra **1**:133; **2**:272

  and the Cyclopes **3**:352–354

  and Cyparissus **1**:134

  and Cyrene **1**:134; **7**:1001

  and Daphne **1**:104, *105, 132*, 133; **3**:341, 365, *367*; **7**:1002; **8**:*1124–1125*; **10**:1417

  Eros's intervention **4**:489

  and Delphi **1**:128–129; **8**:1136

  and Dryope **1**:134

  and Evadne **1**:134

  god of music **1**:130–131

  god of order **1**:131

  and Hyacinthus **1**:133–134; **7**:936

  and Laomedon **6**:805–806

  and Leto **6**:815–816

  link with the sun **5**:*600, 643*; **10**:1344

  and the Muses **7**:925

  musical contests **1**:132; **7**:878–879, 923; **8**:1078; **9**:1257

  names for **1**:129–130

  Phoebus Apollo **1**:129; **10**:1344, 1396

  punished by Zeus **1**:132

  and the Sibyl of Cumae **1**:133

  and Sinope **1**:133

  slaughter of Niobe's children **2**:160; **7**:985, *986*

  and Thalia **1**:134

  tricked by Hermes **5**:672–*673*

Apollo (continued)
  and the Trojan War
    1:132–133; **5**:622
  worshiped in different places
    8:*1136*
Apophis (Apop) **2**:189, *190*;
    4:552
  killed by the sun god **2**:244;
    5:695; **9**:1208, *1209*, 1282,
    1283; **10**:1341
Apoyan Tachi **4**:447
Appu **5**:696
Apsu **3**:403; **7**:868; **10**:1368,
    1369
Apsyrtus **6**:848–849
Apulu **8**:1072
Aqhat **8**:1056
Ara and Irik **10**:1325, 1326
Arachne **1**:91, 104, **141–142**;
    2:171
Arcas **2**:158, 262–263;
    5:653–654; **6**:824, 826;
    7:1001
  and Chrysopelia **4**:441
Arcion **8**:1144
Aremata-Popoa (Short Wave)
    9:1274
Aremata-Rorua (Long Wave)
    9:1274
Ares **2**:148–153**; **5**:651
  and Aprodite **1**:*114*;
    2:150–151; **5**:643, 646–648;
    8:*1121*
  children **1**:116; **2**:*151*;
    8:1121–1122
  a death god **8**:1121
  involvement in the Trojan
    War **2**:151–152; **3**:411;
    5:615, 655; **8**:1069
  Roman equivalent *see* Mars
  trial on the Areopagus **2**:153
Arethusa **1**:105; **7**:*1000*, 1002;
    10:*1420*
Arges **3**:352; **10**:1395, 1396
Argonauts **6**:775–776
  see also Jason, voyage with
    the Argonauts
Argos (giant) **5**:653
Argus **6**:859; **10**:1435–1436
Ariadne **2**:154–155**; **3**:329,
    358; **7**:888
  Bacchus (Dionysus) and
    2:*154*, 155, 218; **3**:*414*,
    416; **10**:1353
  heroine status **3**:394
  Theseus and **2**:154–*155*;

3:329, 358; **8**:1092;
    10:*1352*–1353
Arianrhod **10**:1421–1422
Arinna **5**:692, 693, 699;
    10:1343, *1344*
Arisbe **9**:1164
Aristaeus **7**:1001; **9**:1186
Ariston **1**:118
Arjuna **1**:18; **6**:738
Artemis **2**:156–160**; **6**:780;
    7:914; **10**:1419–1420
  and Actaeon **1**:*20*, 21; **2**:*156*,
    157, *158*; **3**:*409*
  and Agamemnon **1**:49; **2**:159,
    160; **6**:740; **8**:1050
  Bendis and **8**:*1139*
  birth **2**:157; **6**:815
  Britomartis and **2**:247
  Callisto and **2**:262, *263*
  chorus of **2**:157–158
  Hera's battle against **5**:652
  and Iphigeneia **2**:159, 160;
    3:408
  and Leto **6**:815–816
  link with Isis **6**:768
  moon goddess **9**:1278
  and Orion **2**:157; **5**:690;
    8:1055
  Roman equivalent *see* Diana
  slaughter of Niobe's children
    2:160; **7**:985, *986*, *987*
  and the story of Hippolytus
    and Phaedra **1**:116–117
  temples to, *arktoi* **6**:743
Artemis of the Crossroads
    5:620
Arthur, *legendary king of Britain*
    4:508–509; **10**:1422
  and Mordred **4**:448
Artume **4**:447
Artums **8**:1072
Aruru **4**:505
Aryong **6**:795
Asa **1**:40
Asag **7**:983
Asclepius (Aesculapius)
    2:161–162**; **3**:352–353;
    8:*1069*; **10**:1438
  birth **1**:134
  death **1**:131–132
  a demigod **3**:390, *392*
  Hermes and **5**:673–674
  staff **1**:86–87
  temple of (Rome) **4**:498
Asgaya Gigagel **7**:939
Asha Vahishta **1**:102; **6**:747, 748

Asherah **2**:212, 213, 267, 268
  see also Astarte
Ashnan **4**:505
Ashratu *see* Astarte
Ashtar **2**:166, 268
Ashtart *see* Astarte
Ashtoreth *see* Astarte
Ashtoroth *see* Astarte
ashuras **3**:338
Ask and Embla **1**:36;
    6:818–820; **8**:1027
Asops **10**:1308
Asru **4**:445
Assur **7**:870, 874
Astarte (Ashtart; Astoret;
    Ashtoroth; Ashtoreh;
    Ashratu; Qadashu) **1**:24;
    2:163–166**, 268
  cults involving prostitution
    5:718
  see also Inanna; Tanit
Astart-in-the-name-of-Baal
    2:166
Asterios *see* Minotaur
Asterius **7**:885
Astoret *see* Astarte
Astraeia **10**:1334
Astraeus **10**:1396
Astyanax **5**:623, 627; **9**:1167
Astydameia **8**:1096
Astymedusa **8**:1043
Aswapati **6**:739
Atahensic **7**:938, 939
Atalanta **2**:167–168**; **5**:682
Atar **6**:747
Atarrabi **4**:446
Ate **2**:169**
Aten (Aton) **2**:190; **4**:466;
    7:907–908; **10**:*1312*, 1343
Athamas **5**:654; **6**:776
Athena (Pallas) **2**:170–177**;
    3:378; **5**:*656*; **10**:1418, *1419*
  aiding Heracles **2**:172–173
  Athena Ergane **7**:881
  Athena Nike **8**:*1137*
  Athena Parthenos **8**:1083
  Athena Promachos **7**:881
  in battle **2**:172
  and Bellerophon **2**:231
  birth **2**:170–171; **3**:*378*;
    5:597; **10**:1434–1435
  contest with Arachne **1**:91,
    141; **2**:171
  creations of, judged by
    Momos **7**:904

and the defeat of Typhon
    2:171; **10**:*1394*
  dress
    aegis **10**:1433
    battle dress **2**:*171*, *172*, *174*
  and Hephaestus **4**:486; **5**:649
  involvement in the Trojan
    War **2**:151–152, 174; **5**:623,
    655; **10**:1418
    the Trojan Horse **2**:174
  and the Lesser Ajax **1**:52, 54
  and Medusa **8**:1144
  mother of Erichthonius
    4:486; **5**:649
  and Nike **2**:175, *177*; **7**:975
  patron of Athens and gift of
    olive oil **2**:175
  and Poseidon **8**:1148
  Roman equivalent *see*
    Minerva
  statue in the Parthenon
    7:975; **10**:1376
  and Tiresias **10**:1371
  worship of **2**:175–*177*
  see also Paris, Judgment of
Atius Tirawa **7**:939
Atlantids **7**:999
Atlas **2**:178–181**; **4**:*564*; **5**:581;
    10:1374–1375
  Heracles and **2**:178–180;
    5:663–665, 682
  Perseus and **2**:180; **8**:1112
  Pleiades and **8**:1129
Atli **10**:1303, 1402, 1403
Aton *see* Aten
Atrahasis **4**:479, 519
Atreus **1**:48; **2**:182–185**; **6**:855
  House of **2**:*183*; **6**:855–856;
    8:1050
Atropos **4**:*493*–*497*; **5**:598,
    599; **8**:1128
Attis **1**:24; **2**:186–187**; **4**:457,
    509; **7**:933
Atum **2**:188–191**; **4**:466,
    501–502; **10**:*1312*, 1341
  Atum-Re (Re-Atum) **2**:188,
    191
  and the calendar **2**:255
Audhumla (Audumla;
    Audhumbla) **2**:233, 246,
    249–*250*; **4**:568; **10**:*1428*
Augeas **5**:662
Auld Clootie (Auld Cloots)
    3:404
Aurgelmir *see* Ymir
Aurora **4**:485

Ausautas **2**:228

Auseklis **2**:229

Ausrine **2**:224–226, 228, 229

Autolycus **8**:1032; **10**:1307

Automedon **1**:*86*

Autonoe **2**:253

Auxo **5**:582

Avalokitesvara **9**:1174

Avernales **7**:999

Avya **4**:447

Awitelin Tsta **4**:447

Awonawilona **4**:447;
    5:589–590; **7**:939

Azhi Dahaka **1**:127; **6**:747

Azizos **4**:445

Baal **2**:210–215, 267–268;
    10:1312–1313

    death and resurrection **2**:268

    identification with Jupiter
        6:786, 788

    and Lady Asherah of the Sea
        2:164–166

Baalat **1**:25; **2**:268, 269

    Temple of **2**:*269*

Baal Hammon **2**:269

Baal-Peor **4**:446

Baba Yaga **10**:1318, *1321*

Bacchants (Bacchantes) **2**:216,
    217; **7**:931

    see also maenads

Bacchus **2**:216–219; **9**:1231

    and Ariadne **2**:*154*, 155, 218;
        3:*414*

    Greek equivalent *see*
        Dionysus

    as one of the Penates **8**:1100

Balam Ak'ab **6**:842

Balam Quitze **6**:842

Balder **2**:220–223; **9**:1260

    death **1**:18, 34–36;
        2:*220–221*, 260; **4**:516,
        535–536; **5**:633; **6**:822, *823*

    funeral **7**:989

    Hermód's attempt to release
        Balder from the underworld
        5:*676–677*; **8**:1030

Bali (demon) **6**:736

Balius **1**:14, *18*, 85, *86*; **5**:612

Bara, the **1**:26

Barong **10**:1324, *1326*

Baron Samedi **3**:*374*

Bastet **1**:78; **4**:464, *465*, 466

Batara Guru **10**:1324, 1326

Batara Kala **10**:1324, 1326

Baubo **4**:506

Baucis, Philemon and
    6:785–786; **8**:1125

Baugi **4**:568–569, *570*;
    8:1028–1029

Bear **1**:87

Belenus **2**:279

Beli **4**:527–529

Bellerophon **1**:62; **2**:230–232;
    8:1112

Bellona (Duellona) **2**:*152*;
    6:834; **7**:931

Belobog **10**:1318, 1319

Bendigeid Vran *see* Bran the
    Blessed

Bendis **8**:*1139*

Benu bird **2**:191; **4**:550

Beowulf **3**:425; **4**:561–562;
    10:1425

Bergelmir **2**:233–234

Bes **4**:466

beserks **1**:104

Bestla **2**:246; **4**:568; **8**:1024;
    10:1428

Betelgeuse **8**:1056

Bezalel **5**:711–712

Bia **7**:975

Bil **10**:1405

bishopfish **9**:1274

Black Donald **3**:404

Black Emperor **10**:*1311*

Blodughadda **1**:26

Blue Men of the Muir **9**:1273

Boand **7**:966–967

Boannd **2**:279

boddhisatvas **3**:373, 374–375

Bona Dea **4**:516

Bopis Hera **5**:651

Bor **2**:246, 250; **4**:568; **8**:1024;
    10:1428

Boreas **4**:484; **7**:948; **8**:1075;
    10:1313, 1314

Boucolion **6**:805

Bragi **1**:36; **8**:1024

Brahma **3**:316, *318*, 320;
    6:735–736, *737*, 738;
    10:1326

Bran the Blessed (Bendigeid
    Vran) **2**:281

Brekirihunuade **1**:40

Breo Saighead *see* Brigid

Bresal **6**:757

Briareos **4**:564; **10**:1395

Bride *see* Brigid

Brigid (Brighid; Brigindo;
    Brigantia; Bride; Breo
    Saighead) **6**:757; **10**:1422

Brigit **2**:279, 281

Briseis **1**:16, 17, 49–50;
    8:*1094*–1095

Britomartis **2**:158, 247–248;
    10:1419–1420

Brontes **3**:352; **10**:1395, 1396

Brunhild *see* Brynhild

Brynhild (Brunhild) **2**:169;
    4:562; **5**:677; **7**:972; **8**:1026,
    1028; **10**:1302, 1303, 1304,
    1401–1402

Bull of Heaven **4**:571–572;
    6:762

Búri **2**:246, 249–250; **4**:568;
    10:1428, 1429

Burung Une **10**:1326

Byblis **7**:1002

Bylgia **1**:26

Cadmus (Kadmos) **1**:116;
    2:251–253

    founding of Thebes **2**:149,
        251–253; **3**:426

Caenis (Caeneus) **5**:669;
    8:1144

Caha-Paluma **6**:842

Cakixia **6**:842

Calais **5**:*612*; **6**:779

Calchas **1**:49; **5**:619; **6**:740;
    8:1118–1119; **10**:1388, 1390

Calliope **7**:921

Callisto **1**:21, 105; **2**:158,
    262–263; **5**:653–654; **6**:826;
    7:1001; **10**:1334

Calybe **6**:805

Calyce **4**:473

Calypso **2**:178, 264–265; **7**:*999*

Camalotz **6**:842

Camaxtli **6**:845

Camenae **7**:926

Camese **6**:770

Camilla **1**:63

Campe **10**:1374

Canens **6**:773

Capitoline Triad **6**:780

Carme (Karme) **2**:247

Carna **6**:773

Caryatids **2**:176–177; **4**:440,
    441

Cassandra **1**:133; **2**:272–274;
    3:313

    abduction of **1**:50; **2**:174, 273

    death **2**:*274*; **3**:313; **4**:470;
        6:742

    and the Lesser Ajax **1**:54

    and Paris **2**:272–273; **8**:1085

and the Trojan War **2**:*273*;
    10:*1418*

Cassiopeia **1**:75, 76; **3**:424;
    8:1112–1113, 1147

Castalla **1**:105

Castor and Pollux **2**:275–276;
    4:445, *446*; **6**:811, 812–813;
    9:1235

Catamitus **4**:548

Cathbad **6**:757

Cecropian Artemis **7**:931

Cecrops **4**:486, 544; **5**:597;
    9:1190

Celaeno **5**:611, 612, 613, 614;
    8:1131

Celidon **5**:653

Cenchrias **7**:1002

centaurs **1**:*81*, 89

    see also Cheiron

Centaurus **5**:584

Cephalus **4**:483, *484*; **5**:675;
    8:1093

Cepheus **1**:75; **3**:424–425;
    8:1112–1113, 1147

Cerberus **5**:*601*, 603, 607, 665

Ceres **9**:1231, 1235

    Greek equivalent *see* Demeter

Cernunnos **2**:279, *284*; **8**:*1075*

Ceryneian Hind **8**:1131

Ceto **9**:1273

Chac **10**:*1384*, 1385

Chac Mool **9**:*1245*

Chacs, the **10**:1385

Chalchiuhtlicue **2**:205, 209;
    10:1384

Chandra **7**:913

Changing Woman **7**:939, 943

Ch'ang O **3**:*303*, 304, 308

chapshin **6**:791

Chareya **5**:590

Chariclo **10**:1371

Charon **3**:369, *370*; **5**:*605*;
    7:991; **8**:*1022*

    and Psyche **9**:*1191*

Charu **3**:401

Charybdis **8**:1037, *1146*

Chasca **6**:727

Chasca Coyllur **6**:727

Chata **7**:941

Cheiron **1**:14, 89; **3**:339

    and Achilles **1**:14, *16*; **8**:1097

    and Actaeon **1**:20

    and Asclepius **2**:161

    and Jason **6**:775

    and Peleus **8**:1096, *1097*

Chelone **1**:105; **7**:1001–1002

Ch'eng Huang **3**:308, 309

Chen Hsu **3**:308

Chernobog **10**:1318, 1319

Chicksah **7**:941

Chimera **1**:88
  slaying of the **2**:230–*231*;
    8:*1112*

Chineke *see* Chuku

Chirakan-Ixmucane **6**:845

Chloe, Daphnis and **4**:459

Chloris (Flora) **1**:77

Chloris (Meleboea) **7**:986

Choimha **6**:842

Cholban (Chulpan) **3**:296

Chrysaor **5**:581

Chryseis **1**:17, 49, 132; **9**:*1174*
  Criseyde identified as
    10:*1390*

Chryses **9**:1174

Chrysippus **2**:183

Chrysopelia **4**:441

Chrysothemis **2**:185

Chuku (Chineke) **1**:40; **3**:314

Chumong **6**:794, 795

Cilix **2**:251

Cinyras **7**:929; **9**:1174

Circe **3**:310–311; **5**:619; **6**:773,
    849; **8**:1104; **9**:1274;
    10:1372

Cirein crôin **9**:1274

Cleomedes of Astypalaea **3**:392

Cleta **5**:582

Clio **7**:921, *922*, 926

Clitonymus **8**:1094

Clotho **4**:493–494; **5**:598, *599*

Clymene **8**:1022

Clytemnestra **2**:172, 185;
    3:312–313; **6**:813
  Agamemnon and **1**:48, 50,
    51; **5**:634; **8**:1050–1051
  birth **5**:634
  death **3**:313; **4**:*472*
  and the death of Cassandra
    2:273–*274*; **3**:313; **4**:470
  and dualism **4**:445, 446

Clytia **1**:105

Clytie **7**:1002

Clytius **5**:617

Coati **6**:844

Coatlicue **2**:205, 207–208
  moon goddess **3**:*348*

Cocalos **7**:888

Cochamama **6**:727

Cocijo **10**:1385

Cocoamama **6**:727

Coeus **4**:564

Conchobar **6**:757

Concordia, temple to **9**:1236

Connla **9**:1251

Consus **9**:1231

Copacati **6**:727

Cormac mac Art **6**:753

Coronis **1**:134; **2**:151, 161

Coti **1**:40

Cottus **4**:564; **10**:1395

Cotzbalam **6**:842

Coyolxauhqui **2**:205, 208–209;
    3:338; **7**:911

Coyote **3**:376, 404; **7**:939
  and the Great Spirit **5**:587
  and the origin of fire **7**:945

Crathis **8**:1074

Cratos **7**:975

Creon **1**:106, 107;
    8:1041–1042, 1044, 1045

Crescent Moon **10**:1327

Cressida (Criseyde), Troilus and
    3:412; **10**:1388–*1390*

Criseyde *see* Cressida

Cronus **2**:171; **3**:318, 326,
    334–339; **4**:542, 564; **5**:601,
    684; **10**:*1397*, 1431
  and the flood **4**:520
  overthrow of Uranus by
    3:334, *336*; **4**:565;
    10:1373–1374
  and Philyra **3**:*339*
  Roman equivalent *see* Saturn
  Zeus's revenge on **3**:335–336;
    4:565; **5**:601–602, 684;
    10:1374, 1432

Cú Chulainn **6**:752, 755, *757*;
    9:*1226*, 1251; **10**:1401

Cupid **3**:340–343; **6**:*860*;
    9:1231
  Greek counterpart *see* Eros
  and Psyche **3**:341–343;
    9:*1187–1191*

cupids **10**:*1386*, 1387

Curetes **10**:1432

Cybele (Magna Mater) **2**:237;
    4:457; **9**:1231, 1237
  altar consecrated to **7**:*930*
  Attis and **1**:24; **2**:186–*187*;
    4:457
  Greek equivalent *see* Rhea
  mystery cult and worship of
    7:933; **9**:1218, *1219*

Cyclopes **3**:352–357; **4**:564;
    10:1395, 1396
  creation of **3**:318, 334;
    10:1373

killed by Apollo **1**:132
  war against Cronus and the
    Titans **3**:335–336; **4**:565;
    10:1374, 1432
  see also Polyphemus

Cycnus **1**:16; **2**:151; **8**:1117,
    1121

Cyparissus **1**:134; **8**:1125

Cyrene **1**:134; **7**:*1001*

Daedalus **3**:358–361; **5**:*711,
    712*; **7**:887–888; **8**:1149

Daevas *see* devas

Dagda **2**:279; **4**:439; **9**:1161

Daikoku **1**:86

dakinis **1**:80; **4**:457

Damasistratus **8**:1041

Damgalnunna **4**:477

Damkina **10**:1369

Dana **2**:279

Danae **3**:362–364; **5**:580, 581;
    8:1110; **10**:1436–1437

Danu **3**:364

Daphne **3**:365–367
  and Apollo **1**:104, *105*, 132,
    133; **3**:341, 365, *367*;
    7:*1002*; **8**:*1124–1125*;
    10:1417
  Eros's intervention **4**:489
  Leucippus and **3**:365–367;
    8:1130

Daphnis **8**:*1078*
  and Chloe **4**:459

Daramulun **2**:197

Dardanians **1**:28

Dardanus **9**:1164

Dark Thunder **10**:1311

Darth Vader **4**:448

Daw-Kee **5**:587

Dayisun (Dayisud Tengri)
    3:296

Dazhdebog **10**:1318

Dea Dia **9**:1243

Dea Matres (Matronae) **2**:279

Deianeira **5**:665; **8**:1118

Deidamia **1**:15

Deimos **1**:116; **2**:149

Deino **8**:1110

Deiphobos **5**:637; **6**:*857*, 858;
    9:1164

Deipyle **3**:411

deities **3**:378–385

Dekla **2**:228

Delphinus **8**:1144

Demeter **3**:386–389; **5**:*593*
  and the abduction of

Persephone **3**:386, *388*, 389;
    4:504; **5**:602–603; **8**:1106,
    1108; **10**:1311–1312
  and corn **8**:*1124*
  Demeter Erinys **4**:540
  eating part of Pelops **10**:1350
  and Erysichthon **4**:441
  and fertility rituals (Eleusinian
    Mysteries) **4**:506–507, 515;
    9:*1229*
  link with Isis **6**:768
  and Poseidon **8**:1144
  and Triptolemus **3**:386, *387*;
    9:*1229*

demigods and heroes
    3:390–395
  heroes **3**:392–395
  battling dragons **3**:422–424
  compared with giants **4**:564
  cult of Hector **5**:625

Demodocus **7**:926

demons *see* devils

Demophon **3**:387, 389; **4**:506;
    8:1106

Despoina **8**:1144

Deucalion **3**:396–400
  Deucalion (son of king
    Minos) **3**:398
  Deucalion (son of
    Prometheus) **3**:*396–400*;
    4:*521*; **6**:824; **9**:1179

devas (Daevas)
  in ancient myths of India
    3:338
  in Zoroastrianism **3**:402;
    4:443; **6**:747, 748

Devi, many forms **4**:447

devils **3**:401–406
  Dunstan and a **10**:1426
  Japanese **3**:*406*
  Minoan **3**:332
  Native American **3**:406
  in polytheistic cultures
    3:402–403
  Scottish **3**:*404*
  targeting women **3**:406
  in Turkik and Mongol
    religion **3**:296–297
  of the Yekuhana people
    10:1316
  see also Trickster gods

Devi Sri **10**:1325, 1326, 1328

Dhanvantari **9**:1268

Diana **2**:157; **3**:407–410;
    6:780; **9**:1231, *1235*;
    10:1420

Diana Nemorensis (Diana of the Woods) **3**:408; **8**:1072–1073
Roman equivalent *see* Artemis
Dian Cecht **6**:757
Diarmuid **6**:755
Dictes **3**:362
Dictynna **2**:247, 248; **7**:931
Dido, and Aeneas **1**:*31*, 32
Dievas (Praamzius; Satvaras; Prakurimas) **2**:224, 228
Dike **10**:1334, 1435
Dimste **2**:228
Dindymene **9**:1237
Dingo **2**:199
Diomedes, *king of Argos* **2**:151; **3**:**411–412**; **8**:1033
wounding Aphrodite **2**:236; **3**:411
wounding Ares **3**:411; **5**:655; **8**:1069
Diomedes, *king of the Thracians*, eaten by horses **2**:*151*; **5**:662; **8**:1121–1122
Dionysus **3**:**413–418**; **4**:444; **5**:598
adventures of **3**:*415*, 416
double birth **3**:390, 413; **5**:654; **10**:1437
festivals for **3**:417, 418; **5**:669; **7**:931
god of wine **3**:415–416
Hades, parallel with **5**:605
Hermes and **5**:673, *674*
honoring **3**:415
Roman equivalent *see* Bacchus
satyrs and **9**:1257
Silenus **10**:1305
votaries of *see* maenads
Dioscuri *see* Castor and Pollux
Dis **3**:**419–420**; **9**:1231
Greek equivalent *see* Hades
Diti **3**:364
Diuturna **6**:773
Div **10**:1318
divi **9**:1238
djinns **1**:137, 138
Döckálfar (dark elves) **1**:58
Dodol **10**:1318
Dolichenus **6**:786
Dolon **8**:1033
Dolughan Ebügan **3**:296
Dolya **10**:1318
Donar **4**:561

Doris **7**:969; **8**:1022
Dorus **3**:398
Dracula **2**:*238*
Dragon King (Long Vuong; Thuy-tl) **3**:428
dragons **1**:88; **3**:**421–430**
Babylonian
Murussu dragon **6**:*829*; **7**:*954*
see also Tiamat
Chinese **3**:*306*, 421, 427–*428*
Greek, Ladon (dragon of the Hesperides) **3**:425; **5**:663, *681*, *682*
Norse **3**:425–426; **10**:*1300*
drinking the blood of dragons **1**:85, *87*
drugs **3**:402; **6**:747
Dryads **4**:**440–442**; **7**:998, 999
Pomona **7**:999; **8**:**1141–1142**
Dryope **1**:105, 134
Duamutef **1**:110, 111
Duellona *see* Bellona
Dufa **1**:26
Dumuzi **4**:**449–451**, 456–457; **5**:715, 717
Assyrian and Babylonian equivalent *see* Tammuz
Durga **1**:80; **4**:447, *448*
Dwamutef **5**:610
dwarfs, Norse **1**:59
Dyaus (Dyaus Pita) **4**:446–447; **6**:735; **10**:1312
Dyavaprthivi **4**:447
Dylan **9**:1270; **10**:1422

Ea **3**:403; **5**:693, 697; **6**:762, 833; **7**:870; **10**:1369
see also Enki
earth goddess
Minoan **3**:332
Norse **9**:1260–1261, 1262–1263
earth mother **4**:**452–457**
African **4**:452
Aztec **2**:208
Maori **8**:1014, 1015, *1017*
Neanderthal **4**:454–455
Venus figurines **4**:454–455, 502; **9**:1157, 1159
see also mother goddesses
Echidna **3**:422
Echo **4**:**458–459**; **7**:926, 1001
and Narcissus **4**:*458*, 459; **7**:934
and Pan **4**:459; **8**:1075–1076

Egeria **3**:407
Egil **10**:1424
Ehecatl-Quetzalcoatl **9**:1202
Eidothee **9**:1186
Eileithyia **3**:*378*; **5**:651, 659
Einherjar, the, Valkyries and **10**:1400, *1402*
Einodia **6**:742
Eir **10**:1405
Eirene **10**:1435
Eitill **10**:1402, 1403
Ek Chuah **6**:*843*, 845
El **2**:164, 165, 166, 212, 213, 215, 267, 268
Electra **2**:185; **4**:**470–472**; **8**:1022, 1131
Orestes and **4**:*471–472*; **8**:1051, *1053*
Eleios **4**:475
Eleusis **5**:675
El-Gabal **5**:644
elk mother **1**:88, 95, 99
Elpenor **5**:607
elves
in European folklore **1**:59
in Norse mythology (Alfar) **1**:**57–59**
Emathion **10**:1379, 1381
Embla *see* Ask and Embla
Emu, Jabiru and **2**:196, *197*
Enbilulu **4**:477, 505
Endymion **4**:**473–475**
Diana and **3**:*408*
Hypnos and **5**:710
Selene and **9**:*1276*, 1277
Enki **4**:**476–479**, 480, 503, 519; **6**:829; **7**:869, 870
rescue of Inanna **5**:717
see also Ea
Enkidu **3**:371; **4**:*571–572*; **6**:732, 762
Enkimdu **4**:450, 477, 505
Enlil **1**:67; **3**:318–319; **4**:476, **480–482**; **6**:829; **7**:870
and the flood **4**:478–479, 519
Enlil-Marduk (Bel) **4**:480
Ennead, of Heliopolis **2**:189; **9**:1192, 1206
Enyo **2**:152; **8**:1110
Eochaid **6**:757
Eos **2**:148; **4**:**483–485**; **6**:*853*; **10**:1334
and Ares **2**:150–151
and the death of Memnon **10**:*1379*, 1381
and Orion **4**:483; **8**:1055

and Tithonus **4**:484, *485*; **10**:1379–1380, *1381*
Eostre **4**:561
Epaphus **5**:653; **10**:1436
Epeios **2**:174
Epeius **4**:473, 475
Ephialtes **2**:150; **4**:567
Epigoni **3**:411; **8**:1045
Epimetheus **8**:1081; **9**:1180; **10**:1437–1438
Epona **2**:279, *280*
Er **5**:608
Erato **7**:921
Erda **7**:993
Erebus **4**:493
Erechtheus **8**:1146
Ereshkigal **3**:371; **4**:450; **5**:715, 717; **6**:762; **7**:870
Erginus **5**:660
Erichthonius **4**:**486–487**, *544*; **5**:649; **8**:1146; **9**:1190
Erigone **3**:415–416; **10**:1334
Erinyes *see* Furies
Erinys **4**:540
Eris **1**:14, 118; **2**:149; **5**:657, 682; **7**:904; **8**:1085, 1097
Erlik **3**:296, 404
Eros **3**:341; **4**:**488–491**
Roman counterpart *see* Cupid
Erp **10**:1403
Erpr **10**:1402, 1403
Erra **7**:875
Erysichthon **4**:441
Erytheis **5**:681
Esaugetuh Emissee **5**:588
Eshmun **2**:269
Estsanatlehi **4**:445
Esu **1**:44–45
Esus **2**:281
Étain **6**:*755*
Eteocles **1**:106; **8**:1042, 1043–1044
Etzel **7**:972–974
Eudaimonia **5**:582
Eumenides **8**:1051
see also Furies
Eumolpus **8**:1146
Eunomia **10**:1435
Euphorbus **9**:1214–1215
Euphrosyne **5**:582
Europa **2**:251; **3**:*333*; **4**:492; **7**:885; **8**:*1091*; **10**:1435
Eurus **1**:77; **7**:948; **10**:1315

Euryale **5**:580

Eurydice **4**:441; **5**:605, 607; **7**:936; **8**:*1057–1060, 1061*; **9**:1190

Euryganeia **8**:1042

Eurymedusa **7**:927

Eurynome **5**:646; **10**:1313, 1435

Eurystheus **2**:169, 183; **5**:654, 659

and the Labors of Heracles **2**:173, 178; **5**:654–655, 660

Eurytion **7**:928; **8**:1096

Eurytus **8**:1118

Euterpe **7**:921

Evadne **1**:134

Evander **1**:*33*; **9**:1231

Eve **4**:509; **8**:1139

Pandora equated with **8**:*1079*, 1083

Fafnir **1**:*87*; **3**:425–426; **10**:*1300, 1302*

Falstaff **10**:1306

Fand **9**:1270

Fates (Moirai; Parcae; Fata) **4**:493–497; **5**:598, *599*; **7**:993; **10**:1435

Fatua **4**:498

Fauna **4**:498

fauns **1**:82; **9**:1256

Faunus **4**:498–500

Greek equivalent *see* Pan

Faustulus **9**:1221, 1240, 1242, 1244

Favonius **10**:1315

Fedelm **6**:757

Fei Lan **9**:1211

Fenrir **1**:*37*; **5**:633; **8**:1024; **9**:1260

and the apocalypse **1**:*126*; **5**:632; **6**:*817*, 818

chained **9**:1261

Fergus **6**:752, 757

Feronia, festival to **4**:516

Fianna Eireann **9**:1226, 1227

Fides, ritual of **9**:1205

Finn **9**:1226–1227

Fintan **6**:757

Fionn **6**:755, 757

Fisher King **4**:509–510

Fjalar **2**:235–236; **6**:801; **8**:1028; **10**:1405

Flora **1**:77; **7**:*958*; **9**:1231

Fomorii **3**:338

Fon **3**:319

Forseti **1**:36

Fortuna **9**:1231

Fortune, as one of the Penates **8**:1100

Fravashis **6**:748

Fravek and Fravrekain **6**:749

Frey **4**:527–530; **7**:990–991; **9**:1260

and the Alfar (elves) **1**:57

and Gerd **1**:34; **4**:527, *555–556*

ship **7**:991

and the underworld **7**:989

Freya (Gefn; Horn; Mardöll) **1**:37; **4**:527, **531–534**; **7**:991; **9**:1260; **10**:*1366–1367*

depicted as a Valkyrie **10**:1400

Fricka *see* Frigga

Frigga (Fricka) **1**:37; **4**:**535–537**; **10**:1405

and Balder **2**:220–221, 260; **4**:516, 536

fusion with Freya **4**:531

as Odin's wife **4**:535, 536, *537*

Frija **4**:531, 561

Fuflur **8**:1072

Fu Hsi (T'ai Hao) **3**:304, 308

Fu Hsing **3**:308, 309

Fujin **7**:*949*

Fulla **1**:37

Full Moon **10**:1327

Funadama **4**:*518*

Funadama Matsuri festival **4**:*518*

Furies (Erinyes; Furiae; Eumenides; Semnai Theai) **4**:**538–540**, 542; **5**:606; **9**:1231; **10**:1397

and the Harpies **5**:613

and Orestes **4**:*539*; **8**:1051

variant of *see* Ate

Fu Shen **3**:308, 309

Fu-Shou-Lu **3**:309

Gabriel (archangel) **5**:632

Ga-gaah (Wise Crow) **7**:939

Ga-gorib **1**:45

Gaia (Ge) **3**:*321*; **4**:**541–544**; **5**:*594*

and Antaeus **8**:1144–1146

and creation **3**:318; **4**:501, 541–542; **8**:1020

and the Gigantomachy **4**:566

and Hades **5**:602

and overpopulation of the human race **7**:903

Pandora as a epithet for **8**:1082

and Phaethon **8**:1116–1117

rebellion against Uranus **3**:318; **4**:541–542; **10**:1373–1374, 1397

Gailleach **10**:1423

Galahad **10**:*1422*

Galar **6**:801; **8**:1028; **10**:1405

Galas (Galates) **4**:546

Galatea **4**:**545–547**

Galatea (daughter of Eurytius) **4**:547

Galatea (sea nymph) **4**:*545–547*

Acis and **3**:356, *357*; **4**:546, 547

Polyphemus and **3**:356, *357*; **4**:*545–546*, 547

Galatea (statue), Pygmalion and **1**:114–115; **4**:547; **9**:*1196*, 1198

Ganapati **1**:80

Ganesa **1**:*80*, 86; **6**:738

Ganga **6**:738

Ganymede **4**:**548–549**; **5**:615, *616*; **6**:805; **10**:1379

Gargareans **1**:61

Gayomart **6**:748, *749*

Ge *see* Gaia

Geb **2**:188; **3**:*317*; **4**:**550–552**; **7**:994, 995; **9**:1280; **10**:1310, 1398–1399

guardian of the underworld **4**:552

Gediminas **2**:226

Geezhigo-Quae **7**:939

Gefjon (Gefjun; Gefion) **1**:37; **4**:**553–554**; **10**:1405

Gefn *see* Freya

Geirröd **4**:570; **6**:822; **10**:1362

Gengen-Ur **4**:550

Genii Cucullati **2**:279

George, Saint, and the dragon **1**:88; **3**:422, *423*

Gerd **1**:34, 37; **4**:527, **555–556**; **10**:1405

and Frey **1**:34; **4**:527, *555–556*

Germangabis **4**:561

Geryon **4**:568; **6**:772

Geser Khan **3**:296

Geshtinanna **3**:371; **4**:451; **5**:717

Geush Urvan **6**:749

giants **4**:**563–570**

in Asian creation myths **4**:570

Greek **4**:542, *564–568*

see also Cyclopes; Giants; Hecatoncheires; Titans

Norse/Nordic **4**:*568–570*

frost giants and fire giants **4**:570

Thor's encounters with **10**:1360–1362, *1363, 1430*

northern Europe, tale of Vainamoinen **4**:566

Giants (Gigantes) **10**:1397

battle against the gods (Gigantomachy; Gigantomachia) **4**:543–544, *565*, 566–567; **10**:1375, 1432

Zeus's struggle against Otus and Ephialtes **4**:567

Gigantes *see* Giants

Gikuyu **1**:44

Gilfaethwy **1**:104; **10**:1422

Gilling **6**:801

Gitchi Manito **5**:588

Gjalar **2**:235–236

Gjúki **10**:1302

Glauce **6**:779, 851

Glaucus **8**:*1092*; **9**:1274

Gleipnir **1**:37

Glooskap (Nanabozho) **4**:445; **7**:939, 940–941

Gná **10**:1405

God, Biblical **8**:1135

gods and goddesses *see* deities

Goewin **10**:1422

Gog **4**:*569*

Gogmagog **4**:569

Golden Fleece **6**:776

search for *see* Jason, voyage with the Argonauts

Gorgons **5**:**580–581**

Amazons and **1**:64

Govannon **2**:279

Graces **5**:**582–585**

Graeae, the **3**:363; **5**:580; **8**:1110, *1114*

Grandmother Spider Woman **1**:95

Grannus **2**:279

great goddess *see* earth mother

Great Mother **5**:606

Great Spirit **5**:**586–590**; **7**:909, *910*

Green Man **4**:442; **7**:*955*

Grendel **4**:561–562

griffins **1**:88, *90*

Grímhild **10**:1302

Grith **10**:1362

Gucumátz (Gugumátz) **6**:797, 798, 841

Gudrún **10**:1302, 1303, 1402–1403

Gullinborsti **4**:529

Gullintanni *see* Heimdall

Gunnar **10**:1302, 1402

Gunnar Helmingr **4**:529

Gunnlöd **4**:569; **6**:801; **8**:1028, 1029

Gunther **7**:972, 974; **10**:1304

Guqyuivi **4**:447

Gutthorm **10**:1302–1303

Gwdion **1**:104

Gwenhidwy **5**:631

Gwion Bach **6**:801

Gwydion **10**:1422

Gyges **4**:564; **10**:1395

Gylfi **4**:554; **10**:1430

Gymir *see* Aegir

Hades (Polydegmon; Pluton; Pluto) **3**:401, 419–420; **5**:**601–608**

birth **5**:601–602

character **5**:605

and Persephone **3**:386, *388*, 389, 420; **5**:*602–603*; **8**:1106

Roman equivalent *see* Dis

Theseus and Peirithous visit **5**:603; **10**:1354

Haemon **1**:106; **8**:1042

Haemosu **6**:795

Hagen **7**:*972, 974*

Hahgwehdaetgah **4**:445; **7**:938, 939

Hahgwehdiyu **4**:445; **7**:938, 939

Hamadryads **4**:440; **7**:998, 999

Hamdir **10**:1403

Hannahanna **5**:693

Hanuman **1**:80; **6**:738; **8**:*1134*; **10**:1324, 1326, 1327

Hapi 5:609–610

Hapi (Apis; Hepu; sacred bull) **1**:*93*; **5**:610

Ptah and **9**:1195

Hapi (Hapy; Hepy) **1**:110–111; **3**:349; **5**:*609–610*; **7**:979–981

Hapi (son of Horus) **5**:*610*

Harald War-tooth **8**:1026, 1030–1031

Hariti **10**:1323

Harmonia **2**:*251*, 253; **3**:426; **8**:1122

Harpies **1**:31; **5**:**611–614**; **6**:779

Harsomtus **5**:707

Hathor **4**:462, *464*, 466; **5**:*706*, 707; **7**:912, 997

merger with Isis **6**:767

Haumea **8**:1015

Haurvatat **1**:102; **6**:747, 748

Hazzi **5**:693

Heart of Heaven **6**:799, 841, 842, 845

Hebat **5**:693, 699

Hebe **4**:548; **5**:**615–616**, 651

Hecate **3**:*349*; **5**:606, **617–620**; **7**:914, 931; **8**:1128

and Persephone **5**:602, *618*

Hecatoncheires (Hundred-Handed Ones) **4**:564; **10**:1395

creation of **3**:318, 334; **4**:541; **10**:1373

war on Cronus and the Titans **3**:335–336; **4**:565; **10**:*1373*, 1374, 1432

Hector **1**:19; **5**:**621–625**

Achilles and the death of **1**:*17–18*; **5**:*622–623*; **8**:1095; **9**:1166

battle against the Great Ajax **1**:53

cult of **5**:625

and Paris **8**:1087

Hecuba **5**:**626–628**; **9**:1164

Hefring **1**:26

Hegemone **5**:582

Heh **1**:*93*

Heimdall (Gullintanni) **1**:34; **5**:**629–632**; **8**:1024

horn (Gjallarhorn) **5**:*630*, 631, 632

Heitsi-eibib **1**:45

Hel **2**:222; **3**:377; **5**:*633*; **6**:818; **8**:1024, 1030

Hermód and **5**:677

Helen **3**:*394*; **5**:**634–640**; **6**:813

after the Trojan War **5**:*636*, 637–638; **6**:*857, 858*

birth **5**:634; **6**:811–812

as cause of the Trojan War **1**:15, 49; **2**:174; **4**:490; **5**:621, 636

as a cloud image **8**:1086

and Deiphobos **5**:637; **6**:*857*, 858

and dualism **4**:445, 446

in Egypt **5**:638; **8**:1086

Eros and **4**:489–490

giving beauty to a young girl **1**:118–119; **5**:638

as a goddess **5**:638

Homer and **5**:637–638, 640

as an icon **5**:638–640

marriage to Menelaus **6**:*856*, 857

Nemesis and **7**:959, 960–961

Pandora as a model for **8**:1082

Paris's abduction of **1**:15, 118; **2**:174; **5**:621, 636; **8**:*1086–1087*; **9**:*1165*

suitors **1**:52; **5**:713; **6**:857; **8**:1033, 1094, 1118

Theseus's abduction of **2**:275

and tree worship **6**:813

Helenus **1**:31; **5**:627; **8**:1118–1119

Helgi **9**:1266

Heliades **8**:*1117*

Heliconians **4**:440

Helios **1**:129; **5**:**641–644**, 646–648; **8**:1023; **10**:1343–1344, *1345*

and the abduction of Persephone **5**:602, 618

goblet (cup) **5**:642, 662–663

and Phaethon **5**:642; **8**:*1115*–1116, 1117; **10**:1344

and Poseidon **8**:1148

sacred sheep and cattle **5**:642; **8**:1038; **10**:1372

similarity to Re **9**:1211

Helle **5**:674, 678; **6**:776

Hellen **3**:398

Hemithea **1**:16

Hephaestus **2**:151, 170; **5**:**645–649**; **10**:1426–1427

and Athena **4**:486; **5**:649

birth and lameness **5**:*645*–646, 651–652; **10**:1435

creation of the first woman **5**:584, 646; **8**:*1080, 1081*

cult of **5**:649

Dionysus and **3**:417

father of Erichthonius **4**:486; **5**:649

as husband of Aphrodite **1**:113–*114*; **5**:643, 646–648; **7**:951

as husband of one of the Graces **5**:584

link with Prometheus **9**:1182

Roman equivalent *see* Vulcan

Hepy *see* Hapi

Heqet **7**:912

Hera **5**:**650–657**

against Troy and the Trojans **1**:31; **5**:655, 709–710

battle against Artemis **5**:652

birth **5**:650

the birth of Typhon **5**:652; **10**:1394

and Dionysus **3**:413–414; **5**:654

and Echo **4**:458; **7**:1001

and Hephaestus **5**:645–646, 651–652; **10**:1435

and Heracles **2**:172–173; **5**:*654–655*, 659, 660; **6**:785; **7**:1005

intervention in Zeus's love affairs **5**:653–654

revenge on Callisto **2**:158, 262, 263; **5**:653–654; **7**:1001

and Jason **5**:656–657; **6**:775

jealousy and injured pride **5**:655–656

merger with Juno **6**:*780–781*

quarrel with Poseidon **5**:652; **8**:1148

and Tiresias **10**:1371–1372

virgin status **10**:1416

wife of Zeus **5**:650–*653*; **10**:*1435*

Heracles **5**:**658–665**

aided by Athena **2**:172–173

and Alcestis **1**:55; **5**:662

and the Amazons **1**:62; **5**:662, 687

and Atlas **2**:178–180; **5**:663–665, 682

birth **5**:659

and Icarus **5**:711

childhood and education **5**:659–660

cult worship **5**:658–659; **7**:925–926

death and immortality **5**:*664*, 665; **8**:1118

and death of Neleus **7**:971

and death of the sons of Ares

Heracles (continued)
2:151; **8**:1122–1123

fight with Achelous **1**:13;
5:665

fight with Ares **8**:1122–1123

and the Gigantomachy
4:566–567

and Helios's goblet **5**:642,
662–663

and Hera (Juno) **2**:172–173;
5:654–*655*, 659, 660; **6**:785;
7:1005

and death of the sons of Ares
2:151; **8**:1122–1123

and Icarus **5**:711

Labors of **1**:62; **2**:173, 178;
3:425; **5**:655, 658, 659

apples of the Hesperides,
fetching of **2**:178; **3**:425;
5:663–665, 682; **7**:969–
970; **8**:1023; **9**:1181;
10:1387

Augean stables, cleaning of
5:662

belt of Hippolyte, fetching
of **1**:62; **5**:655, 662, 663,
687

birds of the Stymphalian
marshes, shooting of **5**:662

cattle of Geryon, capture
of **4**:568; **5**:642, 655,
662–663; **6**:772

Cerberus, capture of **5**:603,
607, 665

Cretan bull, capture of
5:662

Erymanthion boar, capture
of **5**:661–662, *663*

horses of Diomedes, capture
of **5**:*662*; **8**:1122

Hydra, killing of **5**:*660–661*

Nemean lion, killing of
5:*659*, 660, 663

stag of Ceryneia, capture of
5:661; **8**:1131

and Laomedon **6**:*805*, 806;
9:1164

marriage to Deianeira **5**:665

marriage to Hebe **5**:615–616,
665

and Minerva **7**:883

a mortal and a god **3**:*390*;
7:883

murder of his family **5**:660

and the Muses **7**:925–926

and Nereus **10**:1387

and the Olympic Games
4:514

rescue of Hesione **6**:*806*

rowing contest with Jason
6:777

and the Thespians **5**:660

wrestling match with
Antaeus **4**:568; **5**:*661*;
8:1146

Hercle **8**:1072

Hercules *see* Heracles

Hermanos **8**:1127

Hermaphroditus **5**:**666–669**,
674; **7**:1000; **9**:1169

Hermes **5**:**670–675**

and Aphrodite **5**:666

children **5**:674–675

as a fertility god **4**:502

god of boundaries **5**:670–672

guider of souls in the afterlife
5:605, 670

and herms **5**:*672*

Hestia and **5**:686

importance to brides
5:667–668, 672

link with Priapus **9**:1169

protector of children
5:673–674

Roman equivalent *see*
Mercury

staff and sandals **5**:*670*, 674

a thief **5**:*672–673*, 674, *675*

tricks Apollo **5**:*672–673*

worship of **5**:675

Hermes Psychopompos **5**:670

Hermione **6**:856, 858; **8**:1053

Hermód **2**:221, 222; **5**:633,
676–677; **8**:1030

Hero **5**:**678–680**

heroes *see* demigods and heroes

Herophile **9**:1291

Hesat **7**:997

Hesione **6**:805, *806*; **9**:1164

Hesperethusa **5**:681

Hesperides **5**:**681–682**; **8**:1130
Arethusa **1**:105; **7**:*1000*, 1002;
10:*1420*

golden apples of the **5**:*681*;
7:*1004*

Heracles' quest for **2**:178;
3:425; **5**:663–665, 682;
7:969–970; **8**:1023;
9:1181; **10**:1387

Hestia **5**:**683–686**; **10**:1418
birth **3**:335; **10**:1418

Roman equivalent *see* Vesta

High God **7**:909

Hilaeira **2**:*276*

Himinglaeva **1**:26

Hina (Hine) **8**:1014, 1015,
1016, 1017, *1019*

Hine Ahu One **3**:323

Hine Hauk Ona **8**:1014

Hine Titama **3**:323; **8**:1014

hippocampus **9**:1273

Hippocoon the Usurper **5**:655

Hippodameia (Hippodamia)
2:182, 183; **8**:1050,
1098–1099, 1131

Hippolyte **5**:**687–688**

Heracles and the girdle of
1:62; **2**:149; **5**:655, 662,
663, 687

and Theseus **5**:*687–688*;
10:1354

Hippolytus **3**:407–408;
5:**689–690**; **10**:1420
Artemis and **2**:159; **10**:1420
Phaedra and **1**:*115*, 116–117;
2:231; **8**:1149; **10**:1354,
1420, *1423*

Hippomenes **2**:168; **5**:682

Hipta **5**:616

Hisakitaimisi (Master of
Breath) **7**:939

Hjördis **10**:1300

Hlér *see* Aegir

Höd **2**:220, *221*; **5**:633; **8**:1024;
9:1260

Hoenir **7**:988–989; **10**:1404

Hogni **10**:1302

Holy Boy **1**:87

Horae **1**:112; **10**:1435

Horn *see* Freya

horned gods **8**:*1075*

hortlaks **3**:297

Horus **1**:78, *83*; **4**:466, 467,
550; **5**:**701–708**; **8**:*1065*;
9:1279

eyes **5**:*706–707*, 708

Horus the Elder **5**:701, 703;
9:1210

Horus of Nekhen **5**:*708*

Horus of Pe **5**:*708*

Horus the Younger (the
Child) **5**:701, 703, 704–705;
9:1210

rivalry with Seth
5:705–708; **6**:764; **9**:1208,
1281–1284

sky god **10**:1312

Hou-I **3**:303, 308

household gods, Roman *see*
Lares; Penates; Vesta

Hrönn **1**:26

Hrungnir **10**:1360–1362

Hsi Wang Mu **3**:308

Hu **2**:235

Huang Ti **3**:305, 308

Huarab **3**:322

Hubal **1**:137

Huehueteotl **2**:205

Huitzilopochtli **2**:203, *204*,
205, 207; **9**:1200;
10:1346–1347

battle against siblings **3**:338

birth **2**:208, 209

huldra **1**:59

Huma Tikitiki **8**:1015

Hunahpu and Xbalanque
6:844, 845

Hun Cam and Vucub Cam
6:845, 846; **8**:1047

Hundred-Handed Ones *see*
Hecatoncheires

Hun Hunahpu and Vucub
Hunahpu **6**:846; **8**:1047

Huracan **6**:841–842, 845;
7:948–949

Hwanin **6**:*789*, 792, 793

Hwanung **6**:*789*, 793

Hyacinthus (Hyakinthos)
1:133–134; **3**:395; **7**:936

Hyades **8**:1129

Hydra **5**:*660–661*; **6**:785

Hygieia **2**:161, *162*; **3**:*392*

Hylas **6**:777; **7**:999–1000

Hymen **8**:1058

Hymir **10**:1364

Hyokkose **6**:794, 795

Hyperes **8**:*1130*, 1131

Hyperion **4**:564

Hypnos **5**:584–585, **709–710**;
7:1005

Hyrieus **8**:1131

Iambe **3**:387; **4**:506;
8:1075–1076

Iapetus **2**:178; **4**:564

Iasion **8**:1132

Iaso **2**:161–162

Iasus **2**:168

Iblis **1**:137, 138

Icarius **3**:415–416; **10**:1334

Icarus **3**:358–*360*; **5**:**711–712**;
7:887, 888

Ida **3**:335

Idamantes **5**:714

Idas **2**:276; **6**:812–813

Idomeneus **3**:398; **5:713–714**

Idun **1**:36, 37; **7**:989–990; **9**:1260

Igigi, the *see* Annunaki

Ilia *see* Rhea Silvia

Illapa **6**:727

Illuyankas **3**:422; **5**:694, 695

Ilus **6**:805

Imana **1**:40; **3**:323

Imhotep **9**:1194

Imset (Imsety) **1**:110, 111; **5**:610

Imy-uaf **2**:189

Inanna **1**:67; **4**:485; **5:715–718**; **7**:870
  changing roles **5**:715
  Dumuzi and **4**:449–450, 451, 456–457; **5**:717
  equivalent goddesses **6**:760
    Assyrian and Babylonian *see* Ishtar
    Phoenician *see* Astarte
  and the moon **3**:348
  parallels with Circe **3**:311
  sacred prostitutes of **5**:717
  in the underworld **3**:348, 370–371; **5**:715–717

Inaras **5**:693, 694

Inari **4**:517

Indra **3**:364, 382, 422; **4**:504; **6**:735, *736*, 738; **10**:1312
  and the flood **4**:522

Ing **4**:561

Ino **1**:116; **2**:253; **5**:654; **6**:776; **8**:1093

Inti **6**:726, 727, 728

Inti Illapa **6**:727

Inua **7**:945

Inutoto **8**:1014

Io (mistress of Zeus) **5**:653; **6**:*781*, 859; **8**:1076; **9**:1180; **10**:1435–1436

Io (Polynesian god) **8**:1016

Iobates **2**:230, 231

Iolaus **5**:616, 661

Iole **5**:665; **8**:1118

Ion **3**:398

Ioskeha **7**:938, 939

Iphicles **5**:659; **10**:1436

Iphigeneia **2**:185; **3**:394; **6:740–743**
  Artemis and **2**:159, 160; **3**:408
  becomes Hecate **5**:619

Orestes and **3**:408; **6**:742; **8**:1053
  sacrifice of **1**:16, 49; **2**:159, 160; **3**:312, 408; **4**:470; **6**:740; **8**:1050, 1087

Iphimede **6**:742

Iphis, and Anaxarete **8**:1141–1142

Iqi Balam **6**:842

Iris **10**:1313

Irmin **4**:561

Ishkur **5**:693

Ishtar **4**:485; **6:760–763**; **7**:870
  descent to the underworld **6**:762–763
  equivalent goddesses **6**:760
    Phoenician *see* Astarte
    Sumerian *see* Inanna
  and Gilgamesh **4**:571–572
  and rainbows **10**:1313
  sexual rituals in honor of **6**:763
  symbols **6**:760
  and Tammuz **1**:24; **6**:760–762

Isis **2**:188; **4**:466; **6:764–769**; **7**:*931*; **8**:*1065*
  birth **4**:550
  and the contest between Seth and Horus **5**:705–706; **6**:764; **9**:1282
  cult of **6**:768; **9**:*1178*
  as earth mother **4**:457
  gain of power from Re **6**:764, 766; **9**:1210
  Isis Pelagia (Isis of the Sea) **6**:767
  link with Artemis **6**:768–769
  link with Demeter **6**:768
  merger with the goddess Hathor **6**:767
  merger with the goddess Renenutet **6**:767
  and the moon **6**:768–769
  mysteries of **7**:931, 933
  and Nepthys **7**:962, *964*
  and Osiris **1**:109; **4**:457, 466–467, 503; **5**:704; **6**:764; **8**:1064, *1066*
  roles **6**:766–767
  Romans and **6**:768, *769*; **7**:*933*; **8**:*1138*; **9**:1238
  and the seven scorpions **5**:703
  Temple of Isis at Philae **6**:767
  worship of **6**:767–769; **8**:*1138*

Iskur **4**:505

Ismene **1**:106; **8**:1042, 1045

Istros **8**:1022

Itzamna **6**:842, 845; **10**:*1310*
  see also Gucumàtz; Kukulkan; Quetzalcoatl

Ixchel (Ix Chel) **6**:844, 845; **7**:915

Ixion **5**:584, 652

Ixtab **6**:844–845

Iynx **5**:655; **8**:1076

Izanagi **3**:317–318; **9**:1267–1268

Izanami **3**:317–318; **9**:1267–1268

Iztaccíhuatl **7**:952

Jabiru and Emu, story of **2**:196, *197*

Jade Emperor *see* Yü Ti

Jaguar Baby **8**:1048

Jam *see* Yima

Jambhala *see* Kubera

Jana **6**:773

Janus **6:770–774**, 780

Jason **6:775–779**
  death **6**:779
  voyage with the Argonauts **2**:149; **6**:775–779
  and the Amazons **1**:62
  and Atalanta **2**:167
  and the Harpies **5**:*612*; **6**:779
  and Hecate **5**:619
  and Hera **5**:656–657; **6**:777–778
  and Medea **2**:149, 236; **3**:310, 426; **4**:489; **5**:619; **6**:*778*, 779, *848–849*
  and Orpheus **8**:1057
  ship (the *Argo*) **8**:1126
  and Talos **2**:236
  and Triton **10**:1387
  and Troy **6**:*805*

Jemshid *see* Yima

Jocasta **8**:1040, 1041, 1043, *1044*

Jörmungand **1**:126; **5**:633; **8**:1024, *1026*
  see also Midgard Serpent

Jove *see* Jupiter

Juksáhkká **9**:1266

Juno **6:780–782**; **7**:931; **8**:1073; **9**:1231
  and the Milky Way **5**:659; **10**:*1338*
  and the pomegranate **8**:1109

and rainbows **10**:1313
  wife of Jupiter **6**:783–785

Jupiter (Jove) **3**:*384*; **4**:*504*; **6:783–788**; **9**:1231
  Greek counterpart *see* Zeus
  interaction with mortals **6**:785–786
  Jupiter Dolicenus **6**:*786*
  Jupiter Heliopolitanus **6**:786, *787*
  Jupiter-Mars-Quirinus triad **9**:1233
  love affairs **6**:785
  many names of **6**:787–788
  many shapes **6**:785
  temples to **6**:786–787; **9**:1234

Jurakan **4**:447

Jurate **2**:227, 228

Juturna **6**:773

Kaang **1**:40–*41*, 43

kachinas **1**:73

Kadaklan **10**:1326

Kadmos *see* Cadmus

Kalaturru **5**:717

Kali **3**:402–403; **4**:447; **6**:*732*, 738

Kamala **3**:317

Kamrusepas **5**:693

Kanaloa (Tangaroa) **8**:1013, 1015

Kana'ti (Lucky Hunter) **7**:939, 942

Kane **8**:1014

Kapo **8**:1017

Karma **1**:80

Karme *see* Carme

Kastytis **2**:227–228

Kaupole **2**:228

Kazikamuntu **3**:323

Kedalion **8**:1055

Kelpie **3**:*404*

Keres (Destinies) **4**:493; **8**:1121

Khamba, and Thoibi **5**:679–680

Khasis **5**:711

Khepri (Khepra) **1**:78–79; **7**:*962*; **10**:1341–1342

Khnum (Khmun; Khmun-Re) **4**:466; **5**:610; **7**:981; **9**:1206

Khong Lo **4**:570

Khonsu **4**:466; **7**:912

Khonvum **3**:314–316

Khors **10**:1318

Ki **1**:67; **3**:318; **6**:829

Kilyamama **6**:727

Kim Alji **6**:792
Kingu **3**:403; **6**:831
Kinich Ahau **6**:842
kinoly **1**:74
Kintu **1**:43
Kishar **10**:1369
Kishelemukong **5**:588
Kitsune-Tsuki **3**:406
Kleitos **4**:483
Klytaimestra *see* Clytemnestra
Koboka **2**:197
Köke Möngke Tengri
    (Qormusta) **3**:295, 299
Kólga **1**:26
Kostroma **10**:1318
Kothar **2**:212, 214; **5**:711
Koyash **3**:296
Kraken **9**:1273–1274
Kriemhild **7**:972–974; **10**:1304
Krishna **6**:738
  death **1**:19
Krttika **10**:1340
Kruchina **10**:1318
Kshthathra Vairya (Khshathra
    Vairya) **1**:102; **6**:747, 748
K'u **3**:308
Ku **3**:320; **8**:1013, 1015–1016
Kua **3**:319
Kuan Ti **8**:1140
Kubera (Vaisravana; Jambhala)
    8:1139
Kud **6**:792
K'uei Hsing **3**:308–309
Ku-kapuna **8**:1019
Ku-kekoa **8**:1019
Kukulkan **6**:797–800, 842, 843,
    845; **9**:1199
  see also Quetzalcoatl
Kulla **4**:477, 505
Kuloskap **3**:321; **7**:939
Kumarbi **5**:693, 696, 697;
    10:1398
Kurdalagon **10**:1426
Kurgaru **5**:717
Kurunta **5**:693
Kvasir **2**:235–236; **6**:801;
    8:1028; **10**:1405
Kyknos **8**:1122
Kyniska **3**:394

Lachesis **4**:493, *494*, 496;
    5:598, *599*
Lada **10**:1318
Ladon (dragon of the
    Hesperides) **3**:425; **5**:663,
    681, 682

Lady Ashereh of the Sea
    2:164–166
Lady of the Beasts **3**:409
Laestrygonians **4**:567; **8**:1036
Laius **8**:1040, 1041, *1042*;
    10:1331
Lakshmi **3**:317, *319*; **4**:447;
    6:738; **9**:1268
Lambton Worm **3**:422, 424
Laocoon **6**:802–804; **9**:1174
Laomedon **6**:805–806; **9**:1164
Laonytus **8**:1042
Lara **6**:807, 861
Lares **6**:807–810, 861; **8**:*1101*;
    9:1224
  see also Penates; Vesta
Lat, al- **1**:137–138
Latinus **1**:32; **2**:265; **4**:498
Latinus Silvius **9**:1220
Laukamate **2**:228
Lavinia **1**:*29*, 32–33; **9**:1232
Leander, Hero and **5**:678–*679*,
    680
Leda **2**:275; **5**:634; **6**:811–813;
    10:1437
  children of **4**:445; **5**:634;
    6:811–813; **10**:1437
Leifthrasir *see* Líf and
    Leifthrasir
Lelwani **5**:693
Leto **1**:128; **2**:157; **4**:543;
    5:653; **6**:814–816;
    10:1435
Leuce **5**:603
Leucippe **6**:805
Leucippus, and Daphne
    3:365–367; **8**:1130
Leucothea **8**:1093
Leucothoe **7**:1002
Leucus **5**:714
Leukippos **4**:547
Leviathan **5**:695
Líf and Leifthrasir **1**:126–127;
    5:632; **6**:817
Limniads **1**:103; **7**:999
Limoniads **1**:103; **7**:999
Linus **5**:659; **7**:925
Lir (Llyr) **9**:1186
Lisa **3**:319
Ljosalfar (light elves) **1**:*57*–58
Llefelys **4**:510
Lleu Llaw Gyffes *see* Lugh
Lludd **4**:510
Llwyd **4**:510
Llyr (Lir) **9**:1186
Lodur **6**:818–820, 823

Loki (Loptr) **1**:27, 34–36;
    2:220–*221*, 222, 223;
    6:818–823; **9**:1260
  and the apocalypse
    (Ragnarok) **1**:126; **6**:822,
    823; **10**:1315
  blocks Balder's release from
    Hel **5**:677; **8**:1030
  and the Brising necklace
    (Brísingamen) **4**:533
  character **2**:220; **6**:820–823
  children **6**:818
  and the creation of the first
    humans **6**:818–820
  and the death of Balder
    1:34–36; **2**:220–*221*;
    4:536; **6**:822, *823*
    gods' revenge for **6**:801,
      822, 823
  and Idun **7**:990
  journey to Utgard **9**:1249
  name and images **6**:823
  punishment of **6**:*822*; **7**:948;
    10:*1406*
    the cause of earthquakes
      7:948
  shape-shifting **4**:534; **6**:801,
    818
  and Thor **6**:818; **10**:1361,
    1363
    Thor's hammer **4**:568;
      6:818; **10**:1358–1360,
      1362, 1366
Lone Man **5**:590
Lono **8**:1017
Loptr *see* Loki
Lotus-eaters **8**:1034
Lucifer **3**:410
Lucky Hunter **7**:939, 942
Ludd *see* Nuada
Lugaid *see* Lugh
Lugh (Lug; Lleu Llaw Gyffes;
    Lugh Samildánach; Lugaid)
    2:279, 280, 281, 285;
    6:757, 861
Luna **3**:*344*; **7**:914
Lycaon (first king of Arcadia)
    2:262; **3**:397; **6**:824–826
Lycaon (son of Priam) **9**:1166
Lyceius **1**:130
Lycomedes **10**:1354
Lycorias **1**:105
Lynceus **2**:276; **6**:812–813

Maat **5**:608, 708; **7**:979; **9**:*1172*
Maboya **4**:447

Macha **2**:280, *282*; **6**:753–754,
    757
maenads (potniades; thyiades)
    3:*416*, 418; **6**:827–828;
    7:931
  and Orpheus **8**:1061
  see also Bacchants
Mae Thorani **4**:*452*
Maeve *see* Medb
Magna Mater *see* Cybele
Magog **4**:*569*
Magzor Gyalmo **1**:80
Mahatara **10**:1325, 1326
Mahishasura **4**:*448*
Mahrkusha **6**:749
Mahucutah **6**:842
Mahui-Ike **8**:1016
Maia **2**:178, 262; **8**:1131;
    10:1435
Maíat **4**:466, 469
Malku *see* Melqart
Malsum **3**:406; **4**:445; **7**:939,
    940–941
Mama Huaco **6**:730
Mami Wata **1**:44
Manabozho **7**:940
Manah **1**:137, 138
Manannan Mac Lir **6**:757;
    9:1270, *1271*
Manat, al- **1**:137; **7**:909
Manco Capac **6**:727, 730
Manes **1**:70, *71*
Manetuwak **5**:588
Máni **10**:1405
manitous (great spirits)
    7:939–941
Manu **4**:*522*, 523; **10**:1430
Mara **2**:228; **3**:402, *404*
Mardöll *see* Freya
Marduk **3**:317, 422; **5**:695;
    6:829–833; **7**:870, 873–874;
    10:1369
  battle with Tiamat **3**:317,
    338, 403; **4**:480; **6**:829–*830*,
    831–*833*; **10**:*1368*,
    1369–1370, 1430
  and the constellations
    10:1370
  and the Murussu dragon
    7:*954*
Marena **10**:1318
Maris **8**:1072
Mar'rallang **4**:446
Mars **2**:152–153; **6**:834–839;
    9:1231
  birth **6**:781

father of Romulus and
Remus **6**:835; **9**:1221, 1232,
1240; **10**:1415
Greek equivalent *see* Ares
Jupiter-Mars-Quirinus triad
9:1233
Mars Caecus (blind Mars)
6:837
Mars Ulltor **8**:1072
and Minerva **7**:883
paired with Neptune **7**:967
rituals connected to
6:835–*839*
Marsyas **1**:89, 132, *135*;
7:878–879, 923; **9**:1257,
1258
Masewi and Oyoyewa **7**:939
Mashya and Mashyoi **6**:749
Mashyane **4**:444
Mashye **4**:444
Master of Breath
(Hisakitaimisi) **7**:939
Masters (Mistresses) of the
Animals **9**:1287–1288
Math **1**:104
Math ap Mathonwy **10**:1422
Matronae (Dea Matres) **2**:279
Matsya **1**:80; **4**:*522*
Máttaráhkka **9**:1266
Maui **8**:1015–1016, *1018*
Mawu **3**:319
Mawu-Lisa **1**:40; **3**:319
Meda **5**:714
Medb (Maeve) **6**:752, 755, *757*
Medea **6**:848–851; **8**:1022,
1092
and Hebe **5**:616
and Jason **2**:149, 236; **3**:310,
426; **4**:489; **6**:778, 779,
848–849
murders committed by **6**:779,
849–*851*
and Theseus **6**:851;
10:1351–1352
Medraut *see* Mordred
Medus **6**:851
Medusa
Athena and **8**:1113, 1144
Perseus and **3**:363;
5:580–*581*, 674;
8:1110–1112, 1113
Mefitis **10**:1410
Megaera **4**:540
Megapenthes **6**:856, 858
Megara **5**:660
Mehen **9**:1208

Meilichios **8**:1132
mejenkwaar **3**:406
Melampus **1**:85
Melanion **2**:168; **5**:682
Melanippe **1**:62; **5**:687
Meleager **2**:167–*168*; **4**:495;
8:1122
Meleboea (Chloris) **7**:986
Meles **4**:488
Melete **7**:900, 924
Meliads **4**:440; **10**:1397
Melissa **1**:105
Melpomene **7**:921, *922*
Melqart (Melkart; Melkarth;
Malku) **2**:268, 270
Memnoides **6**:853
Memnon **3**:390; **4**:484;
6:852–854; **10**:1380
death **6**:853; **10**:*1379*,
1380–1381
Menelaus **1**:15–16, 28, 49;
2:174, 185; **5**:634;
6:855–858; **8**:1086, 1087
in the afterlife **5**:638
in Egypt with Helen **5**:638;
6:858
finds Helen after the Trojan
War **5**:*636*, 637; **6**:*857*, *858*
and Proteus **6**:858;
7:969–970; **9**:1186
Menerva (Menrva) **7**:882, 883;
8:1072
Menoeceus **8**:1043; **10**:1372
Menoetes **8**:1043
Men Shen **3**:309
Menthe **1**:105; **5**:603
Menulis **2**:224, 228
Saule and **2**:*228*–229; **7**:914
Mercury **3**:*372*; **6**:859–862;
9:1231
and the afterlife **6**:861–862
Greek equivalent *see* Hermes
as one of the Penates **8**:1100
Meriones **5**:713
Merlin **9**:1252
mermaids and mermen **1**:82;
9:1271–1273
Mermerus **6**:851
Merope **8**:1054–1055, 1131;
10:1307
Mer-ur (Mnevis) **2**:189–191
Metaneira **3**:389; **4**:506; **8**:1106
Metis **2**:170; **5**:597; **8**:1022;
10:1434
Metztli **2**:205
Mezamate **2**:228

Michabo **5**:588
Mictlantecuhtli **2**:205
Midas (Mita) **1**:132;
7:878–880, 923
Silenus and **10**:1305–1306
Midgard Serpent **5**:631, 632,
633; **6**:*817*, 818; **10**:*1362*,
1364
see also Jörmungand
Midir **6**:*755*, 757
Mikelats **4**:446
Milda **2**:228
Miletus **7**:885
Miltiades **1**:53
Mimas **5**:646
mimih spirits **2**:197
Mímir **7**:988–989;
8:1027–1028; **10**:1404–1405
Min **4**:466
Minerva **6**:*809*; **7**:881–884;
9:1231; **10**:1418–1419
Greek equivalent *see* Athena
Minerva Capta **7**:882
Minos **3**:325; **4**:492; **7**:885–890
children **8**:1092
and Daedalus **3**:358–360
death **3**:360
and the death of Britomartis
2:158, 247
judge of the dead **5**:606;
7:888–889, *890*
and the Minotaur **3**:327, 358;
7:887; **8**:1092; **10**:1352
Pasiphae's curse on
8:1092–1093
Poseidon and **7**:886–887;
8:1090, 1149
and Procris **8**:1093
ring retrieved by Theseus
10:1352
Minotaur **1**:78, 79; **2**:154, *155*,
189–191; **3**:327–329, *332*;
7:887; **8**:*1093*; **10**:1352
birth of **3**:358; **5**:711; **7**:887;
8:1149
children fed to **7**:987;
10:1352
as a metaphor **7**:888; **10**:1353
Misenus **10**:1386
Mist-Calf **10**:1360
Mistress of Animals **3**:311, 332
Mita *see* Midas
Mithotyn **8**:1029
Mithras (Mithra) **2**:*237*; **6**:747;
7:*891–895*; **8**:*1070*;
9:1238–1239

killing the cosmic bull **7**:894,
898
Mitra **6**:738
Mixcoatl **2**:205
Mneme **7**:900, 924
Mnemosyne **4**:564; **7**:899–902;
10:1435
Módgud **5**:677
Moirai *see* Fates
Molpadia **1**:63
Momos **7**:903–904
Monster Slayer and Child-of-
Water **7**:939, 943
Mopsos **1**:64; **5**:656
Mordred (Medraut) **4**:448
Morgause **4**:448
Mo Rogrog **8**:1017
Moros **5**:709
Morpheus **5**:710; **7**:919–920
Morrigan **5**:613; **6**:757;
10:1401
Moss Maidens **1**:59
Mot **2**:212, 214–215, 268
death **2**:268–269
Mother of the Corn **7**:931
mother goddesses **3**:*316*–317,
381; **5**:592, 597
Anatolian **3**:*380*
in India **6**:732
see also earth mother
Moyang Kapir **10**:1325–1326
Moyang Melur **10**:1325, 1326
Muh'wäse **7**:940
Muit *see* Mut
Muluku **1**:40
Mulungu **1**:40
Munin **8**:*1025*, 1026
Murussu dragon **6**:*829*; **7**:*954*
Musaeus **7**:923; **9**:1277
Musdamma **4**:505
Muses **7**:921–926
birth of **7**:899–900
and the Graces **5**:582
and the Sirens **7**:926;
9:1269
symbols **1**:*128*
Mut (Muit) **4**:466; **5**:610
Myrina **1**:64
Myrmidons **7**:927–928
Myrrha **1**:22, 116; **5**:690;
7:*929*; **8**:1125
Myrtilus **2**:182–183; **8**:1050,
1099

Nagi Tanka **5**:588–589
Naiads **1**:*103*; **7**:998, 999

Naiads (continued)
  and Hylas **7**:999–1000
  Salmacis **1**:105; **5**:666, *668,
    674*; **7**:1000
  see also Hesperides
Namhae **6**:795–796
Namma **4**:477
Nammu (Ninmah) **1**:67
Namorrodo **2**:199
Nana **2**:186
Nanabozho (Glooskap)
  4:445
Nana Nu'u **8**:1019
Nanauatzin **2**:206; **9**:1200
Nanna **1**:37; **2**:221; **4**:505;
  7:870; **10**:1405–1407
  Babylonian equivalent *see* Sin
Nanshe **4**:477, 505; **7**:984
Nantosuelta **2**:279
Napea (Napaea) **1**:103; **7**:999
Narcissus **7**:934–936
  Echo and **4**:*458, 459*; **7**:934
Narsinh **1**:80
Naru-Kami **7**:949
Nasr **1**:137, 138
Nataraja **7**:*956*
Native Cat **2**:199
nats **10**:*1323*–1324
Natseelit **10**:1313
Naunet **2**:191
Nausicaa **2**:265; **7**:920; **8**:*1038*
Nausinoos **2**:265
Nausithous **2**:265
Nav **10**:1318
Nechtan **7**:966, 967
Neck **1**:59
Nefertem **9**:1193, 1194
Neilos **8**:1022
Neith **4**:466
Neithon **7**:966
Nekhbet **4**:466; **5**:610, 701,
  703
Neleus **7**:971, 986
Nemesis (Retribution) **4**:493;
  5:598, 634; **7**:959–961
Nenaunir **1**:44
Neoptolemus (Pyrrhus)
  8:1053, 1097, 1119;
  9:*1167*
Nephri **5**:610
Nepthys **2**:188; **4**:467;
  7:962–964; **8**:*1065*; **9**:*1284*
  birth **4**:550
  mother of Anubis **1**:108
Neptune **7**:965–968; **9**:1231
  Greek equivalent *see* Poseidon

Nereids **1**:103; **7**:*969, 970,
  998*, 999, 1000; **8**:1022;
  10:1356
  see also Amphitrite; Galatea;
    Metis; Thetis
Nereus **5**:682; **7**:969–970;
  8:1020; **10**:1387
Nergal **7**:870
Nerthus **4**:529; **10**:1405
Nessus **5**:665
Nestor **7**:**971**
Nethuns **7**:966; **8**:1072; **9**:1269
Nethus **4**:561; **7**:991
Ngai **1**:40, 43, 44; **5**:614
Ngalalbal **2**:197
Ngendi **8**:1015
Ngewo **1**:40
Niam **6**:*754*
Nibelung I **7**:974
Nibelungs **7**:972–974
Nicostratus **5**:637; **6**:856
Nidaba (Nisaba) **4**:505; **7**:984
Nídud **10**:1424
Nijole **2**:228
Nike **7**:**975–977**
  Athena and **2**:175, *177*; **7**:975
Nimmug **4**:505
Ningirsu **7**:983
  sisters of **7**:984
Ninhursag (Ninhursaga;
    Ninmah; Belit) **4**:476, 478,
    480; **7**:870, 983, 984
Ninigi **10**:1347
Ninisinna **4**:505
Ninlil **7**:870, 983–984
  see also Ninhursag
Ninmah **7**:870
Ninshubur **5**:717
Ninsun **4**:571, *574*
Ninurta **7**:870, **983–984**
Niobe **1**:13; **2**:160; **7**:985–987;
  10:1349
Niobids, slaughter of **7**:985,
  986
Nisaba *see* Nidaba
Niu **2**:191
Njörd **1**:34; **4**:570; **7**:988–991;
  9:1186; **10**:*1407*
Nokomis (Grandmother) **7**:939
Nomius **1**:130
Nonadieve **2**:228, 229
Norns **4**:497; **7**:992–997
Notus **1**:77; **4**:484; **7**:948;
  10:1314
Nü **3**:319
Nuada (Nudd; Ludd) **9**:1270

Nü Kua **3**:*314*, 319
Numitor **6**:835; **9**:1221, 1231,
  1240–1243
Nun **3**:349; **9**:1195, 1206
Nut **2**:188; **3**:*317*; **4**:550, *552*;
  5:703; **7**:994–997; **9**:1280
  and the calendar **2**:255
  in cow form **7**:996–*997*
  day, night and **3**:*347*; **7**:994
  judge of the dead **7**:996
  personification of the sky
    4:*552*; **7**:994; **10**:*1312,
    1398–1399*
Nux *see* Nyx
Nyama **1**:40, 42
Nyctimus **6**:824
Nymphae Infernae Paludis (the
    Avernales) **7**:999
nymphs **1**:103, 105; **2**:158;
  7:998–1002
  see also Dryads; Naiads;
    Nereids; Oceanids
Nyx (Nux) **3**:352; **4**:493;
  5:709; **7**:1003–1006
Nzame **1**:40

Oceanids **1**:103; **7**:999, 1000;
  8:1020, 1022; **9**:*1183*
Oceanus **3**:352; **8**:1020–1023;
  9:1269
Ocypete **5**:611, 614
Od **4**:534
Odin (Wotan) **1**:27, 34, *36*;
  2:*246*; **4**:*528, 535*;
  8:1024–1031, 1133–1135;
  9:1260
  and the apocalypse **1**:*126*
  and Balder **2**:220
  and Baugi **4**:568–*569*
  and Bergelmir **2**:234
  and the Brising necklace
    (Brísingamen) **4**:533
  and creation **2**:234;
    8:1026–1027
  cult of **9**:1264
  divine possessions **8**:1026
    hall (Valhalla) **3**:377; **4**:534;
      5:676; **8**:1026, *1030*
    horse (Sleipnir) **5**:*676, 677*;
      6:818; **8**:*1030*
    magic ring **4**:555
    ravens **8**:*1025*, 1026
  and Freya **4**:533, 534
  and Frigga **4**:535, 536, *537*
  god of battle **8**:1027
  house of **9**:*1265*

limits of his power
  8:1030–1031
and Mímir **10**:1405
names **8**:1024–1026
personality **10**:1311
quest for wisdom
  8:1027–1029
and the mead of poetry
  4:568–569; **6**:801;
  8:1028–1029
suffering and **6**:801;
  8:1029–1030; **9**:1265
and Ragnarok **5**:631; **8**:1026
sacrifices to **9**:1264
and Thor **8**:1031; **10**:1365
Odosha **10**:1316
Odqan Ghalaqan **3**:295–296
Od Tengri **3**:296
Oduduwa **1**:41
Odur **4**:534
Odysseus (Ulysses)
  8:1032–1039; **10**:1307
  Athena and **2**:172
  childhood **8**:1032
  comparison with Aeneas **1**:30
  death **3**:310; **8**:1038
  and Helen **5**:637, 638; **6**:*858*;
    8:1033
  and Penelope **8**:1033, 1038,
    1104–*1105*
  tomb **8**:1036
  travels after the Trojan War
    and Aeolus **8**:1035–1036
    and Calypso **2**:*264–265*;
      7:*999*; **8**:1038
    and the Ciconians **8**:1034
    and Circe **3**:310, 311;
      8:1036; **10**:1372
    consulting the spirits of
      Hades **2**:238; **8**:1036;
      10:*1371*, 1372
    and the Dodona oak **8**:1126
    and Helios's cattle **5**:642;
      8:1038; **10**:1372
    and the Laestrygonians
      4:567; **8**:1036
    and the Lotus-eaters **8**:1034
    and Nausicaa **7**:920; **8**:*1038*
    and Polyphemus **3**:*354–
      355, 356*; **4**:*567–568*;
      8:*1034–1035*, 1147–1148
    Poseidon and **8**:1038, *1146,
      1147–1148*
    sailing between Charybdis
      and Scylla **8**:1037,
      1146–1147

sees Tantalus in the
underworld **10**:1350
and the Sirens **3**:*393*;
8:*1037*; **9**:1269
and the Trojan War **1**:50;
8:1033–1034
discovery of Achilles **1**:16;
3:*412*
partnership with Diomedes
3:411–*412*; **8**:1033
receives Achilles' armor
1:53, *54*
stealing the Palladium
3:412; **8**:1033
tricking the hermit
Philoctetes **3**:411–412;
8:1119
Oeax **3**:412
Oedipus **8**:**1040–1045**;
10:1372, 1398
and Antigone **1**:106, *107*
death **3**:393
and the Theban Sphinx
6:772; **8**:1042, *1043*;
10:1331
Oeneus **2**:167; **8**:1096
Oengus **6**:751, 755, 757
Oenomaus **2**:182; **4**:514;
8:1050, 1098–1099, 1130,
1131
Oenone **1**:105; **8**:*1085*, 1088
Oenopion **8**:1054–1055
Ogdoad **1**:*93*, 94–95; **3**:344;
9:1192
Oholiab **5**:711–712
Oinoe **5**:656
Oisín **6**:*754*
Oizus **5**:709
Old Clootie (Old Cloots)
3:404
Old Man (the Great Spirit)
5:586
Olofat **8**:1015
Olorun (Olodumare) **1**:40, 44
Olympian gods **5**:598; **10**:1374
war with the Titans
(Titanomachy;
Titanomachia) **2**:178;
3:335–336; **4**:542–*543*, 565;
6:*785*; **10**:*1374*–1378, 1432
Ometeotl **2**:205, 206
Omphale **5**:665
Oneiroi, the **5**:709
oni **3**:*406*
Onjo **6**:794
Ophion **10**:1313

Ops **9**:1231, 1236, 1253, 1254,
1255
Orchomenus **5**:660
Orcus **3**:419
Oreads **1**:103; **4**:440; **7**:999
Oreithyia **8**:1122
Orestes **2**:185; **8**:**1050–1053**
cult of **3**:393
and Electra **4**:*471–472*;
8:1051, *1053*
the Furies and **4**:*539*; **8**:1051,
1053
and Iphigeneia **3**:408; **6**:742;
8:1053
in literature **1**:51; **6**:742
murder of Clytemnestra and
Aegisthus **1**:50; **2**:172
Orion **8**:**1054–1056**
and Artemis **2**:157; **5**:690;
8:1055
birth **8**:1054
a constellation **8**:*1054*,
1055–*1056*, 1065;
10:1338–1339, *1340*
Eos and **4**:483; **8**:1055
and the Pleiades **8**:1129
Orisa **1**:*38*, 44
Ormazd *see* Ahura Mazda
Oro **8**:1015
Orpheus **5**:605, 607; **7**:923,
936; **8**:**1057–1062**; **9**:1190
Orphism and the Orphic
Mysteries **4**:444; **7**:933,
1005; **8**:1061–1062
Orseis **3**:398
Orthus (Orthrus) **5**:663; **6**:772
Orunmila **1**:41
Osiris **2**:188; **4**:466; **5**:703, *706*;
8:**1063–1068**
birth **4**:550; **5**:703; **8**:1063
and the concept of *maat*
8:1065
the dead and **1**:108–109;
2:242–243; **3**:372–373;
4:552; **5**:608; **8**:1065
death of **4**:466–467, 503;
5:704; **8**:1064; **9**:1281
body embalmed **1**:109, *110*
and the moon **7**:912
in the heavens **8**:1065–1066
identified with Re **9**:1209,
1242
images of **8**:1066
Isis and **1**:109; **4**:457,
466–467, 503; **5**:704; **6**:764;
8:1064, *1066*

and the Nile River
7:981–982; **8**:*1063*, 1064
Osiris Khenty-amentiu
8:1066
Osiris Wenen-Nefer **8**:1066
rituals involving **4**:*506*;
8:1067
and Seth **5**:703–704; **7**:982;
8:1064; **9**:1281
Ostara **4**:513, 561
Otr **3**:425, 426; **10**:1303
Otus **2**:150; **4**:567
Ouende **4**:522
Owuo **1**:46–47
Oya **7**:949

Pachacamac **6**:727
Pachamama **6**:727
Padikhonsu **1**:64
Padma **3**:317
Paeon **8**:**1069**
Paeon (a Trojan) **8**:1069
Paeon (god of healing) **1**:129;
8:1069
Paeon (son of Endymion)
4:473, 475; **8**:1069
Paidia **5**:582
Pak **6**:795
Palaemonius **5**:649
Palamedes **8**:1033, 1034
Palinurus **5**:710
Palk **6**:792
Pallas **1**:*33*
Pallas Athena *see* Athena
Pan **2**:217; **5**:*669*, 674;
8:**1074–1078**
and the Battle of Marathon
8:*1076*
and Echo **4**:459;
8:1075–1076
links with Priapus **9**:1169
mistaken for a satyr
9:1257–1258
musical contest with Apollo
1:132; **7**:*879*; **8**:1078
and panic **8**:1075, *1076*
panpipes **7**:1001; **8**:*1074*,
1076, *1078*
and Pitys **8**:1075
and Psyche **8**:*1077*, 1078
Roman equivalent *see* Faunus
and Selene **8**:1075; **9**:1276
and Syrinx **7**:1001; **8**:1076
Panacea **2**:162
Pandaisia **5**:582
Pandareos **5**:613; **10**:1350

Pandia **9**:1277
Pandora **3**:318; **8**:**1079–1084**;
9:1180; **10**:1437–1438
creation of **5**:584, 646;
8:*1080, 1081, 1083*; **9**:1180
Panku **3**:302–303, 308,
319–320; **4**:570
Pannykhis **5**:582
Papa **1**:*123*, 125
Papatuanuku **8**:1014, 1015,
1017
Paphian Aphrodite **7**:931
Parabrahm **3**:382
Pararo **8**:1014
Paris **5**:*622*; **8**:**1085–1089**
abandoned as a baby **5**:621,
627; **8**:1085; **9**:1164
Cassandra and **2**:272–273;
8:1085
and Helen
abduction **1**:15, 49; **2**:174;
4:489–490; **5**:621, 634–
636; **6**:856; **8**:1086–*1087*
relationship with **5**:636–*637*
Judgment of **1**:14, *118*;
2:*173*–174, 272; **5**:634–636,
657, 682; **8**:1085–1086,
1088–1089, 1097
and Oenone **8**:*1085*, 1088
and the Trojan War
8:1087–1088
death **6**:857
the death of Achilles **1**:18,
133; **6**:853; **8**:1088;
10:1357
duel with Menelaus and
rescue by Aphrodite
2:236; **6**:856–857; **8**:1087
Paritegi **6**:793
Parvati **1**:80; **4**:447; **6**:*738*
Pasiphae **3**:*358*; **5**:711; **7**:887;
8:**1090–1093**, 1149
Pasithea **5**:582, 584, 710
Patrimpas **2**:228
Patroclus **1**:14, 16, *17*;
8:**1094–1095**
and Achilles' horses **1**:85
death **1**:133; **5**:622–623;
8:*1095*; **10**:1357
Pazuzu **3**:404
Pegasus **2**:*230*, 231, 232; **5**:*581*;
8:*1112*, 1149
Peirithous **5**:603, 665; **10**:1354
Pele **7**:*952*; **8**:1015
Peleus **7**:928; **8**:**1096–1097**;
10:1357

Peleus (continued)
  marriage to Thetis 1:14;
    7:1000; 8:1097; 9:1181,
    1186; 10:1356
Pelias 1:55, 56; 5:656; 6:775
  death 6:779, 849–851
Pelopia 2:184, 185
Pelops 6:855; 8:1098–1099
  chariot race with Oenomaus
    2:182–183; 8:1050,
    1098–1099, 1131
  cooked in a stew 3:337;
    6:855; 8:1098;
    10:1349–1350
  Hephaestus and 5:646
Pemphredo 8:1110
Penates 8:1100–1103; 9:1224
  see also Lares; Vesta
Penelope 5:638; 8:1033,
    1104–1105
Penthesileia (Penthesilea)
    1:63–64; 5:688
Pentheus 3:416–417; 6:828
Perdix 3:358
Pere 9:1271
Periboea 8:1040
Periphetes 5:649; 10:1351
Perkunas (Perkons) 2:228, 229
Perse 7:1000
Persephone (Proserpina)
    8:1106–1109
  abduction of 3:386, 388, 389,
    420; 5:602–603; 8:1106,
    1108
  and Adonis 1:22, 116
  Eleusinian Mysteries and
    7:931; 8:1106; 9:1229
  and Psyche 3:342
  queen of the underworld
    5:601, 602, 604, 618;
    8:1108, 1109
  and the seasons 3:349, 420;
    4:504–506; 5:717
  showing cycles between
    fertility and death 4:506
Perseus 3:364; 8:1110–1114
  and Andromeda 1:75–76;
    3:424–425, 429; 5:581;
    8:1110, 1112–1113, 1147
  cap of invisibility 7:891
  conception and birth 3:362;
    6:788; 8:1110; 10:1437
  and the Gorgon Medusa
    3:363; 5:580–581, 674;
    8:1110–1112, 1113
  and Pegasus 8:1112

Perun 4:504; 10:1318
Perusa 9:1247
Pessinuntica 7:931
Phaeacians 3:354
Phaedra 1:63, 115, 116–117;
    2:231; 5:687, 689; 8:1092,
    1149; 10:1354, 1420, 1423
Phaenna 5:582
Phaethon 1:122; 4:484; 5:642;
    8:1115–1117; 10:1344
Phanes 7:1005
Phantasos 5:710; 7:919
Pheidippides 8:1076
Pheres 6:851
Phersipnai 8:1072
Philemon, and Baucis
    6:785–786; 8:1125
Philoctetes 3:411–412; 5:665;
    6:857; 8:1118–1120
Philonectes 5:648
Philonoe 2:231, 232; 6:812
Philyra 3:339
Phineus 5:611–612; 6:779
Phlegyas 2:151
Phobetor 5:710; 7:919
Phobos 1:116; 2:149;
    8:1121–1123
Phocus 7:928
Phoebe 2:276; 6:812
Phoebus 3:341; 5:643
Phoebus Apollo 1:129;
    10:1344, 1396
phoenix 1:88
Phoenix, king of the Dolopians
    1:14
Phorcides 5:674
Phorcys 5:619
Phra In 10:1324–1325,
    1326
Phra Sao 10:1325, 1326
Phrastor 8:1042
Phrixus 5:674; 6:776
Phyllis 3:394
Picus 1:91; 4:498; 6:773
Pierus 7:900, 924
Pietas, shrine 9:1236
Pikuolis 2:228
Piryu 6:794
Pittheus 10:1351
Pitys 1:105; 8:1075
Placia 6:805
Pleiades 2:178; 7:999, 1000;
    8:1129–1131
  constellation 6:846; 8:1055,
    1129, 1130; 10:1335, 1340
  names 8:1130

Pleisthenes 2:185
Plexippus 2:167
Pluto see Hades
Pluton see Hades
Plutus (Ploutos) 3:420; 8:1132
Po 8:1013
Podarces see Priam
Podarge 5:611, 612, 614;
    10:1315
Poeas 8:1119
Pokoh 5:588
Polemos 7:977
Poliporthes 8:1032
Polybus 8:1041
Polydectes 3:363; 5:580, 581;
    8:1110, 1113
Polydegmon see Hades
Polydeuces see Castor and
    Pollux
Polydora 8:1097
Polydorus 1:116; 5:626, 627,
    628
Polymede 6:775
Polymestor 5:626, 628
Polymnia 7:921, 924
Polyneices 1:106; 8:1042,
    1043–1045
Polyphemus 3:352
  Galatea and 3:356, 357;
    4:545–546
  Odysseus and 3:354–355,
    356; 4:567–568;
    8:1034–1035, 1147–1148
Polytechnos 5:653
Polyxena 1:16; 5:628
Pomona 7:999; 8:1141–1142
Pontus 8:1020; 9:1268–1269
Popoca 7:952
Popocatepetl 2:205
Porphyrion 4:489, 566–567;
    5:652
Poseidon 8:1143–1150
  and Amphitrite 9:1269
  and Aphrodite 7:951
  and Athena 8:1148
  birth 8:1143
  and Caenis (Caeneus) 5:669;
    8:1144
  and Cassiopeia 1:75; 3:424;
    8:1147
  children 8:1144–1147
  and Demeter 8:1144
  and Erechtheus 8:1146
  and Helios 8:1148
  Hera's quarrel with 5:652;
    8:1148

and Hippolytus 5:689
and Laocoon 6:803–804
and Laomedon 6:805–806
and Minos 7:886–887;
    8:1090, 1149
Poseidon Heliconius 8:1143
Poseidon Hippion (god of
    horses) 8:1149
power over natural forces
    7:948, 965–966; 8:1144
  "courtship" tidal wave
    7:951
Roman equivalent see
    Neptune
and Thetis 1:14; 10:1356
worship of 8:1149–1150
Po Tlen 10:1326, 1329
potniades see maenads
Potter, Harry 4:448
Praamzius see Dievas
Prakurimas see Dievas
Pramzimas 4:521
Priam (formerly Podarces)
    3:394; 5:640; 6:805, 806,
    857; 7:986; 9:1164–1167
  abandonment of Paris 5:621,
    627; 9:1164
  and Aeneas 1:30
  chief wife see Hecuba
  death of 9:1166–1167
  meeting with Achilles 9:1166
Priapus 5:655, 685;
    9:1168–1170; 10:1412
Procris 4:483; 8:1093
Procrustes 3:327; 10:1351
Proetus (Proitus), king of Argos
    2:230
Prometheus 2:170; 3:396;
    9:1179–1184
  chained to a rock 9:1180,
    1182, 1183, 1246; 10:1437
  and Cheiron 1:16
  and the creation of Pandora
    3:318; 8:1080
  creations of, judged by
    Momos 7:904
  and fire 8:1080; 9:1180, 1182,
    1246
  and Heracles 2:178; 5:663;
    9:1181
  parallel with Loki 6:822
Proserpina see Persephone
Proteus 6:858; 7:969–970;
    9:1185–1186
Prthivi 4:446–447
Prudgelmir see Thrùdgelmir

Psyche **9:1187–1191**
  Cupid (Eros) and 3:341–343;
    4:*490*–491; **8:**1078;
    9:*1187*–1191
  Pan and 8:*1077*, 1078
  punished by the Furies 4:*540*
  tasks of 4:491
Ptah 2:191; 4:466;
    9:1192–1195, 1210;
    10:1426
  Ptah-Sokar 9:1192
  Ptah-Sokar-Osiris 9:1192
  Ptah-Tatenen 9:1195
Purusa 10:1430
Pushan 5:672
Pygmalion 1:114–116;
    9:1196–1198
Pylades 4:471–472;
    8:1051–*1053*
Pyramus, and Thisbe 5:679
Pyrrha
  Achilles disguised as 1:14–15
  Deucalion and 3:*397*–399;
    4:*521*; 6:824; 9:1179
Pyrrhus (Neoptolemus)
    8:1053, 1097, 1119; 9:*1167*
Pythia 1:129, *130*; 3:424
Python 1:128, 129, *131*;
    3:*422*–424

Qadashu *see* Astarte
Qat 8:1015
Qebehsenef (Qebhsenuef)
    1:110, 111; 5:610
Qormusta *see* Köke Möngke
    Tengri
Quetzalcoatl 2:203, 205, 209;
    6:797; 8:1049; **9:1199–**
    1203; 10:1382–1384
  a creator god 3:322; 9:1200;
    10:1385
  a twin 4:445
  wind god 7:949; 9:1202
  see also Kukulkan
Quirinus 4:446; **9:1204–1205**,
    1231, 1232, *1233*
  Jupiter-Mars-Quirinus triad
    9:1233

Ra *see* Re
Ragana 2:228
Raiju 3:406
Rainbow Serpents 2:196, *198*;
    4:*523*; 5:614
Rainboy 1:86
Raja Naga 9:1274

Rama 6:738, 739
Rán 1:26; 9:1269–1270
Rangda 10:1324, *1326*
Rangi 1:*123*, 125; 8:1014,
    1015
Ranitokona 8:1015
Rasa 2:228
Rat Woman 1:86
Ravana 6:738; 8:1139
Re (Ra) 1:78, 86; 2:189; 4:466;
    5:644, 695; **9:1206–1211**
  and creation 3:320; 4:550,
    552
  Isis gains power from 6:764,
    766; 9:1210
  Re-Atum (Atum-Re) 2:188,
    191; 9:1209
  revenge on humankind
    9:1211
  Seth and 9:1208, 1282
Re-Amun *see* Amun
Rea Silvia *see* Rhea Silvia
Regin 3:425, 426; 10:1300,
    1302, *1303*
Re-horakhty (Re-"Horus-of-
    the-Two-Horizons") 5:703,
    705, 706; 7:994; 10:*1342*
Renenutet, merger with Isis
    6:767
Resheph 2:268, 270
Rex Nemorensis 3:409
Rhadamanthys 4:492; 5:606;
    7:885; 10:1435
  a judge in the underworld
    7:888
Rhamnubia 7:931
Rhea 3:326, 414; 4:441, 442;
    5:594; 10:1311
  birth of the gods 3:335;
    5:601; 6:783; 10:1374,
    1431–1432
  Roman equivalent
    see Cybele
Rhea Silvia (Rea Silvia; Ilia)
    6:835; **9:1220–1221**, 1232,
    1240; 10:1414–1415
Rhesus 8:1033
Rhiannon 2:279–280
Rhinemaidens 6:*818*; 10:*1400*
Rhodope 1:105
Rhome 9:1240
Rhomulos and Rhomus
    9:1240
Rig 5:631
Rind 10:1425
River-Earl 6:795

Romulus and Remus 4:446;
    9:*1220*, 1221, **1240–1244**;
    10:1415
  and the founding of Rome
    4:446; 6:835; 9:1231–1232,
    1233, 1242–*1244*, 1251
  Romulus taken to heaven
    10:1310
Rongala 8:1017
Rongo 8:1017
Rosmerta 10:1423
Rübezahl 1:*58*, 59
Running Antelope 7:939,
    945–946
Rusalki 10:1320
Ryujin (Luminous Being)
    7:952; 9:1270–1271

Sabrina 2:279
Saga 10:1407
Salacia 7:967
Salmacis 1:105; 5:666, *668*,
    674; 7:1000
Salmoneus 10:1307
Salus, shrine 9:1236
Samas *see* Utu
Sango 1:44
Saoshyant 6:748
Sáráhkka 9:1266
Saramama 6:727
Sarpedon 4:492; 5:709; 7:885;
    10:1435
Satis 7:981
Sat Nam 7:908
Satres 8:1072
Saturn 9:1230, 1231,
    1253–1255
  devouring his children 6:783
  Greek equivalent *see* Cronus
  and Janus 6:770–772
Satvaras *see* Dievas
Satyavan 6:739
satyrs 1:82, 89; 2:216–217;
    3:*413*; 4:*447*; **9:1256–1258**;
    10:1305
  see also Faunus; Marsyas; Pan;
    Silenus
Saule 2:224, *225*, 228
  and Menulis 2:228–229;
    7:914
Saules Meita 7:914
Saules meitas 2:228
Savitri 6:735, 739
Scamander 8:1022
Schoeneus 2:168
Sciron 10:1351

Scylla 5:619; 8:1037, *1092*,
    1146, 1147; 9:*1270*, 1274
sea monsters 8:*1092*;
    9:*1273–1274*
  Charybdis 8:1037, *1146*
  Scylla 5:619; 8:1037, *1092*,
    1146, 1147; 9:*1270*, 1274
sea serpents 3:430; 5:695;
    9:1274
Sebek-Re 9:1206
Sedna 9:1271
Sekhmet 1:78, 108; 4:463–465,
    466; 9:1193, 1194, *1211*
Selene 4:*474*, 475; 7:914;
    8:1075; **9:1275–1278**
Selket 1:85
Selu (Corn) 7:939, 942
Selvans 8:1072
Semara 10:1324, 1326
Semargl 10:1318
Semele 1:21, 116; 2:253; 3:413;
    4:444; 5:654; 10:*1436*, 1437
Semnai Theai *see* Furies
Sequana 2:279
Serapis 6:788; 8:1067
serpents 3:*422*, 430; 8:1139
  Aboriginal Rainbow Serpents
    2:196, *198*; 4:*523*; 5:614
  in apocalypse myths 1:126,
    127
  in Babylonian mythology
    5:695
  in the Biblical Old Testament
    5:695; 8:1139
  in creation mythology 3:*314*,
    319, 321; 5:695
  earth mother depicted as
    4:456
  eating 1:85
  in Egyptian mythology 5:*695*
    see also Apophis
  in Greek mythology
    biting Philoctetes 8:1118,
    1119, *1120*
    symbolism 4:486
  as healers 1:86–87
  Hindu
    cosmic serpent 9:*1268*
    serpent of eternity 3:*319*
  in Hittite mythology 5:694
  Hopi Snake Dancers 1:89
  and Mithraism 7:*897*
  Minoan snake goddesses
    3:*329*, 330
  in Norse mythology 1:126;
    5:631, 632, 633; 6:*817*, 818;

serpents (continued)
8:1024, *1026*; 10:*1362*,
1364
the punishment of Loki
6:*822*; 7:948; 10:*1406*
Olmec deity 8:*1049*
sea serpents 3:430; 5:695;
9:1274
Serpot 1:64
Sesha 1:127
Seshanaga 9:*1268*
Setesuyara 10:1324, 1326
Seth 2:188; 3:402; 4:457, 466,
467, 503; 9:**1279–1284**
animal representations of
9:1280, *1282*
birth 4:550; 9:1280
and the desert 8:1064
and lightning 7:950
and Osiris 5:703–704; 7:982;
8:1064; 9:1281
and Re 9:1208, 1282
rivalry with Horus the
Younger 5:705–708; 6:764;
9:1208, 1281–1284
Sethlans 8:1072
Seven Against Thebes 1:106;
8:1045
Shabbat Hamalka 4:448
Shachihoko 9:1274
Shakti (Kamala; Padma;
Lakshmi) 3:317
Shamash *see* Utu
Shang-Ti 3:302, 308
Shao Hao 3:308
Shapash 2:268; 10:1343
Sharruma 5:693, 698
Sheela-na-gig 4:506
Shekhina 4:448
Shen Nong 3:305, 308
Shen Yi 9:1211
Shou-Hsing 3:*308*, 309
Shu 2:188; 4:463; 7:995;
9:*1207*; 10:1310, 1312, 1399
Shun 3:306, 308
Sia 2:235
Sibil 10:1358
Sibylla 9:1291
Sibzianna 8:1056
Side 5:656
Sidhe, people of the 8:1133
Siduri 4:572
Siegfried *see* Sigurd
Siggeir 1:34; 7:974
Sigmund 7:974; 8:1030;
10:1300, 1304

Sigurd (Siegfried) 1:34, 85, *87*;
3:426; 4:562; 7:972; 8:1030;
10:**1300–1304**, 1402
and the ring 10:1303,
1402–1403
Sigyn 1:37; 6:818, *822*; 7:948
Sila (Silap Inua) 7:939, 945
sileni 10:1305
Silenus 9:1257; 10:**1305–1306**
Silvius 9:1220
Simhamukha 1:80
Sin 3:347; 7:870, 876; 8:1137
Sumerian equivalent *see*
Nanna
Sinfjötli 1:34
Sinis 10:1351
Sinon 6:802–803, 804
Sinope 1:133
Siqiniq 7:911
Sirens 3:*393*; 8:*1037*; 9:*1269*
and the Muses 7:926; 9:1269
Sisyphus 2:149; 5:608; 8:1131;
10:**1307–1308**
Sita 6:738
Siva 3:316; 6:736, 737, 738
cult of (Saivism) 8:1134
as Nataraja, lord of the dance
7:*956*
and Parvati 1:80
rulers as incarnations of
10:1322
Siyamek 6:749
Skadi (Goddess of Snowshoes;
Ski Goddess) 4:531, 570;
7:*989–990*; 10:*1407*
and the torture of Loki
10:*1406*, 1407
Skanda 10:1340
Ski Goddess *see* Skadi
Skírnir 4:527, 555
skogsra 1:59
Skookums 7:939, 945
Skrymir 10:*1363*
Skuld 4:497; 7:*992*
Skywalker, Luke 4:448
Slagfid 10:1424
Sleipnir 5:676, *677*; 6:818;
8:*1030*
snakes *see* serpents
Sobek 5:610; 7:981, *982*
Soko 1:40
Sol Invictus 5:644; 7:933
Solymi, the 2:231
Soma 3:347, 382; 6:735, 738;
7:913
Somnus 5:710

Sonchis 1:123
Sopdet 8:1066
Sopdu 8:1066
Soranus 3:419
Sorli 10:1403
Sothis 5:610
Spartoi 2:253
Spenta Armaiti 1:102; 6:747,
748
Spenta Mainyu 6:747, 748
sphinxes 1:82–83; 5:*611*;
10:**1330–1332**
Great Sphinx at Giza 1:*82*,
83; 10:*1330*–1332
Theban Sphinx 7:926;
8:1041, *1043*
riddle 6:772; 8:1042;
9:1288–1289; 10:1331
Spider People 1:87
spirits
in Aboriginal mythologies
2:196–197, *199*
manitous (great spirits)
7:939–941
Norse
guardian spirits 9:1266
nature spirits 9:1265
see also devas; devils
Sterope 8:1130
Steropes 3:352; 10:1395, 1396
Stheno 5:580
Stribog 10:1318
Strophius 8:1051
Strymo 6:805
Stygian Proserpine 7:931
Styrbjörn 8:1027
Sucellus 2:278–279, *279*
Sülde 3:296
Suleyman (Sulieman) 1:138
Sulis 2:279
Sulis Minerva 2:279; 8:1073
Supay 6:727
Surt 1:126; 9:1260, 1266
Surya 3:382; 5:644; 6:738
Susanowo 10:1345
Suttung 4:569; 6:801; 8:1028,
1029
Suwa 1:137, 138
Svaha 10:1340
Svartálfar (black elves) 1:58–59
Syrinx 1:105; 7:1001; 8:1076

Taakura 8:1018–1019
Ta'aroa 8:1019
Tabu Eriki 8:1017
Tahmuras 6:749

T'ai Ho *see* Fu Hsi
Tailtiu 6:758
Tajin 10:1385
Taku Skanskan 5:589
Taliesin 6:801
Talos 2:*236*; 6:849
Tammuz 1:24; 6:760–762
Sumerian equivalent *see*
Dumuzi
Tane 3:323; 8:1017
Tane Mahuta 8:1014–1015
Tangaroa (Kanaloa) 8:1015,
1016, 1017; 9:1271
Tan'gun 6:792
Tanit (Tinith; Tinnit; Tint)
2:*214, 268*, 269
Tantalus 10:**1349–1350**
Tantalus (son of Thyestes)
2:185
Tantalus (son of Zeus)
cooks Pelops in a stew
3:337; 6:855; 8:1098;
10:1349–1350
eternally punished 5:608;
10:*1349, 1350*
Taqqiq 7:911
Taranis 2:281
T'arhae 6:795–796
Tarhuhiawahku 7:938–939
Taru 5:*691*, 693, 694, 695
Tatenen 9:1195
Taweret 4:*466*; 5:613
Tawiskara 3:406
Ta'xet 4:447
Taygete 8:1131
Ta Yü 3:306, 308
Tecciztecatl 2:206
Tefen 5:703
Tefnut 1:83; 2:188; 3:320;
7:995
Telamon 6:806; 7:928
Telegonus 2:265; 3:310–311;
8:1038, 1104
Telemachus 3:311; 8:1032,
1038
Telephassa 2:251
Telephus 1:16
Telepinu 5:693, 695
Telesto 1:105; 7:1000
Tellus 9:1231, *1238*; 10:1399
Tenes 1:16
Tengri 3:295, 296, 299
Tepeu 6:799, 841
Terpsichore 7:921
Teshub 5:*693*, 696, 697;
10:1398

Tethys, and the Great Bear constellation 2:263
Teucer 6:805
Teutates 2:279, 281
Tezcatlipoca 2:203, 205; 4:445; 6:799; 9:1201; 10:1382, 1385
Thalia 1:134; 5:582; 7:921
Thaltybios 3:312
Thamus 7:900
Thamyris 7:926
Thanatos 2:149; 5:709; 10:1308
Thasus 2:251
Theias 1:22, 116; 7:929
Themis 7:959, 960–961; 10:1376
  as mother of the Fates 4:493; 10:1435
  as mother of the Horae 10:1435
  prophecies concerning Achilles 1:14
Thens, the 10:1325, 1326, 1327
Thersites 1:64
Theseus 10:1351–1355
  abduction of Helen 2:275; 10:1354
  and the Amazons 1:62–63; 5:687–688; 8:1122; 10:1354
  and Ariadne 2:154–155; 3:329, 358; 8:1092; 10:1352–1353
  cult of 3:393
  death 10:1354
  escape from the underworld 5:603, 665; 10:1354
  grave discovered 10:1355
  and Hippolytus 1:116; 5:689
  as king of Athens 10:1353
  and Medea 6:851; 10:1351–1352
  and the Minotaur 1:78; 2:154, 155; 3:327–329, 358; 5:594–595; 7:887; 10:1352–1353, 1355
  as a metaphor 7:888; 10:1353
  and Periphetes 10:1351
  and Phaedra 1:116; 10:1354
  and Procrustes 3:327; 10:1351
  retrieves Minos's ring 10:1352
  and Sciron 10:1351
  and Sinis 10:1351

sword and sandals 10:1351, 1352
Thespius 5:660
Thetis 1:53; 10:1356–1357
  and Achilles 1:14, 15, 17; 6:853; 7:1000; 10:1356–1357
  marriage to Peleus 1:14; 7:1000; 8:1097; 9:1181, 1186; 10:1356
  rescue of Hephaestus 5:645–646; 10:1357
  shape-shifting 9:1185–1186
Theuth 7:900
Thisbe, Pyramus and 5:679
Thjazi 7:989, 990; 10:1407
Thoibi, Khamba and 5:679–680
Thökk, Loki disguised as 2:222; 5:677; 6:818, 822
Thong, Prince 10:1327
Thor 1:34; 4:504, 528, 535; 9:1260; 10:1358–1365
  children 10:1358
  and Christianity 10:1364
  death 10:1364
  and Geirröd 4:570; 6:822; 10:1362
  and Hrungnir 10:1360–1362
  journey to Utgard 9:1249
  and Loki 6:818; 10:1358–1360, 1361, 1363
  and the Midgard Serpent 10:1362, 1364
  and Odin 8:1031; 10:1365
  parallel gods 10:1360
  Jupiter 6:788
  people and places named for 10:1365
  personality and attributes 10:1311, 1358
  possessions
    hall (Bilskírnir) 10:1358
    hammer (Mjöllnir) 4:568; 6:818; 7:991; 9:1264; 10:1358–1360, 1362, 1363, 1364–1365, 1366–1367
  and Skrymir 10:1363
  and Thrym 4:568; 10:1362
  and Utgard-Loki 10:1363
  worship of 10:1364–1365
Thoth 1:79, 93; 3:348; 4:466; 5:608; 7:912, 996
  and the calendar 2:255; 4:550

Thrúdgelmir (Prudgelmir) 2:233, 234, 246
Thrym 4:568; 7:991; 10:1362, 1366–1367
Thunderbird 10:1315
Thyestes 1:48; 2:182, 183–185; 6:855
thyiades see maenads
Tia 4:447
Tiamat 6:831; 10:1368–1370
  battle with Marduk 3:317, 338, 403; 4:480; 6:829–830, 831–833; 10:1368, 1369–1370, 1430
  creation myth involving 3:316–317, 422; 4:480; 5:695; 6:830, 833; 10:1368–1370, 1430
Tien-Mu 7:949
Tilo 1:40
Timagoras 4:488
Timandra 6:812
Timer Kazyk 3:296
Tin (Tinia) 8:1072
Tinaicaboga 8:1018
Tinith see Tanit
Tinnit see Tanit
Tint see Tanit
Tiresias 5:607, 652–653, 669; 7:934; 8:1036, 1043; 10:1371–1372
Tisamenus 6:858; 8:1053
Tisiphone 4:540
Tisna Wati 10:1324, 1326
Titans 4:564; 10:1373–1378
  children of 10:1376
  derivation of Titan 10:1378
  female see Mnemosyne; Phoebe; Rhea; Theia; Themis
  formation 2:235; 3:318, 334; 10:1373
  male see Atlas; Coeus; Cronus; Hyperion; Iapetus; Oceanus; Prometheus
  war with the Olympians (Titanomachy; Titanomachia) 2:178; 3:335–336; 4:542–543, 565; 6:785; 7:1003; 10:1374–1378, 1432
  Zagreus and 4:444; 10:1378
Tithonus 6:805, 806; 10:1379–1381
  Eos and 4:484, 485; 10:1379–1380, 1381

Tityus 4:543; 6:815–816
Tiwaz (Tiw) 2:261; 4:561; 9:1263
  see also Tyr
Tlaloc 2:203, 205, 209; 10:1382–1385
Tlaloques 10:1382, 1384–1385
Tlaltecuhtli 9:1200; 10:1385, 1430
Tmolus 8:1078
To Kabinana 8:1015
Tomam 10:1315
Tomo 3:347–348
Tonacacihuatl 2:206
Tonacatecuhtli 2:206
Tonatiuh 2:203, 205, 206, 209; 7:948; 9:1200
Toxeus 2:167
Trickster gods 6:861
  Aboriginal 2:197
  African 1:44
  Greek, Hermes 5:672–673
  Maori 8:1015–1016, 1018
  Native American 6:861
    Coyote 3:376, 404; 5:587; 7:939, 945
  in Norse mythology 2:220; 6:821
  Roman, Mercury 6:861, 862
Triple Goddess 4:455
Triptolemus 3:386, 387; 4:506; 8:1020–1023; 9:1229
Tritogeneia see Athena
Triton 7:884; 8:1144; 10:1386–1387
tritons 10:1387
Troilus 10:1388–1390
  and Cressida (Criseyde) 3:412; 10:1388–1390
  death 9:1166
Trophonius, oracle of 7:902
Tros 4:548
Troyan 10:1318
Ts'ai Shen 3:308, 309
Tsao Shen 3:308, 309
Tsuki-Yomi 4:446
Tuatha De 6:752, 754–755
Tuatha De Danann 1:125, 126; 3:338, 364
Tucumbalam 6:842
Tulasi 8:1125
Tuli 8:1017
Tullus Hostilius 8:1102; 9:1233, 1234
Tu Matauenga 8:1014, 1015
Turms 8:1072

Turnus **1**:*29*, 33
T'u-ti **3**:308
Tvashtri **10**:1426
twins **4**:*445–446*
Two Ladies **5**:703
Tyche **7**:961; **10**:1334, **1391–1392**
Tydeus **3**:411
Tyndareos **3**:312; **5**:634, 655; **6**:811, 857; **8**:1033
Typhon **3**:422; **7**:948; **10**:**1393–1394**
birth **5**:651, 652
defeat of **2**:171; **4**:495, 543; **10**:1393–1394, 1432–1433
Tyr **1**:36–*37*; **4**:*561*; **8**:1024; **9**:1260, 1261
see also Tiwaz
Tyro **10**:1307
Tzahui **10**:1385
Tzununiha **6**:842

Uga-no-Mitama **4**:517
Uixtocihuatl **10**:1384
Uksáhkká **9**:1266
Ulgan **3**:403–404
Ull **1**:37; **7**:990
Ullikummi **5**:697
Ulysses *see* Odysseus
Umay **3**:295, 296
Una **4**:456
"undead, the" **2**:238
Uni **8**:1072
unicorns **1**:88, *91*
Unkulunkulu **1**:40
Unn (Ud) **1**:26
Urania **7**:921
Uranus **10**:**1395–1399**
and creation **3**:318, 334; **4**:501, 541–542; **10**:1396
giving birth to Aphrodite **1**:112; **10**:1397
overthrow and castration by Cronus **3**:334, *336*; **4**:565; **10**:1373–1374, *1395*, 1397
in Roman mythology **10**:1399
Urash **1**:67; **7**:983
Urcaguary **6**:727
Urd **7**:*992*
Ureia **9**:*1273*
Urker **3**:296
Urshanabi **4**:572
Usas **4**:484
Usins **2**:228
Ustrecha **10**:1318

Utgard-Loki **10**:1363
Utixo **1**:40
Utnapishtim **3**:371, 399; **4**:480, 519, 572
Uttu **4**:505
Utu (Shamash; Samas) **4**:*450*, 505; **7**:870; **9**:1211; **10**:1313, 1342–1343
Uzza, al- **1**:137–138; **7**:909

Vafthrúdnir **2**:234
Vainamoinen **4**:566
Vaisravana *see* Kubera
Vakarine **2**:224, 226
Váli **1**:37
Valkyries **5**:613; **8**:1026; **10**:**1400–1403**
Raven Banner **10**:1401
see also Brynhild
vampires **2**:*238*; **3**:371; **10**:1321
Vanir, the **1**:34; **4**:531; **10**:**1404–1407**
gods included in **10**:1404
gold sacrificed to **4**:532–533
war with the Aesir **4**:531; **7**:988–989; **10**:1404–1405
Vanth **3**:401, *403*
Varah **1**:80
Varuna **6**:735, 738; **7**:*892*; **10**:1312
Vaya **6**:738
Vé **2**:234, 246; **8**:1026–1027
Vejamate **2**:228
Velnias **2**:228
Venus **9**:1231, 1236; **10**:**1408–1411**
and Adonis **10**:1409
affair with Anchises **10**:1408
affair with Mars **1**:*114*
and Cupid **3**:340, *343*
goddess of gardens **10**:1409
Greek equivalent *see* Aphrodite
the name of **10**:1409
as one of the Penates **8**:1100
and Psyche **3**:341, 342; **4**:*540*; **9**:1188, 1189–1190
and purification **10**:1410
temples to **10**:1409–*1411*
Venus Erycina **10**:1410
Venus Genetrix **10**:1411
Venus of Mount Eryx, cult of **10**:1410
Venus Obsequens **10**:1410

Venus Verticordia **10**:1410–1411
Venus Victrix **10**:1411
Verdandi **4**:497; **7**:*992*
Vertumnus **7**:999; **8**:1141, *1142*
Vesta **10**:**1412–1415**
cult of **9**:1176, 1231
Greek equivalent *see* Hestia
vestal virgins and **9**:*1176*; **10**:*1412–1415*
see also Lares; Penates
Vetis **8**:1072
Vichama **6**:727
Victoria **7**:977; **9**:1236
Vídar **1**:37; **5**:632; **8**:1024
Vili **2**:234, 246; **8**:1026–1027
Viracocha **3**:322; **6**:726–*727*, 728, 729
Virbius **3**:407–408; **5**:690; **10**:1420
Vishnu **6**:738
and creation **3**:316, 317, *319*; **6**:736; **9**:*1268*
cult of (Vaishnavism) **8**:1134
and the flood **4**:*522*
incarnations **1**:80, 93; **3**:316
and the tulsi plant **8**:1125
Vohu Mano (or Manah) **6**:747, 748
Voldemort **4**:448
Völsung **1**:34; **7**:974
Völsungs, the **1**:34; **7**:974
Voluptas **4**:491
Vortigern **9**:1252
Vrinda **8**:1125
Vritra (Vrta) **3**:364, 422; **6**:736
Vulcan **7**:952; **9**:1231; **10**:*1425*
creation of the first woman **8**:*1080*, *1081*
Germanic equivalent *see* Wayland
Greek equivalent *see* Hephaestus

Wachilt **10**:1425
Wadd **1**:137, 138
Wadjet **4**:466; **5**:701, 703
Wakan Tanka **5**:589; **7**:909, 939
Wakonda **5**:588
Wanadi **10**:1315–1316
Wanadi II **10**:1316
Wanadi III **10**:1316
Wandjina **2**:*199*; **4**:523
Wang Mu **3**:308
Wayland **10**:**1424–1427**

Wen Ti (Wen Ch'ang) **3**:308, *309*
Wepwawet **1**:111
werewolves **1**:104; **7**:*915*
White Buffalo Calf Woman **7**:939, 941–942
Willow-Flower **6**:795
Winaboozhoo **7**:939–940
Windigo **3**:406
winds, Greek and Roman *see* Anemoi
Winter Thunder **1**:87; **10**:1311
Wise Crow (Ga-gaah) **7**:939
witches **1**:104; **7**:949; **9**:*1277*, *1288*
Wodan (Woden; Wotan) **4**:561
and Mercury **6**:861
see also Odin
Wuali **10**:1323, 1326, 1328
Wurunkatte **5**:693
Wyrd **4**:497

Xanthikos **3**:*321*
Xanthus **1**:14, *18*, 85, *86*; **4**:538; **5**:612; **10**:1314
Xbalanque *see* Hunahpu and Xbalanque
Xecotcovach **6**:841–842
Xenodamus **6**:856
Xib Chac **6**:844, *845*, 846, 847; **9**:*1175*
Xipe Totec **2**:203, 205
Xisuthrus *see* Ziusudra
Xiuhtecuhtli **2**:205
Xochipilli **2**:*205*
Xolotl, a twin **4**:*445*
Xquic **6**:845
Xuthus **3**:398

Yaghuth **1**:137, 138
yaksas **8**:1139
Yakumama **6**:727
Yam **2**:166, 212, 268
conflict with Baal **2**:213–214, 267
Yama **4**:445; **5**:608; **6**:735, 738, 739; **9**:*1216*; **10**:1310
Yani **4**:445; **5**:608
Yao **3**:305–306, 308
Ya'uq **1**:137, 138
Yei deities **7**:*942*–943
yeks **3**:297
Yen Ti **3**:305
Yer-Sub **3**:296
Yima (Jam; Jemshid) **6**:749
Ylvunda Kotta **1**:96

Ymir (Aurgelmir) **2**:234;
9:1260; **10**:**1428–1430**
creation myth concerning
2:233, 246, 249, *250*; **4**:568;
8:1026–1027; **9**:1247, 1268;
10:1429
Yolkai Estsan **4**:445
Yol Tengri **3**:296
Yum Kaax **6**:845
Yuri **6**:794
Yü Ti (Yü Huang Shang Ti)
3:307–308

Zagreus **4**:444; **10**:1378
Zalmoxis **2**:269
Zaltys **2**:228
Zelus **7**:975
Zeme **2**:224, 228
Zemi **4**:447
Zephyrus (Zephyr) **1**:77; **3**:341;
4:484; **7**:948; **9**:1188, *1189*;
10:1314, 1315
Zetes **5**:*612*; **6**:779
Zeus **4**:504; **8**:*1133*;
10:**1431–1438**
and Ares **2**:149; **5**:655
and Asclepius **2**:161;
10:1438

battle against the Giants
10:1432–1433
birth **3**:326, 333, 335; **4**:542;
10:1432
and the birth of Athena
2:170–171; **3**:*378*;
10:1434–1435
and the birth of Dionysus
3:390, 413
character **5**:594
creations of, judged by
Momos **7**:904
and Cronus **3**:326, 335–336,
337; **4**:565; **5**:601–602, 684;
10:1374, 1431–1432
defeat of Typhon **2**:171;
4:495, 543; **5**:652;
10:1393–1394, 1433
early life **3**:*338*
and Crete **3**:*324*, 326, 333
and the flood **4**:*519*, 521
and Hestia **5**:685
and Hypnos **5**:709–710
love affairs **5**:655;
10:1433–1434
Aegina **5**:654; **7**:927
Alcmene **5**:654, 659, 709;
10:1436

Aphrodite **5**:655
Callisto **1**:21; **2**:158, 262,
263; **5**:653–654; **6**:826;
7:1001
Danae **3**:362, *363*; **8**:1110;
10:1436–1437
Electra **8**:1131
Europa **2**:251; **3**:*333*; **4**:*492*;
7:885; **8**:*1091*; **10**:1435
Eurymedusa **7**:927
Eurynome **10**:1435
Ganymede **4**:548–549
Io **5**:653; **6**:*781*; **8**:1076;
9:1180; **10**:1435–1436
Iynx **5**:655
Leda **2**:275; **5**:634; **6**:*811*,
812; **10**:1437
Leto **5**:653; **6**:814–815;
10:1435
Maia **8**:1131
Mnemosyne **7**:899; **10**:1435
Nemesis **7**:961
Semele **3**:413; **5**:654;
10:*1436*, 1437
Taygete **8**:1131
Themis **10**:1435
and Lycaon **6**:824
Nemean Games and **10**:1438

Olympic Games and
10:*1437*, 1438
and Pegasus **8**:1112
and Prometheus
9:1179–1181, 1182, *1183*,
1246; **10**:1437
roles **10**:1433
as god of guests **10**:1434
Roman counterpart *see*
Jupiter
a sky god **10**:1310, 1311,
1312
and Thetis **1**:14; **9**:1181,
1186; **10**:*1356*
thunderbolts **3**:352, *353*
and Tiresias **10**:1371–1372
wife (Hera) **5**:650–*653*;
10:*1435*
Zeus-Chthonios **5**:605
Zeus Horkios **8**:1137
Zeus Xenios **10**:1434
Zhiva **10**:1318
Zipacna **6**:846
Ziusudra (Xisuthrus) **3**:399;
4:519, 520
Zurvan Akarana **6**:746–747,
748

INDEX OF ART AND CULTURE

Page numbers in **bold** refer to main articles; those in *italics* refer to pictures.

Abbate, Noccolò dell', painting of Eros and Psyche **4**:*490*

Abduction of Ganymede, The (Rubens) **4**:*549*

Abildgaard, N.A., painting by **2**:*250*

Achilleid (Statius) **1**:19

Acis and Galatea Hide from the Gaze of Polyphemus (Perrier) **3**:*357*

Acqua, Cesare Dell', *Argonauts, The* **6**:*776*

Adam, Nicolas Sebastien, statue of Prometheus **9**:*1182*

Adam of Bremen **4**:529; **8**:1031; **10**:1364

Aeneas with King Evander and Pallas (da Cortona) **1**:*33*

Aeneas in the Underworld (Rubens) **1**:*32*

Aeneid (Virgil) **1**:32; **7**:*922*
   Aeneas **1**:28; **5**:619; **6**:785, 861; **7**:966; **8**:1101–*1102*
   the Furies **5**:613
   the golden bough **3**:409
   Hecate **5**:618, 619
   Idomeneus **5**:714
   Juno **7**:966
   Jupiter and Juno **6**:780–781
   Laocoon **6**:802
   Latinus **4**:498
   Neptune **7**:966
   Troilus **10**:1388

Aeschylus
   Oresteia trilogy **3**:313; **4**:539; **8**:1052
     Agamemnon **1**:51; **2**:274; **3**:313; **4**:539; **6**:742
     Choephoroe (*The Libation Bearers*) **3**:313; **4**:539
     Eumenides (*The Furies*) **3**:313; **4**:538, 539

Prometheus Bound **7**:926; **8**:1023, 1135; **9**:1180
   Seven Against Thebes, The **8**:1040

Aesop **7**:904

"Aethiopis" (poem) **1**:60; **6**:854

Agamemnon, Mask of **1**:*48*, 49

Agamemnon (Aeschylus) **1**:51; **2**:274; **3**:313; **4**:539; **6**:742, 855; **7**:960

Aiguptiaka (Apion) **1**:84

Ajax (Sophocles) **1**:53

Ajax by the Sea (Sabatelli) **1**:*52*

Alberti, Leon Battista, *Momus* **7**:904

Alcestis (Euripides) **1**:55, 56

Algardi, Alessandro, *Titan* **10**:*1373*

Allegory of Divine Providence (de Cortona) **9**:*1253*

Allegory of Earth (Brueghel the Younger) **4**:*504*

Allegory of Spring (Botticelli) **5**:*582*

Allori, Alessandro
   paintings by
     of Circe **3**:*311*
     of Odysseus and Polyphemus **3**:354, *355*
     of Odysseus and Tiresias **8**:*1036*

Alma-Tadema, Lawrence, *Bacchanal* **2**:*219*

Alvíssmal **10**:1358

Amatoriae Narrationes (Plutarch) **4**:539

Amazons and Her Children, The (Leutze) **1**:*61*

Ammannati, Bartolommeo, sculptures by **6**:*813*; **7**:*967*; **8**:1150

Anahuac (Tylor) **7**:954

Andromeda Chained to the Rocks by the Nereids (Chassériau) **7**:*970*

Anouilh, Jean, *Antigone* **1**:107

Antigone (Anouilh) **1**:107

Antigone (Mendelssohn) **1**:106

Antigone (Sophocles) **1**:106–107

Antoninus Liberalis **8**:1093

Aphrodite of Melos (Venus de Milo) **1**:*117*

Apion, *Aiguptiaka* **1**:84

Apollo Belvedere **1**:*129*

Apollo and Daphne (Bernini) **1**:*132*

Apollo and Daphne (Tiepolo) **3**:*367*

Apollo and Daphne (Zuccari) **1**:*105*

Apollodorus **2**:251
   and the death of Agamemnon **1**:51
   and Hephaestus **5**:646
   and Hermes **5**:673, 674
   and Hippolyte **5**:687–688
   and Idomeneus **5**:714
   Library, The **2**:251
   and Niobe's children **7**:986
   and Menelaus **6**:855, 856
   and Penelope **8**:1104
   and Philoctetes **8**:1120
   and Typhon **10**:1393

Apollonius, *Argonautica* **8**:1069

Apollo a Victor, Sitting on the Dragon (Schütz) **1**:*131*

Apuleius, Lucius, *Metamorphoses (The Golden Ass)* **3**:341; **4**:490; **6**:769; **7**:931; **9**:1178, 1187

Ara Pacis Augustae **8**:*1103*

Arctinus **6**:803

Ares Borghese (sculpture) **2**:*150*

Ares Ludovisi (sculpture) **2**:*148*

Argonautica (Apollonius) **8**:1069

Argonauts, The (Dell' Acqua) **6**:*776*

Aristophanes
   Birds, The **7**:976
   Lysistrata **6**:743; **7**:902

Plutus **8**:1132
   and priests **9**:1176

Aristotle, and Tyche **10**:1392

Armfield, Matthew, illustration of Medea **6**:*851*

Arming of Perseus, The (Burne-Jones) **8**:*1114*

Art of Love, The (Ovid) **1**:56; **3**:341

Astronomica (Hyginus) **9**:1170

Atharva Veda **6**:735

Atreus, Treasury of **2**:*184*

Aurora (Fragonard) **4**:485

Aurora (Reni) **4**:485

Auzon Casket **10**:*1426*

Avestas **6**:746

Babrius **8**:1081

Bacchae, The (Euripides) **6**:828

Bacchanal (Alma-Tadema) **2**:*219*

Bacchanal Before a Temple (Poussin) **4**:*512*

Bacchus (Michelangelo) **2**:*216*, 218

Bacchus and Ariadne (Titian) **3**:*414*

Bacchylides **6**:803

Balders Dod (Ewald) **4**:537

Ballard, J.G., *Drowned World* **4**:526

Banks, Thomas, *Halcyon Discovers Ceyx* **7**:*919*

Banquet des Guédés, Le (Pierre) **3**:*374*

Barbari, Jacopo de', *Sacrifice to Priapus* **9**:*1170*

Barbieri, Giovanni Francesco (Il Guercino), painting of Atlas **2**:*178*, 181

Bardo Thodol **3**:373

Barga, Pietro da, sculpture by **4**:*447*

Batoni, Pompeo Girolamo, painting of Peleus and Cheiron **8**:*1097*

Battling Titans (Platzer) **10**:*1377*

Beccafumi, Domenico, *Deucalion and Pyrrha* **3**:*397*

Beckman, Max **8**:1084

Bell, Charles, *Judgment of Paris* **8**:*1089*

Belleteste, Jean-Antoine, statuette of Apollo and Daphne **8**:*1125*

Bellini, Giovanni, *Feast of the Gods* **9**:*1170*

Benisson, Vittorio, painting of the Terminalia festival **4**:*511*

Benvenuti, Pietro, *Death of Priam, The* **9**:*1167*

Beowulf **4**:561–562
and Heremod **5**:676
and Sigurd **10**:1303
and Wayland **10**:1425

Berlioz, Hector, *Troyens, Les* **6**:804

Bernini, Gian Lorenzo
Apollo and Daphne **1**:*132*
Flight from Troy, The **1**:*30*
Rape of Proserpina, The **5**:*603*
statue of Triton **10**:*1387*

"Bhagavad Gita" ("Song of the Lord") **6**:738

Bible
Adam and Eve **4**:509
apocalyptic visions and Armageddon **1**:120–122; **5**:632
Baal in **2**:214
creation of the world **9**:1193
earthquakes **7**:948
Jacob and Rachel **8**:1127
monotheism and **7**:907
Noah's ark **3**:399; **4**:520–521
serpents **5**:695
story of Joseph (Genesis) **2**:231

Bibliotheca historica (Diodorus Siculus) **1**:64

Birds, The (Aristophanes) **7**:976

Birth of Tragedy from the Spirit of Music, The (Nietzsche) **1**:134

Birth of Venus (Botticelli) **10**:*1409*

Blake, William
Cerberus **5**:*607*
Hecate **5**:*620*

Blinding of Polyphemus, The (Allori) **3**:*355*

Blommer, Nils, *Freya Seeking Her Husband* **4**:*532*

Boccaccio, Giovanni **5**:*628*
Il filostrato **10**:1390
illustration of Oedipus **8**:*1044*
Teseida **5**:*688*

Böcklin, Arnold, painting of Triton and a Nereid **10**:*1386*

Bologna, Giovanni, statue of Mercury **6**:862

Book of Caverns, The **2**:245

book of the dead **1**:79, *111*; **2**:**240–245**; **3**:*373*; **4**:*468*; **7**:*979*; **9**:1195, *1207*
and Nut **7**:995, 996, *997*

Book of Fixed Stars **8**:1056

Book of Gates, The **2**:245

Book of Going Forth by Day, The **2**:240, 242–244

"Book of the Takings, The" **6**:754

Book of What Is in the Underworld, The **2**:244

Bordone, Paris, painting by **2**:*149*

Borel, Antoine Rogat, painting of Thetis and Achilles **10**:*1357*

Bosio, François-Joseph, statue of Heracles and the Hydra **5**:*660*

Botticelli, Sandro
Allegory of Spring **5**:*582*
Birth of Venus **10**:*1409*
Judgment of Paris, The **8**:*1086*
Mars and Venus **6**:*836*

Boyajian, Zabelle C., illustration of Marduk and Tiamat **10**:*1368*

Boyhood Deeds of Cuchulainn, The **9**:*1226*

Brentel, Friedrich, painting of Orpheus **8**:*1059*

Bride of Frankenstein (film) **9**:*1184*

Bronzino, painting of Pygmalion **9**:*1197*

Brueghel the Elder, Jan, painting of Odysseus and Calypso **2**:265

Brueghel the Elder, Pieter, painting of Icarus **5**:712

Brueghel the Younger, Jan, *Allegory of Earth* **4**:*504*

Bruno, Giordano **9**:1217

Bundgaard, Anders, *Gefjon Fountain* **4**:*553*, 554

Burkett, Walter, *Homo Necans* **9**:1245–1246

Burne-Jones, Edward
paintings
Arming of Perseus, The **8**:1114
Danae and the Brazen Tower **3**:*362*
of the Hesperides **7**:*1004*
Pan and Psyche **8**:*1077*, 1078
of Perseus and the Graeae **8**:1114
tapestry of Pomona **8**:*1141*

Byron, Lord
"Don Juan" **5**:680
"Written after Swimming from Sestos to Abydos" **5**:680

Calamis, statue of Poseidon **8**:*1145*, 1150

Calliani, Antonio, painting of Hector and Achilles **1**:*18*

Callimachus
and Euthymus **3**:390
"Hymn to Artemis" **2**:157
and the Pleiades **8**:1130

Campbell, Joseph **6**:773

Camuccini, Vincenzo, painting of Hecuba and Paris **5**:*627*

Camus, Albert, "Myth of Sisyphus, The" **10**:1308

Canova, Antonio
Cupid and Psyche **9**:*1190*
Daedalus and Icarus **5**:*711*
Hebe **5**:*615*
Herm of a Vestal Virgin **10**:*1414*
statue of Theseus and the Minotaur **10**:*1355*
Three Graces **5**:*585*

Capitoline Venus **10**:*1408*

Caravaggio
Head of Medusa, The **5**:*580*
painting of Narcissus **7**:*935*

Carpaccio, Vittore, painting of Amazons **10**:*1354*

Carpeaux, Jean-Baptiste, statue of Philoctetes **8**:*1119*

Carpioni, Giulio, *Realm of Hypnos, The* **5**:*710*

Carracci, Annibale, painting of Polyphemus and Galatea **4**:*545*

Cassoni Campana, Master of the, painting of Pasiphae **8**:*1091*

Catalogues of Women (Hesiod) **8**:*1052*

Catalogue of Heroines **6**:742

Catherwood, Frederick **6**:841

Catullus, and the Muses **7**:923

Cavalori, Mirabello **1**:*29*

Cavattoni, Giovanni, engraving of Cronus **10**:*1397*

caves
paintings in **1**:*92*; **3**:*381*; **8**:*1075*; **9**:1156, *1159*–1161
at Altamira **9**:*1158*, 1160

Cellini, Benvenuto, statue of Danae and Perseus **3**:*364*

Cephalus and Aurora (Poussin) **4**:*485*

Cerberus (Blake) **5**:*607*

Cerne Abbas Giant **4**:502

Cesari, Giuseppe
The Founding of Rome by Romulus **9**:*1243*
painting of Perseus and Andromeda **3**:*429*

Characters (Theophrastus) **5**:*667*

Charon and Psyche (Stanhope) **9**:*1191*

Charon Takes Shadows Across the River (Subleyras) **3**:*370*

Chassériau, Théodore, *Andromeda Chained to the Rocks by the Nereids* **7**:*970*

Chaucer, Geoffrey, *Troilus and Criseyde* **10**:1388–1390

Chaudet, Denis-Antoine, sculpture of Cupid **3**:*340*

Chiari, Fabrizio, *Helios in His Sun Wagon* **5**:*641*

Choephoroe (The Libation Bearers; Aeschylus) **3**:313; **4**:*539*

churches, stave **2**:*222*

Cicero **9**:1173
and augers **9**:*1175*

citharas **8**:1057

Clotho **4**:496

codices
Aztec **2**:*207*
Codex Magliabecchi **3**:*385*
Codex Mendoza **9**:*1173*
Codex Regius **2**:233, *234*; **4**:*554*; **8**:*1029*; **10**:*1403*
see also Poetic Edda
Madrid Codex **6**:*843*

codices (continued)
Vienna Codex **9**:1202
Coffin Texts **2**:242, 243
Colosseum **9**:*1230*
columns, Jupiter **6**:785, 788
"Contendings of Horus and Seth, The" **6**:766
"Cooley Cattle Raid, The" **6**:755
Corot, Jean-Baptiste-Camille, painting of Orpheus and Eurydice **8**:*1060*
Correggio
painting of Danae **6**:*788*
painting of Io **5**:*654*
Cortona, Pietro da
painting of Aeneas **1**:*33*
painting of Saturn **9**:*1253*
Cousin, Jean, the Elder, *Eva Prima Pandora* **8**:*1079*
Coya Pasca **6**:731
Cranach, Lucas, painting of the Judgment of Paris **8**:1088–1089
Crespi, Giuseppe Maria, *Hecuba Blinding Polymnestor* **5**:628
Cretans, The (Euripides) **7**:887
Critias (Plato) **2**:180
Cupid (Chaudet) **3**:*340*
Cupid and Psyche (Canova) **9**:*1190*
Cupid and Psyche (Stanhope) **3**:*342*
Cyclops (Euripides) **3**:356–357; **9**:1258; **10**:1306
Cypria **7**:960–961

Daedalus and Icarus (Canova) **5**:*711*
Daedalus and Icarus (Landon) **5**:*712*
Dalí, Salvador, lithograph of the Judgment of Paris **8**:1089
Danae (Correggio) **6**:*788*
Danae (Titian) **3**:*363*
Danae and the Brazen Tower (Burne-Jones) **3**:*362*
Dance of Apollo and the Muses (Peruzzi) **7**:*921*
Dance of the Maenads (de' Gianuzzi) **6**:*828*
Daniels, Kate, *Niobe Poems, The* **7**:987
Dares the Phrygian **10**:1388
Daumier, Honoré, *Drunken Silenus, The* **10**:*1306*

Dauphin, Charles, *Massacre of Niobe's Children, The* **7**:*986*
David, Jacques-Louis
paintings
Love of Paris and Helen, The **5**:*637*
of Mars and Venus **2**:150
Tears of Andromache **5**:*625*
Death of Achilles, The (Rubens) **7**:*928*
Death of Adonis, The (Mazzuoli) **1**:*25*
Death of Hector and the Triumph of Achilles, The (Calliani) **1**:*18*
Death of Hippolytus, The (Rubens) **5**:*690*
Death of Priam, The (Benvenuti) **9**:*1167*
De Bello Gallico (On the Gallic Wars) (Julius Caesar) **4**:436, 438
De divinatione (Cicero) **9**:*1175*
De Ecclesiasticis Disciplinus (Regino von Prüm) **8**:1073
Delacroix, Eugène, *Furious Medea* **6**:*851*
Delaunay, Robert **8**:1062
De Lingua Latina (Varro) **7**:882
Della Robbia, Andrea **3**:*351*
Delvaux, Laurent **7**:999
Demin, Giovanni, painting of Paris and Hector **5**:*622*
de Morgan, Evelyn
Dryad, The **4**:*440*
Hero Holding the Beacon for Leander **5**:*680*
Mercury **5**:*670*
De renum natura (Lucretius) **6**:743
Deucalion and Pyrrha (Beccafumi) **3**:*397*
Diana and Actaeon (Tiepolo) **1**:*20*
Diana and Callisto (Titian) **2**:262, *263*
Diana of Ephesus (statue) **10**:1419
Dicksee, Frank, painting by **2**:*223*
Dictys of Crete **10**:1388
Dio Cassius **7**:967
Diodorus Siculus (Diodorus of Sicily) **2**:160, 271, 283
and the Amazons **1**:60–61, 64

Bibliotheca historica **1**:64
and Mnemosyne **7**:900
and Phaethon **8**:1116
Dion Chrysostom **4**:436
Dionysiaca (Nonnus) **7**:970; **10**:1378
Dionysius of Helicarnassus
and the Penates **8**:1100–1101
story of Romulus and Remus **9**:1240
Don Juan (Byron) **5**:680
Doolittle, Hilda, "Helen in Egypt" **5**:640
Doré, Gustave, illustration of Minos **7**:*890*
Dracula (Stoker) **10**:1321
Dream of Hecuba, The (de' Gianuzzi) **5**:*626*
Drowned World (Ballard) **4**:526
Drunken Silenus, The (Daumier) **10**:*1306*
Dryad, The (de Morgan) **4**:*440*
du Bellay, Joachim **8**:1083
Dumézil, Georges **6**:745, 820; **9**:1233
Dumont, François, *Titan Struck by Lightning* **10**:*1374*
Duran, Diego, *Historia de los Indios* **9**:*1251*

Education of Cupid, The (Lagrenee) **6**:*860*
Elder Edda see Poetic Edda
Electra (Euripides) **3**:313; **4**:472
Electra (Sophocles) **3**:313; **4**:472; **8**:1052
Elektra (Richard Strauss) **3**:313
Elgin Marbles **5**:*684*
El Greco, *Laocoon* **6**:*804*
Elizabeth of Austria **1**:*19*
Enheduanna **5**:718
Enki and the World Order **7**:877
Ennius
and Ilia **9**:1220
Iphigeneia **6**:743
Enuma Elish **3**:317, 403, 421–422; **6**:*830*; **7**:873; **10**:1368, 1430
Epic Cycle **6**:854
Epic of Gilgamesh see Gilgamesh, Epic of
Epicureans, and Tyche **10**:1392
Erasmus of Rotterdam **8**:1083
Erechtheum **2**:176–177; **4**:*441*
Panathenaea festival and **4**:514

"Ethiopis" *see* "Aethiopis"
Eumenides (Aeschylus) **3**:313; **4**:538, 539
Euphorion **6**:803
Euripides **5**:598
Alcestis **1**:55, 56
Bacchae, The **6**:828
Cretans, The **7**:887
Cyclops **3**:356–357; **9**:1258; **10**:1306
Helen **5**:638; **8**:1086
Heracles **10**:1355
Hippolytus **1**:117; **5**:689
Medea **6**:779, 851
Oresteia **8**:1052
Electra **3**:313; **4**:472
Iphigeneia Among the Taurians (Iphigeneia in Tauris) **3**:312; **4**:539; **6**:742
Iphigeneia at Aulis **2**:159; **6**:740–742, 856
Orestes **5**:640
Phaethon **5**:643
Suppliant Women **10**:1355
Trojan Women, The **5**:625
and Ganymede **4**:549
and Hecuba **5**:627, 628
and Helen **5**:640; **6**:858; **8**:1088
works about Bellerophon **2**:231–232
Evans, Arthur **3**:329–330; **7**:*889*
Eva Prima Pandora (Cousin the Elder) **8**:*1079*
Ewald, Johannes, *Balders Dod* **4**:537
Exekias **1**:*62*
Eyrbyggia Saga **10**:1363
Eyvind, *Hákonarmál* **5**:676

Fabius Pictor **9**:1240
Faerie Queene, The (Spenser) **5**:585, 640
"Fáfnismál" (poem) **10**:1303
Fall of Icarus, The (Saraceni) **3**:*360*
Fall of Phaethon, The (Giordano) **8**:*1116*
Fall of the Titans (Rubens) **10**:*1375*
Fantastic Cave Landscape with Odysseus and Calypso (Brueghel the Elder) **2**:265
Farnese Hercules (Glykon) **3**:*390*

Fasti (Ovid) **6**:861; **9**:1170

Fates, The (Goya) **4**:*495*

Faust, myth of **5**:640

Feast of the Gods (Bellini) **9**:1170

Ferrari, Luca, painting of Zeus and Semele **10**:*1436*

Ferroni, Egisto, painting of Psyche and Zephyrus **9**:*1189*

Feuerbach, Anselm

Iphigeneia **6**:*740*

Judgment of Paris, The **1**:*118*

Finding of Erichthonius, The (Rubens) **4**:*487*

First New Chronicle and Good Government, The (Poma de Ayala) **6**:*730*

Flateyjarbók **4**:529; **8**:1027

Flaxman, John **8**:1084

illustration of Tiresias **10**:*1372*

Flaying of Marsyas, The (Titian) **1**:*135*

Flight from Troy, The (Bernini) **1**:*30*

Ford, H.J.

illustration of Odysseus and Calypso **7**:*999*

illustration of Paris and Oenone **8**:*1085*

Founding of Rome by Romulus, The (Cesari) **9**:*1243*

Fragonard, Jean-Honoré, painting by **4**:*485*

Franchville, Pierre de, statue of Orpheus **8**:*1057*

François Vase (Kleitias) **5**:585; **8**:1097

Frankenstein (Shelley) **9**:1184

Franks Casket **10**:1426

Frazer, James **6**:773–774

Golden Bough, The **3**:409

Freud, Sigmund **7**:936; **8**:1044

Freya Seeking Her Husband (Blommer) **4**:*532*

Friggia (Gustav III) **4**:*537*

Furious Medea (Delacroix) **6**:*851*

Gaia Hypothesis **1**:101; **4**:457, 544; **7**:957

Gallic Wars, The (Julius Caesar) **2**:280–281

Garcilaso de Vega, Gomez **6**:730

Gefjon Fountain (Bundgaard) **4**:*553*, 554

Gehrts, Johannes, painting of Hel **5**:*633*

Gennep, Arnold Van **9**:1222, 1228

Geoffrey of Monmouth **4**:554

Historia regum Britanniae **3**:427

Georgics (Virgil) **8**:1059

Gerald of Wales **9**:1248

Gerda (Tegnér) **4**:556

Germania (Tacitus) **4**:529, 559; **9**:1263; **10**:1405

Gérôme, Jean-Lèon, *Pygmalion and Galatea* **9**:*1196*

Gesta Danorum **8**:1026

Gesta Hammaburgensis ecclesiae pontificum (Adam of Bremen) **4**:529

Giaccarelli, Antonio, plaster relief **9**:*1166*

Gianuzzi, Pippi de'

Dance of the Maenads **6**:*828*

Dream of Hecuba, The **5**:*626*

Olympus **6**:*785*

Gide, André, *Prometheus Misbound* **9**:1184

Gilgamesh, Epic of **3**:371, 399; **4**:480, **571–574**; **6**:763; **7**:869

An **1**:67

flood myth **4**:519

Ishtar **6**:760–762

Gimbutas, Marija **4**:454; **8**:1075

Giordano, Luca

paintings

of Diana and Endymion **3**:*408*

The Fall of Phaethon **8**:*1116*

of Ulysses and Calypso **2**:*265*

Giorgi, Giovan Battista, mosaic depicting Apollo **1**:*128*

Glaser, Eduard **1**:137

Gluck, Christoph **6**:743

Glykon, Farnese Hercules **3**:*390*

Goethe, Johann Wolfgang von, *Iphigeneia* **4**:497

Golden Ass, The see *Metamorphoses (The Golden Ass)* (Apuleius)

Golden Bough, The (Frazer) **3**:409

Gorgophone **8**:1114

Gosforth cross **9**:1265

Goya, Francisco

Fates, The **4**:*495*

painting of Cronus (Saturn) **3**:*335*, 338–339

Graduate, The (novel and movie) **2**:231

Graves, Robert

and Hebe **5**:616

and Hestia **5**:685

Great Sphinx, at Giza **1**:*82*, 83; **10**:*1330*–1332

Gregory of Nazianzus **8**:1083

Grien, Hans Baldung, woodcut of witches **9**:*1288*

Grignion, Charles, sculpture of Hades **5**:*606*

"Grímnismál" (poem) **10**:1430

Guercino, Il see Barbieri, Giovanni Francesco

Guérin, Pierre-Narcisse

paintings

of Clytemnestra **3**:*313*

of Eos and Cephalus **4**:*484*

Morpheus and Iris **7**:*920*

Phaedra and Hippolytus **10**:*1423*

Guide to Greece (Pausanias) **7**:961; **8**:1149

Gundestrup Cauldron **8**:1075

Gunst, Philip van, painting of Perseus and Medusa **5**:*581*

Hákonarmál (Eyvind) **5**:676

Halcyon Discovers Ceyx (Banks) **7**:*919*

Hárbardsljód **8**:1031; **10**:1358

Hauptmann, Gerhart **6**:743

Hávamál **8**:1029, 1030

Head of Medusa, The (Caravaggio) **5**:*580*

Hebe (Canova) **5**:*615*

Hecate (Blake) **5**:*620*

Hecuba Blinding Polymnestor (Crespi) **5**:*628*

Heemskerck, Maerten van, painting of Ares and Aprodite **2**:150; **5**:649

Hegel, Georg Wilhelm Friedrich **1**:106

Heiss, Johann, painting of Pandora **8**:*1081*

"Helen in Egypt" (Hilda Doolittle) **5**:640

Helen (Euripides) **5**:638; **8**:1086

Helen on the Steps of Troy (Moreau) **5**:*638*

Helios in His Sun Wagon (Chiari) **5**:*641*

Hendrich, Hermann, *Rhinemaidens, The* **10**:*1400*

Henryson, Robert, *Testament of Cresseid, The* **10**:1390

Hera Barberini **5**:*652*

Heracles (Euripides) **10**:1355

Heracles on the Pyre (Reni) **5**:*664*

Hercules Killing the Dragon of the Hesperides (dello Sciorina) **5**:*682*

Herm of a Vestal Virgin (Canova) **10**:1414

Herodotus **4**:466

and the Amazons **1**:60, 61

and Helen **5**:638

History **5**:638; **8**:1065

and the Iranians **6**:744–745

and sexual rituals in honor of Ishtar **6**:763

Hero Holding the Beacon for Leander (de Morgan) **5**:*680*

Herter Ernst, statue of the dying Achilles **1**:*19*

Hesiod

Catalogues of Women **8**:1052

Catalogue of Heroines **6**:742

and Elysium **3**:372

and the four winds **1**:77; **7**:948

and the Graces **5**:582

and the Harpies **5**:611

and Hephaestus **5**:645–646

and heroes **3**:392

and the Hesperides **5**:681

and the Muses **7**:922, 923

and Poseidon **8**:1143

see also *Theogony*; *Works and Days*

Hippolytus (Euripides) **1**:117; **5**:689

Hisham ibn al-Kalbi, *Kitab al-asnam* **1**:137

Historia de gentibus septentrionalibus (Magnus) **4**:*535*

Historia de los Indios (Duran) **9**:*1251*

Historia regum Britanniae (Geoffrey of Monmouth) **3**:427

History (Herodotus) **5**:638; **8**:1065

History of the Lombards (Paul the Deacon) **4**:535
History of Things in New Spain (de Sahagún) **9**:1201
Homer **8**:1035
  and the elysian fields **3**:372
  and the four winds **1**:77
  and Helen **5**:637–638, 640
  and Hephaestus **5**:645
  and the Muses **7**:921–922
  and Poseidon **8**:1144
  and the underworld (Hades) **5**:607–608; **9**:1214
  see also Iliad; Odyssey
Homeric Hymns
  "Hymn to Aphrodite" **10**:1380
  "Hymn to Demeter" **5**:618; **8**:1106–1108
  "Hymn to Hermes" **5**:672, *673*; **7**:900
  "Hymn to Hestia" **5**:686
  "Hymn to Pan" **8**:1074
  "Hymn to Selene" **9**:1276
Homo Necans (Burkett) **9**:1245–1246
Horace, *Odes*, and the Neptunalia **7**:968
Howard, Henry, painting of the Pleiades **8**:*1131*
Hrozny, Friedrich **5**:699
Hunt of Meleager and Atalanta, The (Rubens) **2**:168
Hyginus **10**:1334
  Astronomica **9**:1170
hymns, Homeric *see* Homeric Hymns
Hyndluljód **5**:631, 676

Ibn Fadlan **9**:1264
I Ching (Book of Changes) **3**:*305*
Idomeneo, rè di Creta (Mozart) **5**:714
Iliad (Homer) **8**:1035
  Achilles **1**:18
  the Amazons **1**:61, 62, 63
  Ares **2**:149
  Bellerophon **2**:230
  Cassandra **2**:274
  the Furies **4**:538
  the Graces **5**:582
  the Great Ajax **1**:52–53
  Hebe **5**:615
  Hector **5**:621, 625
  Hecuba **5**:627

Helen **5**:640
Helen and Paris **5**:636–637
Hypnos **7**:1005
Idomeneus **5**:713
the Lesser Ajax **1**:53
Niobe **7**:986
Paeon **8**:1069
Paris **8**:1087
Peleus **8**:1097
Troilus **10**:1388
the Trojan War **5**:595
"Il Penseroso" (Milton) **7**:920
Imru' Al-qays Ibn Hujr **1**:138
Ingres, Jean-Auguste-Dominique, painting of Zeus and Thetis **10**:*1356*
Iphigeneia (Ennius) **6**:743
Iphigeneia (Feuerbach) **6**:*740*
Iphigeneia (Goethe) **4**:497
Iphigeneia at Aulis (Euripides) **2**:159; **6**:740–742, 856
Iphigeneia in Aulis (Gluck) **6**:743
Iphigeneia in Brooklyn (Schickele) **6**:743
Iphigeneia in Tauris (Gluck) **6**:743
Iphigeneia in Tauris (*Iphigeneia Among the Taurians*; Euripides) **3**:312; **4**:539; **6**:742
Iphigenie in Aulis (Hauptmann) **6**:743
Iphigenie in Delphi (Hauptmann) **6**:743
Iryon **6**:790
Ishtar Gate **6**:*760, 763, 829*; **7**:*876*

Jacomb-Hood, George Percy, illustration of Hermód and Balder **5**:677
Jacopo della Quercia, sculpture of Rhea Silvia **9**:*1220*
Janus and Juno (Zelotti) **6**:*771*
Jason Swearing Eternal Affection to Medea (de Troy) **6**:*849*
Jeune Homme et la Mort, Le (Petit) **7**:*936*
Jordaens, Jacob, *Ulysses in the Cave of Polyphemus* **3**:*354*
Joyce, James, *Ulysses* **8**:1039
Judgment of Paris (Bell) **8**:1089
Judgment of Paris (Rubens) **8**:1089

Judgment of Paris, The (Botticelli) **8**:*1086*
Judgment of Paris, The (Feuerbach) **1**:*118*
Juno Showering Gifts on Venice (Veronese) **6**:*782*
Jupiter columns **6**:785, 788

Kapoor, Anish, *Marsyas* **1**:135
Kauffmann, Angelica, *Legend of Cupid and Psyche, The* **9**:*1188*
Keats, John, *Endymion* **4**:475
Kim Pusik **6**:790
Kipling, Rudyard, *Puck of Pook's Hill* **10**:1427
Kitab al-asnan (Hisham ibn al-Kalbi) **1**:137
Klee, Paul, drawing of Pandora's box **8**:1084
Klinger, Max, sculpture of Cassandra **2**:272
Krafft, Johann Peter, *Oedipus and Antigone at Colonus* **1**:*107*
Kraken Wakes, The (Wyndham) **4**:526

Lagrenee, Louis Jean François, *Education of Cupid, The* **6**:*860,*
La Hire, Laurent de, painting of Theseus **10**:*1351*
Lairesse, Gerard de painting by **2**:265
  painting of Dido and Aeneas **1**:*31*
Lamine, Peter Simon, statue of Faunus **4**:*499*
Landon, Charles-Paul, *Daedalus and Icarus* **5**:*712*
Laocoon (El Greco) **6**:*804*
Laocoon Group, The **6**:802
Larsson, Carl, *Midwinter Sacrifice* **4**:530
Last Judgment, The (Michelangelo) **3**:*419*
Lastman, Pieter, painting of Jupiter and Juno **6**:*781*
Latona and the Lycian Peasants (van Poelenburg) **6**:*815*
Leda and the Swan (Rubens) **6**:*811*
Ledberg Stone **6**:823
Legenda aurea (de Voragine) **3**:*423*

Legend of Cupid and Psyche, The (Kauffmann) **9**:*1188*
Lehmann, Karl, painting of Prometheus **9**:*1183*
Lehner, Mark **10**:1332
Leighton, Frederick paintings
  of Electra **4**:*470*
  of Mnemosyne **7**:*900*
  of Persephone **3**:*388*
  of Perseus and Pegasus **8**:*1112*
Lens, Cornelis Andries, *Zeus and Hera* **5**:*651*
Leroux, Hector, *The Vestal Virgins* **10**:*1414*
Leutze, Emanuel Gottlieb, *Amazon and Her Children, The* **1**:*61*
Levi, Eliphas **4**:*443*
Library, The (Apollodorus) **2**:251; **7**:986
"Lied vom hürnen Seyfrid, Das" (poem) **10**:1303–1304
Lincoln, Bruce **9**:1249
Livy **9**:1175
  and the ritual of Fides **9**:1205
  Romulus and Remus **9**:1240
Lokasenna **1**:27; **6**:822–823; **10**:1361
Loki Bound (Winge) **6**:822
Longus, story of Pan and Echo **4**:459
Lorrain, Claude, painting of Apollo and Hermes **5**:*673*
Lovelock, James **1**:101; **4**:544; **7**:957
Love of Paris and Helen, The (David) **5**:*637*
Lucan **2**:281, 283
Lucretius, *De rerum natura* **6**:743
Lugal-e **7**:983–984
Lysistrata (Aristophanes) **6**:743; **7**:902

Mabinogi (*Mabinogion*) **1**:104; **2**:280, 286; **4**:510
Mackennal, Edgar Bertram, sculpture of Circe **3**:*310*
Madrid Codex **6**:*843*
Magnus, Olaus, *Historia de gentibus septentrionalibus* **4**:535
Mahabharata **6**:737–738, 739; **10**:1340

Malory, Thomas **10**:1422

Manetti, Rutilio, *Perseus and Andromeda* **8**:*1147*

Manship, Paul, statue of Prometheus **9**:*1181*

Mariette, Auguste **9**:1195

Marmor Parium **3**:*399*

Mars Disarmed by Venus and the Graces (David) **2**:150

Mars and Venus (Botticelli) **6**:*836*

Mars and Venus Caught in the Net (van Heemskerck) **2**:150

Marsyas (Kapoor) **1**:135

Massacre of Niobe's Children, The (Dauphin) **7**:*986*

Mazzoni, Sebastiano, *Three Fates, The* **4**:*496*

Mazzuoli, Giuseppe, *Death of Adonis, The* **1**:*25*

Medea (Euripides) **6**:779, 851

Medea (Sandys) **6**:*848*

Meleager and Atalanta (Rubens) **2**:*168*

Memnon, Colossi of **6**:*854*

Menander **10**:1392

Mendelssohn, Felix, *Antigone* **1**:106

menhirs **9**:*1160*, 1163

Mercury (de Morgan) **5**:*670*

Metamorphoses (Ovid) *see* Ovid, *Metamorphoses*

Metamorphoses (The Golden Ass) (Apuleius) **3**:341; **4**:490; **6**:769; **7**:931

 Cupid and Psyche **3**:341–343; **9**:1187

 and the Isis Mysteries **7**:931; **9**:1178

Michelangelo

 Last Judgment, The **3**:*419*

 paintings

 Sibyls **9**:*1171, 1293*

 Piabba del Campidoglio **2**:*275*

 sculptures, *Bacchus* **2**:*216*, 218

Midsummer Night's Dream, A (Shakespeare) **3**:340; **5**:688; **10**:1355

Midwinter Sacrifice (Larsson) **4**:530

Milton, John

 "Il Penseroso" **7**:920

 and Pandora **8**:1083

 Paradise Lost **2**:166; **7**:907

Minga, Andreo del, painting of Deucalion and Pyrrha **4**:*521*

Minotaur, The (Watts) **3**:*332*

Mnemosyne (Rossetti) **10**:*1398*

Momus (Alberti) **7**:904

Moreau, Gustave

 Helen on the Steps of Troy **5**:*638*

 painting of Diomedes **2**:*151*

 painting of Oedipus and the Sphinx **8**:*1043*

 painting of Orpheus's head **8**:*1062*

Morpheus and Iris (Guérin) **7**:*920*

Morris, William, tapestry of Pomona **8**:*1141*

Morte d'Arthur, Le (Malory) **10**:1422

Mourning Becomes Electra (O'Neill) **3**:313; **4**:472

Mozart, Wolfgang Amadeus, *Idomeneo, rè di Creta* **5**:714

Musaeus **5**:680

Mussard, Pierre, engraving of Laocoon **6**:*803*

Mutilation of Uranus, The (Vasari) **10**:*1395*

My Fair Lady (musical and film) **1**:115–116; **9**:*1198*

Myth of Erra, The **7**:875, 877

Mythologiae (Natalis Comitis) **5**:*617*

"Myth of Sisyphus, The" (Camus) **10**:1308

Naevius, Gnaeus **10**:1409

Nanak **7**:908–909

Nemesis' Triumph Over Sin (Veronese) **7**:*959*

Neptune Calming the Tempest (Rubens) **7**:*965*, 967

Nibelungenlied ("Song of the Nibelungs") **4**:*562*; **7**:*972*, 974; **10**:1304

Nietzsche, Friedrich, *The Birth of Tragedy from the Spirit of Music* **1**:134

Nike of Paionios **7**:977

Nilometers **7**:*980*

Niobe Poems, The (Daniels) **7**:987

Niobid Painter **7**:*985*, 987

Niobid of the Sallustian Gardens **7**:987

Nome, François de, painting of Persephone **8**:*1109*

Nonnus, *Dionysiaca* **7**:970; **10**:1378

obelisks, Egyptian **4**:469

Odes (Horace), and the Neptunalia **7**:968

Odyssey (Homer) **8**:1035

 Achilles' spirit in the underworld **1**:18

 Calypso **2**:264, *265*

 and Crete **3**:325

 the Cyclopes **3**:354–355

 the eating of Helios's cattle **5**:642

 the Harpies **5**:614

 Helen **5**:637–638

 Heracles **5**:658

 the oracle of Dodona **8**:1126

 Orestes **8**:1052

 Penelope **8**:1104, 1105, 1108

 Tantalus **10**:1350

Oedipus and Antigone at Colonus (Krafft) **1**:*107*

Oedipus at Colonus (Sophocles) **1**:106; **3**:393; **8**:1040; **10**:1355

Oedipus the King (Sophocles) **1**:106; **8**:1040, 1042

Oghuznama **3**:294

Olympus (de' Gianuzzi) **6**:*785*

O'Neill, Eugene **2**:160

 Mourning Becomes Electra **3**:313; **4**:472

On the Gallic Wars (De Bello Gallico) (Julius Caesar) **4**:436, 438

Oresteia **8**:1052

 see also Aeschylus, *Oresteia* trilogy; Euripides, *Oresteia*

Orestes (Euripides) **5**:640

Origen

 and Mithraism **7**:897

 and Pandora **8**:1083

 and rebirth **9**:1217

Origin of the Milky Way, The (Tintoretto) **10**:*1338*

Orphica, the **8**:1061

Oseberg ship **7**:*991*

Ovid

 The Art of Love **1**:56; **3**:341

 and Cupid **3**:341

 and Daphne **3**:367

 and Echo **4**:458

 Fasti **6**:861; **9**:1170

and the Lares **6**:807, 809

and Memnon **6**:853

Metamorphoses **1**:104; **3**:341, 356, *415*; **4**:441

 Actaeon **1**:20

 Arachne **1**:91, 141

 Aurora **4**:485

 Caenis **8**:1144

 flood myth **4**:*519*

 Hermaphroditus **5**:666

 Icarus **5**:712

 Juno **6**:781

 Morpheus **7**:919–920

 Myrrha **7**:929

 Narcissus **7**:934

 Niobe **7**:987

 Orpheus **8**:1059

 Pan and Syrinx **8**:1076

 Phaethon **8**:1116

 Pomona **8**:1141

 Poseidon **8**:1144

 Proteus **9**:1185

 Pygmalion **1**:114–115

 the Muses **7**:923

 Perseus **2**:180

paintings, rock *see* rock paintings

Pajou, Augustin, *Psyche Abandoned* **9**:*1187*

Pandora's Box (film) **8**:1084

Pandora's Box (Panofsky) **8**:1083

Panofsky, Irwin and Dora, *Pandora's Box* **8**:1083

Pan and Psyche (Burne-Jones) **8**:*1077*, 1078

Paradise Lost (Milton) **2**:166; **7**:907

Parion Marble **3**:*399*

Parthenon **2**:175–176, *177*

 Elgin Marbles **5**:*684*

 statue of Athena in **7**:975; **10**:1376

Patinir, Joachim de, painting of Charon **8**:*1022*

Paul the Deacon, *History of the Lombards* **4**:535

Pausanias **2**:159–160, 231, 251–253; **4**:475; **6**:812

 and Cleomedes of Astypalaea **3**:392

 and the Cumaaean Sibyl **9**:1292

 and Daphne **3**:365–367

 and Euthymus **3**:390

 and griffins **1**:88

Pausanias (continued)
Guide to Greece **7**:961;
8:1149
and Hecate **5**:620
and Idomeneus **5**:713
and Iphigeneia **5**:619
and the Memnoides **6**:853
and Mnemosyne **7**:902
and the Muses **7**:900, 902,
924
and Narcissus **7**:934–935
and Niobe **7**:986
and Pan **8**:1078
and Pasiphae **8**:1093
Penrose, J. Doyle, painting of
Loki **10**:*1406*
Pericles **2**:175
Perrier, François
*Aeneas and His Companions
Fighting the Harpies* **5**:613
painting of Acis and Galatea
3:*357*
Perseus and Andromeda (Manetti)
8:*1147*
Perseus Frees Andromeda
(Wtewael) **1**:*75*
Perseus Releases Andromeda
(Rubens) **8**:1114
Peruzzi, Baldassare, *Dance of
Apollo and the Muses* **7**:*921*
Petit, Roland, *Le Jeune Homme
et la Mort* **7**:936
Petronias **9**:1292
Peyron, Jean Francois Pierre,
painting of Alcestis **1**:*56*
Phaedrus (Plato) **7**:900
Phaethon (Euripides) **5**:643
Phidias (Pheidias) **2**:175, *177*
bust of Zeus **8**:*1133*
statue of Athena **7**:975;
10:1376
statue of Nemesis **7**:960, 961
statue of Zeus **10**:1438
Philoctetes (Sophocles) **8**:1120
phobias **8**:1123
Picart, Bernard
engravings
of Eos and Tithonus
10:*1381*
of Lycaon **6**:*824*
of Phineus and the Harpies
5:*612*
of Tantalus **10**:*1350*
illustration of Myrrha **7**:*929*
print of Cassandra **2**:*273*
Picasso, Pablo **10**:1355

Pierre, André, *Le Banquet des
Guédés* **3**:*374*
Pindar **2**:231
and Elysium **3**:372
and the Graces **5**:584
and Hecuba **5**:627
and the Muses **7**:902
Pythian Odes **3**:365
and Tyche **10**:1391–1392
Pinturicchio, fresco of
Penelope **8**:*1105*
Pittoni, Giovanni Battista,
painting by **2**:*156*
Plath, Sylvia **4**:472
Plato
and apocalyptic beliefs **1**:123
and Atlantis **2**:181; **4**:524;
7:951
a demigod **3**:390
and the overthrow of Uranus
10:1397
Phaedrus **7**:900
Republic
and the Fates **4**:496
and the soul **9**:1215
and the underworld **5**:608
and sacrificial rituals **6**:824
Symposium **1**:56
and Tyche **10**:1392
Platzer, Ignác, *Battling Titans*
10:*1377*
Plautus, and the Lares **6**:807
Plautus, Titus Maccius **10**:1409
Pliny the Elder, and Neptune
7:967
Pliny the Younger, ghost stories
3:373
Plutarch **2**:271; **4**:466
Amatoriae Narrationes **4**:539
and Cronus **3**:335–336
and moonlight **9**:1276
and Nut's womb **5**:703
and Phobos **8**:1122
and Saturn **6**:783
story of Seth's killing of
Osiris **9**:1281
Plutus (Aristophanes) **8**:1132
Poelenburg, Cornelis van,
*Latona and the Lycian
Peasants* **6**:*815*
Poetic Edda (*Elder Edda*) **2**:220,
233, *234*; **4**:554; **10**:1403,
1425
and Aegir's feast **1**:27
and Frey **4**:527
and Gerd **4**:555

and Hoenir **1**:36
"Lokasenna" **4**:554
and Thrym **10**:1366
Thrymskvida **10**:1366
and Tyr **1**:*37*
Völuspá **2**:246; **3**:320; **5**:631;
6:817, 818–820; **10**:1315,
1430
poetry
blood as inspiration for
2:235–236
Greek **5**:640; **7**:902
in Norse mythology **6**:801;
10:1405
Pollainolo, Antonio, painting of
Heracles and Antaeus **5**:*661*
Polybius **10**:1392
Polyclitus, statue of Diomedes
3:*411*
Polydorus, sculpture of
Odysseus **8**:*1033*
Polygnotus, painting of
Memnon **6**:854
Poma de Ayala, Guaman **6**:730
Popul Vuh **6**:797, 841, 846,
847; **9**:1268
Posidonius **4**:436
Poussin, Nicolas
paintings
of Aurora **4**:485
Bacchanal Before a Temple
4:*512*
of Echo and Narcissus
4:*459*
of Endymion **4**:*473*
of Galatea and Acis **4**:547
*Triumph of Neptune and
Amphitrite, The* **7**:967
of Zeus and the goat
Amaltheia **10**:*1433*
Praxiteles, sculpture of Hermes
and Dionysus **5**:*674*, 675
Primitive Culture (Tylor) **1**:100
Proclus, and Philoctetes **8**:1120
Prometheus Bound (Aeschylus)
7:926; **8**:1023, 1135; **9**:1180
Prometheus Misbound (Gide)
9:1184
Prometheus Unbound (Shelley)
9:1184
Prose Edda (Snorri Sturluson)
2:220, 233, 234, 249, 250;
10:1403, 1405
Aegir **1**:27
the afterlife **3**:377
Frey **4**:529

Freya **4**:533
Frigga **4**:535, 537
Gerd **4**:555
"Gylfaginning" chapter, and
Gefjon **4**:553
Heimdall **5**:629
Hermód **5**:676, 677
Loki **6**:818
Njörd and Skadi **7**:990
Thor **10**:1358
Ymir **10**:1430
Proserpina (Rossetti) **5**:*602*
Psyche Abandoned (Pajou)
9:*1187*
Puck of Pook's Hill (Kipling)
10:1427
Punishment of Eros (fresco)
4:*491*
Purification of Mercury, The **6**:*862*
"Pursuit of Diarmuid and
Grainne, The" **6**:755
Pygmalion (Shaw) **1**:115; **9**:1198
Pygmalion and Galatea
(Gérôme) **9**:*1196*
pyramids
Egyptian **4**:*462*
Mayan **6**:797, *800, 840, 844*
see also ziggurats
Pyramid Texts **1**:108; **2**:242,
243; **6**:764; **7**:994; **8**:1064
and the eyes of Horus **5**:707
and Seth **9**:1281, 1284
Pythagoras and Pythagoreans,
and transmigration of souls
(rebirth) **3**:374; **7**:924, 931;
9:1214–1215, *1217*
Pythian Odes **3**:365

Quellinus, Erasmus, painting of
Odysseus and Diomedes
3:*412*
Quincy, Quatremère de, shield
8:*1023*
Quintus Ennius **7**:882
Quintus Smyrnaeus **6**:803

Rackham, Arthur
illustrations
Alberich and Hagen **7**:*972*
Brynhild **10**:*1401*
Freya **1**:*36*
Fricka **4**:*537*
Loki and the Rhine
maidens **6**:*818*
Midas **7**:*878*
the Norns **7**:*992*

Odin **1**:*36*

Pandora **8**:*1082*

Siegfried and Brunhild
4:*562*

Sigurd drinking dragon's
blood **1**:*87*

Thor **10**:*1358*

Ramayana **6**:738–739; **10**:1324

Rape of Europa, The (de Vos)
3:*333*

Rape of Proserpina, The (Bernini)
5:*603*

Raphael
painting of Galatea **4**:*547*
painting of St. George **3**:*423*

Realm of Hypnos, The (Carpioni)
5:*710*

Redon, Odilon, painting of
Polyphemus and Galatea
4:*546*

Regino von Prüm, *De
Ecclesiasticis Disciplinus*
8:1073

"Reginsmál" (poem) **10**:1303

Regnault, Jean-Baptiste
paintings by
of Theseus and Ariadne
2:*155*
of Xanthus and Balius **1**:*86*

Religion Romaine de Vénus, La
(Schilling) **10**:1409

Rembrandt
paintings
of Actaeon and Callisto
1:*21*
of Athena **2**:*171*
of Diana **2**:*160*

Reni, Guido
Heracles on the Pyre **5**:*664*
paintings by **2**:*168*; **4**:*485*

Renoir, Pierre-Auguste,
painting of Diana and
Actaeon **3**:*409*

Republic see Plato, *Republic*

Rhinegold and the Valkyrie, The
(Rackham) **4**:*534*

Rhinemaidens, The (Hendrich)
10:*1400*

Rígsthula **5**:631

Rig Veda **3**:422; **5**:*672*; **6**:735;
7:892

Ring des Nibelungen, Der
(Wagner) **1**:*127*; **4**:*537, 562*;
7:972

rock carvings, Scandinavian
9:*1260*, 1261

rock paintings, Aborigine
2:*196, 197, 199*

Rodriguez, Diego, painting of
the forge of Vulcan **8**:*1080*

Rök Stone **9**:*1263*

Roman Antiquities (Dionysius of
Helicarnassus) **8**:1100–1101

Roman de Troie (de Sainte-
Maure) **10**:1390

Romano, Giulio
painting of the Trojan Horse
8:*1034*
*Vulcan Forging the Arms of
Achilles* **5**:*646*

Ronsard, Pierre **8**:1083

Rossetti, Dante Gabriel
Mnemosyne **10**:*1398*
painting of Pandora **8**:*1084*
Proserpina **5**:*602*

Rowling, J.K. **4**:448

Royal Commentaries of the Inca
(Garcilasco de Vega) **6**:730

Rubens, Peter Paul
paintings **3**:339
Achilles **7**:*928*
Aeneas **1**:*32*
Bellona **2**:*152*
Castor and Pollux **2**:*276*
earth mother Cybele **4**:*453*
Erichthonius **4**:*487*
Fall of the Titans **10**:*1375*
Ganymede **4**:*549*
Hippolytus **5**:*690*
Judgment of Paris **8**:*1089*
Leda and the Swan **6**:*811*
Meleager and Atalanta
2:*168*
Midas, Apollo, and Pan
7:*879*
Neptune **7**:*965*, 967
Persephone **8**:*1109*
Perseus Releases Andromeda
8:1114
Saturn (Cronus) **3**:*334*, 339
Thetis and Achilles **1**:*15*

Sabatelli, Francesco, painting of
Ajax **1**:*52*

Sacrifice of Iphigeneia, The
(Tiepolo) **6**:*742*

Sacrifice to Priapus (de' Barbari)
9:*1170*

*Saga of the Volsungs see Völsunga
Saga*

Sahagún, Bernardino de **2**:208,
209

History of Things in New Spain
9:1201

Sainte-Maure, Benoît de,
Roman de Troie **10**:1390

Salmacis and Hermaphroditus
(Spranger) **5**:*668*

Salvi, Niccoló, Trevi Fountain
7:*966*; **8**:1150

Salviati, Cecchino, painting of
the Fates **5**:*599*

Sama Veda **6**:735

Samguk Sagi **6**:790

Samguk Yusa **6**:790

Sandys, Frederick, *Medea* **6**:848

San Giovanni, Giovanni de
fresco of Hebe and
Ganymede **5**:*616*
painting of Eos **4**:*485*

Sappho **8**:1061
and Helen **5**:638
poem to Aphrodite **1**:114

Saraceni, Carlo, *Fall of Icarus,
The* **3**:*360*

*Saturn Devouring One of His
Children* (Goya) **3**:*335,*
338–339

Saturn Devouring a Son
(Rubens) **3**:*334*

satyr plays **9**:1258

Saxo Grammaticus **4**:529;
8:1026, 1029; **9**:1265;
10:1365, 1407

Scaiaro, Giovanni, painting of
Paris and Helen **8**:*1087*

Scenes from the Trojan War (de'
Gianuzzi) **5**:*626, 628*

Schiavonetti, Luigi, engraving
of Idomeneus **5**:*713*

Schilling, Robert, *Religion, La
Romaine de Vénus* **10**:1409

Schliemann, Heinrich **1**:*49*

Schram, Alois, *Vestal Virgin, The*
10:*1412*

Schubert, Franz **6**:743

Schütz, Sebastian, picture of
Apollo and Python **1**:*131*

Schwind, Moritz von, painting
of Psyche **4**:*540*

Sciorina, Lorenzo della,
painting of Heracles **5**:*682*

Scott, Stephen, "Tears of
Niobe, The " **7**:*987*

Secret History of the Mongols, The
3:*294*

"Secret Name of Re, The"
6:764, 766

Seven Against Thebes, The
(Aeschylus) **8**:*1040*

Shabaka Stone **9**:*1192–1193*

Shakespeare, William
and Falstaff **10**:1306
A Midsummer Night's Dream
3:*340*; **5**:*688*; **10**:1355
Troilus and Cressida **10**:1390

Shaman, The (Vitebsky) **9**:*1289*

Shan Hai Ching **3**:428

Shelley, Mary Wollstonecraft,
Frankenstein **9**:1184

Shelley, Percy Bysshe,
Prometheus Unbound **9**:1184

Shepherd, George, painting of
Gog and Magog **4**:*569*

Shield, The (Menander)
10:*1392*

shinhwa **6**:790–791, *792–796*

Sibylline Books **9**:1234

Siegfried (Wagner) **10**:*1300*

Simonides, and Hippolyte
5:*687*

Sisyphus (Titian) **10**:*1307*

Skáldskaparmál (Snorri
Sturluson) **6**:801

Skallagrímsson, Egill **2**:250

Snorri Sturluson **8**:1029;
9:1265
and the Aesir **1**:34
and funeral pyres **9**:1264
and the Norns **7**:992
and Odin **8**:1024
Skáldskaparmál **6**:801
and Ymir **10**:1429
Ynglinga Saga **4**:529, 536, 553,
555
see also Prose Edda

Sockburn hogback **6**:823

Socrates, link with Silenus
10:1306

Solon, laws of **5**:598

"Song of the Lord" ("Bhagavad
Gita") **6**:738

"Song of the Nibelungs" *see
Nibelungenlied*

"Song of Noble Siegfried,
The" **10**:1303–1304

"Songs of Isis and Nephthys,
The" **7**:964

Songs of the Kings, The
(Unsworth) **6**:743

Sophocles **5**:598; **6**:803
Ajax **1**:53
Antigone **1**:106–107
Electra **3**:313; **4**:472; **8**:1052

Sophocles (continued)
  Oedipus at Colonus **1**:106;
    3:393; **8**:1040; **10**:1355
  Oedipus the King **1**:106;
    8:1040
  and Philoctetes **8**:1120
Spagnolo, Lo *see* Crespi,
  Giuseppe Maria
Spell of the Twelve Gates, The
  2:244–245
Spenser, Edmund, *The Faerie
  Queene* **5**:585, 640
Spranger, Bartholomeus
  painting of Glaucus and
    Scylla **8**:*1092*
  Salmacis and Hermaphroditus
    5:*668*
Stanhope, John Roddam
    Spencer
  Charon and Psyche **9**:*1191*
  Cupid and Psyche **3**:*342*
Star Trek: Voyager (TV series)
  8:1039
Star Wars (film) **4**:448
Statius, *Achilleid* **1**:19
stelae **8**:*1065*, 1067; **9**:*1195*,
  1279; **10**:*1312*
Stephens, John Lloyd **6**:841
Sterrett, Virginia Frances,
  Tanglewood Tales **2**:252
Stesichorus **5**:634, 638; **8**:1052
Stoics, and Tyche **10**:1392
Stoker, Bram, *Dracula* **10**:1321
Strabo, and priestesses to
  Aphrodite **1**:119
Stratton, Helen, illustration of
  Freya **10**:*1366*
Strauss, Richard **3**:313; **4**:472
Stuck, Franz von
  painting of Athena, Hera, and
    Aphrodite **5**:*656*
  painting of Helen **5**:*634*
  Wounded Amazon **1**:*65*
Subleyras, Pierre, painting of
  Charon **3**:*370*
Sun Chariot **7**:*989*
Suppliant Women (Euripides)
  10:1355
Sutasoma (Tantular) **10**:1323
Symposium (Plato) **1**:56
syncretism **2**:165; **9**:1209–1210,
  1278

Tacitus **4**:*559*, 560; **8**:1027
  Germania **4**:529, 559; **9**:*1263*;
    10:1405

Tagliolini, sculpture of Jupiter
  4:*504*
"Táin, The" ("The Cooley
  Cattle Raid") **6**:755
Taliesin **1**:105
Tanglewood Tales (Sterrett) **2**:252
Tantular, *Sutasoma* **10**:1323
tarot cards **3**:*401*
Tears of Andromache (David)
  5:*625*
"Tears of Niobe, The" (Scott)
  7:987
Tegnér, Esias **4**:556
Tennyson, Alfred, Lord,
  "Tithonus" **10**:1381
Teseida (Boccaccio) **5**:*688*
Testament of Cresseid, The
  (Henryson) **10**:1390
Theocritus
  and Pan **8**:1074
  story of Polyphemus and
    Galatea **4**:545–546
Theogony (Hesiod) **1**:77; **3**:352;
  4:488, 501, 564; **5**:641;
  7:1005
  and creation **8**:1020; **10**:1373
  and the Fates **4**:493; **5**:598
  and the Furies **4**:538
  and Hecate **5**:617
  Hittite influence on **5**:697
  and Nemesis **7**:959
  and Nereus **7**:969
  and Nike **7**:975
  and Pandora **8**:1079–1081
Theophrastus
  Characters **5**:667
  and mandrake collectors
    8:1127
tholos **2**:162
Thompson, Bob **8**:1089
Thórdarson, Sighvat **1**:57
Three Fates, The (Mazzoni)
  4:*496*
*Three Goddesses: Athena, Hera,
  and Aphrodite* (von Stuck)
  5:*656*
Three Graces (Canova) **5**:*585*
Thrymskvida **10**:1362
Thucydides **1**:53
Tibaldi, Pellegrino, paintings of
  Polyphemus **3**:354, *356*;
  4:*567*
Tibullus, and household gods
  6:808
Tiepolo, Giovanni Battista
  Apollo and Daphne **3**:*367*

Diana and Actaeon **1**:*20*
painting of the Trojan Horse
  8:*1089*
Sacrifice of Iphigeneia, The
  6:*742*
Venus Receives Mars **5**:*648*
tiles, monster-mask, Korean
  6:*792*
Timaeus **8**:1103
Timaeus (Plato) **2**:180
Tintoretto
  Origin of the Milky Way, The
    10:*1338*
  painting of Arachne **1**:*141*
  *Vulcan Surprises Venus and
    Mars* **1**:*114*
Tischbein, Johann Heinrich,
  painting by **2**:*169*
Titan (Algardi) **10**:*1373*
Titan Struck by Lightning
  (Dumont) **10**:*1374*
"Tithonus" (Tennyson)
  10:1381
Titian
  paintings by **2**:160, 218–219
  Bacchus and Ariadne **3**:*414*
  Danae **3**:*363*
  Diana and Callisto **2**:262,
    263
  Flaying of Marsyas, The
    1:*135*
  Sisyphus **10**:*1307*
  of Venus and Adonis **1**:*24*
  Venus Blindfolding Cupid
    3:*343*
Trevi Fountain **7**:*966*; **8**:1150
*Triumph of Neptune and
  Amphitrite, The* (Poussin)
  7:*967*
Troilus and Cressida
  (Shakespeare) **10**:1390
Troilus and Criseyde (Chaucer)
  10:1388–1390
Trojan Women (Euripides) **5**:625
  and Ganymede **4**:549
  and Hecuba **5**:627, 628
  and Helen **5**:640; **6**:858;
    8:1088
Troyens, Les (Berlioz) **6**:804
Troy, Jean-François de, painting
  of Jason and Medea **6**:*849*
Troy (movie) **1**:19
Tuby, Jean-Baptiste, fountain
  6:*814*
Turner, J.M.W., painting of
  Lake Nemi **3**:*410*

Tylor, Edward Burnett **1**:69,
  100–*101*; **7**:954

Ulysses (Joyce) **8**:*1039*
Ulysses and Calypso (Giordano)
  2:*265*
*Ulysses in the Cave of
  Polyphemus* (Jordaens) **3**:*354*
Ulysses and the Cyclops (Tibaldi)
  3:*356*
Union of Water with Earth, The
  (Rubens) **4**:*453*
Unsworth, Barry **6**:743
Upanishads **7**:913; **9**:1216
Ur, Standard of **7**:*984*
Utagawa Kunisada, painting
  of Amaterasu **10**:*1346*

"Vafthrúdnismál" (poem)
  10:1430
Van Dyck, Anthony, painting
  of Marsyas **9**:*1258*
Varro, Marcus Terentius **7**:882
Vasari, Giorgio, *The Mutilation
  of Uranus* **10**:*1395*
Vedas, the **6**:735, 737
  Rig Veda **3**:422; **5**:672; **6**:735;
    7:892; **10**:1430
  and Yama **5**:608
Velàzquez, Diego, painting
  of Arachne **1**:*142*
Velde, Adriaen van de,
  Vertumnus and Pomona
    8:*1142*
Venus Blindfolding Cupid
  (Titian) **3**:*343*
Venus de Milo **1**:*117*
Venuses (prehistoric figurines)
  4:454–455, 502; **9**:1157,
    1159
Venus of Laussel **3**:346;
  4:455, 502, 503; **7**:*919*;
    9:1228
Venus of Lespugue **4**:502;
  9:*1157*
Venus of Willendorf **4**:455,
  502, *503*; **9**:1157
*Venus and Mars, Victory
  and Cupid* (Bordone)
  2:*149*
Venus Receives Mars (Tiepolo)
  5:*648*
Veronese, Paolo
  Nemesis's Triumph Over Sin
    7:*959*
  painting of Juno **6**:*782*

Vertumnus and Pomona (van de Velde) **8**:*1142*

Vestal Virgin, The (Schram) **10**:*1412*

Vestal Virgins, The (Leroux) **10**:*1414*

Viani, Antonio Maria, painting of Apollo **5**:*600*

Vienna Codex **9**:1202

Virgil
and Charon **5**:605
and Elysium **3**:372; **5**:608
Georgics, and Orpheus **8**:1059
and Hephaestus **5**:646
see also Aeneid

Vitebsky, Piers, *Shaman, The* **9**:*1289*

Vogel, Hermann **6**:*810*

Völsunga Saga **4**:537; **8**:1026; **10**:1303, 1304
and Brynhild **10**:1401–1402

"Volundarkvida" **10**:1425

Völuspá (poem) **2**:246; **3**:320; **5**:631; **6**:817, 818–820; **10**:1315, 1430

Vos, Maerten de, *Rape of Europa, The* **3**:*333*

Vulcan Forging the Arms of Achilles (Romano) **5**:*646*

Vulcan Surprises Venus and Mars (Tintoretto) **1**:*114*

Wagner, Richard
Der Ring des Nibelungen **1**:127; **4**:537, 562; **7**:972
Siegfried **10**:*1300*

"Waldere" (poem) **10**:1425

Warka vase **5**:*715*

Warrior's Husband, The **5**:688

Watts, George Frederic, *The Minotaur* **3**:*332*

Weber, Max **9**:1171–1172

Wicar, Jean Baptiste Joseph paintings
of Electra **4**:*471*
of Jupiter **3**:*384*

Winged Victory of Samothrace, The **7**:*977*

Winge, M.E., *Loki Bound* **6**:*822*

Woolley, Leonard **4**:*524*

Works and Days (Hesiod)
and the end of the world **1**:123
and Nemesis **7**:959
and Pandora **8**:1079, 1081–1082
and the Pleiades **8**:1130

Wounded Amazon (van Stuck) **1**:*65*

Wrathful Jupiter, The (Wicar) **3**:*384*

writing
Canaanite **2**:266
Egyptian **4**:467
Mongol **3**:293–294
Sumerian **4**:*476*; **7**:869–870
Turkic **3**:293–294

types
cuneiform **4**:*476*; **7**:870, *877*
demotic **4**:467
hieratic **2**:243; **4**:467

Wtewael, Joachim, *Perseus Frees Andromeda* **1**:*75*

Wyndham, John, *The Kraken Wakes* **4**:526

Yajur Veda **6**:735

Ynglinga Saga (Snorri Sturluson) **4**:529, 536, 553, 555

Zelotti, Giambattista, *Janus and Juno* **6**:*771*

Zeus and Hera (Lens) **5**:*651*

ziggurats **1**:*66–67*; **4**:*478*

Zuccari, Federico and Taddeo, *Apollo and Daphne* **1**:*105*

INDEX OF PLACES

Page numbers in **bold** refer to main articles; those in *italics* refer to pictures.

AFRICA

Abu Simbel **9**:1192, *1194*
Abydos (Ibdju) **7**:982;
   8:1067–1068
Africa **1:38–47**
Akhetaton **10**:1343
ancestor worship **1**:70, 73–74
Ashanti people **1**:42, 46–47
   sky god **3**:383; **10**:1310
Atlas Mountains **2**:*180*
Avaris **9**:1284
belief in rebirth **9**:1212
Carthage, and Baal **2**:*214*
   creation myths **1**:40–41;
     3:314–316, 319, 323
   death and the afterlife
     1:*46–47*; **3**:376
Crocodilopolis **7**:981
Dendera, Nilometer **7**:*980*
Edfu, temple **9**:1210
Egypt **4:460–469**
   the afterlife **1**:74, 109–110;
     3:*371*, 372–373, *375*;
     4:552; **5**:608; **7**:979,
     996; **9**:*1194*
   agriculture, the harvest **7**:963
   Amazon story **1**:64
   animal-headed deities
     1:*78–79*, *83*; **4**:*465*, *466*;
     5:*702*, *708*; **10**:*1393*
   animal worship **1**:93
   Anubis and the dead **1**:*88*,
     108–111; **3**:*375*; **4**:466
   boats in religion **4**:*463*
   book of the dead **1**:*79*, *111*;
     2:240–245; **3**:373; **4**:*468*;
     7:979; **9**:1195, *1207*
   calendars **2**:254–255, *256*,
     257
   coffins and sarcophaguses
     1:*110*; **4**:*552*; **6**:*768*; **7**:*995*
   concept of *maat* (divine
     balance) **5**:708; **7**:979;
     8:1065
   creation myths **1**:94–95;

     2:188–189, 191; **3**:320;
     4:465, 501–502, 550, *551*;
     6:832; **7**:994
   day and night in legend
     3:344
   drama **7**:964
   eye amulets **5**:*707*
   and fertility of the earth
     4:*506*, *507*, 508
   food libations for the dead
     5:707
   geographical influence
     4:461–462
   gods **4**:462–*465*, 466
   influence on Greece **5**:597
   Lower and Upper **4**:461;
     7:981; **9**:*1208*, 1283
   mummification **1**:88,
     109–110; **3**:*371*, *375*
   nature deities **1**:102
   Nile River **3**:349, *350*;
     4:*507*; **5**:609; **7:978–982**;
     10:1336
   periods of history **4**:464
   pharaohs **2**:189; **4**:461, 465,
     550; **5**:701; **9**:1174, 1283,
     1284
   priests **9**:*1177–1178*, 1195
   ruled by Macedonian Greeks
     7:964
   sacrifice **4**:469
   Saint Katarina monastery
     7:*907*
   scorpions revered **1**:85
   and the soul **1**:109; **3**:370
   sources of mythology
     4:466–467
   sphinxes **1**:*82–83*
   stars **10**:1336–1337
   temples **4**:467–*469*; **5**:*704*;
     9:1177–1178
   tombs **2**:240, *241*, *245*; **4**:461,
     462
   ushabtis and shawabtis **2**:*244*
Fan people **1**:45, 47
flood myths **4**:522
Giza
   Great Sphinx **1**:*82*, 83;
     10:*1330–1332*
   pyramids **4**:*462*; **10**:1330

Heliopolis (Iunu)
   and Atum **2**:188, 189;
     4:501–502
   cult of Re **9**:1206
   Ennead of **2**:189; **9**:1192,
     1206
Ibdju (Abydos) **7**:982;
   8:1067–1068
Idfu
   festival **5**:704
   temple **5**:*704*
Karnak
   statues of Sekhmet **9**:*1194*
   Temple of Amun **9**:1177
Kikuyu people **1**:44; **8**:1126;
   10:1426
Liberia, myth about death **1**:47
Luba people, and the moon
   7:913
Lunda people, the sun and the
   moon **7**:913
Madagascar
   ancestor worship **1**:74
   creation myth **1**:46; **3**:323
   souls of ancestors **1**:45–46
Memphis, and the god Ptah
   9:1192–1195
monotheism **7**:909
Nigeria
   creator deity of the Ibo
     3:314–316
   creator deity of the Yoruba
     1:41
Nile River **3**:349, *350*; **4**:*507*;
   5:609; **7:978–982**; **10**:1336
   Hapi as god of **5**:609–610;
     7:979–981
   Osiris and **7**:981–982;
     8:*1063*, 1064
Nubia **4**:462
Nubt **9**:1284
Philae, Temple of Isis **6**:*767*
San people, myths **1**:40–*41*, 45;
   7:911–912
Sbeitla **7**:*881*
Sierra Leone, creation myth
   1:40
Thebes (Egypt)
   litany featuring Re **9**:*1208*
   sarcophagus lid from **4**:*552*

Thugga **3**:*353*
Tunisia, Sbeitla **7**:*881*
Ubangui people **1**:45
Yoruba people **1**:41, *44–45*
   ancestor-worship **1**:*69*
Zulu people **1**:45

ASIA

EASTERN ASIA

Beijing
   Nine Dragon Wall **3**:*428*
   Summer Palace **3**:*430*
Central Asia and the Steppes
   3:292–299
China **3:300–309**
   ancestor worship **1**:71–73
   burials **3**:*300–302*
   calendar **2**:*254*, 256–*257*;
     3:348
   constellations **10**:1337
   creation myths **3**:302–303,
     314, 319–320, 428;
     4:570
   flood myth **4**:522–523
   ginseng **8**:1127
   gods **3**:307–*309*
   Great Wall of **3**:*300*
   hunting rule **3**:350
   Khotan **1**:79–80
   months **3**:348
   mountains **3**:*307*
   mythical emperors of the
     Golden Age **3**:304–306
   planets **10**:*1337*
   rivers **3**:306
   sea monster **9**:1274
   sky god **10**:*1311*
   and the structure of the
     world **3**:303–304
   yin and yang **3**:302, *304*
Chinhan **6**:794
Gobi Desert **3**:292
Japan
   Ainu **1**:94; **3**:381
   ancestor worship **1**:72, 73
   animal sacrifice **1**:94
   animal worship **3**:381

constellations **10**:1337–1338, 1339, 1340

creation myth **3**:317–318; **9**:1267–1268

demons **3**:*406*

festivals **4**:*517–518*; **10**:1347

flag **10**:1347

imperial family **10**:*1347*

rites of passage **9**:*1227*

Shinto **3**:316, 317–318; **4**:517

weddings **9**:*1227*

Koguryo **6**:789, 794

Korea **6:789–796**

  animism and magic **6**:*792–794*

  categories of myths **6**:790–791

  epics of the Three Kingdoms **6**:794–795

  kings of Silla **6**:*794, 795–796*

  solhwa **6**:790, 795

  Three Kingdoms **6**:789–*790*

Mongolia **3**:*293*

  shamans **9**:*1290*

Mount T'aebaek **6**:*789, 793*

Paekche **6**:789, 794

Silla **6**:789, 794–*795*

Tai Shan (mountain) **3**:307

Taklimakan Desert **3**:292

Tibet

  apocalypse myth **1**:127

  book of the dead **3**:373

  reincarnation belief **3**:374–375; **9**:1212

SOUTHERN ASIA

Andaman Islands, Moon Man **3**:347–348

Angkor Thom **10**:1322, *1324*

Angkor Wat **10**:*1322*, 1324

  effigy of Yama **9**:*1216*

Bali

  cremation of the dead **9**:*1215*

  theatrical masks **10**:*1326*

Borneo

  creation myth **10**:1326–*1327*

  myth about the moon **10**:1327

Cambodia

  Angkor Thom **10**:1322, *1324*

  Angkor Wat **9**:*1216*; **10**:*1322*, 1324

  merging of Hinduism and Buddhism **10**:1323

myth concerning the origin of **10**:1327

statue of Ganesa **1**:*80*

Celebes, and the origin of death **3**:376

Harappa **6**:734

India **6:732–739**

  animal sacrifice **1**:94; **6**:737

  Aryans **6**:734–735

  battle between *ashuras* and *devas* **3**:338

  belief in reincarnation **9**:1215–1217

  Birhor **1**:103

  calendars **2**:257–258

  creation myth **3**:317

  death and the afterlife **5**:608; **7**:913

  Dravidian civilization **3**:364

  Indus Valley (Harappan) civilization **3**:*316*; **6**:732–734, *739*

  myths **3**:317; **6**:737–738

  the Rig Veda **3**:422; **5**:672; **6**:735; **7**:892

  sacrifice of the original man **9**:1247

  shamans **9**:1285

  Stone Age civilizations **6**:732

  totemism **1**:103

Indonesia

  ancestor worship **10**:1328–1329

  belief in a soul **10**:1328

  Islam in **10**:1323

Java

  deities **10**:1324

  myth about volcanoes **10**:1327

Kashmir, shamans **9**:1285

Laos

  creation myth **10**:1327

  flood myth **4**:521

Mahabalipuram **4**:*525*

Malaysia

  and the afterlife **10**:1329

  ancestor worship **1**:73

  myth about civilized behavior **10**:1325–1326

Mohenjo-Daro **6**:732, *734–735*

Myanmar

  belief in the afterlife **10**:1329

  belief in the soul **10**:1328

  nats (spirits) **10**:*1323*–1324

  and the origin of countries **10**:1327

Nias, ancestor worship **10**:1328–1329

Southeast Asia **10:1322–1329**

  and the afterlife **10**:1329

  ancestor worship **10**:1328–1329

  creation myths **10**:1326–*1327*

  deities **10**:1324–*1326*

  religions **10**:1322–1323

  rice myths **10**:1327–*1328*

  and the soul **10**:1328

Sulawesi

  Bada people **10**:1323

  burials **10**:*1329*

  care for the ancestors **10**:1329

  rice myth **10**:1328

Sumatra **10**:1324

Thailand

  creation myth **10**:1327

  deities **10**:1324–1325

  flood myth **4**:521

  rice myth **10**:1327–1328

Vietnam

  Confucianism **10**:1323

  creation myth **4**:570

  dragons **3**:*421*, 428

WESTERN ASIA

Akkad (Agade) **7**:870

Akkadian Empire **7**:870–871

Alacahüyük, Sphinx Gate **5**:*696*

Anatolia

  Hittites **5:691–700**; **10**:*1344*

  mother goddess **3**:*380*

  pomegranates **8**:1109

Aphrodisias **9**:*1179*

Arabia **1:136–140**

  animism **1**:137–138

  deities **1**:137

  early cultures **1**:136–137

  Islam **1**:*138*, 140

Baalbek **2**:*215*

Babylon **6**:833

  calendar **2**:255–256

  fall of **7**:876

  Ishtar Gate **6**:*760*, 763, *829*; **7**:*876*

  sexual ritual **6**:763

Babylonia

  calendars **2**:255–256

  creation myth **3**:316–317, 403, 421–422; **5**:695; **6**:830, 833; **10**:1368–1370

First Dynasty of Babylon **7**:871–872

neo-Babylonian Empire **7**:875–876

  sexual ritual **6**:763

  social structure **7**:872

Black Sea **3**:400

Byblos **1**:24–25; **9**:1281

  temples **2**:*269, 270*, 271

Canaan and Phoenicia **2:266–271**

  gods **2**:212, 266–271

  human sacrifice in Phoenicia **2**:271

  Phoenicia **2**:*266–267*

Carthage, human sacrifice **2**:*271*

Catalhüyük (Catal Huyuk) **5**:606; **9**:*1163*

  bull cult **9**:1162–1163

  earth-mother worship **4**:455–456

Central Asia and the Steppes **3:292–299**

Cyrene **7**:*1001*

Euphrates River **4**:*477*; **6**:*832*; **7**:868; **10**:1370

Girsu **7**:871

Hattushash **5**:699, *700*; **10**:*1344*

Iran **6:744–749**

  apocalypse myth **1**:127

  deities **1**:102; **6**:746–747, *748, 749*

  Zoroastrianism **3**:402; **4**:443–444; **6**:744, 745–749

Iraq

  and the earth mother **4**:*454*

  ziggurats **1**:*66*

  see also Mesopotamia

Jerash **6**:*808*

Jericho, Neolithic burials **9**:1162

Jordan

  Jerash **6**:*808*

  temple to Artemis **2**:*159*

Kish **7**:869

Kullah **1**:*66*

Lagash **7**:869, 983

Lebanon, temple to Jupiter Heliopolitanus **6**:*787*

Mecca **1**:140

  black stone of **1**:*139*

Mesopotamia **7:868–877**

  and the afterlife **3**:370–371

  Akkadian Empire **7**:870–871

Mesopotamia (continued)
Amorites **7**:871
Aramaean invasions **7**:872–873
Assyrians **7**:873–875
astrology **1**:68
astronomy **1**:68
attitude toward scorpions **1**:85
Chaldeans **7**:874, 875
creation myth **4**:477–478, 480; **6**:832
and divination **1**:67–68
flood myth **3**:399; **4**:*480*, 519, *520*, 572; **7**:950–951; **10**:1313
gods **1**:*102–103*; **7**:868–869, 870, 877; **10**:1342–1343
Jews **7**:877
Kassites **7**:872
Third Dynasty of Ur **7**:871
trading contacts **7**:869
ziggurats **4**:*478*
Mittani **5**:691–692
Mount Zagros **6**:*746*
Nimrod, Mount, stone head of Tyche **10**:*1391*
Nineveh **7**:*874*
Nippur **4**:480, *482*; **7**:869
Palmyra (*now* Tadmur), temple to Baal **2**:*210*
Saphon, Mount **2**:*212*, 213, 215
Scythia, Amazons **1**:60
Sinai, Saint Katarina monastery **7**:*907*
Sumeria **6**:829
belief in the underworld **5**:606–607
calendars **4**:479
cities **7**:869
creation myths **3**:318–319; **4**:477–478
demons **3**:404
flood myths **3**:399; **4**:478–479, 519–520
gods **4**:478; **6**:829
nature deities **1**:102
rituals and ceremonies **4**:479; **5**:717–718
urban and fertility deities **4**:503, 505
writing **4**:*476*; **7**:869–870
Syria
sun god **1**:*140*
wall painting of Gaia **4**:*542*

Tabriz, painting of a giant **4**:*563*
Tarsus, worship of Mithras **7**:893
Tigris River **7**:*868*, 983; **10**:*1370*
Troy **1**:28
excavation of **1**:49
fall of **2**:174, *273*; **5**:626; **6**:804
Hector as the symbol of **5**:623–624
Laomedon and **6**:*805*, 806
Turkey
Aphrodisias **1**:*119*
Midas's tomb **7**:880
Tyre
and Astarte **2**:*164*
and Melqart **2**:270
Ugarit (*now* Ras Shamra) **2**:164, 210, *213*
fertility goddess **4**:*501*
sun god **10**:1343
Ur **7**:869
ancient flood **4**:*524*
ziggurats **1**:66–67; **4**:*478*
Uruk **7**:869, *871*
temple to Anu **1**:68
temple to Inanna **5**:*718*
Yazilikaya, Hittite carving **5**:*694*

AUSTRALIA, NEW ZEALAND, AND THE PACIFIC

Australia **2**:**192–201**
Cook Islands **8**:*1012*, 1014, *1016*–1019, *1140*
Darling River **2**:201
Easter Island **8**:*1015*
Hawaii **9**:*1272*
creation myth **8**:1013–1014
Kauai **9**:*1272*
Kimberley **2**:201
Marshall Islands, female demons (mejenkwaar) **3**:406
Metung **2**:199
New Zealand, Maori **1**:*123*, 125; **3**:319, 320; **8**:*1014*–1016, *1018*
Oceania **8**:**1012–1019**
Polynesia **8**:1012, 1013–1014, *1140*

creation myths **3**:*320*, 323; **8**:1013–1015, *1016*; **9**:1271
land-of-long-ago **9**:*1272*
Mount Kilauea **7**:*952*
myths about volcanoes **7**:952
sea gods **9**:1271
sea monsters **9**:1274

EUROPE

Achelous River **1**:13
Aegina, and Britomartis **2**:247, 248
Alba Longa **8**:1102
Altamira, cave paintings **9**:*1158*, 1160
Anglesey, Roman invasions of **4**:*438*, 439
Arcadia **4**:441
and Pan **8**:1074, 1078
Argos **5**:652
Hybristika festival **5**:669
marriage ritual **5**:667
Aricia (modern Ariccia) **3**:408, 409; **9**:1234
Athens
Acropolis **2**:175–*177*; **5**:*596*; **7**:975, *976*
the assembly **9**:1173
Athena as patron of **2**:*175*
City Dionysia festival **3**:417, 418
democracy **5**:597–598
and Deucalion's grave **3**:399
founding of **5**:596–597
Gaia and **4**:544
laws of Solon **5**:598
metics **4**:488
Parthenon **2**:175–176, *177*; **7**:975
Roman Forum **1**:77
and Sparta **5**:598
Temple of Hephaestus **5**:*649*; **9**:1182; **10**:1355
Temple of Olympian Zeus **10**:*1438*
theater of Dionysus **3**:*418*
Tower of Winds **1**:77
worship of Athena **2**:175–*177*; **5**:596–597
Balkans, ancestors' graves reopened **10**:1321
Baltic, the **2**:**224–229**
Belarus, supreme being **10**:1319

Britain, Roman invasion of **4**:438–439
Carnac **9**:*1160*, 1163
Cephalonia, tomb of Odysseus? **8**:1036
Corfu (Corcyra), mythological formation of **10**:1397, *1399*
Corinth **10**:*1308*
Crete **3**:**324–333**; **7**:889
earthquakes and volcanic eruption **3**:325, 328; **7**:890, 951–952
fertile goddess figurines **4**:502
mythological origins of the Cretans **3**:326
palace of Knossos **3**:*327*, *329*–330, 358; **7**:*885*, 886, 889–890; **10**:*1353*
worship of Britomartis **2**:248
Cyclades, female figurines **5**:*592*
Delos **1**:128
and Leto **6**:814, 816
worship of Apollo **8**:*1136*
Delphi
oracle (the Pythian Sibyl) **1**:128–129, *130*; **7**:924; **9**:*1171*, 1177, *1291*, 1293–*1294*; **10**:*1421*
temple **3**:*400*; **5**:*594*
Denmark, Tolland Man **9**:*1262*
Dicte, Mount **3**:326, 333; **5**:*594*; **7**:886; **10**:*1432*
Dodona **4**:442; **8**:1126; **9**:1177; **10**:1433
Eleusis **3**:387; **4**:*508*; **5**:*618*
England
Lindow Man **2**:283; **9**:*1252*
Stonehenge **9**:*1162*
Wayland's Smithy **10**:*1427*
Epidaurus, sanctuary of Asclepius **2**:162
Etna, Mount **2**:171; **5**:646, 652; **10**:*1394*
France
Le Puy **1**:*98*
Return of the Gleaners ritual **7**:917
Germany, elves **1**:59
Greece **5**:**591–600**
Achaeans **5**:593, 594–595; **10**:1311
and the afterlife **3**:369, *370*, *372*; **5**:606, 607–608; **7**:888–889, *890*, 991; **9**:1214; **10**:1310

the age of invasions
(1900–1500 BCE)
5:593–594
alphabet **2**:212–213, 253
attitudes toward sleep **5**:710
Bronze Age (Helladic period)
5:593
calendar **2**:260–261
city-states **5**:595, 596, 598
classical **5**:595
mythology **5**:598–600
creation myths **3**:318,
334–335; **4**:501, 541–542;
8:1020; **10**:1313, 1396
"Dark-age" **5**:594–595
day and night legend **3**:346
Eleusinian Mysteries **3**:385,
386, 389; **4**:506–507, 515;
7:931, 933; **9**:*1229*, 1278
family tree of deities **8**:*1134*
flood myth **2**:262; **3**:397–398,
399; **4**:*519*, 521; **9**:1179
forms of worship **5**:*594*
Golden Age of Cronus **3**:336
and the hearth **5**:592,
683–684, 686; **10**:1418
influence of Egypt on **5**:597
Ionians **5**:593, 595
men in society **5**:598, 668
museums **7**:925
mystery cults **7**:**930–933**;
8:1137
and natural catastrophes
1:122–123
nature deities **1**:102
Olympian gods **5**:598
Orphism and the Orphic
Mysteries **4**:444; **7**:933,
1005; **8**:1061–1062
Pelasgians **5**:592, 650;
10:1311
personification in myths
7:1005–1006
poetry **5**:640; **7**:902
pre-Olympian gods **7**:1005
priests **9**:1175–1176, 1237
sacrifices **2**:159–160, *235*,
237; **3**:337; **6**:824–826;
9:1245–*1247*, 1249
sea monsters **8**:*1092*, *1146*;
9:*1270*, 1273, 1274
sky gods **10**:1310, 1311
Stone Age **5**:591–592
weddings and marriage
5:667–668, 672; **7**:976;
10:1416

winds **1**:77; **10**:*1314*, 1315
women in society **5**:584, 668;
8:1091
Helice **8**:1144
Helicon, Mount, and the
Muses **7**:922, 923, 925
Heraculaneum
bas-relief from **8**:*1050*
bust of a satyr from **9**:*1257*
Herculaneum, mural showing
Galatea **4**:546
Hlesey **1**:27
Iceland **9**:*1259*; **10**:*1365*
worship of Frey **4**:529
worship of Thor **10**:1364
Ida, Mount **3**:*324*, 326, 333;
10:*1432*
Ireland **6**:**750–759**
ancestor worship **1**:70–71
"boyhood deeds" stories
9:*1226*–1227
carvings representing fertility
4:506
Celts **6**:751
Christianity **6**:751–752, *759*
classes (cycles) of myths
6:752–753
class system of the gods **6**:753
elves **1**:59
fertility of the land **4**:510
festivals **6**:757–759
gods and heroes **6**:*757*
horse sacrifice **9**:1248
measurement of time **6**:757
myths **6**:*753*, *754–757*
name changes of the gods
6:753–754
Neolithic tomb at
Newgrange **6**:750, 751,
752, 757; **9**:*1161*, 1163
and number three **6**:759
origin myths **6**:754–755
people of the Sidhe **8**:1133
tale types **6**:754
virgin goddess **10**:1422
Isturitz **9**:1159
Italy, cult of Isis **6**:768; **9**:1238
Kos **2**:162; **5**:667
Krivichi, cremations **10**:1321
Kurgan, earthworks **10**:1321
Lake Nemi **3**:408, *410*
Lampsacus **9**:1170
La Salette, apparition at
1:*124*
Lascaux, cave **9**:1160–1161
Lavinium **1**:33; **8**:1101–1103

Lemnos **5**:646, 649
women of **1**:117–118; **6**:776
Le Puy **1**:*98*
Letoon, and Leto **6**:816
Leuke **1**:64
Lithuania, flood myth **4**:521
London, Gog and Magog
4:*569*
Lycaon, Mount **6**:824, 826
Malta, terra-cotta goddess
found in **4**:*502*
Messene **6**:*826*
Mycenae
burial mask **5**:*595*
graves **1**:*50*; **3**:*369*
overthrow of the Minoans
10:1353
Schliemann and **1**:*49*
Treasury of Atreus **2**:*184*
Newgrange **6**:750, 751, *752*,
757; **9**:*1161*, 1163
Olympia, Temple of Zeus
2:181; **8**:1099; **10**:*1438*
Olympus, Mount **5**:*591*, 593,
646; **10**:1316, 1375, 1417
Orchomenus **5**:585
Ostia, *mithraea* **7**:895–896
Othrys, Mount **10**:1375
Paestum
Temple of Neptune **7**:*968*
temple to Hera **5**:*657*
Palaikastro, worship of Zeus
10:*1432*
Palestrina (Praeneste), engraved
mirror found in
10:1408–1409
Paphos, worship of Aphrodite
1:119
Parthenios, Mount **8**:1078
Peloponnese Peninsula **2**:*182*,
183; **8**:*1099*
Pergumum, Altar of Zeus
4:497; **5**:620; **10**:1378
Pharos **9**:*1185*, 1186
Phlios **5**:616
Pompeii
fresco of Aphrodite and Ares
8:*1121*
fresco of Bacchus **2**:*218*
fresco of a banquet scene
9:*1204*
fresco of Cassandra **10**:*1418*
fresco of Eros **4**:*491*
fresco of Priam, Menelaus,
Helen and Deiphobos
6:*857*

mural of Galatea **4**:546
and Priapus **9**:*1168*, 1170
wall painting of Pasiphae
8:*1093*
Praeneste (Palestrina), engraved
mirror found in
10:1408–1409
Puzzuoli, cave of the Cumaean
Sibyl **9**:*1292*
Rhamnous, temple of Nemesis
7:*961*
Rhine River **10**:*1304*
Rhodes
Colossus of **5**:642
cult of Helios **5**:642
Rome **9**:**1230–1239**
augers **9**:1175
Augustan Altar of Peace (Ara
Pacis Augustae) **8**:*1103*
Bacchanalia scandal **2**:217
Campus Martius **7**:967, 968
Colosseum **9**:*1230*
first kings **9**:1220,
1232–1233, *1234*
Forum **9**:*1237*
Forum gates **6**:774
foundation myths **4**:446;
6:835; **9**:1231–1232, *1233*,
1242–*1244*
Golden Age **9**:1253–1254,
1255
and the hearth **10**:1412
House of the Vestal Virgins
10:*1415*
Latin League **9**:1234
patricians **9**:1235
and the rape of the Sabine
women **9**:1232
Regia (royal palace) **6**:838,
839
the Remoria **9**:1243
a republic **9**:1234–1235
ritual of Fides **9**:1205
Santa Constanza **2**:219
saved from the Sabines
6:772–773
senate **9**:1172–1173
temple of Apollo **1**:*133*
temple of Diana **3**:410
temple of Janus **6**:836
temple of the Lares **6**:810
temple of Mithras **7**:*895*
temple of Quirinus **9**:1205
temple of Vesta **10**:1412,
1421
temples on Tiber Island **4**:498

Rome (continued)
  temples to Heracles
    7:925–926
  temples to Juno 6:782
  temples to Jupiter 6:786–787;
    9:1234
  temples to Mars 6:835, 837
  temples to Minerva 7:882,
    884
  temples to Venus
    10:1410–1411
  Trajan's forum 9:1205
  vestal virgins 9:1176;
    10:1412–1415, 1420–1421
Russia, the moon and weather
  lore 7:917, 918
Samothrace 1:64
Santorini (Thera) 3:325, 328,
  330; 7:890, 951; 10:1387
Scandinavia 9:1259–1266
  Christianity 2:222–223;
    9:1264–1265; 10:1360,
    1364
  family tree of deities 8:1135
  human sacrifice 4:529;
    9:1262, 1264
  Rök Stone 9:1263
  ships 7:988, 989
  worship of Frey 4:529
Scotland
  Blue Men of the Muir
    9:1273
  devils 3:404
Selinunte 10:1435
Siberia
  animal worship 1:95–99
  creation myth 3:403–404
  elk mother 1:88, 95, 96
  Evenki people 1:96, 99
  Ket people 10:1315
  Orochey people 1:96
  shamanism 1:96
Sjaelland 4:554
Slavs 10:1317–1321
Sounion, temple of Poseidon
  8:1149, 1150
Sparta 5:598
  Carneia festival 9:1275
  Hyakinthia festival 3:395
  marriage ritual 5:667
  and the Muses 7:923
  tree worship 6:813
Stonehenge 9:1162
Tanum, rock carvings 9:1260
Tarquinia, Tomb of the Bulls
  10:1389

Temesa 3:390–392
Thebes (Greece)
  founding of 2:149, 251–253;
    3:426
  statues of Amenhotep III
    6:853–854
  temple of Heracles 5:659
  Tiresias and 10:1372
Thera (Santorini) 3:325, 328,
  330; 7:890, 951; 10:1387
Thrace 2:152
  Amazons 1:60
Tifata, Mount 3:410
Trois Frères, Les, cave painting
  at 9:1159, 1161
Troezen 8:1130, 1131
Troyes Frères, Les, cave painting
Uppsala 4:529, 530
Vilnius, Tale of the Castle of
  2:226
Wales
  dragon 3:427
  elves 1:59
  fertility of the land 4:510
  story of Arianrhod
    10:1421–1422
Wildenmannlisloch 9:1159
Zákinthos 2:182

NORTH, CENTRAL, AND
SOUTH AMERICA

Alaska, Tlingit people 9:1274
Badlands 7:953
Celilo Falls 7:937–938
Chichén Itzá 6:799
  ball games 6:847; 8:1047
  cenotes 6:845, 846
  High Priest's Grave 6:800
  New Year ceremony 6:847
  statue of Chac Mool 9:1245
  statue of Xib Chac 9:1175
  Temple of Kukulkan 6:797,
    798, 799, 843, 847
Chile, the Araucanians
  7:915
Copán 6:841
Cuzco 6:724, 726
Day of the Dead 4:517
Ecuador, flood myth 4:523
Greenland, moon-god 3:347
La Mojarra, Olmec inscriptions
  at 8:1047–1048
La Venta 8:1046, 1047, 1049
Machu Picchu 6:725, 726;
  10:1348

Mexico
  Aztecs 2:202–209
  Maya 6:840–847
  Olmecs 8:1046–1049
Monument Valley 10:1316
Mount Shasta 5:588, 590
San Lorenzo 8:1046, 1047,
  1049
Tenochtitlán 2:202, 203, 204
  temple Teocalli 10:1384
Teotihuacán
  Temple of Quetzalcoatl
    9:1200, 1202
  and Tlaloc 10:1382, 1385
Tikal 6:844
Tula 9:1201
Tulúm, temple at 7:913
Uxmal 6:840
  Palace of the Governor 6:843
Xochicalco, Temple of the
  Feathered Serpent 9:1199
Zapotec, ball court 8:1047

MYTHICAL AND
LEGENDARY PLACES

Acheron 5:606
Agharti 1:127
Aina-momomaakane 9:1272
Alfheim 1:57
Asgard 8:1027
  bridge to 1:34
  Freya and the walls of 4:534;
    8:1030
Atlantis 2:180–181; 3:328;
  4:523, 524; 7:951
  Amazons and 1:64
Bifröst 1:34, 126; 5:629,
  631–632; 10:1313
Bilskírnir 10:1358
Blessed, Isles of the 5:608;
  6:783; 9:1214
Booyan 9:1271
Cocytus 5:606
elysian fields (Elysium) 3:372;
  5:608; 10:1310
Esharra 10:1370
Garden of the Hesperides
  2:178
Ginnungagap 2:233, 246, 249;
  8:1024; 10:1428, 1430
Gjöll River 5:677
Hades (place of the dead)
  5:605, 606, 607–608; 7:991;
  9:1214

Cerberus and 5:601, 607
Orpheus in 8:1058–1060
Hanan Pacha 6:728
Hel 5:633
Hippocrene fountain 8:1112
Hunland 10:1300
Jötunheim 2:234; 5:631;
  8:1027; 10:1429
Kun Iun 3:307
Lethe 5:608
Lyonesse 4:524
Midgard 8:1027
Muspellsheim 4:568; 10:1428
Niflheim 4:568; 5:633;
  10:1428, 1429
Ogygia 2:264
Okolnir 2:234
otherworld, Celtic 2:283, 284
Phlegethon 5:606
Pusat Tasik 9:1274
Ryugu 9:1270
Sessrúmnir 4:534
Sheol 9:1219
Styx River 3:369, 370; 5:605,
  606; 7:991; 8:1022; 9:1191
  Achilles dipped in 10:1357
Symplegades 6:777
Tartarus 3:337; 5:608; 7:1005;
  10:1373
  Tantalus punished in 10:1350
Tlalocan 10:1382, 1385
Tuat 9:1206, 1208
Tyno Helig 4:524
Uku Pacha 6:728
underworld (land of the dead)
  5:606–607, 608
  Egyptian 2:242, 244; 5:608
  Greek (Hades) 5:605, 606,
    607–608; 7:991
  Cerberus and 5:601, 607
  Orpheus in 8:1058–1060
  Inanna's descent to the 3:348,
    370–371; 5:715–717
  Ishtar's descent to 6:762–763
  Norse 2:221–222; 5:633,
    676–677; 7:989
Utgard 4:568
Vaitarami River 5:608
Valhalla 3:377; 4:534; 5:676;
  8:1026, 1030
  the Valkyries in 10:1400
Vanaheim 4:531; 10:1404
Vígríd 1:126

INDEX OF PEOPLES AND SOCIETY

Page numbers in **bold** refer to main articles; those in *italics* refer to pictures.

Abaluyia people, and the first humans **3**:323
Aborigines, Australian **2**:*192–201*
and animal-headed figures **1**:81
art **2**:*196, 198, 199*
ceremonies and rituals **2**:*195*, 200, 201
blood-drinking **2**:239
and the Dreamtime (Dreaming) **2**:194, 196–197
earth mother **4**:456
flood myths **4**:523
mythical tracks across the desert **2**:199, *201*
myths **2**:195
and constellations **2**:*200*; **8**:1055
creation **2**:194, 196–197
explaining songs, dances, and art **2**:200–201
of morality **2**:196, 197
and places **2**:198–199
variations in **2**:201
the ownership of places **2**:199–200
religions **2**:193–194
animism **2**:194
totemism **1**:92; **2**:194–*196*
sacred places **2**:*193*, 195
the Southern Pleiades (constellation) **10**:1340
spirits **2**:196–198, *199*
Abraham **7**:*906*, 907
Achaeans **5**:593, 594–595; **10**:1311
Achilles' heel **1**:19
aconite plants **5**:607
acorns **4**:442
Adonia festival **5**:678
Aebutius, Publius **2**:217

Aeolians **5**:593
Africa **1**:**38–47**
Ahmose **9**:1210
Ainu **1**:94; **3**:381
Akhenaten *see* Amenhotep IV
Alexander the Great
and Achilles **1**:19
and the Amazons **1**:64–65
and Oceanus **8**:1023
and Zoroastrianism **6**:746
Allca Cuna (Virgins of the Sun) **6**:*731*
alphabets
Etruscan **2**:253
Greek **2**:212–213, 253; **7**:926
Phoenician **2**:213
Roman **2**:253
Amenhotep II **10**:1332
Amenhotep III (Amenophis III) **6**:853–*854*
Amenhotep IV (Akhenaten; Akhenaton) **4**:514; **5**:610; **10**:1332
and monotheism **2**:190; **7**:907, *908*; **9**:1210; **10**:*1343*
Amorites **7**:871
Anatolians **5**:593
mother goddess **3**:*380*
Ancus Marcius **9**:1233
Anfs **1**:140
Anglo-Saxons **4**:558
Beowulf legend **3**:425; **4**:561–562; **10**:1425
and Easter **4**:513
temples **4**:561
animals **1**:**84–91**
attitudes toward **1**:85–86
in Celtic mythology **2**:*286*
communication with humans **1**:84–85
and death **1**:*88*
earth mother as **4**:456
and the flood **4**:520
in Greek mythology
Pegasus **8**:*1112*
seducing women **8**:*1091*

as guides **3**:410
as healers **1**:86–87
hunters and **3**:*381*, 409–410; **7**:*943, 944*
imaginary **1**:87–88
dragons **3**:**421–430**
griffins **1**:88, *90*
phoenix **1**:88
unicorns **1**:88, *91*
mythic hybrids **1**:89
human-headed animal figures **1**:81–83
as guides **3**:410
totem **1**:103
Central Asian **3**:297, *298*
transformations **1**:89–91, 104
Ankhs **2**:*188*
Annales Maximi **9**:1234
Antiochus I **7**:893
Antiochus III **9**:1175
Apollonius of Tyana **7**:902
Apollo Program **1**:*134*
apples, and ancestor worship **1**:70, 71
Arabia **1**:**136–140**
Aramaeans **7**:872–873
Araucanians **7**:915
Archelaus **7**:923
Ardashir I **4**:*444*
arktoi **6**:*743*
Aryans, in India **6**:734–735
Ashanti people **1**:42, 46–47
sky god **3**:383; **10**:1310
Assyrians **7**:873–875
asterims **10**:1333
astrology **8**:1137
Mesopotamian **1**:68
Romans and **8**:1123
see also zodiac
astronomy, Mesopotamian **1**:68
augurs **5**:697
Augustus **4**:438; **9**:1237
and the Lares **6**:810
as Pontifex Maximus **9**:*1236*
and the Temple of Apollo **1**:133

Aus **1**:138
Australia **2**:**192–201**
Aztecs **2**:**202–209**
calendar **2**:203
capital city (Tenochtitlán) **2**:202, 203, *204*; **10**:*1384*
codices **2**:207; **9**:1203
Codex Magliabecchi **3**:*385*
Codex Mendoza **9**:*1173*
Vienna Codex **9**:1202
creation myths **2**:206; **3**:322; **10**:1430
the Five Suns (worlds or ages) **2**:*209*; **10**:1382–1384
creation of the fifth world **10**:1385
flood myth **2**:209
gods and goddesses **2**:203, *205, 206, 207*–209; **3**:*348*
human sacrifice **2**:204–206, *208*, 238–239; **3**:*385*; **9**:1200, 1249, *1251*; **10**:1347
children **10**:1384
Jaguar Knights **8**:1048
and the planet Venus **9**:1202
priests **2**:203–204, *239*; **9**:*1173*

Bada people **10**:1323
Balboa, Vasco Núñez de **6**:725
ball games
Mayan **6**:*847*
Olmec **8**:*1047*
Balts, the **2**:**224–229**
and the Baltic Sea **2**:227–228
festivals **2**:226
gods and goddesses **2**:224–226, *228–229*
human sacrifice **2**:227
religious beliefs **2**:226
religious leaders **2**:227
surviving traditions **2**:229
Battle Ax people **10**:1367
bears, remains of, in prehistoric caves **9**:1158–1159

Bedouin **1**:138

bezoars **3**:294

birth *see* childbirth

Black Death, rats and **1**:86

blacksmiths, in myth and
    legend **10**:*1426–1427*

Blaise, Saint **10**:*1317*

boats
    and death **7**:*991*
    in Egyptian religion **4**:*463*
    see also ships

bones, of sacrificed animals,
    cracked **9**:1249

Boniface, Saint **9**:1265

Brasidas **3**:395

bronze, used on Crete **3**:324

Bronze Age
    Greek **5**:593
    Scandinavian **9**:*1260,*
        1261–1263

Buddha (Gautama Buddha)
    7:909, 957; **9**:1216–1217;
    10:1327
    Mara (evil demon) and **3**:402

Burgundians **4**:557, *558*

Caesar, Julius
    calendar **2**:261
    and the Celts **2**:280–281, 283
    and the druids **4**:436–437

calendars **2**:**254–261**
    Aztec **2**:203
    Babylonian **2**:255–256
    Celtic **2**:258–259, 285; **3**:348
    Chinese **2**:*254,* 256–*257;*
        3:348
    Egyptian **2**:254–255, *256,*
        257
    Greek **2**:260–261
    Gregorian **2**:261
    of India **2**:257–258
    Julian **2**:*261;* **6**:770
    Mayan **2**:259–260
    and the moon **3**:346, 347
    Navajo **3**:350–351
    Roman **2**:*260,* 261; **6**:770;
        9:1233
    Sumerian **4**:479

Canaan and Phoenicia
    2:**266–271**

caves **3**:380–*381*
    paintings in **1**:92; **3**:*381;*
        8:*1075;* **9**:1156, *1159*–1161
        at Altamira **9**:*1158,* 1160
    remains of prehistoric bears
        9:1158–1159

Celts **2**:**277–286**
    and the afterlife **3**:375
    ancestor worship **1**:70–71
    apocalypse myth **1**:*125*–126
    Battle of Moytura **3**:338
    calendar **2**:258–259, 285;
        3:348
    Christian influence on **2**:285
    Cosmic Tree **3**:409
    cult of the severed head
        2:*281*
    divination rituals **1**:71
    festivals **2**:285; **4**:512–513
    gods and goddesses
        2:278–*280;* **6**:753, 861
        Roman interpretation
            2:280–281
    graves **3**:*368;* **6**:861–862
    Hallstatt culture **2**:277; **3**:*368*
    in Ireland **6**:751, 753
    kings, and fertility of the land
        4:510
    language **2**:277
    La Tène culture **2**:277–278
    metalwork **2**:277
    mythology, animals in **2**:*286*
    the otherworld **2**:283, 284
    sacrifice
        horse **9**:1248
        human **2**:239, 281, *283;*
            9:1249–1251, *1252*
    and the seasons **3**:348
    virginity in mythology
        10:*1421–1423*
    see also druids

cenotes **6**:845, *846*

Central Asia and the Steppes
    3:**292–299**

Chaldeans **7**:874, 875

childbirth
    Artemis and **1**:15
    rites of passage and
        9:1222–1223

China **3**:**300–309**

cicadas **4**:484; **10**:1379–1380,
    1381

Cimmeranians **9**:1292

Cimon **3**:393; **10**:1355

Cincinnatus, Lucius Quinctius
    6:836

Claudius, *Roman emperor*
    4:438

Clovis, baptism **9**:*1225*

coffins and sarcophaguses
    Egyptian **1**:110; **4**:*552;* **6**:768;
        7:*995*

Greek **5**:*623;* **7**:*899;* **8**:*1052,*
    1076
    Roman **5**:*605, 689;* **8**:*1098*

coins, Roman **6**:*773,* 774, *838,*
    859; **7**:*884;* **8**:*1032*

Constantia **2**:219

Constantine **7**:897

constellations **10**:1333–1334
    Andromeda **1**:*76*
    Aquarius **4**:549
    Aquila **4**:549; **10**:1337
    Auriga **4**:487; **5**:690
    in Babylonian mythology
        10:1370
    Boötes **10**:1334
    Canis Major **8**:1056; **10**:1334
    Canis Minor **8**:1056
    Cassiopeia **1**:76
    Cepheus **1**:76
    Chinese **10**:1337
    Corona Borealis **3**:416;
        10:1353
    Cygnus **6**:812; **8**:1117
    Draco **5**:682
    Gemini **6**:813
    Great Bear (Ursa Major)
        1:21; **2**:158, *262,* 263;
        5:654; **6**:826; **7**:1001;
        10:1334, 1336–1337
        the Big Dipper **10**:1334,
            1338, 1339, 1340
        Japanese name for
            10:1337–1338
    Japanese **10**:1337–1338, 1339,
        1340
    Little Bear (Ursa Minor)
        2:158
        Japanese name for
            10:1337–1338
    Lyra **8**:1061; **10**:1337
    named for Greek myths
        10:1335
    Orion **8**:*1054,* 1055–*1056,*
        1065; **10**:1338–1339, *1340*
    Perseus **1**:*76;* **8**:1114
    Pleiades **6**:846; **8**:1055, *1129,*
        1130; **10**:*1335,* 1340
    Scorpius **8**:1056
    Southern Cross **2**:*200*
    Southern Pleiades **10**:1340
    Taurus **8**:1056
    Virgo **10**:1334

corn **8**:1124
    Aztec myth **10**:1384

Cortés, Hernán **9**:1202, *1203*

Crete **3**:**324–333;** **7**:889

crossroads
    Hecate and **5**:*619,* 620
    Lares and **6**:*808*

cyclones **7**:948–949

Cyrus II (Cyrus the Great)
    6:744; **7**:876, 877
    tomb **7**:*893*

daffodils **7**:*936*

Daidala festival **5**:652

dances
    Aboriginal **2**:200
    Hopi
        and ancestor worship **1**:73
        Snake Dancers **1**:89
    Kiowa, Sun Dance **5**:*586,* 587

Darius I **6**:746

Darwinism, social **1**:100

Dayak people, creation myth
    10:*1326–1327*

Day of the Dead **4**:*517*

days
    and nights **3**:344–*346*
    of the week, Norse **2**:260;
        4:537

disability, Greeks and **5**:*645,*
    646

Diwali **2**:258

Dogon people **8**:*1071*

Dorians **5**:593; **10**:1311

Drake, Francis **9**:1273

drama, in Egypt **7**:964

dreams **7**:920

druids **2**:284–285; **4**:**436–439**
    and the afterlife **3**:375;
        4:439
    and oak trees **4**:*442*
    and sacrifice **2**:239; **4**:439;
        9:*1248, 1252*

Dunstan, Saint **10**:1426

earth, supported in space **7**:947

earthquakes, beliefs about
    7:947–*948;* **8**:1144;
    10:1399

Easter **4**:513

Egypt **4**:**460–469**

Elamites **6**:744; **7**:874, 875

Electra complex **4**:471

elements, worship of the, by
    the Slavs **10**:1317–1318

Elymians **10**:1410

Empedocles **9**:1215

Eskimos
    shamans **9**:*1287*
    see also Inuit

Etruscans 8:*1073*
 alphabet 2:253
 and divination 8:1070–1071
 goddess of death 3:401,
  403
 goddess Menrva 7:*882–883*
 and Rome 9:*1230–1231*
Eumenes II 10:1378
Euthymus 3:390, 392
Evenki people 1:96, 99
Ewe people, sun and moon
  myth 10:1348

Fan people 1:45, 47
fate, in the Greek world
  10:1391
feng shui 3:427–428
Feriae Latinae 6:787
fertility 4:**501–510**;
  8:1138–1139
 mandrake plant and 8:1126,
  1127
 Norse fertility deities 4:529,
  531
fetiales 6:838
Finnic people 9:1259–1260
fire
 origin, Native American
  myth 7:945
 worshiped in Arabia 1:138
flowers, in Greek mythology
  7:*936, 1002*
Franks 4:557, *558*
Frisians 4:557, *558*

Galations 2:278
Galli 2:187; 9:1237
garlic 8:1127, *1128*
Genghis Khan 3:*294,* 297–298
Germanic peoples 4:**557–562**
 apocalypse myth 1:127
 fertility deity 4:529
Gilgamesh 3:371; 4:482, *571,*
  573; 6:760–762, 763
ginseng 8:1127
Gleaners, Return of the 7:*917*
Götar people 4:557, *558*
Greece 5:**591–600**
Gudea 7:871

Hallstatt culture 2:277
hallucinogens
 shamans and 9:*1289*
 witches and 9:*1288*
Hammurabi 4:573; 6:831;
  7:871–872, *873*

handicap, physical *see* disability
hats, Phrygian 2:*186;* 7:*891,*
  893
Hatshepsut 9:*1210;* 10:*1332*
Hattians 5:692–693
 influence on Hittite myths
  5:694–695
hearth
 the Greeks and the 5:592,
  683–684, 686; 10:*1418*
 the Romans and the 10:1412
Heraia (games for women)
  5:657
herms 5:*619, 672;* 6:*859;*
  9:1169
hierodules 2:271
Himyarites 1:137
Himyar 1:138
Hippocrates 2:162
hippopotamuses, Horus and
  Seth as 9:*1282*
Hirpini 6:835–836; 8:1071
Hirsenti 8:1071
Hittites 5:**691–700**
 capital city 10:*1344*
 gods and goddesses
  5:692–*694*
 kingship 5:697–699
 modern knowledge of 5:699
 myths 5:694–695, 696, 699
  the dragon Illuyankas 3:*422;*
   5:694, 695
  the Kumarbi Cycle
   5:696–697
 religion 5:697
 influence of 5:699–700
 women in society 5:*699*
Holy Grail 4:509–510
horses
 Boreas (north wind) as
  10:1313
 Diomedes eaten by horses
  2:*151;* 5:662; 8:1121–1122
 immortal horses of Achilles
  1:*18,* 85, *86;* 5:612
 Pegasus 8:*1112*
 Poseidon Hippion (god of
  horses) 8:1149
 sacrificed 9:*1248*
 Sleipnir (Odin's horse)
  5:*676, 677;* 6:818; 8:*1030*
houses
 Roman, shrines to household
  gods 6:*808–809, 810;*
  8:*1100, 1101;* 9:*1224*
 Slavic tree spirits in 10:*1319*

Hudhayl 1:138
Huns 3:297
hunter-gatherers
 animal deities 3:381
 and months of the year
  3:349–351
hunting
 by the Inuit 7:945
 by Native Americans 3:350;
  7:*943, 944–*945
 honoring Dionysus 3:415
 rituals involving sacrifice 1:94
 rules of 3:350
Hurrians 5:693–694
 influence on Hittite myths
  5:694, 696
hurricanes 7:948–949
Hushedar 6:748
Hybristika festival 5:669
Hyksos, and Seth 3:402; 9:1284

Ibo peoples, creator deity 3:314
Inca 6:**724–731**
 festivals 6:*729*
 gods 6:726–728
  sun god 6:726;
   10:1347–1348
 Machu Picchu 6:*725, 726;*
  10:1348
 myths 6:729
  birth of the Inca Empire
   6:729–730
  creation myth 3:322; 4:523;
   6:729
  flood 4:523; 6:729
 the Quechua tradition 6:731
 religion 6:730–731
 sacrifice 6:*728*
 the Spaniards and 6:725–726
  chroniclers of Inca culture
   6:*730*
 worship of *huaca* 6:728
incest 10:1398, 1421
India 6:**732–739**
Indus Valley (Harappan)
  civilization 6:732–734, 737,
  739
 collapse 6:734
 mother goddess 3:*316*
interpretatio Romana 6:861
Inuit
 hunting by 7:945
 moon and sun deities 7:911;
  10:1346
 sea deities 9:1271
 spirits 7:945

Ionians 5:593, 595
Iran 6:**744–749**
Ireland 6:**750–759**
Irenaeus, Saint 7:906
Isia, the 6:769
Isthmian Games 8:1144,
  1149–1150; 10:1307
Itzá 6:799

jaguar cult 8:1048–1049
jars, canopic 1:110–111; 5:*610*
Jayavarman II 10:1322
Jayavarman VII 10:1322, *1324*
Jesus Christ
 and the apocalypse 1:121
 Norse mythology and
  Balder 2:222, 223
  Odin 8:1029–1030; 9:1265
 and Orpheus 8:1058
Jingo, *Empress of Japan*
  9:1270–1271
Julia Domna 10:1412, 1415
Jupiter (planet), named 10:1335

Ka-aper 9:*1177*
Kachin people
 belief in the afterlife 10:1329
 and the soul 10:1328
Kalb 1:138
Kassites 7:872
Ket people, and the south wind
  10:1315
Khafre 9:1206
 pyramid 10:1330
 and the Sphinx 10:1330,
  1332
Khasekhemwy 9:1279
Khaywan 1:138
Khazraj 1:138
Khoikhoi people 1:45
Khufu, funerary boat 4:*463*
Kikuyu people 1:44; 8:1126
Korea 6:**789–796**
Kunai people 2:199
kykeon 3:387, 389; 4:508

labyrinths (mazes) 3:360–*361*
 Minoans and 3:330–331
 and the Minotaur myth
  3:358; 5:595; 8:1091;
  10:*1352*
lamba 1:*74*
La Tène culture 2:277–278
Latin League 9:1234
laurel 3:*365,* 367; 8:1124–*1125*
lightning 7:*950*

Lindow Man **2**:283; **9**:*1252*
lingams **6**:737
lingam symbol **4**:502
Locrians, and Ajax **1**:54
Lombards **4**:535
Ludi Neptunales **7**:968
Ludi Romani (Roman games)
    6:787
Ludi Saeculares (Sacred Games)
    3:420
lunatics, the moon and **7**:914
Lycurgus **9**:1172

magic
    in Korean mythology **6**:792
    sympathetic **9**:1160–1161
Malagasy people, ancestor
    worship **1**:74
Mamertines **6**:836
mandrake plant **8**:1126–*1127*
Maori
    apocalypse myths **1**:*123*, 125
    creation myths **3**:319, 320;
        8:1014–1015
    flutes **8**:*1014*
    trickster god **8**:1015–1016,
        1018
Marcus Aurelius **8**:*1072*
marriage **9**:*1227*–1228;
    10:1416
    see also weddings
Marsi **6**:836
Mars (planet) **10**:1336
Mary (Virgin Mary)
    apocalypse myths and **1**:*124*
    apparition at La Salette **1**:*124*
Masai people **1**:*42*, *43*–44;
    9:*1223*, 1224
    rain god **5**:614
masks
    of Anubis, and burial rituals
        1:110
    Aztec **2**:*206*
    Greek
        Agamemnon **1**:*48*, 49
        Demeter **3**:*386*
        Mycenaean burial mask
            5:*595*
Maya **6**:**840–847**
    ball games **6**:*847*; **8**:1047
    beliefs about the earth **6**:842;
        7:947
    beliefs about the universe
        6:842
    bloodletting **6**:846; **8**:1049;
        9:1174–1175

calendar **2**:*259*–260
creation myths **3**:322; **6**:797,
    799, 841–842; **7**:948–949;
    9:1268
deities **6**:841, *843*, 844, *845*;
    9:*1245*
    sky gods **10**:1310
festivals **4**:517
Great Cycles, and the
    apocalypse **1**:122
human sacrifice **6**:797,
    799–800, 845–847; **9**:*1245*
kings and queens **6**:844
and the night sky **6**:846
    planet Venus **6**:843
and the Olmecs **8**:1048
periods of civilization
    6:840–841
priests **9**:1173–*1175*
pyramids **6**:*797*, *800*, *840*,
    844
Spanish conquest of **6**:847
and suicide **6**:844–845
maypole dancing **4**:513
Mayta Capac **6**:724–725
mazes *see* labyrinths
Medes **6**:744
megaliths (stone monuments)
    9:*1163*, 1228
    at Carnac **9**:*1160*, 1163
    Irish **6**:*750*, 752; **7**:916
    Stonehenge **9**:*1162*
meiligmata **8**:*1132*
menstrual cycles
    first menstruation
        9:1224–1226
    synchronization **7**:916
Mercury (planet) **10**:1335
Merovingians **4**:*560*
Mesolithic Age
    in India **6**:732, 750
    time-reckoning **7**:916
Mesopotamia **7**:**868–877**
Milky Way **5**:659; **8**:1116;
    10:*1338*
Minaeans **1**:137
Minoans **5**:712
    art **7**:889
    bronze **3**:324
    cave and mountain
        sanctuaries **3**:333; **7**:886
    cults **3**:331
        bull **3**:*327*, *331*
    deities **3**:332
        adopted by the Greeks
            2:247–248

mother goddess **3**:321, 325
    snake goddesses **3**:*329*, 330
    double-ax symbols on pillars
        3:*326*, 330
    earthquakes and volcanic
        eruptions **3**:325, 328; **7**:890,
        951–952; **10**:1353
    overthrown by the
        Myceneans **10**:1353
    palaces **3**:330–331
        Knossos **3**:*327*, *329*–330,
            358; **7**:*885*, *886*, *889*–890;
            10:*1353*
        mazes **3**:330–331
    religion **3**:325
miscarriage, Japanese Buddhism
    and **3**:406
mistletoe **4**:*516*; **9**:*1252*
mithraea **7**:894, 895–896,
    897–898, 933
Moabite people, and dualism
    4:446
Mochica **1**:*102*
Mongols **3**:293–*294*
    apocalypse myth **1**:127
    creation myths **3**:297
    demons **3**:296–297
    gods **3**:295–296
    Huns **3**:297
    life after death **3**:299
    Oghuzes **3**:297
    shamanism **3**:294–*295*, 299
    shrines **3**:*299*
    Uighurs **3**:297
    writing **3**:293–294
Montezuma II **9**:*1203*
months **3**:344, *351*
    cycles **3**:348
    names **3**:349–350
moon **7**:**911–918**;
    9:1275–1276, 1277
    African myth **10**:1348
    creation of **7**:915–916
    cycles, effects of **7**:916–917
    deities **3**:*344*, 348; **7**:913;
        8:1137
        Aztec **3**:*348*; **7**:911
        Baltic **2**:*228*–229; **7**:914
        Chinese **3**:*303*, 304
        Egyptian **3**:348; **7**:*912*
        Greek **3**:348, *349*; **7**:914;
            9:*1275*–*1278*
        Inca **6**:727
        Indian (Vedic) **7**:913
        Inuit **7**:911; **10**:1346
        Mayan **7**:915

Mesopotamian **7**:870, 876;
    8:1137; **3**:348
    Roman **3**:407, 410; **7**:914;
        9:1278
Dyak myth (from Borneo)
    10:1327
and lunacy **7**:*914*
lunar cycles **3**:345, 346–348
the man in the, Native
    American myth **7**:945–946
and the weather **7**:917–918
worshiped by the Slavs
    10:1319–1320
morning star *see* Venus
    (planet)
Mother Shipton **1**:124
mountains **10**:1316
    in China **3**:*307*
Muhammad **7**:909
Muratos people, flood myth
    4:523
Mursilis I **5**:691
Mursilis II **5**:698
museums, Greek **7**:925
myrrh **1**:22, 25

Nabonidus **7**:876
narcissi **7**:935, *936*
Native Americans **7**:**937–946**
    Algonquians
        hunters **7**:*944*
        myth of Glooskap and
            Malsum **7**:940–941
        supreme deity **7**:940
    ancestor worship **1**:73
    and animals **1**:92, 93
        as healers **1**:87
    apocalypse myths **1**:*122*,
        123–124
    Arapaho, creation myth
        5:586–587
    Athabascan, hunting rules
        3:350
    calendar **2**:*258*
    Cherokee, myth of Kana'ti
        and Selu **7**:942
    Choctaw, land of **7**:941
    creation myths **3**:314, 321;
        5:586–587, 589–590; **7**:939,
        941; **10**:1313
    Crow, creation myth **5**:586
    death and the afterlife **9**:*1218*
    and devils **3**:406
    Great Plains **7**:937, *943*, *953*
        Legend of the Buffalo
            Dance **7**:943–944

Great Spirit **5:586–590**;
7:*909, 910*

Haida Indians, dual death god
4:447

Hopi
ancestor worship **1**:73
apocalypse myth **1**:*122*, 124
fertility god **4**:*510*

hunters' concern for the
hunted **7**:*943, 944*–945

Iroquois, spirit entities
7:938–939

Kiowa
and the Great Spirit **5**:*586*,
587
Sun Dance **5**:*586*, 587

Leni Lenape (Delaware),
manitous **7**:939

manitous (great spirits)
7:939–941

monotheism **7**:909, 910

Navajo
calendar **3**:350–351
creation myth **10**:1313
day and night in legend
3:344–346
Flint Chant **1**:87
healing animals in
mythology **1**:87
hunting rule **3**:350
and Monument Valley
10:*1316*
and the moon **3**:347
Mountain Way story **1**:97
rainbows **10**:1313
Rat Man and Rainboy
ritual **1**:86
storm gods **10**:1311
and winds **10**:1313–1314
Yei deities **7**:942–943

Ojibwa
and the Great Spirit
5:587–588
nocturnal spearfishing
7:939–940

Onondaga, apocalypse myth
1:123
and the origin of death
3:376

Pawnee
stars and the seasons
10:1339–1340
storm god **10**:*1315*

Pueblo Indians **7**:*940*
ancestor worship **1**:73
and healing animals **1**:87

religion in the modern world
7:946

rituals **1**:86, 95; **7**:*946*
Blessing Way rites **7**:943
Sun Dance **5**:*586*, 587;
7:*910*

sacred locations **7**:937–938

Seneca
apocalypse myth **1**:123
and sky people **10**:1315

Sioux **7**:*941*
Great Spirit **5**:588–589,
590; **7**:*909*
and healing animals **1**:87
White Buffalo Calf Woman
7:941–942
and tornadoes **7**:949–950
totem poles **1**:*104*

Tuscaroras **7**:939

Zuni, Great Spirit and
creation **5**:589–590

natural forces **7:947–952**

Neanderthals
burials **3**:381; **4**:454; **9**:*1156,*
1157–1158
and cave bears **9**:1158–1159

Nebuchadnezzar II **7**:876

Nefertiti **6**:*765*

Nemean Games **10**:1438

Neolithic Age **9**:1161–*1163*
death and the afterlife **9**:1162
gods and goddesses **3**:383;
4:*502*; **9**:1162
in Greece **5**:591–592
in India **6**:732
in Ireland **6**:*750*, 752
passage tomb at Newgrange
6:750, 751, *752*, 757;
9:*1161*, 1163
megaliths (stone monuments)
6:*750*; **9**:1163
at Carnac **9**:*1160*, 1163
in Ireland **6**:*750*, 752
Stonehenge **9**:*1162*

Neptune (planet), named
10:1336

Nero **9**:1294

nidughans **3**:*295*

nightshade, deadly **8**:1128

Nilometers **7**:*980*

Noah **3**:399; **4**:520–521

northern lights **10**:1400, *1403*

Nubilior, Marcus Fulvius **7**:925

Numa Pompilius **8**:1102;
9:1205, 1233; **10**:1412

nymphaeums **7**:998

Oceania **8:1012–1019**

Oedipus complex **8**:1044

Oghuzes **3**:297

Olaf, *king of Sweden* **2**:223

Olaf Tryggvason **10**:1364

olive oil, Athens and **2**:175

Olmecs **8:1046–1049**
worship of Tlaloc **10**:1385

Olympic Games **4**:473, 475,
513, 514–515; **9**:1249;
10:*1437*, 1438

omophagia **3**:415

onions **8**:1127–1128

Orochey people, and animal
mothers **1**:96

Osorkon II **5**:*706*

Ossetes **6**:745

Ostrogoths **4**:558

Paleolithic Age **9**:1157–1161
horned god **8**:1075
time-reckoning **7**:*916*
see also Neanderthals

Panhellenic Games **3**:395

Parthians **6**:744

Paul, Saint **10**:*1317*

peacocks **1**:86; **10**:1436

Pelasgians **5**:592, 650; **10**:1311

Pentheus, *king of Thebes* **2**:216

Peribsen **9**:1279

Persians **6**:744
Mithraism **7**:892–893

pharaohs **2**:189; **4**:461, 465;
9:1284
association with the gods
9:1174, 1206, 1279, 1283
as Heirs of Geb **4**:550
depicted as sphinxes **10**:1330,
1332
priesthood **9**:1174
royal titles **5**:701; **9**:1206,
1279, 1284
tombs **7**:995–996

Philip II of Macedonia **7**:923

Phoenicians **2**:212–213

Piceni **8**:1071

Picentes **6**:836

Pierus **7**:924

pillars
depicting Hecate **5**:*619*
Germanic religious artifacts
4:560–561
herms **5**:*619, 672*; **6**:859;
9:1169
phallus-like **4**:502

pine trees **8**:1075

Pizarro, Francisco **6**:725–726

planets **10**:*1337*
named **10**:1334–1336, 1396

plants **8:1124–1128**,
1138–1139
used by shamans **9**:*1286*,
1289
see also trees

Pluto (planet), named **10**:1336

polis **5**:598

pomegranates **8**:*1106*, 1108,
1109

pomerium **6**:837–838

Pompey the Great
and the Amazons **1**:65
temple to Venus **10**:1411

pontifex maximus **9**:1235,
1236
and the vestal virgins
10:1412, 1414

prehistoric man *see* hunter-
gatherers; Mesolithic Age;
Neolithic Age; Paleolithic
Age

prytaneion **5**:686

Pyrrhus of Epirus **1**:28

Pythian Games **1**:129; **3**:*365*;
4:514

Quechua **6**:731

Quiché tribe **6**:797, 841

quipus **6**:724

Quraysh **1**:138

rainbows **10**:*1313*

Ramses II **9**:1192
funerary temple **9**:*1172*

Ramses III **6**:*768*; **7**:873, *963*

Ramses VI, tomb **3**:*347*

rats, attitudes toward **1**:85–86

revenge killings **1**:50–51

Romans **9:1230–1239**
the afterlife **5**:*605*
Elysium **3**:372; **5**:608
the Last Judgment **3**:420
Lethe **5**:608
ancestor worship **1**:70, *71*
calendars **2**:*260*, 261; **6**:770;
9:1233
and the Celts **2**:278, 279
druids **4**:*438*–439
and Christianity **8**:1070,
1071
deities **9**:1231, 1236
three-group system **9**:1233
two names **8**:1072

Romans (continued)
emperors
divine **9**:1238
as priests **9**:1172, *1236*
empire **9**:1236–1237
festivals **4**:515–516
Agonium **6**:774
Anna Perenna **7**:968
Bacchanalia **4**:516; **7**:931
Compitalia **6**:808, 810
Consualia **4**:516; **9**:1205
Day of Slaves **10**:1420
Feriae Latinae **6**:787
Hilaria **2**:187
to Jupiter **6**:787
Larentalia **4**:516
to the Lares **6**:808, 810
Ludi Neptunales **7**:968
Ludi Romani **6**:787
Lupercalia **4**:*500*, 516
Matronalia **6**:782
Megalesia **9**:1237
Mercuralia **6**:861
military season **6**:838–839
Neptunalia **7**:967, 968
Opuconsivia **9**:1254
Parilia **4**:*515*
Quinquatrus **7**:884
Quirinalia **9**:1205
Robigalia **9**:1205
Rustic Vinalia **10**:1410
Saturnalia **4**:515, 516;
6:770–772; **9**:1254–*1255*
Terminalia **4**:*511*
to Jupiter **6**:787
to the Lares **6**:808, 810
Vestalia **10**:1412
Vulcanalia **4**:516
household gods, shrines to
6:808–*809*, 810; **8**:1100,
1101; **9**:*1224*
invasion of the British Isles
4:438–439
Mithraism **6**:747; **7**:894–898;
9:1238–1239
mother goddess **4**:*455, 457*
paganism **8**:1071
priests and priestesses **9**:1175,
1235
emperors as priests **9**:1172,
1236
flamens (flamines)
9:1204–1205
Galli **2**:187; **9**:1237
and reincarnation **5**:608;
10:1313

religion **7**:931
and sacrifice **1**:*94*; **2**:237;
9:*1251*
to Mars **6**:834, *839*
superstitions **6**:803
weddings and marriage
10:1416, *1417*
and household gods
9:1224
winds **1**:77
rune stones, Viking **10**:*1405*

Sabaeans **1**:136–137
Sabines, attack on Rome
6:772
Saint Elmo's fire **2**:276; **6**:813
Sakai people, and the afterlife
10:1329
Samhain **1**:70–71; **4**:512;
6:758–759
Sami **9**:1259–1260, 1265, 1266
shamans **9**:1249
thunder god images **10**:1362
San people
myths **1**:*40–41*
about the moon **7**:911–912
Sapa Inca **6**:730
sarcophaguses *see* coffins and
sarcophaguses
Sargon **7**:870–871
Sassanian Empire **6**:744, *745*,
746
Saturn (planet) **9**:*1254*
moons **10**:1378
named **10**:1335
Saxons **4**:557, 558
Scandinavia **9**:**1259–1266**
scorpions **1**:85
sea **9**:**1267–1274**
Blue Men of the Muir
9:1273
Celtic gods **9**:1270, *1271*
Greek gods of **9**:1268–1269
Glaucus **8**:*1092*; **9**:1274
Nereus **7**:**969–970**
Nethuns **9**:1269
Oceanus **8**:**1020–1023**;
9:1269
Phorcys **5**:619
Pontus **9**:1268–1269
Poseidon **8**:**1143–1150**;
9:1269
Proteus **6**:858; **7**:969–970;
9:**1185–1186**
Triton **7**:884; **8**:1144;
10:**1386–1387**

Greek sea nymphs
Nereids **1**:103; **7**:*969, 970,
998*, 999, 1000; **8**:1022
Sirens **3**:*393*; **8**:*1037*;
9:*1269*
Japanese gods of, Ryujin
7:952; **9**:1270–1271
mermaids and mermen **1**:82;
9:1271–1273
Norse gods of
Aegir **1**:**26–27**; **9**:1269
Njörd **7**:989; **10**:1407
Polynesian gods **9**:1271
Roman gods of, Neptune
7:**965–968**
sea monsters **8**:*1092*;
9:*1273–1274*
Charybdis **8**:*1037, 1146*
Scylla **5**:619; **8**:1037, *1092,
1146*, 1147; **9**:*1270*, 1274
sea serpents **3**:430; **5**:695;
9:1274
sea witches **9**:1273
seals, Mesopotamian **7**:*874*
seasons **3**:348–349
Baal and **2**:215
Greek myths
Adonis **5**:717
Persephone **3**:389, 420;
4:504–506; **8**:1106–1108
modern **3**:351
Sumerian mythology,
Dumuzi and **5**:717
Sedna (planet or planetoid),
named **10**:1336, 1396
Seleucids **6**:744
senate, Roman **9**:1172–1173
Sennacherib **7**:875
Serbs, and the moon **10**:1319
Servius Tullius **9**:1233, 1234
Sesostris (Senusret) I, *king of
Egypt* **2**:*188*
Seti I **8**:1068; **10**:1332
temple of **9**:*1281*
tomb **10**:*1336*
Shalmaneser III **7**:875
Shan people, and earthquakes
7:947–948
ships
Broighter **9**:*1271*
Scandinavian **7**:*988*, 989,
991
see also boats
Shoki, spirit of **3**:406
Sif **10**:1358
Silk Road **3**:*293*

sky **10**:**1309–1316**
gods
of the Ashanti people **3**:383;
10:1310
Canaanite **10**:1312–1313
Chinese **10**:*1311*
Egyptian **10**:*1312*,
1398–1399
Greek **10**:1310, 1311
Indo-European
10:1311–1312
Mayan **10**:*1310*
Mesopotamian **10**:1313
of the Navajo **10**:1311
Norse **10**:1311
paradise in the **10**:1310
sky people **10**:1315–1316
Slavs **10**:**1317–1321**
apocalypse myth **1**:127
creation myths **10**:1318–1319
deities **10**:1318–1319
festivals and holidays **10**:1320,
1321
moon worship **10**:1319–1320
rituals for the dead **10**:1321
sacrifices made by **10**:1320
shrines **10**:1320
and the unclean dead
10:1321
and vampires **10**:1321
social Darwinism **1**:100
solhwa **6**:790, 795
Solon **1**:123
Southeast Asia **10**:**1322–1329**
sparagmos **3**:415
Sparta, League of **8**:1053
standing stones, in Ireland
6:*750*
stars **10**:**1333–1340**
Arcturus **2**:263; **6**:826
Capella **3**:*338*
evening star *see* Venus (planet)
Milky Way **5**:659; **8**:1116;
10:*1338*
morning star *see* Venus
(planet)
Sirius (Dog Star)
Egyptians and **2**:255; **6**:766;
8:1065–1066; **10**:1336
Greeks and **6**:772
see also constellations
Stepterion **1**:129
Stone Age
Middle *see* Mesolithic Age
New *see* Neolithic Age
Old *see* Paleolithic Age

Sulla, Lucius Cornelius **9**:1294; **10**:1411

sun **10**:**1341–1348**

  African myth **10**:1348

  Chinese mythology **3**:303

  deities **8**:1137

    Aztec **10**:1346–1347

    Baltic **2**:228, *229*

    Chinese **9**:1211

    Egyptian **2**:*189*, 190, 242; **5**:644, 703; **7**:907, *908*; **9**:1206–1208, *1209*; **10**:*1341*–*1342*

    Greek **5**:*641*–*644*; **10**:1343–1344, *1345*

    Hindu **5**:644

    Hittite **5**:695; **10**:1343, *1344*

    Inca **6**:726; **10**:1347–1348

    Inuit **7**:911; **10**:1346

    Japanese **3**:316; **10**:*1345*–*1346*

    Mayan **6**:842; **9**:1211

    Mesopotamian **4**:*450*; **9**:1211; **10**:1342–1343

    Native American **10**:1346

    Syrian **1**:*140*; **5**:644

  eclipses, and Baltic mythology **2**:*228*–229

  Greek mythology and Apollo **5**:*600*

    Phaethon **5**:642; **8**:*1115*–*1116*

  Mayans and **6**:842

  Norse mythology and **9**:1261–1262

  Roman mythology **5**:644

superstitions

  and the fall of Troy **6**:803

  Roman **6**:803

surfboard, the first **8**:*1019*

Suryavarman II **10**:1322, 1324

Svear people **4**:557, *558*

Tarquinius Priscus, Lucius **9**:1233

Tarquinius Superbus (Tarquin the Proud) **9**:1233, 1292

Tegeans **8**:1053

Teotihuacános **8**:1048, 1049

Thalestris **1**:65

Theodosius I **9**:1294

Thespians **5**:660; **7**:923

thunderstones **10**:1364

thunder and thunderstorms **7**:949

Thuringians **4**:557, *558*

Thutmose I **9**:1210

Thutmose IV **10**:1332

thyrsos **3**:414, 415, 418

tidal waves **7**:951–952

Tiglath-pileser III **7**:875

Tiwanaku civilization **6**:726–727

tjets **6**:764

Tlingit people, sea monster **9**:1274

toga virilis **6**:808

Tolland Man **9**:*1262*

Toltecs

  myths, Kukulkan **6**:843

  and Quetzalcoatl **8**:1049; **9**:*1201, 1202*

totem poles **1**:*104*

trees

  banyan **8**:1126

  baobab **8**:*1126*

  Christmas **4**:559

  cypress **8**:1125

  Dryads and **4**:440–442

  Hamadryads and **7**:998

  laurel **3**:367; **7**:1002; **8**:*1124*–*1125*

  linden **8**:1125

  myrrh **8**:1125

  mythological

    Ished Tree **2**:*190*

    of the Kikuyu people **8**:1126

    World Tree **3**:321–322, *323*; **5**:631; **6**:817; **7**:992; **8**:1029, 1126; **9**:1265, 1286

    Yggdrasil **3**:321–322, *323*; **5**:631; **6**:817; **8**:1126

  oak **3**:*407*, 409; **4**:441, *442*, 560; **8**:1125

at Dodona **4**:442; **8**:1126; **9**:*1177*; **10**:*1433*

  pine **8**:1075

  poplar **8**:1117

  spirits **10**:*1319*

  sycamore **7**:*996*, 997

Tuccia **10**:*1421*

Tungus **6**:789

Turks **3**:293–294

  creation myth **3**:297

  demons **3**:296–297

  gods **3**:295–296

  and life after death **3**:299

  shamanism **3**:294, 299

  writing **3**:293–294

Tutankhamen **2**:190; **4**:*467*; **9**:1210

  treasures from tomb of **2**:*244*; **9**:1194

  canopic jars **1**:110–111

  funeral mask **4**:460

Ubangui people **1**:45

Uighurs **3**:297

Umbrians

  foundation myth **8**:1071

  religious rituals **8**:1072

Unas **9**:*1280*

Uranus (planet) **10**:1336, *1396*

Vedism **6**:735–736

Venus (planet; morning star; evening star) **10**:*1335*, 1336, *1410*

  Astarte and **2**:163

  Maya and **6**:843

  named **10**:1336

  Quetzalcoatl and **9**:1201, *1202*, 1203

Vikings **9**:1264

  burial **3**:*377*

  rune stones **10**:*1405*

  shield bosses **10**:*1404*

Villca Umu **6**:731

virginity **10**:**1416–1423**

  Daphne's wish for **3**:367

  in Norse mythology, Gefjon **4**:554

Virgins of the Sun (Allca Cuna) **6**:*731*

Virgo Vestalis Maxima **10**:1412

Visigoths **4**:557–558

volcanoes **7**:*952*

  Javan myth about **10**:1327

Warpalaurus **5**:*691*

weddings

  in Greece **5**:667–668, 672; **7**:976

  Roman **10**:1416, *1417*

  and household gods **9**:1224

  see also marriage

weeks, days of the, Norse **2**:260; **4**:537

whetstone, in Norse myths **10**:1362

winds, beliefs about **1**:77; **7**:*948*–*950*; **10**:1313–1315

women

  and the earth mother **4**:452–454

  in Greek society **5**:584, 668; **8**:1091

Wulfstan, *archbishop* **5**:632

xenia **8**:1086

Xerxes I **3**:367; **6**:746

years **3**:344

  cycles **3**:348

Yekuhana, sky people and creation **10**:1315–1316

yoga **6**:737, *739*; **7**:*905*

Yoruba people **1**:41, *44*–*45*

  ancestor-worship **1**:*69*

Yuan Xiao **2**:*257*

zodiac **3**:348; **10**:*1339*

  Aries **1**:94, *95*

  Taurus **1**:94

Zoroaster **6**:745–746, 748

Zulu people **1**:45

INDEX OF HISTORY AND LEGEND

Page numbers in **bold** refer to main articles; those in *italics* refer to pictures.

Amenhotep IV (Akhenaten; Akhenaton) **2**:190; **4**:514; **5**:610; **7**:907, *908*; **9**:1210; **10**:1332, *1343*
Anglesey, Roman invasions of **4**:*438*, 439
Arthur, *legendary king of Britain* **4**:508–509; **10**:1422
Athens
    founding of **5**:596–597
    and Sparta **5**:598
Augustus **1**:32, 133; **4**:438; **6**:810; **9**:*1236*-1237

Babylon **6**:833
    fall of **7**:876
Babylonia
    First Dynasty of Babylon **7**:871–872
    neo-Babylonian Empire **7**:875–876
Black Death, rats and **1**:86
Britain, Roman invasion of **4**:438–439
Buddha (Gautama Buddha) **3**:402; **7**:909, 957; **9**:1216–1217; **10**:1327

Caesar, Julius **2**:261, 280–281, 283; **4**:436–437
Celts **2**:277–286
    Hallstatt culture **2**:277; **3**:*368*
    in Ireland **6**:751, 753
    La Tène culture **2**:277–278
Cicero **9**:1173, 1175
Crete **3**:**324–333**
    earthquakes and volcanic eruption **3**:325, 328; **7**:890, 951–952

Drake, Francis **9**:1273

Egypt **4**:**460–469**
    influence on Greece **5**:597
    periods of history **4**:464
    pharaohs **2**:189; **4**:461, 465, 550; **5**:701; **9**:1174, 1283, 1284
    ruled by Macedonian Greeks **7**:964
Evans, Arthur **3**:329–330; **7**:*889*

flood myths, historical basis for **3**:400; **4**:520, *524*–525

Genghis Khan **3**:*294*, 297–298
Germanic peoples, migrations of **4**:557–558
Greece **5**:**591–600**
    the age of invasions (1900–1500 BCE) **5**:593–594
    Bronze Age (Helladic period) **5**:593
    "Dark-age" **5**:594–595
    influence of Egypt on **5**:597
    Stone Age **5**:591–592

Hallstatt culture **2**:277
Hammurabi **4**:573; **6**:831; **7**:871–872, *873*
Hannibal, retreat from Rome **2**:187

Inca **6**:**724–731**
    Spanish conquest of **6**:725–726
India **6**:**732–739**
    arrival of Aryans **6**:734–735
    Dravidian civilization **3**:364
    Indus Valley (Harappan) civilization **3**:*316*; **6**:732–*734*, *739*
    Stone Age civilizations **6**:732
Isthmian Games **8**:1144, 1149–1150; **10**:1307

Jayavarman II **10**:1322
Jayavarman VII **10**:1322, 1324
Jesus Christ **1**:121; **2**:222, 223; **8**:1029–1030; 1058; **9**:1265

Kadesh, battle of **5**:692
Korea **6**:**789–796**
    kings of Silla **6**:*794*, *795*–796
    Three Kingdoms **6**:789–*790*

Lake Regillus, Battle of **2**:276
La Tène culture **2**:277–278
Latin League **9**:1234

Marathon, Battle of **8**:*1076*
Maya **6**:**840–847**
    kings and queens **6**:844
    and the Olmecs **8**:1048
    periods of civilization **6**:840–841
    Spanish conquest of **6**:847
Mesopotamia **7**:**868–877**
    Akkadian Empire **7**:870–871
    Aramaean invasions **7**:872–873
    Assyrians **7**:873–875
    Third Dynasty of Ur **7**:871
Milvian Bridge, Battle of **7**:897
Montezuma II **9**:*1203*
Moytura, Battle of **3**:338
Muhammad **7**:909

Nebuchadnezzar II **7**:876
Nefertiti **6**:*765*
Nero **9**:1294

Oceania, settlement of **8**:1012–1013
Oceanids **1**:103; **7**:
Olympic Games **4**:473, 475, *513*, 514–515; **9**:1249; **10**:*1437*, 1438

Panhellenic Games **3**:395
Patrick, Saint **2**:*285*; **9**:1271

Pompey the Great **1**:65; **10**:1411
Pythian Games **1**:129; **3**:*365*; **4**:514

Ramses II **9**: *1172;* 1192
Rome **9**:**1230–1239**
    empire **9**:1236–1237
    first kings **9**:1220, 1232–1233, *1234*
    foundation myths **4**:446; **6**:835; **9**:1231–1232, *1233*, 1242–*1244*
    invasion of the British Isles **4**:438–439
    Latin League **9**:1234

Sabines, attack on Rome **6**:772
Sabine women, rape of the **9**:1232
Salamis, Battle of **1**:53; **7**:976
Sargon **7**:870–871
Sassanian Empire **6**:744, *745*, 746
Scandinavia **9**:**1259–1266**
    introduction of Christianity **9**:1264-1265
    settlement of **9**:1259-1260
Sparta, League of **8**:1053
Stonehenge **9**:*1162*

Thebes (Greece)
    founding of **2**:149, 251–253; **3**:426
Tiwanaku civilization **6**:726–727
Trojan War, historical basis for **5**:595
Troy **1**:28
    excavation of **1**:49
Tutankhamen **1**:110–111; **2**:190, *244*; **4**:*460*; *467*; **9**:1194, 1210

Woolley, Leonard **4**:*524*

INDEX OF WORSHIP AND RITUAL

Page numbers in **bold** refer to main articles; those in *italics* refer to pictures.

afterlife **3**:370–371
  Celts, druids, and **3**:375; **4**:439
  Egypt **1**:74, 109–110; **3**:*371*, 372–373, *375*; **4**:552; **5**:608; **7**:979, 996; **9**:1194
  fertility and **4**:507–508
  Germanic peoples and **3**:377
  Greeks and **3**:369, *370*, *372*; **5**:606, 607–608; **7**:888–889, *890*, 991; **9**:1214; **10**:1310
  Incas and **6**:728
  Indian **5**:608; **7**:913
  Indus Valley civilization and **6**:732
  Koreans and **6**:793
  Mesopotamians and **3**:370–371
  Native Americans **9**:*1218*
  Norse beliefs **3**:377; **7**:993; **9**:1264
  Romans and the Last Judgment **3**:420
  Southeast Asia **10**:1329
  Turks, Mongols, and the **3**:299
  for warriors **3**:377
  Zoroastrianism and **6**:748–749
Agonium festival **6**:774
All Worlds, Church of **8**:1073
ancestor worship **1**:**69–74**; **10**:1328–1329
  animism and **1**:69, 101
animal worship **1**:**92–99**
animism **1**:**100–105**; **3**:380
  Aborigines and **2**:194
  and ancestor worship **1**:69, 101
  Arabs and **1**:137
  Koreans and **6**:792
  polytheism and **8**:1135–1136

Anna Perenna feast **7**:968
Aphrodisiac festival **4**:514
Armilustrium, festival of the **6**:839
asvamedha **9**:1248
augurs **9**:1175

Bacchanalia (Bacchic Mysteries; *orgia*) **2**:217; **3**:385, 418; **4**:516; **7**:931
baptism **9**:1223–1224, *1225*
Beltane, festival of **4**:513; **6**:758
blood **2**:**235–239**
  bloodletting
    Maya and **6**:846; **8**:1049; **9**:1174–1175
    Olmecs and **8**:1049
  drinking **2**:239
    of dragons' **1**:85, *87*
    vampires and **2**:238; **3**:371
Buddhism **7**:909; **8**:1135
  animal-headed deities **1**:79–80
  festivals **4**:517
  Japanese, demons (*oni*) **3**:*406*
  Mara (evil demon) and **3**:402, *404*
  and nature **7**:*957*
  reincarnation and rebirth of the soul **3**:374–375, *376*; **9**:*1212*
  in Southeast Asia **10**:1322–1323
  Tibetan
    the Dalai Lama **9**:1174, 1212
    the Panchen Lama **3**:375
  Wheel of Life **3**:*404*; **9**:*1212*
burial
  in caves **3**:381
  Celtic **3**:*368*; **6**:861–862
  Chinese **3**:300–*302*
  Egyptian **5**:707
  Greek **3**:*369*; **5**:592
  Neanderthal **3**:381; **4**:454; **9**:*1156*, 1157–1158

  in Neolithic societies **9**:1162, 1163
  in Sulawesi **10**:*1329*
  Viking **3**:*377*

cannibalism, Greeks and **6**:824–826
Capac Raimi festival **6**:729
Carneia festival **9**:1275
Catholicism, the Mass as a sacrifice **9**:1249
ceremonies *see* rituals and ceremonies
Chacs **9**:*1175*
Charitesea festival **5**:585
Christianity
  in Africa **1**:39
  and the afterlife **3**:377
  animal-headed figures **1**:81
  and the apocalypse **1**:120–121
  Bacchus and **2**:219
  baptism **9**:1223–1224, *1225*
  born-again believers **9**:1217–1218
  and the Celts **2**:285–286
  confirmation ceremony **9**:1224
  and the decline of mystery cults **7**:933
    Mithraism **7**:897–898
  and the druids **4**:439
  Easter **3**:347; **4**:513
  in Ireland **6**:751–752, *759*
  a monotheistic religion **7**:905–*907*, 908, 910
  and Native Americans **5**:590
  in Polynesia **8**:1017–1018
  priests **9**:1172
  the resurrection of Christ **9**:1212
  in the Roman Empire **8**:1070, 1071
  saints **8**:1135

  in Scandinavia **2**:*222*–223; **9**:*1264*–1265; **10**:*1360*, 1364
  see also Catholicism
Christmas **4**:*516*; **7**:933
  Chrismas trees **4**:559
churching of women **9**:1223
circumcision **9**:1224
Compitalia festival **6**:808, 810
confirmation ceremony **9**:1224
Confucianism
  Five Classics **3**:305
  in Korea **6**:*791*
  in Southeast Asia **10**:1323
Consualia festival **4**:516; **9**:1205
Coptic sect **9**:1224
Corybantis **9**:1237
cosmogenic myths *see* creation myths
couvade **9**:1222–1223
creation myths **3**:**314–323**, 403–404; **4**:523–524
  of the Aborigines **2**:194, 196–197
  African **1**:40–41, 46; **3**:314–316, 319, 323
  Aztec **2**:206; **3**:322; **10**:1430
  Babylonian **3**:316–317, 403, 421–422; **5**:695; **6**:830, 833; **10**:1368–1370
  blood and **2**:235
  Central Asian **3**:297
  Chinese **3**:302–303, *314*, 319, 428; **4**:570
  dragons in **3**:421–422
  Egyptian **1**:94–95; **2**:188–189, 191; **4**:465, 501–502, 550, *551*; **6**:832; **7**:994; **9**:1192–1193
  fertilizing myths **4**:501–502
  Greek **3**:*397*, 398; **4**:501, *521*, 541–542; **8**:1020; **10**:1429–1430
  Hinduism and **3**:316, *319*, 320; **6**:736; **9**:*1268*
  Inca **3**:322; **4**:523; **6**:729

creation myths (continued)
Japanese **3**:317–318;
9:1267–1268
Maori **3**:319, 320;
8:1014–1015
Mayan **3**:322; **6**:797, 799,
841–842; **7**:948–949; **9**:1268
Mesopotamian **4**:477–478,
480; **6**:832
Native American **3**:314, 321;
5:586–587, 589–590; **7**:939,
941; **10**:1313
Norse **2**:233, 234, 246,
249–*250*; **8**:1026–1027
Polynesian **3**:*320*, 323;
8:1013–1015, *1016*; **9**:1271
Siberian **3**:403–404
Slavic **10**:1318–1319
Southeast Asian
10:1326–*1327*
Sumerian **3**:318–319;
4:477–478
Vietnamese **4**:570
of the Yekuhana people
10:1315–1316
Zoroastrian **3**:314;
4:443–444; **6**:747, *749*
cremation **3**:368, 369
cults **8**:1137
bull
Apis cult in Memphis
9:1195
at Catalhüyük **9**:1162–1163
Minoan **3**:*327, 331*
mystery *see* mystery cults
cycles **3**:**344–351**

Day of the Dead **4**:*517*
death **3**:**368–377**
African myths **1**:46–47
and ancestor worship **1**:69–70
belief in a spirit or soul
3:369–370
boats and **7**:*991*
book of the dead **1**:*79, 111*;
2:**240–245**; **3**:373; **4**:*468*;
7:979; **9**:1195, *1207*
and Nut **7**:995, 996, *997*
cremation **3**:368, 369
deities of the dead **3**:*374*
festivities for the dead **4**:*517*
ghosts **3**:372, 373
in Polynesian mythology
8:1019
Gilgamesh's quest for
immortality **3**:371

Mayan death rituals **6**:*797*,
799–800, 844–847
see also sacrifice
mourners, wearing black
9:*1228*
mummification **1**:88,
109–110; **3**:369, *371*
Anubis and **1**:88, *109*; **3**:*375*
Native Americans and
dual death god **4**:447
the origin of death **3**:376
Sioux Ghost Keeping
Ceremony **7**:942
origins of death **3**:376
reincarnation *see* rebirth
rites of passage **9**:1228
Slavs and **10**:1321
suicide, Mayans and
6:844–845
see also afterlife; ancestor
worship; burial; sacrifice
Dionysia festival **3**:417, 418;
7:931
divination
in Arabia **1**:138
Celtic **1**:71
Etruscan **8**:1070–1071
in Greece **9**:1175–1176
in Mali, Dogon people
8:*1071*
Mesopotamian **1**:67–68
in Norse mythology, the
Norns **7**:993
in Rome **9**:1175
see also oracles
dualism **4**:**443–448**; **7**:*956*,
957–958
Arab religions and **1**:138

Easter Sunday **3**:347
eggs, in creation mythology
3:319–320
egunguns **3**:382
Eleusinian Mysteries **3**:385,
386, 388; **4**:506–507, 515;
7:931, 933; **9**:*1229*
Plutus and **8**:1132
Selene and **9**:1278
Eternal Source, Church of
the **8**:1073
etiological myths **9**:1180
euhemerism **3**:302

Feast of Fools (Quirinalia
festival) **9**:1205
Feraferia **8**:1073

festivals **4**:**511–518**
Baltic **2**:226
Celtic **2**:285; **4**:512–513
Chinese, New Year **2**:*257*
for the dead **4**:*517*
Egyptian, Sed **4**:*514*; **5**:708
Greek **4**:513–515
Adonia **5**:678
Aphrodisiac festival **4**:514
choruses at **2**:157–158
the Cronia **3**:337
Daidala **5**:652
for Dionysus **3**:417, 418;
5:669; **7**:931
for the Graces **5**:585
Halieia **5**:642
for Hephaestus **5**:649
Heraia (games for women)
5:657
Hyakinthia **3**:395
Isthmian games **8**:1144,
1149–1150
Lycosoura **6**:824
Olympic Games **4**:473, 475,
513, 514–515; **9**:1249;
10:*1437*, 1438
Oschophoria **7**:987
Panathenaea **4**:513–514;
10:1353, 1376
for Poseidon **8**:1144,
1149–1150
Pythian Games **1**:129;
3:*365*; **4**:514
Stepterion **1**:129
Thesmophoria **3**:386, 389;
5:585
see also Eleusinian Mysteries
Inca **6**:*729*
Irish **6**:757–759
Japanese **4**:517–*518*; **10**:1347
Mayan **4**:517
Phoenician **2**:271
Roman **4**:515–516
Agonium **6**:774
Anna Perenna **7**:968
Bacchanalia **4**:516; **7**:931
Compitalia **6**:808, 810
Consualia **4**:516; **9**:1205
Day of Slaves **10**:1420
Feriae Latinae **6**:787
Hilaria **2**:187
of Jupiter **6**:787
Larentalia **4**:516
of the Lares **6**:808, 810
Ludi Neptunales **7**:968
Ludi Romani **6**:787

Lupercalia **4**:*500*,
516
Matronalia **6**:782
Megalesia **9**:1237
Mercuralia **6**:861
military-season **6**:838–839
Neptunalia **7**:967, 968
Openconsivia **9**:1254
Parilia **4**:*515*
Quinquatrus **7**:884
Quirinalia **9**:1205
Robigalia **9**:1205
Rustic Vinalia **10**:1410
Saturnalia **4**:515, 516;
6:770–772; **9**:1254–*1255*
Terminalia **4**:*511*
Vestalia **10**:1412
Vulcanalia **4**:516
Slavic **10**:1320, 1321
flamens (flamines) **9**:1204–1205
future, telling the *see* divination

Ghost Keeping Ceremony
7:942
ghosts **3**:372, 373
in Polynesian mythology
8:1019
graves *see* death and the
afterlife, burial

Halloween **2**:285; **4**:512
Hanal Pixan **4**:517
heads, severed, Celtic cult
2:*281*
Hilaria festival **2**:187
Hinduism **6**:736–737
apocalypse myth **1**:127
and creation **3**:316, *319*, 320;
6:736; **9**:*1268*
deities **3**:382, *383*; **8**:1134,
1135, 1136
animal-headed **1**:*80*
dragons **3**:422
fertility symbols **4**:502
flood myth **4**:*522*, 523
Mahabharata **6**:737–738,
739
monotheism **7**:908
myth concerning the Pleiades
10:1340
polytheism **8**:1134, 1135
pre-Aryan influences **6**:737
the *Ramayana* **6**:738–739
rebirth of the soul **3**:374;
9:*1215*, 1216
serpents **3**:*319*; **9**:*1268*

in Southeast Asia **10**:1322
and the tulsi plant
8:1125–1126
universe **3**:*322*
and yoga **7**:*905*
Holy Trinity **7**:906; **8**:1140
Hyakinthia festival **3**:395

idolatry **1**:138
Imbolc (Oimelg) festival **4**:513;
6:758; **10**:1422
Inti Raimi festival **6**:*729*
Ished tree **2**:*190*
Islam
in Africa **1**:38–39
in Arabia **1**:*138*, 140
the black stone of Mecca
1:*139*
circumcision **9**:1224
monotheism **7**:905–*907*, 908,
909, 910
in Southeast Asia **10**:1323

Jainism **9**:1217
Jews *see* Judaism
Judaism
the afterlife **9**:1219
animal-headed figures **1**:81
circumcision **9**:1224
the devil/demons **3**:402
and monotheism **7**:905–907,
908, 910

Karma **6**:737
Koljada festival **10**:1320, 1321
Kupalo festival **10**:1320

Larentalia festival **4**:516; **9**:1205
Lughnasadh, festival of **4**:513;
6:758
Lupercalia festival **4**:*500*, 516
Lycosoura festival **6**:824

Maslenica festival **10**:1320
Mass, as a sacrifice **9**:1249
Matronalia festival **6**:782
Megalesia festival **9**:1237
Mercuralia festival **6**:861
metempsychosis *see* rebirth
Mithraism **6**:747; **7**:891–898,
933; **8**:*1070*; **9**:1238–1239
modalism **7**:906
monism **7**:957
monotheism **3**:380; **7**:905–910;
8:1133, 1135
and devils **3**:402

dualism as an element of
7:957–958
in Egypt **2**:190; **7**:907, *908*;
9:1210; **10**:*1343*
ethical and intellectual **7**:905
mummification **1**:88, *109*–110;
3:369, *371*
Anubis and **1**:88, *109*; **3**:*375*
mystery cults **7**:930–933;
8:1137
of Mithras (Mithraism) **7**:894,
895, 896–898, 933; **8**:*1070*;
9:1239
Orphism and the Orphic
Mysteries **4**:444; **7**:933,
1005; **8**:1061–1062; **9**:1214
and Villa of the Mysteries
7:*932, 933*
see also Eleusinian Mysteries;
rites of passage

nature religions **7**:953–958
see also animism
Neptunalia festival **7**:967, 968
Norse culture
sacrifice **1**:57
stave churches **2**:*222*

October Horse sacrifice **6**:839
Oimelg (Imbolc) festival **4**:513;
6:758; **10**:1422
omophagia **6**:827
Oneness, concept of **7**:906
Opeconsivia festival **9**:1254
Opening of the Mouth
ceremony **9**:1195
oracle bones **3**:302
oracles **7**:920; **9**:1176–1177;
10:1421
at Delphi (Pythian Sibyl)
1:128–129, *130*; **7**:924;
9:*1171*, 1177, *1291*,
1293–*1294*; **10**:1421
oracle of Dodona **8**:1126
oracle of Trophonius **7**:*902*
Temple of Amphiaurus **3**:*395*
see also Sibyl
orgia see Bacchanalia
ornithomancy **1**:138; **8**:1071
Orphism and the Orphic
Mysteries **4**:444; **7**:933,
1005; **8**:1061–1062; **9**:1214
Oschophoria festival **7**:987

paganism **8**:1070–1073
Pagan Way **8**:1073

palingenesis *see* rebirth
Panathenaea festival **4**:513–514;
10:1353, 1376
pantheism **3**:380
Parilia festival **4**:*515*
Perun's Day **10**:1320
phyllomancy **4**:442
polytheism **3**:380; **8**:1133–1140
and devils **3**:402–403,
404–406
supreme deity **8**:*1133*–1135
predetermination **7**:993
prehistoric religion
9:1156–1163
cave paintings **1**:92; **3**:*381*;
8:1075; **9**:1156, *1159*–1161
at Altamira **9**:*1158*, 1160
and the earth mother
4:454–455
Neanderthal burials **3**:381;
4:454; **9**:*1156*, 1157–1158
priests and priestesses
9:1171–1178
Aztec **2**:203–204, *239*;
9:*1173*
Egyptian **9**:*1177*–1178, 1195
Galli **2**:187; **9**:1237
in Greek myth **9**:*1174*
Mayan **9**:1173–*1175*
Roman **9**:1175, 1235
emperors as priests **9**:1172,
1236
flamens (flamines)
9:1204–1205
Galli **2**:187; **9**:1237
vestal virgins **9**:1176;
10:1412–1415, 1420–1421
virgin priestesses **10**:1421
vestal virgins **9**:1176;
10:1412–1415, 1420–1421
see also oracles; shamans
Pythian Sibyl *see* Sibyl, oracle
at Delphi

Quinquatrus festival **7**:884
Quirinalia festival (Feast of
Fools) **9**:1205

Radunica festival **10**:1320
rebirth (reincarnation;
transmigration of souls)
2:285; **3**:374–375, *376*;
9:1212–1219
Buddhism and **3**:374–375,
376; **9**:*1212*
Greeks and **10**:1313

Orphism **8**:1062; **9**:1214
Pythagorus/Pythagoreans
3:374; **7**:924, 931;
9:1214–1215, *1217*
Hinduism and **6**:737
Romans and **5**:608; **10**:1313
Reformed Druids of North
America **8**:1073
religion, evolution of? **7**:954,
956–957
resurrection **9**:1212, 1219
rites of passage **7**:930;
9:1222–1229
Aborigines, blood-drinking
2:239
Greek, and the Lares **6**:808
initiation of shamans **9**:1287,
1289
Masai **1**:*42*; **9**:*1223*, 1224
mystery cults **7**:930
Roman, before and after war
6:836–837
see also mystery cults
rituals and ceremonies
of the Aborigines **2**:*195*, 200,
201
blood-drinking **2**:239
African **1**:41–43
ancestor worship **1**:70–71, 72,
73
Babylonian, sexual ritual
6:763
of the Balts **2**:226
childbirth ritual **9**:1222–1223
Egyptian, for the dead **9**:1195
French, Return of the
Gleaners **7**:*917*
funerals **3**:371–372
Egyptian **1**:110; **4**:552
Slavic **10**:1321
Greek
for Adonis **1**:25
Bacchanalia (*orgia*) **2**:217;
3:385, 418
at Deucalion's grave **3**:399
sport as a religious ritual
9:1249
Thesmophoria festival
3:386, 389; **5**:585
weddings and marriage
rituals **5**:667–668, 672;
7:976; **10**:1416
see also Eleusinian Mysteries
Korean **6**:*791*
Native American **1**:86, 95;
7:*946*

rituals and ceremonies
(continued)
Blessing Way rites **7**:943
Sun Dance **5**:*586*, 587;
7:*910*
Roman
ritual of Fides **9**:1205
Ver Sacrum rite **6**:835–836
shamanic rituals **9**:1289–1290
Sumerian **4**:479; **5**:717–718
Umbrian **8**:1072
see also festivals; mystery cults;
rites of passage; sacrifice
Robigalia festival **9**:1205
Rusal'naia Week **10**:1320
Rustic Vinalia festival **10**:1410

sacrifice **2**:237–238;
9:1245–1252
to ancestors **2**:238
animal **1**:*94*; **9**:1246–1247
and cracked bones **9**:1249
donkeys **9**:1170
horses **9**:*1248*
Egyptians and **4**:469
foundation offerings
9:1251–1252
Greeks and **2**:*235*, 237; **3**:337;
9:1245–*1247*, 1249
in Greek mythology **2**:238
human sacrifice **3**:337
to Artemis **2**:159–160
to Zeus **6**:824–826
human **2**:237
in Africa **1**:47
Aztecs and **2**:204–206, *208*,
238–239; **3**:*385*; **9**:1200,
1249, *1251*; **10**:1347, 1384
Balts and **2**:227
Carthaginians and **2**:*271*
Celts and **2**:239, 281, *283*;
9:1249–1251
druids and **2**:239; **4**:439
Greeks and **3**:337
Incas and **6**:728

Indus Valley civilization
6:732
Lindow Man **9**:1252
Mayans and **6**:*797*,
799–800, 845–847;
9:1174–*1175*
Minoan **3**:331
Phoenicians and **2**:271
in Scandinavia **4**:529;
9:*1262*, 1264
Slavic **10**:1320
Tollund Man **9**:1262
Turks, Mongols, and **3**:299
Incas and **6**:728
in India **1**:94; **6**:737
myth **9**:1247
Norse **1**:57; **4**:532–533;
9:1264
in the Roman Empire **1**:*94*;
2:237; **9**:*1251*
to Mars **6**:834, *839*
self-sacrifice **9**:1251
St. Egorij Day **10**:1320
Saivism **8**:1134
samsara **3**:*376*
Saturnalia festival **4**:515, 516;
6:770–772; **9**:1254–*1255*
scapulimancy **3**:302
Sed festival **4**:*514*; **5**:708
Semik festival **10**:1321
shamans **3**:381–382;
9:1171–1172, *1274*,
1285–1290
in Africa **1**:*40*, 41–43, 45
and animals **1**:91
and the "otherworld" **3**:370
in Siberia **1**:*96*
the first shamans **1**:99
Turks, Mongols, and
3:294–*295*, 299
shawabtis (shabtis) **2**:244
Shinto
creation myth **3**:317–318
festivals **4**:517
supreme deity **3**:316

Sibyl **9:1291–1294**
oracle at Delphi (Pythian
Sibyl) **1**:128–129, *130*;
7:*924*; **9**:*1171*, 1177, *1291*,
1293–*1294*; **10**:1421
Persian **9**:1291–1292, *1293*
Sibyl of Cumae **1**:133;
9:1291, *1292*
Sikhism
and monotheism **7**:908
and reincarnation **9**:1217
Sitowa festival **6**:729
Sokchonje **6**:*791*
soul
belief in a **3**:369–370
Southeast Asian belief in
10:1328
transmigration of the *see*
rebirth
sparagmos **6**:827
Stepterion festival **1**:129
Strinennia festival **10**:1320
subordinationism **7**:906
suicide, Mayans and **6**:844–845
Sun Dance ritual **5**:*586*, 587;
7:*910*
Suovetaurilia ceremony
6:834

Tango-no-Sekku **4**:518
Taoism **3**:303
gods **3**:307–309
Taurobolium **2**:237; **9**:1218
temples
Anglo-Saxon **4**:561
Baltic **2**:226
Egyptian **4**:467–*469*; **5**:*704*;
9:1177–1178
Greek
on the Acropolis
2:175–*177*; **5**:596; **7**:975,
976
Temple of Amphiaurus
3:*395*
to Hera **5**:657

Mayan **6**:*797*, *800*, 843, 847
Phoenician **2**:*269*, *270*, 271
Roman, to Diana **3**:408, 410
Terminalia festival **4**:*511*
theosophy **9**:1217
Thesmophoria festival **3**:386,
389; **5**:585
totemism **1**:103–105
Aborigines and **1**:*92*;
2:194–*196*
totem animals **1**:103
Central Asian **3**:297, *298*
Trinity (Holy Trinity) **7**:906;
8:1140
Tubilustrium, festival of the
6:838

ushabtis **2**:*244*

Vaishnavism **8**:1134
Ver Sacrum ("Sacred Spring")
6:835–836; **8**:1071
Vestalia festival **10**:1412
vestal virgins **9**:*1176*;
10:1412–1415, 1420–1421
Viking Brotherhood **8**:1073
voodoo religion
evil devils **3**:404
souls **3**:370
Vulcanalia festival **4**:516

Wheel of Life, Buddhist **3**:*404*;
9:*1212*

Zoroastrianism **6**:744, 745–749
the afterlife **6**:748–749
creation myths **3**:314;
4:443–444; **6**:747, *749*;
9:1268
and dualism **4**:443–444
evil spirits **3**:402; **4**:443; **6**:747
monotheism **7**:908

COMPREHENSIVE INDEX

Page numbers in **bold** refer to main articles; those in *italics* refer to pictures.

Abaluyia people, and the first humans **3**:323
Abbate, Noccolò dell', painting of Eros and Psyche **4**:*490*
Abduction of Ganymede, The (Rubens) **4**:*549*
Abena **1**:42
Abildgaard, N.A., painting by **2**:*250*
Aborigines, Australian **2**:*192–201*
art **2**:*196, 198, 199*
ceremonies and rituals **2**:*195*, 200, 201
blood-drinking **2**:239
and the Dreamtime (Dreaming) **2**:194, 196–197
earth mother **4**:456
flood myths **4**:523
mythical tracks across the desert **2**:199, *201*
myths **2**:195
and constellations **2**:*200*; **8**:1055
creation **2**:194, 196–197
explaining songs, dances, and art **2**:200–201
of morality **2**:196, 197
and places **2**:198–199
variations in **2**:201
ownership of places **2**:199–200
religions **2**:193–194
animism **2**:194
totemism **1**:92; **2**:*194–196*
sacred places **2**:*193*, 195
Southern Pleiades (constellation) **10**:1340
spirits **2**:196–198, *199*
Abraham **7**:*906*, 907
Abu Simbel **9**:1192, *1194*
Abydos (Ibdju) **7**:982; **8**:1067–1068
Abzu **6**:830; **7**:868
Acantha **1**:105
Acastus **6**:779; **8**:1096

Acca Larentia **9**:1240
Achaeans **5**:593, 594–595; **10**:1311
Achaeus **3**:398
Achelous **1**:13; **5**:665
Achelous River **1**:13
Acheron **5**:606
Achilleid (Statius) **1**:19
Achilles **1**:**14–19**; **3**:390; **7**:1000; **9**:1181, 1186
and the Amazon queen **1**:*62*, 64
comparison with Aeneas **1**:30
death of Achilles **1**:18, 133; **5**:622; **6**:853; **7**:*928*, 1000; **8**:1088; **10**:1357
death of Hector **1**:*17–18*; **5**:*622–623*; **8**:1095; **9**:1166
death of Lycaon **9**:1166
death of Memnon **6**:853; **10**:1380–1381
death of the sons of Priam **9**:1164–*1166*
death of Troilus **9**:1166; **10**:1388
disguised as a girl **1**:14–15, 16; **3**:*412*; **10**:1357
dispute with Agamemnon **1**:17, 19; **2**:*169*, 174; **7**:*971*; **8**:1094–1095
education by Cheiron **1**:14, *16*; **8**:1097
friendship with Patroclus **1**:133; **5**:622, 623; **8**:1094, 1095; **10**:1357
immortal horses **1**:*18, 85, 86*; **5**:612
marriage to Helen **5**:638
and the Myrmidons **7**:*928*
shield **8**:1020, *1023*
Thetis and **1**:14, *15*, 17; **6**:853; **7**:1000; **10**:1356–*1357*
and the Trojan War **1**:15–16, 50; **6**:853
Achilles' heel **1**:19
Acis **3**:356, *357*; **4**:546
Acis and Galatea Hide from the Gaze of Polyphemus (Perrier) **3**:*357*

aconite plants **5**:607
acorns **4**:442
Acqua, Cesare Dell', *The Argonauts* **6**:*776*
Acrisius **3**:362, 363; **8**:1110, 1114; **10**:1436
Actaeon **1**:**20–21**
and Artemis (Diana) **1**:20, 21; **2**:*156*, 157, *158*; **3**:*409*
Acusilaus **8**:1032
Adam of Bremen **4**:529; **8**:1031; **10**:1364
Adam and Eve **4**:509
Adam, Nicolas Sebastien, statue of Prometheus **9**:*1182*
Aditi **6**:738
Admete **5**:687
Admetus **1**:*55*, 132; **4**:495; **5**:662
Adonia festival **5**:678
Adonis **1**:**22–25**
and Aphrodite (Venus) **1**:22–24, 25, 116; **7**:936; **10**:1409
birth **1**:22, 116; **7**:*929*
a Canaanite and Phoenician god **2**:268, 269–270, 271
death of **1**:116; **2**:150
and the seasons **5**:717
Adrasteia **3**:335; **7**:*959, 961*
Adroa **4**:447
Aeacus **5**:606, 654; **6**:806; **7**:*927–928*; **8**:1096
a judge in the underworld **7**:888
Aebutius, Publius **2**:217
Aed **6**:757
Aedon **5**:653
Aeetes **3**:426; **6**:*777*, 848
Aegeus **3**:327, 329; **9**:*1291*; **10**:*1351*, 1352, 1353
Aegina **5**:654; **7**:927
and Britomartis **2**:247, 248
Aegir (Hlér; Gymir) **1**:**26–27**; **9**:1269
and the apocalypse **1**:126
Aegisthus **1**:50; **2**:183; **3**:313; **8**:1050–*1051*; **10**:1349
Aegle **5**:681
Aello **5**:611, 614

aconite plants **5**:607
Aeneas **1**:**28–33**; **3**:390, 409; **6**:785, 861
death **1**:33
and Dido **1**:*31*, 32; **6**:785
and the foundation of Rome **9**:1232
Juno and **6**:780–781
and the Penates **8**:1101–*1102, 1103*
Romanization of **1**:28
ship caught in a storm **10**:*1314*
and the Trojan War **1**:28–30
in the underworld **1**:32; **9**:1292
wanderings with the Trojans **3**:313
and the Harpies **5**:612, *613*
Aeneas with King Evander and Pallas (da Cortona) **1**:*33*
Aeneas Silvius **9**:1220
Aeneas in the Underworld (Rubens) **1**:*32*
Aeneid (Virgil) **1**:32; **7**:*922*
Aeneas **1**:28; **5**:619; **6**:785, 861; **7**:*966*; **8**:1101–*1102*
the Furies **5**:613
the golden bough **3**:409
Hecate **5**:618, 619
Idomeneus **5**:714
Juno **7**:966
Jupiter and Juno **6**:780–781
Laocoon **6**:802
Latinus **4**:498
Neptune **7**:966
Troilus **10**:1388
Aeode **7**:900
Aeolians **5**:593
Aeolus **3**:398; **8**:1035–1036
Aerope **2**:183, 184
Aesacus **1**:91; **9**:1164
Aeschylus
Oresteia trilogy **3**:313; **4**:539; **8**:1052
Agamemnon **1**:51; **2**:274; **3**:313; **4**:539; **6**:742
Choephoroe (*The Libation Bearers*) **3**:313; **4**:539
Eumenides (*The Furies*) **3**:313; **4**:538, 539

Aeschylus (continued)
Prometheus Bound **7**:926; **8**:1023, 1135; **9**:1180
Seven Against Thebes, The **8**:1040
Aesculapius *see* Asclepius
Aesir **1**:34–37; **4**:531, 554
war with the Vanir **4**:531; **7**:988–989; **10**:1404–1405
Aesop **7**:904
Aether **3**:352
"Aethiopis" (poem) **1**:60; **6**:854
Aethlius **4**:473
Aethon **3**:398
Aethra **8**:1130; **10**:*1351*
Aetolus **4**:473, 475
Africa **1**:38–47
ancestor worship **1**:70, 73–74
Ashanti people **1**:42, 46–47
sky god **3**:383; **10**:1310
belief in rebirth **9**:1212
creation myths **1**:40–41; **3**:314–316, 319, 323
death and the afterlife **1**:46–47; **3**:376
Fan people **1**:45, 47
flood myths **4**:522
Khoikhoi people **1**:45
Kikuyu people **1**:44; **8**:1126; **10**:1426
Luba people, and the moon **7**:913
Lunda people, the sun and the moon **7**:913
monotheism **7**:909
San people, myths **1**:40–*41*; **7**:911–912
Sbeitla **7**:*881*
Ubangui people **1**:45
Yoruba people **1**:41, *44–45*
ancestor-worship **1**:*69*
Zulu people **1**:45
afterlife **3**:370–371
Celts, druids and **3**:375; **4**:439
Egypt **1**:74, 109–110; **3**:*371*, 372–373, *375*; **4**:552; **5**:608; **7**:979, 996; **9**:1194
fertility and **4**:507–508
Germanic peoples and **3**:377
Greeks and **3**:369, *370, 372*; **5**:606, 607–608; **7**:888–889, *890*, 991; **9**:1214; **10**:1310
Incas and **6**:728
Indian **5**:608; **7**:913
Indus Valley civilization and **6**:732

Koreans and **6**:793
Mesopotamians and **3**:370–371
Native Americans **9**:*1218*
Norse beliefs **3**:377; **7**:993; **9**:1264
Romans and the Last Judgment **3**:420
Southeast Asia **10**:1329
Turks, Mongols, and the **3**:299
for warriors **3**:377
Zoroastrianism and **6**:748–749
Agade *see* Akkad
Agamemnon **1**:48–51; **6**:855–856
and Artemis **1**:49; **2**:159, 160; **6**:740
and Ate **2**:*169*
and Cassandra **1**:50; **2**:273–274; **3**:313; **4**:470; **6**:742; **8**:1051; **10**:1418
in literature **1**:51
Mask of **1**:*48*, 49
murdered by Clytemnestra and Aegisthus **1**:50, *51*; **2**:185, 273–274; **3**:*313*; **4**:470; **5**:634
sacrifice of Iphigeneia **1**:16, 49; **2**:159, 160; **3**:312, 408; **4**:470; **6**:740, 856; **8**:1050, 1087
and the Trojan War **1**:49–50; **7**:920
abduction of Chryseis **9**:1174
dispute with Achilles **1**:17, 19; **2**:*169*, 174; **7**:*971*; **8**:1094–1095
Agamemnon (Aeschylus) **1**:51; **2**:274; **3**:313; **4**:539; **6**:742, 855; **7**:960
Aganippe **1**:105
Agas **3**:402
Agave (Aguae) **2**:216, 253; **3**:417
Agdistis **2**:186; **9**:1237
Agenor **1**:76; **2**:251; **8**:1113
Agharti **1**:127
Aglaea **5**:582, 584
Aglaurus **2**:150; **4**:486, *487*
Agni **3**:382, 403; **6**:735, 738; **10**:1340
Agonium festival **6**:774
Ahau-Kin **9**:1211

Ah Ciliz **6**:845
Ah Cuxtal **6**:845
Ahmose **9**:1210
Ah Peku **6**:845
Ah Puch **6**:845
Ahriman *see* Angra Mainyu
Ahura **4**:443
Ahura Mazda (Ormazd) **3**:314, *402*; **4**:443, *444*; **6**:*744*, 746–747, *748*, 749
Ai **3**:296
Aiantis **1**:53
Aidos **7**:959, 961
Aiguptiaka (Apion) **1**:84
Aina-momomaakane **9**:1272
Ainu **1**:94; **3**:381
Aithalides **9**:1214–1215
Ajax **1**:52–54
Ajax of Locris (Little Ajax; Lesser Ajax; Locrian Ajax) **1**:*52*, 53–54; **2**:174, 273, 274
Telamonian Ajax (Great Ajax) **1**:52, *53, 54*
Ajax (Sophocles) **1**:53
Ajax by the Sea (Sabatelli) **1**:*52*
Akhenaten *see* Amenhotep IV
Akhetaton **10**:1343
Akkad (Agade) **7**:870
Akkadian Empire **7**:870–871
Alacahüyük, Sphinx Gate **5**:*696*
Alaghom Naom **6**:845
Alalus **5**:693
Alaska, Tlingit people **9**:1274
Ala Tala **10**:1323, 1326, 1328
Alba Longa **8**:1102
Al-Basti (Red Mother) **3**:297
Alberich **7**:*972*, 974
Alberti, Leon Battista, *Momus* **7**:904
Alcestis **1**:55–56, 132; **4**:495; **5**:662
Alcestis (Euripides) **1**:55, 56
Alcibiades **5**:672
Alcinous **8**:1038
Alcmene **3**:394; **5**:654, 659, 709; **10**:1436
Alcyone **8**:1131
Alcyoneus **4**:566, 568
Alecto **4**:540
Alectryon **1**:114
Alexander the Great
and Achilles **1**:19
and the Amazons **1**:64–65
and Oceanus **8**:1023

sacrifice to Phobos **8**:1122
and Zoroastrianism **6**:746
Alexikakos **1**:130
Alf **10**:1300
Alfar **1**:57–59
Alfheim **1**:57
Algardi, Alessandro, *Titan* **10**:*1373*
Alignak **9**:1271
Al-Karisi (Red Woman) **3**:297
Allah **7**:909
Allat **7**:*909*
Allca Cuna (Virgins of the Sun) **6**:*731*
Allegory of Divine Providence (de Cortona) **9**:*1253*
Allegory of Earth (Brueghel the Younger) **4**:*504*
Allegory of Spring (Botticelli) **5**:*582*
Allori, Alessandro
paintings by
of Circe **3**:*311*
of Odysseus and Polyphemus **3**:354, *355*
of Odysseus and Tiresias **8**:*1036*
All Worlds, Church of **8**:1073
Almaqah **1**:137
Alma-Tadema, Lawrence, *Bacchanal* **2**:*219*
alphabets
Etruscan **2**:253
Greek **2**:212–213, 253; **7**:926
Phoenician **2**:213
Roman **2**:253
Alpheus **7**:1002; **10**:*1420*
Altamira, cave paintings **9**:*1158*, 1160
Althaea **2**:168; **4**:495
Alvíssmal **10**:1358
Amairgen **1**:105
Amaltheia **1**:105; **3**:326, 335, *338*; **10**:*1433*
Ama no Uzume **10**:1345–1346
Amaterasu **3**:316; **4**:446; **10**:1345–*1346*, 1347
Ise-Jingu shrine **10**:*1347*
Amatoriae Narrationes (Plutarch) **4**:539
Amazons **1**:60–65; **2**:231; **8**:1122
Heracles and **1**:62; **5**:662, 687
Theseus and **1**:62–63; **5**:*687–688*; **8**:*1122*; **10**:*1354*

Amazons and Her Children, The (Leutze) **1**:*61*
Amei Awi **10**:1326
Amemait **1**:*111*
Amenhotep II **10**:1332
Amenhotep III (Amenophis III) **6**:853–*854*
Amenhotep IV (Akhenaten; Akhenaton) **4**:514; **5**:610; **10**:1332
  and monotheism **2**:190; **7**:*907, 908*; **9**:1210; **10**:*1343*
Amenti **3**:373
Ameretat **1**:102; **6**:747, 748
Amesa Spentas **3**:402; **6**:747
Amida Buddha **7**:909
Amma **1**:40
Ammannati, Bartolommeo, sculptures by **6**:*813*; **7**:967; **8**:1150
Am-mut **5**:608
Amorgen **6**:757
Amorites **7**:871
Amotken **3**:314
Amphiaraus **3**:394, *395*
Amphictyon **3**:398
Amphinomus **8**:1104
Amphion **7**:985
Amphitrite **7**:965, 970; **8**:1144, *1148*
  and Theseus **10**:1352
Amphitryon **5**:654, 709
Amulius **6**:835; **9**:*1221*, 1231–1232, 1240, 1241–1242; **10**:1414–1415
Amun (Amen; Amun-Re; Re-Amun) **2**:190; **4**:463, 466; **6**:788; **7**:994; **9**:*1172*, 1206, 1209; **10**:1342
Amycus **6**:777
Amyklas **7**:986
An **1**:*66–68*; **3**:318; **4**:476, 480; **7**:870, *872*
  see also Anu
Anahita **6**:*747*
Anahuac (Tylor) **7**:954
Anansi **1**:42
Ananta **3**:*319*
Anat **2**:164, 166, 212, 267, 268; **8**:1056
  and Baal **2**:166, 213, 215, 268
Anatolia
  Hittites **5**:**691–700**; **10**:*1344*
  mother goddess **3**:380
Anatolians **5**:593
  mother goddess **3**:380

Anaxarete, Iphis and **8**:1141–1142
ancestor worship **1**:**69–74**; **10**:1328–1329
  animism and **1**:101
Anchises **1**:28, *30*, 31, 32; **2**:158
Anchurus **7**:879
Ancus Marcius **9**:1233
Andaman Islands, Moon Man **3**:347–348
Androcles **1**:*84–85*
Androgeos **7**:887; **8**:1092
Andromache **5**:621
Andromeda **1**:*75–76*; **7**:*970*
  Perseus and **1**:*75–76*; **3**:424–425, *429*; **5**:581; **8**:*1110, 1112*–1113, *1147*
Andromeda Chained to the Rocks by the Nereids (Chassériau) **7**:*970*
Andvari **10**:1303
Anemoi **1**:**77**
Anfs **1**:140
Angatch **1**:46
angatra **1**:74
angkors **10**:1322
Angkor Thom **10**:1322, *1324*
Angkor Wat **10**:*1322*, 1324
  effigy of Yama **9**:*1216*
Anglesey, Roman invasions of **4**:438, 439
Anglo-Saxons **4**:558
  Beowulf legend **3**:425; **4**:561–562; **10**:1425
  and Easter **4**:513
  temples **4**:561
Angra Mainyu (Ahriman) **3**:*402*; **4**:443, *444*; **6**:746–747, 748, 749
Angrboda **6**:818; **10**:1404
animal-headed figures **1**:**78–83**
  Australian Aboriginal **1**:81
  Buddhist **1**:79–80
  Egyptian **1**:78–*79*, *83*; **4**:*465, 466*; **5**:*702, 708*; **10**:*1393*
  Greek *see* Minotaur
  Hindu **1**:*80–81*
  Judeo-Christian **1**:81
  Mesopotamian **1**:79
  Animal Mothers **1**:87
animals **1**:**84–91**
  attitudes toward **1**:85–86
  in Celtic mythology **2**:286
  communication with humans **1**:84–85
  and death **1**:*88*

earth mother as **4**:456
and the flood **4**:520
as guides **3**:410
as healers **1**:86–87
hunters and **3**:*381*, 409–410; **7**:*943, 944*
imaginary **1**:87–88
  dragons **3**:**421–430**
  griffins **1**:88, *90*
  phoenix **1**:88
  unicorns **1**:88, *91*
mythic hybrids **1**:89
  human-headed animal figures **1**:81–83
totem **1**:103
  Central Asian **3**:*297, 298*
transformations **1**:89–91, 104
animal worship **1**:**92–99**
animism **1**:**100–105**; **3**:380
  Aborigines and **2**:194
  and ancestor worship **1**:69
  Arabs and **1**:137
  Koreans and **6**:792
  polytheism and **8**:1135–1136
Ankhs **2**:*188*
Annales Maximi **9**:1234
Anna Perenna feast **7**:968
Annunaki (Igigi), the **1**:67; **7**:877
Anouilh, Jean, *Antigone* **1**:107
Anshar **10**:1369
Antaeus **4**:568; **5**:*661*, 663; **8**:1144–1146
Anteia (Stheneboea) **2**:230, 232
Antenor **10**:1388
Antero Vipunen **4**:566
Anthas **8**:*1130*, 1131
Antheia **5**:582
Anticlia **10**:1307
Anticlus **8**:1034
Antigone (daughter of Eurytion) **7**:928; **8**:1096
Antigone (daughter of Oedipus) **1**:**106–107**; **8**:1042, *1045*
Antigone (Anouilh) **1**:107
Antigone (Mendelssohn) **1**:106
Antigone (Sophocles) **1**:106–107
Antinous **8**:1104
Antiochus I **7**:893
Antiochus III **9**:1175
Antiope **1**:62–63; **5**:*687*, 688; **8**:*1122*; **10**:1354
Antoninus Liberalis **8**:1093
Antum **1**:67

Anu **5**:693, 696; **10**:1398
  see also An
Anubis **1**:78, **108–111**; **4**:466; **8**:*1065*
  a guide for the dead **5**:703
  a judge of the dead **1**:*111*; **5**:608
  and mummification **1**:88, *109*; **3**:*375*
  representations of **1**:*88*, 109
Anukis **7**:981
Ao **8**:1013
Aoede **7**:924
Aphaea (Aphaia) **2**:247, *248*
Aphrodisiac festival **4**:514
Aphrodisias **9**:*1179*
Aphrodite **1**:**112–119**; **2**:148; **5**:*656*
  and Adonis **1**:22–*24*, 25, 116; **7**:936
  and Aeneas **1**:28
  and Ares **1**:*114*; **2**:150–151; **5**:643, 646–648; **8**:*1121*
  children **1**:116
  birth **1**:*112*; **10**:1397, *1409*
  and brides **5**:667
  creation **3**:318, 334
  and the Graces **5**:*582*
  and Helios **5**:643
  and Hermes **5**:666
  and Hippolytus **1**:116; **10**:1354
  love affair with Zeus **5**:655
  mother of Eros **4**:488, *491*
  and Myrrha **7**:929
  and Pasiphae **8**:1091
  and Poseidon's "courtship" tidal wave **7**:951
  and Priapus **9**:1168
  and Psyche **4**:491
  and Pygmalion **1**:115; **9**:*1197*, 1198
  rescues Paris **2**:236; **6**:857
  Roman equivalent *see* Venus
  squeaking sandal **7**:*904*
  symbols of **1**:115
  wife of Hephaestus **1**:113–*114*; **5**:643, 646–648; **7**:951
  and the women of Lemnos **1**:117–118
  worship of **1**:119
  see also Paris, Judgment of
Aphrodite of Melos (Venus de Milo) **1**:*117*

Apion, *Aiguptiaka* **1**:84
Apis (Hapi; Hepu) **1**:93; **5**:610
  Ptah and **9**:1195
apocalypse myths **1**:**120–127**
  Aztec **2**:209
  Celtic **1**:*125–126*
  Germanic **1**:127
  Greek **1**:123
  Iranian **1**:127
  Maori **1**:*123*, 125
  Mayan **1**:122
  Mother Shipton and **1**:124
  Native American **1**:123–124
  Norse *see* Ragnarok
  Virgin Mary and **1**:*124*
Apocatequil **6**:727
Apollo **1**:**128–135**; **9**:1231
  adopted by the Romans
    8:1136; **9**:*1239*
  Apollo Grannus **2**:279
  Apollo Medicus **1**:133
  Apollo Mithras **6**:746
  battle against Python **1**:128,
    129, *131*; **3**:422–424
  birth **1**:128; **2**:157; **6**:815
  Clytie and **7**:1002
  conspiracy against Zeus **1**:131
  and Coronis **1**:134; **2**:161
  cult of **1**:129, 133;
    9:1235–1236
  curse on Cassandra **1**:133;
    2:272
  and the Cyclopes **3**:352–354
  and Cyparissus **1**:134
  and Cyrene **1**:134; **7**:1001
  and Daphne **1**:104, *105, 132*,
    133; **3**:341, 365, *367*;
    7:1002; **8**:*1124–1125*;
    10:1417
    Eros's intervention **4**:489
  and Delphi **1**:128–129;
    8:1136
  and Dryope **1**:134
  and Evadne **1**:134
  god of music **1**:130–131
  god of order **1**:131
  and Hyacinthus **1**:133–134;
    7:936
  and Laomedon **6**:805–806
  and Leto **6**:815–816
  link with the sun **5**:*600, 643*;
    10:1344
  and the Muses **7**:925
  musical contests **1**:132;
    7:878–*879*, 923; **8**:1078;
    9:1257

names for **1**:129–130
Phoebus Apollo **1**:129;
  10:1344, 1396
punished by Zeus **1**:132
and the Sibyl of Cumae
  1:133
and Sinope **1**:133
slaughter of Niobe's children
  2:160; **7**:985, *986*
and Thalia **1**:134
tricked by Hermes
  5:672–*673*
and the Trojan War
  1:132–133; **5**:622
worshiped in different places
  8:*1136*
Apollo Belvedere **1**:*129*
Apollo and Daphne (Bernini)
  1:*132*
Apollo and Daphne (Tiepolo)
  3:*367*
Apollo and Daphne (Zuccari)
  1:*105*
Apollodorus **2**:251
  and Agamemnon **1**:51
  and Hephaestus **5**:646
  and Hermes **5**:673, 674
  and Hippolyte **5**:687–688
  and Idomeneus **5**:714
  The Library **2**:251
  and Menelaus **6**:855, 856
  and Niobe's children **7**:986
  and Penelope **8**:1104
  and Philoctetes **8**:1120
  and Typhon **10**:1393
Apollonius, *Argonautica* **8**:1069
Apollonius of Tyana **7**:902
Apollo Program **1**:*134*
*Apollo a Victor, Sitting on the
  Dragon* (Schütz) **1**:*131*
Apophis (Apop) **2**:189, *190*;
  4:552
  killed by the sun god **2**:244;
    5:695; **9**:1208, *1209*, 1282,
    1283; **10**:1341
Apoyan Tachi **4**:447
apples, and ancestor worship
  1:*70, 71*
Appu **5**:696
Apsu **3**:403; **7**:868; **10**:1368,
  1369
Apsyrtus **6**:848–849
Apuleius, Lucius, *Metamorphoses
  (The Golden Ass)* **3**:341;
  4:490; **6**:769; **7**:931; **9**:1178,
  1187

Apulu **8**:1072
Aqhat **8**:1056
Arabia **1**:**136–140**
  animism **1**:137–138
  deities **1**:137
  early cultures **1**:136–137
  Islam **1**:*138*, 140
Arachne **1**:91, 104, **141–142**;
  2:171
Ara and Irik **10**:1325, 1326
Aramaeans **7**:872–873
Ara Pacis Augustae **8**:*1103*
Araucanians **7**:915
Arcadia **4**:441
  and Pan **8**:1074, 1078
Arcas **2**:158, 262–263;
  5:653–654; **6**:824, 826;
  7:1001
  and Chrysopelia **4**:441
Archelaus **7**:923
Arctinus **6**:803
Ardashir I **4**:*444*
Areion **8**:1144
Aremata-Popoa (Short Wave)
  9:1274
Aremata-Rorua (Long Wave)
  9:1274
Ares **2**:**148–153**; **5**:651
  and Aphrodite **1**:*114*;
    2:150–151; **5**:643, 646–648;
    8:*1121*
  children **1**:116; **2**:*151*;
    8:1121–1122
  a death god **8**:1121
  involvement in the Trojan
    War **2**:151–152; **3**:411;
    5:615, 655; **8**:1069
  Roman equivalent *see* Mars
  trial on the Areopagus **2**:153
Ares Borghese (sculpture)
  2:*150*
Ares Ludovisi (sculpture) **2**:*148*
Arethusa **1**:*105*; **7**:*1000*, 1002;
  10:*1420*
Arges **3**:352; **10**:1395, 1396
Argo (ship) **8**:1126
Argonautica (Apollonius)
  8:1069
Argonauts **6**:775–776
  see also Jason, voyage with the
    Argonauts
Argonauts, The (Dell 'Acqua)
  6:*776*
Argos **5**:652
  Hybristika festival **5**:669
  marriage ritual **5**:667

Argos (giant) **5**:653
Argus **6**:859; **10**:1435–1436
Ariadne **2**:**154–155**; **3**:329,
  358; **7**:888
  and Bacchus (Dionysus)
    2:*154*, 155, 218; **3**:*414*, 416;
    10:1353
  heroine status **3**:394
  and Theseus **2**:154–*155*;
    3:329, 358; **8**:1092;
    10:*1352*–1353
Arianrhod **10**:1421–1422
Aricia (modern Ariccia) **3**:408,
  409; **9**:1234
Arinna **5**:692, 693, 699;
  10:1343, *1344*
Arisbe **9**:1164
Aristaeus **7**:1001; **9**:1186
Ariston **1**:118
Aristophanes
  The Birds **7**:976
  Lysistrata **6**:743; **7**:902
  Plutus **8**:1132
  and priests **9**:1176
Aristotle, and Tyche **10**:1392
Arjuna **1**:18; **6**:738
arktoi **6**:743
Armageddon, Battle of **1**:121;
  5:632
Armfield, Matthew, illustration
  of Medea **6**:*851*
Armilustrium, festival of the
  6:839
Arming of Perseus, The (Burne-
  Jones) **8**:1114
Artemis **2**:**156–160**; **6**:780;
  7:914; **10**:1419–1420
  and Actaeon *see* Actaeon, and
    Artemis
  and Agamemnon **1**:49; **2**:159,
    160; **6**:740; **8**:1050
  and Bendis **8**:*1139*
  birth **2**:157; **6**:815
  and Britomartis **2**:247
  and Callisto **2**:262, *263*
  chorus of **2**:157–158
  Hera's battle against **5**:652
  and Hippolytus **1**:116–117
  and Iphigeneia **2**:159, 160;
    3:408
  and Leto **6**:815–816
  link with Isis **6**:768
  moon goddess **9**:1278
  and Orion **2**:157; **5**:690;
    8:1055
  Roman equivalent *see* Diana

slaughter of Niobe's children
2:160; 7:985, *986, 987*
temples to, *arktoi* 6:743
Artemis of the Crossroads
5:620
Arthur, *legendary king of Britain*
4:508–509; 10:1422
and Mordred 4:448
Art of Love, The (Ovid) 1:56;
3:341
Artume 4:447; 8:1072
Aruru 4:505
Aryans, in India 6:734–735
Aryong 6:795
Asa 1:40
Asag 7:983
Asclepius (Aesculapius)
2:161–162; 3:352–353;
8:*1069*; 10:1438
birth 1:134
death 1:131–132
a demigod 3:390, *392*
Hermes and 5:673–674
staff 1:86–87
temple of (Rome) 4:498
Asgard 8:1027
bridge to 1:*34*
Asgaya Gigagel 7:939
Ashanti people 1:42, 46–47
sky god 3:383; 10:1310
Asha Vahishta 1:102; 6:747, 748
Asherah 2:212, 213, 267, 268
see also Astarte
Ashnan 4:505
Ashratu *see* Astarte
Ashtar 2:166, 268
Ashtart *see* Astarte
Ashtoreth *see* Astarte
Ashtoroth *see* Astarte
ashuras 3:338
Ask and Embla 1:36;
6:818–820; 8:1027
Asops 10:1308
Asru 4:445
Assur 7:870, 874
Assyrians 7:873–875
Astarte (Ashtart; Astoret;
Ashtoroth; Ashtoreth;
Ashratu; Qadashu) 1:24;
2:163–166, 268
cults involving prostitution
5:718
see also Inanna; Tanit
Astart-in-the-name-of-Baal
2:166
asterims 10:1333

Asterius *see* Minotaur
Asterius, *king of Crete* 7:885
Astoret *see* Astarte
Astraeia 10:1334
Astraeus 10:1396
astrology 8:1137
Mesopotamian 1:68
Romans and 8:1123
see also zodiac
Astronomica (Hyginus) 9:1170
astronomy
Mesopotamian 1:68
see also planets; stars
Astyanax 5:623, 627; 9:1167
Astydameia 8:1096
Astymedusa 8:1043
asvamedha 9:1248
Aswapati 6:739
Asynjur, the 1:37
Atahensic 7:938, 939
Atalanta 2:167–168; 5:682
Atar 6:747
Atarrabi 4:446
Ate 2:169
Aten (Aton) 2:190; 4:466;
7:*907–908*; 10:*1312*, 1343
Athamas 5:654; 6:776
Atharva Veda 6:735
Athena (Pallas) 2:170–177;
3:378; 5:*656*; 10:1418, *1419*
Athena Ergane 7:881
Athena Nike 8:*1137*
Athena Parthenos 8:1083
Athena Promachos 7:881
and Bellerophon 2:231
birth 2:170–171; 3:*378*;
5:597; 10:1434–1435
contest with Arachne 1:91,
141; 2:171
creations of, judged by
Momos 7:904
and the defeat of Typhon
2:171; 10:1394
dress
aegis 1433
battle dress 2:171, *172, 174*
and Hephaestus 4:486; 5:649
involvement in the Trojan
War 2:151–152, 174; 5:623,
655; 10:1418
the Trojan Horse 2:174
and the Lesser Ajax 1:*52*, 54
and Medusa 8:1144
mother of Erichthonius
4:486; 5:649
and Nike 2:175, *177*; 7:975

patron of Athens and gift of
olive oil 2:*175*
and Poseidon 8:1148
Roman equivalent *see*
Minerva
statue in the Parthenon
7:975; 10:1376
and Tiresias 10:1371
worship of 2:175–177
see also Paris, Judgement of
Athens
Acropolis 2:175–177; 5:*596*;
7:975, *976*
the assembly 9:1173
Athena as patron of 2:*175*
City Dionysia festival 3:417,
418
democracy 5:597–598
and Deucalion's grave 3:399
founding of 5:596–597
Gaia and 4:544
laws of Solon 5:598
metics 4:488
Parthenon 2:175–176, *177*;
7:975
Roman Forum 1:77
and Sparta 5:598
Temple of Hephaestus 5:*649*;
9:1182; 10:1355
Temple of Olympian Zeus
10:*1438*
theater of Dionysus 3:*418*
Tower of Winds 1:77
worship of Athena
2:175–*177*; 5:596–*597*
Atius Tirawa 7:939
Atlantids 7:999
Atlantis 2:180–181; 3:328;
4:*523*, 524; 7:951
Amazons and 1:64
Atlas 2:178–181; 4:*564*; 5:581;
10:1374–1375
Heracles and 2:178–180;
5:663–665, 682
Perseus and 2:180; 8:1112
Pleiades and 8:1129
Atlas Mountains 2:*180*
Atli 10:1303, 1402, 1403
Aton *see* Aten
Atrahasis 4:479, 519
Atreus 1:48; 2:182–185; 6:855
House of 2:*183*; 6:855–856;
8:1050
Treasury of 2:*184*
Atropos 4:*493–497*; 5:598,
599; 8:1128

Attis 1:24; 2:186–187; 4:457,
509; 7:933
Atum 2:188–191; 4:466,
501–502; 10:1312, 1341
Atum-Re (Re-Atum) 2:188,
191
and the calendar 2:255
Audhumla (Audumla;
Audhumbla) 2:233, 246,
249–*250*; 4:568; 10:*1428*
Augeas 5:662
augurs 5:697; 9:1175
Augustus 4:438; 9:1237
and the *Aeneid* 1:32
and the Lares 6:810
as Pontifex Maximus 9:*1236*
and the Temple of Apollo
1:133
Auld Clootie (Auld Cloots)
3:404
Aurgelmir *see* Ymir
Aurora 4:485
Aurora (Fragonard) 4:485
Aurora (Reni) 4:485
aurora borealis 10:1400, *1403*
Aus 1:138
Ausautas 2:228
Auseklis 2:229
Ausrine 2:224–226, 228, 229
Australia 2:192–201
see also Aborigines, Australian
autochthons 3:336–337
Autolycus 8:1032; 10:1307
Automedon 1:*86*
Autonoe 2:253
Auxo 5:582
Auzon Casket 10:*1426*
Avalokitesvara 9:1174
Avaris 9:1284
Avernales 7:999
Avestas 6:746
Avya 4:447
Awitelin Tsta 4:447
Awonawilona 4:447;
5:589–590; 7:939
Axis Mundi 3:294
Azhi Dahaka 1:127; 6:747
Azizos 4:445
Aztecs 2:202–209
calendar 2:203
capital city (Tenochtitlán)
2:202, 203, *204*; 10:*1384*
codices and 2:*207*; 9:1203
Codex Magliabecchi 3:*385*
Codex Mendoza 9:*1173*
Vienna Codex 9:1202

Aztecs (continued)
creation myths **2**:206; **3**:322;
10:1430
the Five Suns (worlds or ages)
2:*209*; **10**:1382–1384
creation of the fifth world
10:1385
flood myth **2**:209
gods and goddesses **2**:203,
205, 206, 207–209; **3**:*348*
human sacrifice **2**:204–206,
208, 238–239; **3**:*385*;
9:1200, 1249, *1251*; **10**:1347
children **10**:1384
and the planet Venus **9**:1202
priests **2**:203–204, *239*;
9:*1173*

Baal **2**:**210–215**, 267–268;
10:1312–1313
death and resurrection **2**:268
identification with Jupiter
6:786, 788
and Lady Asherah of the Sea
2:164–166
Baalat **1**:25; **2**:268, 269
Temple of **2**:*269*
Baalbek **2**:*215*
Baal Hammon **2**:269
Baal-Peor **4**:446
Baba Yaga **10**:1318, *1321*
Babrius **8**:1081
Babylon **6**:833
calendar **2**:255–256
fall of **7**:876
Ishtar Gate **6**:*760*, 763, *829*;
7:*876*
sexual ritual **6**:763
Babylonia
calendars **2**:255–256
capital city *see* Babylon
creation myth **3**:316–317,
403, 421–422; **5**:695; **6**:830,
833; **10**:1368–1370
First Dynasty of Babylon
7:871–872
neo-Babylonian Empire
7:875–876
sexual ritual **6**:763
social structure **7**:872
Bacchae, The (Euripides) **6**:828
Bacchanal (Alma-Tadema)
2:*219*
Bacchanal Before a Temple
(Poussin) **4**:*512*
Bacchanalia (Bacchic

Mysteries; *orgia*) **2**:217;
3:385, 418; **4**:516; **7**:931
Bacchants (Bacchantes) **2**:216,
217; **7**:931
see also maenads
Bacchus **2**:**216–219**; **9**:1231
and Ariadne **2**:*154*, 155, 218;
3:*414*
Greek equivalent *see*
Dionysus
as one of the Penates **8**:1100
Bacchus (Michelangelo) **2**:*216*,
218
Bacchus and Ariadne (Titian)
3:*414*
Bacchylides **6**:803
Bada people **10**:1323
Badlands **7**:*953*
Balam Ak'ab **6**:842
Balam Quitze **6**:842
Balboa, Vasco Núñez de **6**:725
Balder **2**:**220–223**; **9**:1260
death **1**:18, 34–36;
2:220–*221*, 260; **4**:516,
535–536; **5**:633; **6**:822, *823*
funeral **7**:989
Hermód's attempt to release
from the underworld
5:*676–677*; **8**:1030
Balders Dod (Ewald) **4**:537
Bali
cremation of the dead **9**:*1215*
theatrical masks **10**:*1326*
Bali (demon) **6**:736
Balius **1**:14, *18*, 85, *86*; **5**:612
Balkans, ancestors' graves
reopened **10**:1321
Ballard, J.G., *Drowned World*
4:526
ball games
Mayan **6**:*847*
Olmec **8**:*1047*
Baltic, the **2**:**224–229**
Balts, the **2**:224–*229*
and the Baltic Sea **2**:227–228
festivals **2**:226
gods and goddesses
2:224–226, 228–229
human sacrifice **2**:227
religious beliefs **2**:226
religious leaders **2**:227
surviving traditions **2**:229
Banks, Thomas, *Halcyon
Discovers Ceyx* **7**:*919*
Banquet des Guédés, Le (Pierre)
3:*374*

banyan trees **8**:1126
baobab trees **8**:*1126*
baptism **9**:1223–1224, *1225*
Bara, the **1**:26
Barbari, Jacopo de', *Sacrifice to
Priapus* **9**:*1170*
Barbieri, Giovanni Francesco
(Il Guercino), painting of
Atlas **2**:*178*, 181
Bardo Thodol **3**:373
Barga, Pietro da, sculpture by
4:*447*
Barong **10**:1324, *1326*
Baron Samedi **3**:*374*
Bastet **1**:78; **4**:464, *465*, 466
Batara Guru **10**:1324, 1326
Batara Kala **10**:1324, 1326
Batoni, Pompeo Girolamo,
painting of Peleus and
Cheiron **8**:*1097*
Battle Ax people **10**:1367
Battling Titans (Platzer) **10**:*1377*
Baubo **4**:506
Baucis, Philemon and
6:785–786; **8**:1125
Baugi **4**:568–569, *570*;
8:1028–1029
Bear **1**:87
bears, remains of, in prehistoric
caves **9**:1158–1159
Beccafumi, Domenico,
Deucalion and Pyrrha **3**:*397*
Beckman, Max **8**:1084
Bedouin **1**:138
Beijing
Nine Dragon Wall **3**:*428*
Summer Palace **3**:*430*
Belarus, supreme being
10:1319
Belenus **2**:279
Beli **4**:527–529
Bell, Charles, *Judgment of Paris*
8:1089
Bellerophon **1**:62; **2**:**230–232**;
8:1112
Belleteste, Jean-Antoine,
statuette of Apollo and
Daphne **8**:*1125*
Bellini, Giovanni, *Feast of the
Gods* **9**:1170
Bellona (Duellona) **2**:*152*;
6:834; **7**:931
Belobog **10**:1318, 1319
Beltane, festival of **4**:513; **6**:758
Bendigeid Vran *see* Bran the
Blessed

Bendis **8**:*1139*
Benisson, Vittorio, painting of
the Terminalia festival **4**:*511*
Benu bird **2**:191; **4**:550
Benvenuti, Pietro, *Death of
Priam, The* **9**:*1167*
Beowulf **3**:425; **4**:561–562;
10:1425
Beowulf **4**:561–562
and Heremod **5**:676
and Sigurd **10**:1303
and Wayland **10**:1425
Bergelmir **2**:**233–234**
Berlioz, Hector, *Troyens, Les*
6:804
Bernini, Gian Lorenzo
Apollo and Daphne **1**:*132*
Flight from Troy, The **1**:*30*
Rape of Proserpina, The **5**:*603*
statue of Triton **10**:*1387*
Bes **4**:466
beserks **1**:104
Bestla **2**:246; **4**:568; **8**:1024;
10:1428
Betelgeuse **8**:1056
Bezalel **5**:711–712
bezoars **3**:294
"Bhagavad Gita" ("Song of the
Lord") **6**:738
Bia **7**:975
Bible
Adam and Eve **4**:509
apocalyptic visions and
Armageddon **1**:120–122;
5:632
Baal in **2**:214
creation of the world **9**:1193
earthquakes **7**:948
God **8**:1133, 1135
Jacob and Rachel **8**:1127
Joseph **2**:231
monotheism and **7**:907
Noah's ark **3**:399; **4**:520–521
serpents **5**:695
Bibliotheca historica (Diodorus
Siculis) **1**:64
Bifröst **1**:*34*, 126; **5**:*629*,
631–632; **10**:1313
Bil **10**:1405
Bilskírnir **10**:1358
Birds, The (Aristophanes) **7**:976
birth *see* childbirth
*Birth of Tragedy from the Spirit of
Music, The* (Nietzsche) **1**:134
Birth of Venus (Botticelli)
10:*1409*

bishopfish **9**:1274

Black Death, rats and **1**:86

Black Donald **3**:404

Black Emperor **10**:*1311*

Black Sea **3**:400

blacksmiths, in myth and legend **10**:1426–1427

Blaise, Saint **10**:*1317*

Blake, William
Cerberus **5**:*607*
Hecate **5**:*620*

Blessed, Isles of the **5**:608; **6**:783; **9**:1214

Blinding of Polyphemus, The (Allori) **3**:355

Blodughadda **1**:26

Blommer, Nils, *Freya Seeking Her Husband* **4**:*532*

blood **2**:235–239
bloodletting
the Maya and **6**:846; **8**:1049; **9**:1174–1175
Olmecs and **8**:1049
drinking **2**:239
of dragons **1**:85, *87*
vampires and **2**:238; **3**:371
see also sacrifice

Blue Men of the Muir **9**:1273

Boannd (Boand) **2**:279; **7**:966–967

boats
and death **7**:*991*
in Egyptian religion **4**:*463*
see also ships

Boccaccio, Giovanni **5**:*628*
Il filostrato **10**:*1390*
illustration of Oedipus **8**:*1044*
Teseida **5**:*688*

Böcklin, Arnold, painting of Triton and a Nereid **10**:*1386*

boddhisatvas **3**:373, 374–375

bogeymen **9**:1262

Bologna, Giovanni, statue of Mercury **6**:862

Bona Dea **4**:516

bones, of sacrificed animals, cracked **9**:1249

Boniface, Saint **9**:1265

Book of Caverns, The **2**:245

book of the dead **1**:*79*, *111*; **2**:240–245; **3**:373; **4**:*468*; **7**:*979*; **9**:1195, *1207*
and Nut **7**:995, 996, *997*

Book of Fixed Stars **8**:1056

Book of Gates, The **2**:245

Book of Going Forth by Day, The **2**:240, 242–244

"Book of the Takings, The" **6**:754

Book of What Is in the Underworld, The **2**:244

Booyan **9**:1271

Bopis Hera **5**:651

Bor **2**:246, 250; **4**:*568*; **8**:1024; **10**:1428

Bordone, Paris, painting by **2**:*149*

Boreas **4**:484; **7**:*948*; **8**:1075; **10**:1313, 1314

Borel, Antoine Rogat, painting of Thetis and Achilles **10**:*1357*

Borneo
creation myth **10**:1326–*1327*
myth about the moon **10**:1327

Bosio, François-Joseph, statue of Heracles and the Hydra **5**:*660*

Botticelli, Sandro
Allegory of Spring **5**:*582*
Birth of Venus **10**:*1409*
Judgment of Paris, The **8**:*1086*
Mars and Venus **6**:*836*

Boucolion **6**:805

bough, golden **3**:409

Boyajian, Zabelle C., illustration of Marduk and Tiamat **10**:*1368*

Boyhood Deeds of Cú Chulainn, The **9**:*1226*

Bragi **1**:36; **8**:1024

Brahma **3**:316, *318*, 320; **6**:735–736, *737*, 738; **10**:1326

Bran the Blessed (Bendigeid Vran) **2**:281

Brasidas **3**:395

Brekirihunuade **1**:40

Brentel, Friedrich, painting of Orpheus **8**:*1059*

Breo Saighead *see* Brigid

Bresal **6**:757

Briareos **4**:564; **10**:1395

Bride *see* Brigid

Bride of Frankenstein (film) **9**:*1184*

Brigid (Brighid; Brigindo; Brigantia; Bride; Breo Saighead) **6**:757; **10**:1422

Brigit **2**:279, 281

Briseis **1**:16, 17, 49–50; **8**:*1094*–1095

Brísingamen *see* Brising necklace

Brising necklace (Brísingamen) **4**:532, *533*; **10**:1366–1367

Britain, Roman invasion of **4**:438–439

Britomartis **2**:158, **247**–248; **10**:1419–1420

Brontes **3**:352; **10**:1395, 1396

bronze, used on Crete **3**:324

Bronze Age
Greek **5**:593
Scandinavian **9**:*1260*, 1261–1263

Bronzino, painting of Pygmalion **9**:*1197*

Brueghel the Elder, Jan, painting of Odysseus and Calypso **2**:265

Brueghel the Elder, Pieter, painting of Icarus **5**:712

Brueghel the Younger, Jan, *Allegory of Earth* **4**:*504*

Brunhild *see* Brynhild

Bruno, Giordano **9**:1217

Brynhild (Brunhild) **2**:169; **4**:562; **5**:677; **7**:*972*; **8**:1026, *1028*; **10**:1302, 1303, 1304, 1401–1402

Buddha (Gautama Buddha) **7**:909, 957; **9**:1216–1217; **10**:1327
Mara (evil demon) and **3**:402

Buddhism **7**:909; **8**:1135
animal-headed deities **1**:79–80
festivals **4**:517
Japanese, demons (*oni*) **3**:406
Mara (evil demon) and **3**:402, *404*
and nature **7**:*957*
reincarnation and rebirth of the soul **3**:374–375, *376*; **9**:*1212*
in Southeast Asia **10**:1322–1323
Tibetan
the Dalai Lama **9**:1174, 1212
the Panchen Lama **3**:375
Wheel of Life **3**:*404*; **9**:*1212*

Bull of Heaven **4**:571–572; **6**:762

Bundgaard, Anders, *Gefjon Fountain* **4**:*553*, 554

Burgundians **4**:557, *558*

Búri **2**:246, **249**–250; **4**:*568*; **10**:1428, 1429

burial
in caves **3**:381
Celtic **3**:*368*; **6**:861–862
Chinese **3**:300–*302*
Egyptian **5**:707
Greek **3**:369; **5**:592
Neanderthal **3**:381; **4**:454; **9**:*1156*, 1157–1158
in Neolithic societies **9**:1162, 1163
in Sulawesi **10**:*1329*
Viking **3**:*377*

Burkett, Walter, *Homo Necans* **9**:1245–1246

Burne-Jones, Edward
paintings
The Arming of Perseus **8**:1114
Danae and the Brazen Tower **3**:*362*
of the Hesperides **7**:*1004*
Pan and Psyche **8**:*1077*, 1078
of Perseus and the Graeae **8**:*1114*
tapestry of Pomona **8**:*1141*

Burung Une **10**:1326

Byblis **7**:1002

Byblos **1**:24–25; **9**:1281
temples **2**:*269*, 270, 271

Bylgia **1**:26

Byron, Lord, and Leander **5**:680

Cadmus (Kadmos) **1**:116; **2**:**251**–253
founding of Thebes **2**:149, 251–253; **3**:426

Caenis (Caeneus) **5**:669; **8**:1144

Caesar, Julius
calendar **2**:261
and the Celts **2**:280–281, 283
and the druids **4**:436–437

Caha-Paluma **6**:842

Cakixia **6**:842

Calais **5**:*612*; **6**:779

Calamis, statue of Poseidon **8**:*1145*, 1150

Calchas **1**:49; **5**:619; **6**:740; **8**:1118–1119; **10**:1388, 1390

calendars **2**:**254–261**
Aztec **2**:203
Babylonian **2**:255–256
Celtic **2**:258–259, 285; **3**:348
Chinese **2**:*254*, 256–*257*;
3:348
Egyptian **2**:254–255, *256*,
257
Greek **2**:260–261
Gregorian **2**:261
of India **2**:257–258
Julian **2**:*261*; **6**:770
Mayan **2**:*259–260*
Navajo **3**:350–351
Roman **2**:*260*, 261; **6**:770;
9:1233
Sumerian **4**:479
Calliani, Antonio, painting of
Hector and Achilles **1**:*18*
Callimachus
and Euthymus **3**:390
"Hymn to Artemis" **2**:157
and the Pleiades **8**:1130
Calliope **7**:921
Callisto **1**:21, 105; **2**:158,
262–263; **5**:653–654; **6**:826;
7:1001; **10**:1334
Calybe **6**:805
Calyce **4**:473
Calydonian boar hunt
2:*167–168*; **8**:*1096*, 1122
Calypso **2**:178, **264–265**; **7**:*999*
Camalotz **6**:842
Camaxtli **6**:845
Cambodia
Angkor Thom **10**:1322, *1324*
Angkor Wat **9**:*1216*; **10**:*1322*,
1324
merging of Hinduism and
Buddhism **10**:1323
myth concerning the
origin of **10**:1327
Camenae **7**:926
Camese **6**:770
Camilla **1**:63
Campbell, Joseph **6**:773
Campe **10**:1374
Camuccini, Vincenzo, painting
of Hecuba and Paris **5**:627
Camus, Albert, "Myth of
Sisyphus, The" **10**:1308
Canaan and Phoenicia
2:**266–271**
gods **2**:212, 266–271
human sacrifice in Phoenicia
2:271

Canens **6**:773
cannibalism, Greeks and
6:824–826
Canova, Antonio
sculptures
Cupid and Psyche **9**:*1190*
Daedalus and Icarus **5**:*711*
Hebe **5**:*615*
Herm of a Vestal Virgin
10:*1414*
statue of Theseus and the
Minotaur **10**:*1355*
Three Graces **5**:*585*
Capac Raimi festival **6**:729
Capitoline Triad **6**:780
Capitoline Venus **10**:*1408*
Caravaggio
painting of Narcissus **7**:*935*
Head of Medusa, The **5**:*580*
Carme (Karme) **2**:247
Carna **6**:773
Carnac **9**:*1160*, 1163
Carneia festival **9**:1275
Carpaccio, Vittore, painting of
Amazons **10**:*1354*
Carpeaux, Jean-Baptiste, statue
of Philoctetes **8**:1119
Carpioni, Giulio, *Realm of
Hypnos, The* **5**:*710*
Carracci, Annibale, painting of
Polyphemus and Galatea
4:*545*
Carthage
and Baal **2**:*214*
human sacrifice **2**:*271*
Caryatids **2**:176–177; **4**:440,
441
Cassandra **1**:133; **2**:**272–274**;
3:313
abduction of **1**:*50*; **2**:*174*,
273
death **2**:*274*; **3**:313; **4**:470;
6:742
and the Lesser Ajax **1**:54
and Paris **2**:272–273; **8**:1085
and the Trojan War **2**:*273*;
10:*1418*
Cassiopeia **1**:75, 76; **3**:424;
8:1112–1113, 1147
Cassoni Campana, Master of
the, painting of Pasiphae
8:*1091*
Castalla **1**:105
Castor and Pollux **2**:**275–276**;
4:445, *446*; **6**:811, 812–813;
9:1235

Catalhüyük (Catal Huyuk)
5:606; **9**:*1163*
bull cult **9**:1162–1163
earth-mother worship
4:455–456
Catalogues of Women (Hesiod)
8:1052
Catalogue of Heroines **6**:742
Catamitus **4**:548
Cathbad **6**:757
Catherwood, Frederick **6**:841
Catholicism, the Mass as a
sacrifice **9**:1249
Catullus, and the Muses **7**:923
Cavalori, Mirabello, painting of
Lavinia **1**:*29*
Cavattoni, Giovanni, engraving
of Cronus **10**:*1397*
caves **3**:380–381
paintings in **1**:*92*; **3**:*381*;
8:*1075*; **9**:*1156*, *1159*–1161
at Altamira **9**:*1158*, 1160
remains of prehistoric bears
9:1158–1159
Cecropian Artemis **7**:931
Cecrops **4**:486, 544; **5**:597;
9:1190
Celaeno **5**:611, 612, 613, 614;
8:1131
Celebes, and the origin of
death **3**:376
Celidon **5**:653
Celilo Falls **7**:937–938
Cellini, Benvenuto, statue of
Danae and Perseus **3**:*364*
Celts **2**:**277–286**
and the afterlife **3**:375
ancestor worship **1**:70–71
apocalypse myth **1**:*125*–126
Battle of Moytura **3**:338
calendar **2**:258–259, 285;
3:348
Christian influence on **2**:285
Cosmic Tree **3**:409
cult of the severed head
2:*281*
divination rituals **1**:71
festivals **2**:285; **4**:512–513
gods and goddesses
2:*278–280*; **6**:753, 861
Roman interpretation
2:280–281
graves **3**:368; **6**:861–862
Hallstatt culture **2**:277;
3:*368*
in Ireland **6**:751, 753

kings, and fertility of the land
4:510
language **2**:277
La Tène culture **2**:277–278
metalwork **2**:*277*
mythology, animals in **2**:*286*
the otherworld **2**:283, 284
sacrifice
horse **9**:1248
human **2**:239, 281, *283*;
9:1249–1251, *1252*
and the seasons **3**:348
virginity in mythology
10:1421–1423
see also druids
Cenchrias **7**:1002
cenotes **6**:845, *846*
centaurs **1**:*81*, 89
see also Cheiron
Centaurus **5**:584
Central Asia and the Steppes
3:**292–299**
Cephalonia, tomb of Odysseus?
8:1036
Cephalus **4**:483, *484*; **5**:675;
8:1093
Cephalus and Aurora (Poussin)
4:485
Cepheus **1**:75; **3**:424–425;
8:1112–1113, 1147
Cerberus **5**:*601*, 603, *607*, 665
Cerberus (Blake) **5**:*607*
ceremonies *see* rituals and
ceremonies
Ceres **9**:1231, 1235
Greek equivalent *see* Demeter
Cerne Abbas Giant **4**:502
Cernunnos **2**:279, *284*; **8**:*1075*
Ceryneian Hind **8**:1131
Cesari, Giuseppe
*Founding of Rome by Romulus,
The* **9**:*1243*,
painting of Perseus and
Andromeda **3**:*429*
Ceto **9**:1273
Chac **10**:*1384*, 1385
Chac Mool **9**:*1245*
Chacs **9**:*1175*; **10**:1385
Chalchiuhtlicue **2**:205, 209;
10:1384
Chaldeans **7**:874, 875
Chandra **7**:913
Changing Woman **7**:939, 943
Ch'ang O **3**:*303*, 304, 308
chapshin **6**:791
Characters (Theophrastus) **5**:667

Chareya **5**:590

Chariclo **10**:1371

chariot race, Pelops versus
Oenomaus **8**:1098–1099

Charitesea festival **5**:585

Charon **3**:369, *370*; **5**:*605*;
7:991; **8**:*1022*
and Psyche **9**:*1191*

Charon and Psyche (Stanhope)
9:*1191*

*Charon Takes Shadows Across the
River* (Subleyras) **3**:*370*

Charu **3**:401

Charybdis **8**:1037, *1146*

Chasca **6**:727

Chasca Coyllur **6**:727

Chassériau, Théodore,
*Andromeda Chained to the
Rocks by the Nereids* **7**:*970*

Chata **7**:941

Chaucer, Geoffrey, *Troilus and
Criseyde* **10**:1388–1390

Chaudet, Denis-Antoine,
sculpture of Cupid **3**:*340*

Cheiron **1**:14, 89; **3**:339
and Achilles **1**:14, *16*; **8**:1097
and Actaeon **1**:20
and Asclepius **2**:161
and Jason **6**:775
and Peleus **8**:1096, *1097*

Chelone **1**:105; **7**:1001–1002

Ch'eng Huang **3**:308, 309

Chen Hsu **3**:308

Chernobog **10**:1318, 1319

Chiari, Fabrizio, *Helios in His
Sun Wagon* **5**:*641*

Chichén Itzá **6**:799
ball games **6**:*847*; **8**:1047
cenotes **6**:845, *846*
High Priest's Grave **6**:*800*
New Year ceremony **6**:847
statue of Chac Mool **9**:*1245*
statue of Xib Chac **9**:*1175*
Temple of Kukulkan **6**:*797,
798,* 799, 843, 847

Chicksah **7**:941

childbirth
Artemis and **1**:15
rites of passage and
9:1222–1223

Chile, the Araucanians **7**:915

Chimera (Chimaera) **1**:88
slaying of the **2**:230–*231*;
8:1112

China **3**:**300–309**
ancestor worship **1**:71–73

burials **3**:300–*302*

calendar **2**:*254*, 256–*257*;
3:348

constellations **10**:1337

creation myths **3**:302–303,
314, 319–320, 428; **4**:570

flood myth **4**:522–523

ginseng **8**:1127

gods **3**:307–*309*

Great Wall of **3**:*300*

Khotan **1**:79–80

months **3**:348

mountains **3**:*307*

mythical emperors of the
Golden Age **3**:304–306

planets **10**:*1337*

rivers **3**:306

sea monster **9**:1274

sky god **10**:*1311*
and the structure of the
world **3**:303–304

yin and yang **3**:302, *304*

Chineke *see* Chuku

Chinhan **6**:794

Chirakan-Ixmucane **6**:845

Chloe, Daphnis and **4**:459

Chloris **1**:77

Chloris (Meleboea) **7**:986

Choephoroe (*The Libation
Bearers*; Aeschylus) **3**:313;
4:539

Choimha **6**:842

Cholban (Chulpan) **3**:296

Christianity
in Africa **1**:39
and the afterlife **3**:377
animal-headed figures **1**:81
and the apocalypse
1:120–121
Bacchus and **2**:219
baptism **9**:1223–1224, *1225*
born-again believers
9:1217–1218
and the Celts **2**:285–286
confirmation ceremony
9:1224
and the decline of mystery
cults **7**:933
Mithraism **7**:897–898
and the druids **4**:439
Easter **3**:347; **4**:513
in Ireland **6**:751–752, *759*
a monotheistic religion
7:905–907, 908, 910
and Native Americans **5**:590
in Polynesia **8**:1017–1018

priests **9**:1172
the resurrection of Christ
9:1212
in the Roman Empire
8:1070, 1071
saints **8**:1135
in Scandinavia **2**:222–223;
9:*1264*–1265; **10**:*1360,*
1364
see also Catholicism

Christmas **4**:516; **7**:933
Chrismas trees **4**:559

Chrysaor **5**:581

Chryseis **1**:17, 49, 132; **9**:*1174*
Criseyde identified as
10:*1390*

Chryses **9**:1174

Chrysippus **2**:183

Chrysopelia **4**:441

Chrysothemis **2**:185

Chuku (Chineke) **1**:40; **3**:314

Chumong **6**:794, 795

churches, stave **2**:222

churching of women **9**:1223

cicadas **4**:484; **10**:1379–1380,
1381

Cicero **9**:1173
and augers **9**:1175

Cilix **2**:251

Cimmeranians **9**:1292

Cimon **3**:393; **10**:1355

Cincinnatus, Lucius Quinctius
6:836

Cinyras **7**:929; **9**:1174

Circe **3**:**310–311**; **5**:619; **6**:773,
849; **8**:1104; **9**:1274;
10:1372

circumcision **9**:1224

Cirein crôin **9**:1274

citharas **8**:1057

Claudius, *Roman emperor* **4**:438

Cleomedes of Astypalaea
3:392

Cleta **5**:582

Clio **7**:921, *922,* 926

Clitonymus **8**:1094

Clotho **4**:493–494, 496; **5**:598,
599

Clovis, baptism **9**:*1225*

Clymene **8**:1022

Clytemnestra **2**:172, 185;
3:**312–313**; **6**:813
Agamemnon and **1**:48, 50,
51; **5**:634; **8**:1050–1051
birth **5**:634
death **3**:313; **4**:*472*

and the death of Cassandra
2:273–*274*; **3**:313; **4**:470
and dualism **4**:445, 446

Clytia **1**:105

Clytie **7**:1002

Clytius **5**:617

Coati **6**:844

Coatlicue **2**:205, 207–208
moon goddess **3**:348

Cocalos **7**:888

Cochamama **6**:727

Cocijo **10**:1385

Cocoamama **6**:727

Cocytus **5**:606

codices
Aztec **2**:207
Codex Magliabecchi **3**:*385*
Codex Mendoza **9**:*1173*
Codex Regius **2**:233, *234*;
4:554; **8**:1029; **10**:1403
see also Poetic Edda
Madrid Codex **6**:843
Vienna Codex **9**:1202

Coeus **4**:564

coffins and sarcophaguses
Egyptian **1**:110; **4**:*552*; **6**:*768*;
7:*995*
Greek **5**:*623*; **7**:*899*; **8**:*1052,
1076*
Roman **5**:*605*, 689; **8**:*1098*

Coffin Texts **2**:242, 243

coins, Roman **6**:773, 774, *838,
859*; **7**:*884*; **8**:*1032*

Colosseum **9**:*1230*

columns, Jupiter **6**:785, 788

Compitalia festival **6**:808, 810

Conchobar **6**:757

Concordia, temple to **9**:1236

confirmation ceremony **9**:1224

Confucianism
Five Classics **3**:305
in Korea **6**:791
in Southeast Asia **10**:1323

Connla **9**:1251

Constantia **2**:219

Constantine **7**:897

constellations **10**:1333–1334
Andromeda **1**:76
Aquarius **4**:549
Aquila **4**:549; **10**:1337
Auriga **4**:487; **5**:690
in Babylonian myth **10**:1370
Boötes **10**:1334
Canis Major **8**:1056; **10**:1334
Canis Minor **8**:1056
Cassiopeia **1**:76

Cepheus **1**:76

Chinese **10**:1337

Corona Borealis **3**:416; **10**:1353

Cygnus **6**:812; **8**:1117

Draco **5**:682

Gemini **6**:813

Great Bear (Ursa Major) **1**:21; **2**:158, *262*, 263; **5**:654; **6**:826; **7**:1001; **10**:1334, 1336–1337

the Big Dipper **10**:1334, 1338, 1339, 1340

Japanese name for **10**:1337–1338

Japanese **10**:1337–1338, 1339, 1340

Little Bear (Ursa Minor) **2**:158

Japanese name for **10**:1337–1338

Lyra **8**:1061; **10**:1337

named for Greek myths **10**:1335

Orion **8**:*1054*, 1055–*1056*, 1065; **10**:1338–1339, *1340*

Perseus **1**:*76*; **8**:1114

Pleiades **6**:846; **8**:1055, *1129*, 1130; **10**:*1335*, 1340

Scorpius **8**:1056

Southern Cross **2**:*200*

Southern Pleiades **10**:1340

Taurus **8**:1056

Virgo **10**:1334

Consualia festival **4**:516; **9**:1205

Consus **9**:1231

"Contendings of Horus and Seth, The" **6**:766

Cook Islands **8**:*1012*, 1014, *1016*, 1017, 1018–1019, *1140*

"Cooley Cattle Raid, The" **6**:755

Copacati **6**:727

Copán **6**:841

Coptic sect **9**:1224

Corfu (Corcyra), mythological formation of **10**:1397, *1399*

Corinth **10**:*1308*

Cormac mac Art **6**:753

corn **8**:1124

Aztec myth **10**:1384

Coronis **1**:134; **2**:151, 161

Corot, Jean-Baptiste-Camille, painting of Orpheus and Eurydice **8**:*1060*

Correggio

painting of Danae **6**:*788*

painting of Io **5**:*654*

Cortés, Hernán **9**:1202, *1203*

Cortona, Pietro da

painting of Aeneas **1**:*33*

painting of Saturn **9**:*1253*

Corybantis **9**:1237

cosmogenic myths *see* creation myths

Coti **1**:40

Cottus **4**:564; **10**:1395

Cotzbalam **6**:842

Cousin, Jean, the Elder, *Eva Prima Pandora* **8**:*1079*

couvade **9**:1222–1223

Coya Pasca **6**:731

Coyolxauhqui **2**:205, 208–209; **3**:338; **7**:911

Coyote **3**:376, 404; **7**:939

and the Great Spirit **5**:587

and the origin of fire **7**:945

Cranach, Lucas, painting of the Judgment of Paris **8**:1088–1089

Crathis **8**:1074

Cratos **7**:975

creation myths **3**:**314–323**, 403–404; **4**:523–524

of the Aborigines **2**:194, 196–197

African **1**:40–41, 46; **3**:314–316, 319, 323

Aztec **2**:206; **3**:322; **10**:1430

Babylonian **3**:316–317, 403, 421–422; **5**:695; **6**:830, 833; **10**:1368–1370

blood and **2**:235

Central Asian **3**:297

Chinese **3**:302–303, *314*, 319, 428; **4**:570

dragons in **3**:421–422

Egyptian **1**:94–95; **2**:188–189, 191; **4**:465, 501–502, 550, *551*; **6**:832; **7**:994; **9**:1192–1193

Greek **3**:*397*, 398; **4**:501, *521*, 541–542; **8**:1020; **10**:1429–1430

Hinduism and **3**:316, *319*, 320; **6**:736; **9**:*1268*

Inca **3**:322; **4**:523; **6**:729

Japanese **3**:317–318; **9**:1267–1268

Maori **3**:319, 320; **8**:1014–1015

Mayan **3**:322; **6**:797, 799, 841–842; **7**:948–949; **9**:1268

Mesopotamian **4**:477–478, 480; **6**:832

Native American **3**:314, 321; **5**:586–587, 589–590; **7**:939, 941; **10**:1313

Norse **2**:233, 234, 246, 249–*250*; **8**:1026–1027

Polynesian **3**:*320*, 323; **8**:1013–1015, *1016*; **9**:1271

Siberian **3**:403–404

Slavic **10**:1318–1319

Southeast Asian **10**:1326–*1327*

Sumerian **3**:318–319; **4**:477–478

Vietnamese **4**:570

of the Yekuhana people **10**:1315–1316

Zoroastrian **3**:314; **4**:443–444; **6**:747, *749*

cremation **3**:368, 369

Creon **1**:106, 107; **8**:1041–1042, 1044, 1045

Crescent Moon **10**:1327

Crespi, Giuseppe Maria, *Hecuba Blinding Polymnestor* **5**:628

Cressida (Criseyde), Troilus and **3**:412; **10**:1388–*1390*

Cretans, The (Euripides) **7**:887

Crete **3**:**324–333**; **7**:889

earthquakes and volcanic eruption **3**:325, 328; **7**:890, 951–952

fertile goddess figurines **4**:502

mythological origins of the Cretans **3**:326

palace of Knossos **3**:*327*, *329*–330, 358; **7**:*885*, *886*, *889*–890; **10**:*1353*

worship of Britomartis **2**:248

see also Minoans

Criseyde *see* Cressida

Critias (Plato) **2**:180

Crocodilopolis **7**:981

Cronus **2**:171; **3**:318, 326, **334–339**; **4**:542, 564; **5**:601, 684; **10**:*1397*, 1431

and the flood **4**:520

overthrow of Uranus by **3**:334, *336*; **4**:565; **10**:1373–1374

and Philyra **3**:*339*

Roman equivalent *see* Saturn

Zeus's revenge on **3**:335–336; **4**:565; **5**:601–602, 684; **10**:1374, 1432

crossroads

Hecate and **5**:*619*, 620

Lares and **6**:*808*

Cú Chulainn (Cúchulainn) **6**:752, 755, *757*; **9**:*1226*, 1251; **10**:1401

cults **8**:1137

bull

Apis cult in Memphis **9**:1195

at Catalhüyük **9**:1162–1163

Minoan **3**:*327*, *331*

mystery *see* mystery cults

Cumont, Franz **7**:891

Cupid **3**:**340–343**; **6**:*860*; **9**:1231

Greek counterpart *see* Eros

and Psyche **3**:341–343; **9**:*1187*–1191

Cupid (Chaudet) **3**:*340*

Cupid and Psyche (Canova) **9**:*1190*

Cupid and Psyche (Stanhope) **3**:*342*

cupids **10**:*1386*, 1387

Curetes **10**:1432

Cuzco **6**:724, *726*

Cybele (Magna Mater) **2**:237; **4**:457; **9**:1231, 1237

altar consecrated to **7**:*930*

Attis and **1**:24; **2**:186–*187*; **4**:457

Greek equivalent *see* Rhea

mystery cult and worship of **7**:933; **9**:1218, *1219*

Cyclades, female figurines **5**:*592*

cycles **3**:**344–351**

Cyclopes **3**:**352–357**; **4**:564; **10**:1395, 1396

and Apollo **1**:132

creation of **3**:318, 334; **10**:1373

descendant of *see* Polyphemus

war against Cronus and the Titans **3**:335–336; **4**:565; **10**:1374, 1432

Cyclops (Euripides) **3**:356–357; **9**:1258; **10**:1306

Cycnus **1**:16; **2**:151; **8**:1117, 1121

Cyparissus **1**:134; **8**:1125

Cypria **7**:960–961

Cyrene **1**:134; **7**:*1001*
Cyrus II (Cyrus the Great) **6**:744; **7**:876, 877
   tomb **7**:*893*

Daedalus **3**:**358–361**; **5**:*711, 712*; **7**:*887–888*; **8**:*1149*
Daedalus and Icarus (Canova) **5**:*711*
Daedalus and Icarus (Landon) **5**:*712*
Daevas *see* devas
Dagda **2**:279; **4**:439; **9**:1161
Daidala festival **5**:652
Daikoku **1**:86
dakinis **1**:80; **4**:457
Dalai Lama **3**:375; **9**:1174, 1212, 1214
Dalí, Salvador, lithograph of the Judgment of Paris **8**:1089
Damasistratus **8**:1041
Damgalnunna **4**:477
Damkina **10**:1369
Dana **2**:279
Danae **3**:**362–364**; **5**:580, 581; **8**:1110; **10**:1436–1437
Danae (Correggio) **6**:*788*
Danae (Titian) **3**:*363*
Danae and the Brazen Tower (Burne-Jones) **3**:*362*
Dance of Apollo and the Muses (Peruzzi) **7**:*921*
Dance of the Maenads (de' Gianuzzi) **6**:*828*
dances
   Aboriginal **2**:200
   Hopi
      and ancestor worship **1**:73
      Snake Dancers **1**:89
   Kiowa, Sun Dance **5**:*586*, 587
Daniels, Kate, *The Niobe Poems* **7**:987
Danu **3**:364
Daphne **3**:**365–367**
   and Apollo **1**:104, *105*, *132*, *133*; **3**:341, 365, *367*; **7**:1002; **8**:*1124–1125*; **10**:1417
   Eros's intervention **4**:489
   Leucippus and **3**:365–367; **8**:1130
Daphnis **8**:*1078*
   and Chloe **4**:459
Daramulun **2**:197
Dardanians **1**:28
Dardanus **9**:1164

Dares the Phrygian **10**:1388
Darius I **6**:746
Dark Thunder **10**:1311
Darling River **2**:201
Darth Vader **4**:448
Darwinism, social **1**:100
Daumier, Honoré, *Drunken Silenus, The* **10**:*1306*
Dauphin, Charles, *Massacre of Niobe's Children, The* **7**:*986*
David, Jacques-Louis paintings
   Love of Paris and Helen, The **5**:*637*
   of Mars and Venus **2**:150
   Tears of Andromache **5**:*625*
Daw-Kee **5**:587
Dayak people, creation myth **10**:*1326–1327*
Day of the Dead **4**:517, *517*
Dayisun (Dayisud Tengri) **3**:296
days
   and nights **3**:344–*346*
   of the week, Norse **2**:260; **4**:537
Dazhdebog **10**:1318
Dea Dia **9**:1243
Dea Matres (Matronae) **2**:279
death **3**:**368–377**
   African myths **1**:46–47
   and ancestor worship **1**:69–70
   belief in a spirit or soul **3**:369–370
   boats and **7**:*991*
   books of the dead **1**:79, 111; **2**:**240–245**; **3**:373; **4**:*468*; **7**:979; **9**:1195, *1207*
   and Nut **7**:995, 996, *997*
   cremation **3**:368, 369
   deities of the dead **3**:*374*
   festivities for the dead **4**:*517*
   ghosts **3**:372, 373
      in Polynesian mythology **8**:1019
   Gilgamesh's quest for immortality **3**:371
   Mayan death rituals **6**:*797*, 799–800, 844–847
      see also sacrifice
   mourners, wearing black **9**:*1228*
   mummification **1**:88, *109*–110; **3**:369, *371*
      Anubis and **1**:88, *109*; **3**:*375*

Native Americans and
   dual death god **4**:447
   the origin of death **3**:376
   Sioux Ghost Keeping Ceremony **7**:942
origins of death **3**:376
reincarnation *see* rebirth
rites of passage **9**:1228
Slavs and **10**:1321
suicide, Mayans and **6**:844–845
see also afterlife; burial; ancestor worship; sacrifice
Death of Achilles, The (Rubens) **7**:*928*
Death of Adonis, The (Mazzuoli) **1**:*25*
Death of Hector and the Triumph of Achilles, The (Calliani) **1**:*18*
Death of Hippolytus, The (Rubens) **5**:*690*
Death of Priam, The (Benvenuti) **9**:*1167*
De Bello Gallico (On the Gallic Wars) (Julius Caesar) **4**:436, 438
De divinatione (Cicero) **9**:*1175*
De Ecclesiasticis Disciplinus (Regino von Prüm) **8**:*1073*
Deianeira **5**:665; **8**:1118
Deidamia **1**:15
Deimos **1**:116; **2**:149
Deino **8**:1110
Deiphobos **5**:637; **6**:*857*, 858; **9**:1164
Deipyle **3**:411
deities **3**:**378–385**
Dekla **2**:228
Delacroix, Eugène, *Furious Medea* **6**:*851*
Delaunay, Robert **8**:1062
De Lingua Latina (Varro) **7**:*882*
Della Robbia, Andrea **3**:*351*
Delos **1**:128
   and Leto **6**:814, 816
   worship of Apollo **8**:*1136*
Delphi
   oracle (the Pythian Sibyl) **1**:128–129, *130*; **7**:924; **9**:*1171*, 1177, *1291*, 1293–*1294*; **10**:*1421*
   temple **3**:*400*; **5**:*594*
Delphinus **8**:1144
Delvaux, Laurent **7**:*999*
Demeter **3**:**386–389**; **5**:*593*

and the abduction of Persephone **3**:386, *388*, 389; **4**:504; **5**:602–603; **8**:1106, *1108*; **10**:1311–1312
   and corn **8**:*1124*
   Demeter Erinys **4**:540
   eating part of Pelops **10**:1350
   and Erysichthon **4**:441
   and fertility rituals (Eleusinian Mysteries) **4**:506–507, 515; **9**:*1229*
   link with Isis **6**:768
   and Poseidon **8**:1144
   and Triptolemus **3**:386, *387*; **9**:*1229*
demigods and heroes **3**:**390–395**
   heroes **3**:392–395
      battling dragons **3**:422–424
      compared with giants **4**:564
      Hector, cult of **5**:625
Demin, Giovanni, painting of Paris and Hector **5**:*622*
Demodocus **7**:926
demons *see* devils
Demophon **3**:387, 389; **4**:506; **8**:1106
de Morgan, Evelyn
   Dryad, The **4**:*440*
   Hero Holding the Beacon for Leander **5**:*680*
   Mercury **5**:*670*
Denmark, Tolland Man **9**:*1262*
De rerum natura (Lucretius) **6**:*743*
Description of Greece (Pausanias) **7**:*961*
Desderah, Nilometer **7**:*980*
Despoina **8**:1144
Deucalion **3**:**396–400**
   Deucalion (son of king Minos) **3**:398
   Deucalion (son of Prometheus) **3**:*396–400*; **4**:*521*; **6**:824; **9**:1179
Deucalion and Pyrrha (Beccafumi) **3**:*397*
devas (Daevas)
   in ancient myths of India **3**:338
   in Zoroastrianism **3**:402; **4**:443; **6**:747, 748
Devi, many forms **4**:447
devils **3**:**401–406**
   demons
      Japanese **3**:*406*

devils (continued)
Minoan **3**:332
in polytheistic cultures
3:402–403
in Turkik and Mongol
religion **3**:296–297
of the Yekuhana people
10:1316
Native American **3**:406
Saint Dunstan and a **10**:1426
Scottish **3**:*404*
targeting women **3**:406
Devi Sri **10**:1325, 1326, 1328
Dhanvantari **9**:1268
Diana **2**:*157*; **3**:**407–410**;
6:780; **9**:1231, *1235*;
10:1420
Diana Nemorensis (Diana
of the Woods) **3**:408;
8:1072–1073
Greek equivalent *see* Artemis
Diana and Actaeon (Tiepolo)
1:*20*
Diana and Callisto (Titian)
2:*262, 263*
Diana of Ephesus (statue)
10:*1419*
Dian Cecht **6**:757
Diarmuid **6**:755
Dicksee, Frank, painting by
2:*223*
Dicte, Mount **3**:326, 333;
5:594; **7**:886; **10**:1432
Dictes **3**:362
Dictynna **2**:247, 248; **7**:931
Dictys of Crete **10**:1388
Dido, and Aeneas **1**:*31, 32*
Dievas (Praamzius; Satvaras;
Prakurimas) **2**:224, 228
Dike **10**:1334, 1435
Dimste **2**:228
Dindymene **9**:1237
Dingo **2**:199
Dio Cassius **7**:967
Diodorus Siculus (Diodorus of
Sicily) **2**:160, 271, 283
and the Amazons **1**:60–61, 64
Bibliotheca historica **1**:*64*
and Mnemosyne **7**:900
and Phaethon **8**:1116
Diomedes, *king of Argos* **2**:151;
3:**411–412**; **8**:1033
wounding Aphrodite **2**:236;
3:411
wounding Ares **3**:411; **5**:655;
8:1069

Diomedes, *king of the Thracians*,
eaten by horses **2**:*151*;
5:662; **8**:1121–1122
Dion Chrysostom **4**:436
Dionysiaca (Nonnus) **7**:970;
10:1378
Dionysia festival **3**:417, 418;
7:931
Dionysius of Helicarnassus
and the Penates **8**:1100–1101
story of Romulus and Remus
9:1240
Dionysus **3**:**413–418**; **4**:444;
5:598
adventures of **3**:*415*, 416
double birth **3**:390, 413;
5:654; **10**:1437
festivals for **3**:417, 418; **5**:669;
7:931
god of wine **3**:415–416
Hermes and **5**:673, *674*
honoring **3**:415
parallel with Hades **5**:605
Roman equivalent *see*
Bacchus
satyrs and **9**:1257
Silenus **10**:1305
votaries of *see* maenads
Dioscuri *see* Castor and Pollux
Dis **3**:**419–420**; **9**:1231
Greek equivalent *see* Hades
disability, Greeks and **5**:*645*,
646
Diti **3**:364
Diuturna **6**:773
Div **10**:1318
divi **9**:1238
divination
in Arabia **1**:138
Celtic **1**:71
Etruscan **8**:1070–1071
in Greece **9**:1175–1176
in Mali, Dogon people
8:*1071*
Mesopotamian **1**:67–68
in Norse mythology, the
Norns **7**:993
in Rome **9**:1175
see also oracles
Diwali **2**:258
djinns **1**:137, 138
Döckálfar (dark elves) **1**:58
Dodol **10**:1318
Dodona **4**:442; **8**:1126; **9**:1177;
10:1433
Dogon people **8**:*1071*

Dolichenus **6**:786
Dolon **8**:1033
dolphins, in Roman mythology
3:*415*, 416
Dolughan Ebügan **3**:296
Dolya **10**:1318
Donar **4**:561
Don Juan (Byron) **5**:680
Doolittle, Hilda, "Helen in
Egypt" **5**:640
Doré, Gustave, illustration
of Minos **7**:*890*
Dorians **5**:593; **10**:1311
Doris **7**:969; **8**:1022
Dorus **3**:398
Dracula **2**:*238*
Dracula (Stoker) **10**:1321
Dragon King (Long Vuong;
Thuy-tl) **3**:428
dragons **1**:88; **3**:**421–430**
Babylonian
Murussu dragon **6**:*829*;
7:*954*
see also Tiamat
Chinese **3**:*306*, 421, 427–428
Greek, Ladon (dragon of the
Hesperides) **3**:425; **5**:663,
681, 682
Norse **3**:425–426; **10**:*1300*
drinking the blood of
dragons **1**:85, *87*
Drake, Francis **9**:1273
Dream of Hecuba, The (de'
Gianuzzi) **5**:*626*
dreams **7**:920
Drowned World (Ballard) **4**:526
drugs **3**:402; **6**:747
druids **2**:284–285; **4**:**436–439**
and the afterlife **3**:375; **4**:439
and oak trees **4**:*442*
and sacrifice **2**:239; **4**:439;
9:*1248, 1252*
Drunken Silenus, The (Daumier)
10:*1306*
Dryads **4**:**440–442**; **7**:998, 999
Dryad, The (de Morgan) **4**:*440*
Dryope **1**:105, 134
dualism **4**:**443–448**; **7**:*956,*
957–958
Arab religions and **1**:138
Duamutef **1**:110, 111
du Bellay, Joachim **8**:1083
Duellona *see* Bellona
Dufa **1**:26
Dumézil, Georges **6**:745, 820;
9:1233

Dumont, François, *Titan Struck
by Lightning* **10**:*1374*
Dumuzi **4**:**449–451**, 456–457;
5:715, 717
Assyrian and Babylonian
equivalent *see* Tammuz
Dunstan, Saint **10**:1426
Duran, Diego, *Historia de los
Indios* **9**:*1251*
Durga **1**:80; **4**:447, *448*
Dwamutef **5**:610
dwarfs, Norse **1**:59
Dyaus (Dyaus Pita) **4**:446–447;
6:735; **10**:1312
Dyavaprthivi **4**:447
Dylan **9**:1270; **10**:1422

Ea **3**:403; **5**:693, 697; **6**:762,
833; **7**:870; **10**:1369
see also Enki
Earth, supported in space **7**:947
earth goddess
Minoan **3**:332
Norse **9**:1260–1261,
1262–1263
earth mother (great goddess)
4:**452–457**
African **4**:452
Aztec **2**:208
Maori **8**:1014, 1015, *1017*
Neanderthal **4**:454–455
Venus figurines **4**:454–455,
502; **9**:1157, 1159
see also mother goddesses
earthquakes, beliefs about
7:*947–948*; **8**:1144; **10**:1399
Easter **3**:347; **4**:513
Easter Island **8**:*1015*
Echidna **3**:422
Echo **4**:**458–459**; **7**:926, 1001
and Narcissus **4**:*458, 459*;
7:934
and Pan **4**:459; **8**:1075–1076
eclipses
lunar **7**:*937*; **10**:1320
solar, Baltic mythology and
2:*228–229*
Ecuador, flood myth **4**:523
Edfu, temple **9**:1210
Education of Cupid, The
(Lagrenee) **6**:*860*
Egeria **3**:407
eggs, in creation mythology
3:319–320
Egil **10**:1424
egunguns **3**:*382*

Egypt **4**:460–469

the afterlife **1**:74, 109–110;
3:*371*, 372–373, *375*; **4**:*552*;
5:*608*; **7**:979, 996; **9**:1194

agriculture, the harvest **7**:963

Amazon story **1**:64

animal-headed deities
1:*78–79*, *83*; **4**:*465*, 466;
5:*702*, *708*; **10**:1393

animal worship **1**:93

Anubis and the dead **1**:*88*,
108–111; **3**:*375*; **4**:466

boats in religion **4**:*463*

book of the dead **1**:*79*, *111*;
2:**240–245**; **3**:373; **4**:*468*;
7:979; **9**:1195, *1207*

calendars **2**:254–255, *256*,
257

coffins and sarcophaguses
1:110; **4**:*552*; **6**:*768*; **7**:*995*

concept of *maat* (divine
balance) **5**:708; **7**:979;
8:1065

creation myths **1**:94–95;
2:188–189, 191; **3**:320;
4:465, 501–502, 550, *551*;
6:832; **7**:994

day and night in legend **3**:344

drama **7**:964

eye amulets **5**:*707*

and fertility of the earth
4:*506*, *507*, 508

food libations for the dead
5:*707*

gods **4**:462–*465*, 466

influence on Greece **5**:597

Lower and Upper **4**:461;
7:981; **9**:*1208*, 1283

mummification **1**:88,
109–110; **3**:*371*, *375*

Nile River **3**:349, *350*; **4**:*507*;
5:*609*; **7**:**978–982**; **10**:1336

periods of history **4**:464

pharaohs **2**:189; **4**:461, 465,
550; **5**:*701*; **9**:1174, 1283,
1284

priests **9**:*1177–1178*, 1195

ruled by Macedonian Greeks
7:964

sacrifice **4**:469

Saint Katarina monastery
7:*907*

and the soul **1**:109; **3**:370

sources of mythology
4:466–467

sphinxes **1**:*82–83*

stars **10**:1336–1337

temples **4**:467–*469*; **5**:*704*;
9:*1177–1178*

tombs **2**:240, *241*, *245*; **4**:*461*,
462

ushabtis and shawabtis **2**:*244*

Ehecatl-Quetzalcoatl **9**:1202

Ehrenfels Castle **7**:*974*

Eidothee **9**:1186

Eileithyia **3**:*378*; **5**:651, 659

Einherjar, the, Valkyries and
10:1400, *1402*

Einodia **6**:742

Eir **10**:1405

Eirene **10**:1435

Eitill **10**:1402, 1403

Ek Chuah **6**:*843*, 845

El **2**:164, 165, 166, 212, 213,
215, 267, 268

Elamites **6**:744; **7**:874, 875

Elder Edda see *Poetic Edda*

Electra **2**:185; **4**:**470–472**;
8:1022, 1131

Orestes and **4**:*471–472*;
8:1051, *1053*

Electra (Euripides) **3**:313; **4**:472

Electra (Sophocles) **3**:313;
4:*472*; **8**:1052

Electra complex **4**:471

Eleios **4**:475

Elektra (Richard Strauss) **3**:313

elements, worship of the, by
the Slavs **10**:1317–1318

Eleusinian Mysteries **3**:385,
386, 388; **4**:506–507, 515;
7:931, 933; **9**:*1229*

Plutus and **8**:1132

Selene and **9**:1278

Eleusis **3**:387; **4**:*508*; **5**:*618*,
675

El-Gabal **5**:644

Elgin Marbles **5**:*684*

El Greco, *Laocoon* **6**:*804*

elk mother **1**:88, 95, 99

Elpenor **5**:607

elves
in European folklore **1**:59
in Norse mythology (Alfar)
1:**57–59**

Elymians **10**:1410

elysian fields (Elysium) **3**:*372*;
5:*608*; **10**:1310

Emathion **10**:1379, 1381

Embla see Ask and Embla

Empedocles **9**:1215

Emu, Jabiru and **2**:196, *197*

Enbilulu **4**:477, 505

Endymion **4**:**473–475**

Diana and **3**:*408*

Hypnos and **5**:710

Selene and **9**:*1276*, 1277

England
Lindow Man **2**:283; **9**:*1252*

Stonehenge **9**:1162

Wayland's Smithy **10**:*1427*

Enheduanna **5**:718

Enki **4**:**476–479**, 480, 503, 519;
6:829; **7**:869, 870

rescue of Inanna from the
underworld **5**:717

see also Ea

Enkidu **3**:371; **4**:*571–572*;
6:732, 762

Enkimdu **4**:450, 477, 505

Enki and the World Order **7**:877

Enlil **1**:67; **3**:318–319; **4**:476,
480–482; **6**:829; **7**:870

and the flood **4**:478–479, 519

Enlil-Marduk (Bel) **4**:480

Ennead, of Heliopolis **2**:189;
9:1192, 1206

Ennius
and Ilia **9**:1220

Iphigeneia **6**:743

Enuma Elish **3**:317, 403,
421–422; **6**:*830*; **7**:873;
10:1368, 1430

Enyo **2**:152; **8**:1110

Eochaid **6**:757

Eos **2**:148; **4**:**483–485**; **6**:*853*;
10:1334

and Ares **2**:150–151

and the death of Memnon
10:*1379*, 1381

and Orion **4**:483; **8**:1055

and Tithonus **4**:484, *485*;
10:1379–1380, *1381*

Eostre **4**:561

Epaphus **5**:653; **10**:1436

Epeios **2**:174

Epeius **4**:473, 475

Ephialtes **2**:150; **4**:567

Epic Cycle **6**:854

Epic of Gilgamesh see *Gilgamesh,
Epic of*

Epicureans, and Tyche **10**:1392

Epidaurus, sanctuary of
Asclepius **2**:162

Epigoni **3**:411; **8**:1045

Epimetheus **8**:1081; **9**:1180;
10:1437–1438

Epona **2**:279, *280*

Er **5**:608

Erasmus of Rotterdam **8**:1083

Erato **7**:921

Erda **7**:993

Erebus **4**:493

Erechtheum **2**:176–177; **4**:*441*

Panathenaea festival and
4:514

Erechtheus **8**:1146

Ereshkigal **3**:371; **4**:450; **5**:715,
717; **6**:762; **7**:870

Erginus **5**:660

Erichthonius **4**:**486–487**, *544*;
5:649; **8**:1146; **9**:1190

Erigone **3**:415–416; **10**:1334

Erinyes *see* Furies

Erinys **4**:540

Eris **1**:14, 118; **2**:149; **5**:657,
682; **7**:904; **8**:1085, 1097

Erlik **3**:296, 404

Eros **3**:341; **4**:**488–491**

Roman counterpart *see*
Cupid

Erp **10**:1403

Erpr **10**:1402, 1403

Erra **7**:875

Erysichthon **4**:441

Erytheis **5**:681

Esaugetuh Emissee **5**:588

Esharra **10**:1370

Eshmun **2**:269

Eskimos
shamans **9**:*1287*

see also Inuit

Estsanatlehi **4**:445

Esu **1**:44–45

Esus **2**:281

Étain **6**:*755*

Eteocles **1**:106; **8**:1042,
1043–1044

Eternal Source, Church of the
8:1073

"Ethiopis" *see* "Aethiopis"

etiological myths **9**:1180

Etna, Mount **2**:171; **5**:646, 652;
10:1394

Etruscans **8**:*1073*

alphabet **2**:253

and divination **8**:1070–1071

goddess of death **3**:401, *403*

goddess Menrva (Minerva)
7:882–883

and Rome **9**:1230–1231

Etzel **7**:972–974

Eudaimonia **5**:582

euhemerism **3**:302

Eumenes II **10**:1378

Eumenides **8**:1051

see also Furies

Eumenides (Aeschylus) **3**:313; **4**:538, 539

Eumolpus **8**:1146

Eunomia **10**:1435

Euphorbus **9**:1214–1215

Euphorion **6**:803

Euphrates River **4**:*477*; **6**:*832*; **7**:868; **10**:1370

Euphrosyne **5**:582

Euripides **5**:598

Alcestis **1**:55, 56

Bacchae, The **6**:828

and Bellerophon **2**:231–232

Cretans, The **7**:887

Cyclops **3**:356–357; **9**:1258; **10**:1306

Helen **5**:638; **8**:1086

Heracles **10**:1355

Hippolytus **1**:117; **5**:689

Medea **6**:779, 851

Oresteia **8**:1052

Electra **3**:313; **4**:472

Iphigeneia Among the Taurians (*Iphigeneia in Tauris*) **3**:312; **4**:539; **6**:742

Iphigeneia at Aulis **2**:159; **6**:740–742, 856

Orestes **5**:640

Phaethon **5**:643

Suppliant Women **10**:1355

Trojan Women, The **5**:625

and Ganymede **4**:549

and Hecuba **5**:627, 628

and Helen **5**:640; **6**:858; **8**:1088

Europa **2**:251; **3**:*333*; **4**:*492*; **7**:885; **8**:*1091*; **10**:1435

Eurus **1**:77; **7**:948; **10**:1315

Euryale **5**:580

Eurydice **4**:441; **5**:605, 607; **7**:936; **8**:1057–*1060*, *1061*; **9**:1190

Euryganeia **8**:1042

Eurymedusa **7**:927

Eurynome **5**:646; **10**:1313, 1435

Eurystheus **2**:169, 183; **5**:654, 659

and the Labors of Heracles **2**:173, 178; **5**:654–655, 660

Eurytion **7**:928; **8**:1096

Eurytus **8**:1118

Euterpe **7**:921

Euthymus **3**:390, 392

Evadne **1**:134

Evander **1**:*33*; **9**:1231

Evans, Arthur **3**:329–330; **7**:*889*

Eva Prima Pandora (Cousin the Elder) **8**:*1079*

Eve **4**:509; **8**:1139

Pandora equated with **8**:*1079*, 1083

Evenki people **1**:96, 99

Ewald, Johannes, *Balders Dod* **4**:537

Ewe people, sun and moon myth **10**:1348

Exekias **1**:*62*

Eyrbyggia Saga **10**:1363

Eyvind, *Hákonarmál* **5**:676

Fabius Pictor **9**:1240

Faerie Queene, The (Spenser) **5**:585, 640

Fafnir **1**:*87*; **3**:425–426; **10**:*1300, 1302*

"Fáfnismál" (poem) **10**:1303

Fall of Icarus, The (Saraceni) **3**:*360*

Fall of Phaethon, The (Giordano) **8**:*1116*

Fall of the Titans (Rubens) **10**:*1375*

Falstaff **10**:1306

Fand **9**:1270

Fan people **1**:45, 47

Fantastic Cave Landscape with Odysseus and Calypso (Brueghel the Elder) **2**:265

Farnese Hercules (Glykon) **3**:*390*

Fasti (Ovid) **6**:861; **9**:1170

Fata *see* Fates

fate, in the Greek world **10**:1391

Fates (Moirai; Parcae; Fata) **4:493–497**; **5**:598, *599*; **7**:993; **10**:1435

Fates, The (Goya) **4**:*495*

Fatua **4**:498

Fauna **4**:498

fauns **1**:82; **9**:1256

Faunus **4:498–500**

Greek equivalent *see* Pan

Faust, myth of **5**:640

Faustulus **9**:1221, 1240, 1242, 1244

Favonius **10**:1315

Feast of Fools (Quirinalia festival) **9**:1205

Feast of the Gods (Bellini) **9**:1170

Fedelm **6**:757

Fei Lan **9**:1211

feng shui **3**:427–428

Fenrir **1**:*37*; **5**:633; **8**:1024; **9**:1260

and the apocalypse **1**:*126*; **5**:632; **6**:*817*, 818

chained **9**:1261

Feraferia **8**:1073

Fergus **6**:752, 757

Feriae Latinae **6**:787

Feronia, festival to **4**:516

Ferrari, Luca, painting of Zeus and Semele **10**:*1436*

Ferroni, Egisto, painting of Psyche and Zephyrus **9**:*1189*

fertility **4:501–510**; **8**:1138–1139

mandrake plant and **8**:1126, 1127

Norse fertility deities **4**:529, *531*

festivals **4:511–518**

Baltic **2**:226

Celtic **2**:285; **4**:512–513

Chinese, New Year **2**:257

for the dead **4**:*517*

Egyptian, Sed **4**:*514*; **5**:708

Greek **4**:513–515

Adonia **5**:678

Aphrodisiac festival **4**:514

choruses at **2**:157–158

the Cronia **3**:337

Daidala **5**:652

for Dionysus **3**:417, 418; **5**:669; **7**:931

for the Graces **5**:585

Halieia **5**:642

for Hephaestus **5**:649

Heraia (games for women) **5**:657

Hyakinthia **3**:395

Isthmian games **8**:1144, 1149–1150

Lycosoura **6**:824

Olympic Games **4**:473, 475, *513*, 514–515; **9**:1249; **10**:*1437*, 1438

Oschophoria **7**:987

Panathenaea **4**:513–514; **10**:1353, 1376

for Poseidon **8**:1144, 1149–1150

Pythian Games **1**:129; **3**:*365*; **4**:514

Stepterion **1**:129

Thesmophoria **3**:386, 389; **5**:585

see also Eleusinian Mysteries

Inca **6**:*729*

Irish **6**:757–759

Japanese **4**:517–*518*; **10**:1347

Mayan **4**:517

Phoenician **2**:271

Roman **4**:515–516

Agonium **6**:774

Anna Perenna **7**:968

Bacchanalia **4**:516; **7**:931

Compitalia **6**:808, 810

Consualia **4**:516; **9**:1205

Day of Slaves **10**:1420

Feriae Latinae **6**:787

Hilaria **2**:187

to Jupiter **6**:787

Larentalia **4**:516

to the Lares **6**:808, 810

Ludi Neptunales **7**:968

Ludi Romani **6**:787

Lupercalia **4**:*500*, 516

Matronalia **6**:782

Megalesia **9**:1237

Mercuralia **6**:861

military season **6**:838–839

Neptunalia **7**:967, 968

Openconsivia **9**:1254

Parilia **4**:*515*

Quinquatrus **7**:884

Quirinalia **9**:1205

Robigalia **9**:1205

Rustic Vinalia **10**:1410

Saturnalia **4**:515, 516; **6**:770–772; **9**:1254–*1255*

Terminalia **4**:*511*

Vestalia **10**:1412

Vulcanalia **4**:516

Slavic **10**:1320, 1321

fetiales **6**:838

Feuerbach, Anselm

Iphigeneia **6**:*740*

Judgment of Paris, The **1**:*118*

Fianna Eireann **9**:1226, 1227

Fides, ritual of **9**:1205

Fimbul Winter **1**:126

Finding of Erichthonius, The (Rubens) **4**:*487*

Finn **9**:1226–1227

Finnic people **9**:1259–1260

Fintan **6**:757

Fionn **6**:755, 757

fire
origin, Native American myth **7**:945
worshiped in Arabia **1**:138

First New Chronicle and Good Government, The (Poma de Ayala) **6**:*730*

Fisher King **4**:509–510

Fjalar **2**:235–236; **6**:801; **8**:1028; **10**:1405

flamens (flamines) **9**:1204–1205

Flateyjarbók **4**:529; **8**:1027

Flaxman, John **8**:1084
illustration of Tiresias **10**:*1372*

Flaying of Marsyas, The (Titian) **1**:*135*

Flight from Troy, The (Bernini) **1**:*30*

flood myths **3**:399–400; **4**:519–526; **7**:950–951
African **4**:522
Australian Aboriginal **4**:523
Aztec **2**:209
Biblical **3**:399
Chinese **4**:522–523
Greek **2**:262; **3**:397–398, *399*; **4**:*519*, 521; **9**:1179
Hindu **4**:*522*, 523
historical basis **3**:400; **4**:520, *524–525*
Inca **4**:523; **6**:729
Japanese god of tidal waves **7**:952
Lithuanian **4**:521
Mesopotamian **3**:399; **4**:*480*, 519, *520*, 572; **7**:950–951; **10**:1313
Polynesian **8**:1019
Southeast Asian **10**:1327
Sumerian **3**:399; **4**:478–479, 519–520
in Thai and Lao mythology **4**:521

Flora **1**:77; **7**:*958*; **9**:1231

flowers, in Greek mythology **7**:*936, 1002*

Fomorii **3**:338

Fon **3**:319

Ford, H.J.
illustration of Odysseus and Calypso **7**:*999*
illustration of Paris and Oenone **8**:*1085*

Forseti **1**:36

Fortuna **9**:1231

Fortune, as one of the Penates **8**:1100

Founding of Rome by Romulus, The (Cesari) **9**:*1243*

Fragonard, Jean-Honoré, painting by **4**:485

France
Le Puy **1**:*98*
Return of the Gleaners ritual **7**:917

Franchville, Pierre de, statue of Orpheus **8**:*1057*

François Vase (Kleitias) **5**:585; **8**:1097

Frankenstein (Shelley) **9**:1184

Franks **4**:557, *558*

Franks Casket **10**:1426

Fravashis **6**:748

Fravek and Fravrekain **6**:749

Frazer, James **6**:773–774
The Golden Bough **3**:409

Freud, Sigmund **7**:936; **8**:1044

Frey **4**:527–530; **7**:990–991; **9**:1260
and the Alfar (elves) **1**:57
and Gerd **1**:34; **4**:527, *555–556*
ship **7**:991
and the underworld **7**:989

Freya (Gefn; Horn; Mardöll) **1**:37; **4**:527, **531–534**; **7**:991; **9**:1260; **10**:*1366*–1367
depicted as a Valkyrie **10**:1400

Freya Seeking Her Husband (Blommer) **4**:*532*

Fricka *see* Frigga

Frigga (Fricka) **1**:37; **4**:**535–537**; **10**:1405
and Balder **2**:220–221, 260; **4**:516, 536
fusion with Freya **4**:531
as Odin's wife **4**:535, 536, *537*

Friggia (Gustav III) **4**:537

Frija **4**:531, 561

Frisians **4**:557, *558*

Fuflans **8**:1072

Fu Hsi (T'ai Hao) **3**:304, 308

Fu Hsing **3**:308, 309

Fujin **7**:*949*

Fulla **1**:37

Full Moon **10**:1327

Funadama **4**:*518*

Funadama Matsuri festival **4**:*518*

Furies (Erinyes; Furiae; Eumenides; Semnai Theai) **4**:**538–540**, 542; **5**:606; **9**:1231; **10**:1397
and the Harpies **5**:613
and Orestes **4**:*539*; **8**:1051
variant of *see* Ate

Furious Medea (Delacroix) **6**:*851*

Fu Shen **3**:308, 309

Fu-Shou-Lu **3**:309

future, telling the *see* divination

Gabriel (archangel) **5**:632

Ga-gaah (Wise Crow) **7**:939

Ga-gorib **1**:45

Gaia (Ge) **3**:*321*; **4**:**541–544**; **5**:*594*
and Antaeus **8**:1144–1146
and creation **3**:318; **4**:501, 541–542; **8**:1020
and the Gigantomachy **4**:566
and Hades **5**:602
and overpopulation of the human race **7**:903
Pandora, as an epithet for **8**:1082
and Phaethon **8**:1116–1117
rebellion against Uranus **3**:318; **4**:541–542; **10**:1373–1374, 1397

Gaia (spacecraft) **4**:544

Gaia Hypothesis **1**:101; **4**:457, 544; **7**:957

Gailleach **10**:1423

Galahad **10**:*1422*

Galar **6**:801; **8**:1028; **10**:1405

Galas (Galates) **4**:546

Galatea **4**:**545–547**
Galatea (daughter of Eurytius) **4**:547
Galatea (sea nymph) **4**:*545–547*
Acis and **3**:356, *357*; **4**:546, 547
Polyphemus and **3**:356, *357*; **4**:*545–546*, 547
Galatea (statue), Pygmalion and **1**:114–115; **4**:547; **9**:*1196*, 1198

Galations **2**:278

Galli **2**:187; **9**:1237

Gallic Wars, The (Julius Caesar) **2**:280–281

Ganapati **1**:80

Ganesa **1**:*80*, 86; **6**:738

Ganga **6**:738

Ganymede **4**:**548–549**; **5**:615, *616*; **6**:805; **10**:1379

Garcilaso de Vega, Gomez **6**:730

Garden of the Hesperides **2**:178

Gargareans **1**:61

garlic **8**:1127, *1128*

Gayomart **6**:748, *749*

Ge *see* Gaia

Geb **2**:188; **3**:*317*; **4**:**550–552**; **7**:994, 995; **9**:1280; **10**:1310, 1398–1399
guardian of the underworld **4**:552

Gediminas **2**:226

Geezhigo-Quae **7**:939

Gefjon (Gefjun; Gefion) **1**:37; **4**:**553–554**; **10**:1405

Gefjon Fountain (Bundgaard) **4**:*553*, 554

Gefn *see* Freya

Gehrts, Johannes, painting of Hel **5**:*633*

Geirröd **4**:570; **6**:822; **10**:1362

Gengen-Ur **4**:550

Genghis Khan **3**:*294*, 297–298

Genii Cucullati **2**:279

Gennep, Arnold Van **9**:1222, 1228

Geoffrey of Monmouth **4**:554
Historia regum Britanniae **3**:427

George, Saint, and the dragon **1**:88; **3**:422, *423*

Georgics (Virgil) **8**:1059

Gerald of Wales **9**:1248

Gerd **1**:34, 37; **4**:527, **555–556**; **10**:1405
and Frey **1**:34; **4**:527, *555–556*

Gerda (Tegnér) **4**:556

Germangabis **4**:561

Germania (Tacitus) **4**:529, 559; **9**:1263; **10**:1405

Germanic peoples **4**:**557–562**
apocalypse myth **1**:127
fertility deity **4**:529

Germany, elves **1**:59

Gérôme, Jean-Lèon, *Pygmalion and Galatea* **9**:*1196*

Geryon **4**:568; **6**:772

Geser Khan **3**:296

Geshtinanna **3**:371; **4**:451; **5**:717

Gesta Danorum **8**:1026

Gesta Hammaburgensis ecclesiae pontificum (Adam of Bremen) **4**:529

Geush Urvan **6**:749

Ghost Keeping Ceremony **7**:942

ghosts **3**:372, 373
  in Polynesian mythology **8**:1019

Giaccarelli, Antonio, plaster relief **9**:*1166*

giants **4**:**563–570**
  in Asian creation myths **4**:570
  Greek **4**:542, *564–568*
    see also Cyclopes; Giants; Hecatoncheires; Titans
  Norse **4**:*568–570*
    frost giants and fire giants **4**:570
    Thor's encounters with **10**:1360–1362, *1363*, *1430*
  northern Europe, tale of Vainamoinen **4**:566

Giants (Gigantes) **10**:1397
  Battle Against the (Gigantomachy; Gigantomachia) **4**:543–544, *565*, 566–567; **10**:1375, 1432
  satyrs' role in **9**:1257
  Zeus's struggle against Otus and Ephialtes **4**:567

Gianuzzi, Pippi de'
  Dance of the Maenads **6**:*828*
  The Dream of Hecuba **5**:*626*
  Olympus **6**:*785*

Gide, André, *Prometheus Misbound* **9**:1184

Gigantes *see* Giants

Gigantomachy (Gigantomachia; Battle Against the Giants) **4**:543–544, *565*, 566–567; **10**:1375, 1432
  satyrs' role in **9**:1257

Gikuyu **1**:44

Gilfaethwy **1**:104; **10**:1422

Gilgamesh **3**:371; **4**:482, *571-*574; **6**:760–762, 763

Gilgamesh, Epic of **3**:371, 399; **4**:480, **571–574**; **6**:763; **7**:869
  and An **1**:67

flood myth **4**:519
  and Ishtar **6**:760–762

Gilling **6**:801

Gimbutas, Marija **4**:454; **8**:1075

Ginnungagap **2**:233, 246, 249; **8**:1024; **10**:1428, 1430

ginseng **8**:1127

Giordano, Luca
  paintings
    of Diana and Endymion **3**:*408*
    Fall of Phaethon, The **8**:*1116*
    of Ulysses and Calypso **2**:*265*

Giorgi, Giovan Battista, mosaic depicting Apollo **1**:*128*

Girsu **7**:871

Gitchi Manito **5**:588

Giza
  Great Sphinx **1**:*82*, 83; **10**:*1330*–1332
  pyramids **4**:*462*; **10**:1330

Gjalar **2**:235–236

Gjallarbrú **5**:677

Gjöll River **5**:677

Gjúki **10**:1302

Glaser, Eduard **1**:137

Glauce **6**:779, 851

Glaucus **8**:*1092*; **9**:1274

Gleaners, Return of the **7**:*917*

Gleipnir **1**:37

Glooskap (Nanabozho) **4**:445; **7**:939, 940–941

Gluck, Christoph **6**:743

Glykon, Farnese Hercules **3**:*390*

Gná **10**:1405

Gobi Desert **3**:292

God, Biblical **8**:1135

gods and goddesses *see* deities

Goethe, Johann Wolfgang von, *Iphigeneia* **4**:497

Goewin **10**:1422

Gog **4**:*569*

Gogmagog **4**:569

Golden Ass, The see Metamorphoses (The Golden Ass; Apuleius)

Golden Bough, The (Frazer) **3**:409

Golden Fleece **6**:776
  search for *see* Jason, voyage with the Argonauts

Gorgons **5**:**580–581**
  Amazons and **1**:64

Gorgophone **8**:1114

Gosforth cross **9**:1265

Götar people **4**:557, *558*

Govannon **2**:279

Goya, Francisco
  The Fates **4**:*495*
  painting of Cronus (Saturn) **3**:*335*, 338–339

Graces **5**:**582–585**

Graduate, The (novel and movie) **2**:231

Graeae, the **3**:363; **5**:580; **8**:1110, *1114*

Grandmother Spider Woman **1**:95

Grannus **2**:279

graves *see* death and the afterlife, burial

Graves, Robert
  and Hebe **5**:616
  and Hestia **5**:685

great goddess *see* earth mother

Great Mother **5**:606

Great Sphinx, at Giza **1**:*82*, 83; **10**:*1330*–1332

Great Spirit **5**:**586–590**; **7**:*909*, *910*

Greece **5**:**591–600**
  Achaeans **5**:593, 594–595; **10**:1311
  and the afterlife **3**:369, *370*, *372*; **5**:606, 607–608; **7**:888–889, *890*, 991; **9**:1214; **10**:1310
  the age of invasions (1900–1500 BCE) **5**:593–594
  alphabet **2**:212–213, 253
  and androgyny **5**:668–669
  Bronze Age (Helladic period) **5**:593
  calendar **2**:260–261
  city-states **5**:595, 596, 598
  classical **5**:595
    mythology **5**:598–600
  creation myths **3**:318, 334–335; **4**:501, 541–542; **8**:1020; **10**:1313, 1396
  "Dark-age" **5**:594–595
  day and night legend **3**:346
  Eleusinian Mysteries **3**:385, 386, 389; **4**:506–507, 515; **7**:931, 933; **9**:*1229*, 1278
  family tree of deities **8**:*1134*
  female choruses **2**:157–158
  festivals *see* festivals, Greek

flood myth **2**:262; **3**:397–398, *399*; **4**:*519*, 521; **9**:1179
  forms of worship **5**:*594*
  Golden Age of Cronus **3**:336
  and the hearth **5**:592, *683*–684, 686; **10**:1418
  influence of Egypt on **5**:597
  Ionians **5**:593, 595
  men in society **5**:598, 668
  museums **7**:925
  and music **7**:924
  mystery cults **7**:**930–933**; **8**:1137
  and natural catastrophes **1**:122–123
  nature deities **1**:102
  Olympian gods **5**:598
  Orphism and the Orphic Mysteries **4**:444; **7**:933, 1005; **8**:1061–1062
  Pelasgians **5**:592, 650; **10**:1311
  personification in myths **7**:1005–1006
  poetry **5**:640; **7**:902
  pre-Olympian gods **7**:1005
  priests **9**:1175–1176, 1237
  rituals and ceremonies *see* rituals and ceremonies, Greek
  sacrifices **2**:159–160, 235, 237; **3**:337; **6**:824–826; **9**:1245–*1247*, 1249
  sea monsters **8**:*1092*, *1146*; **9**:*1270*, 1273, 1274
  sky gods **10**:1310, 1311
  Stone Age **5**:591–592
  weddings and marriage **5**:667–668, 672; **7**:976; **10**:1416
  winds **1**:77; **10**:*1314*, 1315
  women in society **5**:584, 668; **8**:1091
  see also Athens

Greenland, moon-god **3**:347

Green Man **4**:442; **7**:*955*

Gregory of Nazianzus **8**:1083

Grendel **4**:561–562

Grien, Hans Baldung, woodcut of witches **9**:*1288*

griffins **1**:88, *90*

Grignion, Charles, sculpture of Hades **5**:*606*

Grímhild **10**:1302

"Grímnismál" (poem) **10**:1430

Grith **10**:1362

guardian spirits, Norse 9:1266
Gucumátz (Gugumátz) 6:797, 798, 841
Gudea 7:871
Gudrún 10:1302, 1303, 1402–1403
Guercino, Il see Barbieri, Giovanni Francesco
Guérin, Pierre-Narcisse
  paintings
  of Clytemnestra 3:313
  of Eos and Cephalus 4:484
  Morpheus and Iris 7:920
  Phaedra and Hippolytus 10:1423
Guide to Greece (Pausanias) 8:1149
Gullinborsti 4:529
Gullintanni see Heimdall
Gundestrup Cauldron 8:1075
Gunnar 10:1302, 1402
Gunnar Helmingr 4:529
Gunnlöd 4:569; 6:801; 8:1028, 1029
Gunst, Philip van, painting of Perseus slaying Medusa 5:581
Gunther 7:972, 974; 10:1304
Guqyuivi 4:447
Gutthorm 10:1302–1303
Gwdion 1:104
Gwenhidwy 5:631
Gwion Bach 6:801
Gwydion 10:1422
Gyges 4:564; 10:1395
Gylfi 4:554; 10:1430
Gymir see Aegir

Hades (place of the dead) 5:605, 606, 607–608; 7:991; 9:1214
  Cerberus and 5:601, 607
  Orpheus in 8:1058–1060
Hades (Polydegmon; Pluton; Pluto) 3:401, 419–420; 5:601–608
  birth 5:601–602
  character 5:605
  and Persephone 3:386, 388, 389, 420; 5:602–603; 8:1106
  Roman equivalent see Dis
  Theseus and Peirithous visit 5:603; 10:1354
Haemon 1:106; 8:1042
Haemosu 6:795

Hagen 7:972, 974
Hahgwehdaetgah 4:445; 7:938, 939
Hahgwehdiyu 4:445; 7:938, 939
Hákonarmál (Eyvind) 5:676
Halcyon Discovers Ceyx (Banks) 7:919
Halloween 2:285; 4:512
Hallstatt culture 2:277
hallucinogens
  shamans and 9:1289
  witches and 9:1288
Hamadryads 4:440; 7:998, 999
Hamdir 10:1403
Hammurabi 4:573; 6:831; 7:871–872, 873
Hanal Pixan 4:517
Hanan Pacha 6:728
handicap, physical see disability
Hannahanna 5:693
Hannibal, retreat from Rome 2:187
Hanuman 1:80; 6:738; 8:1134; 10:1324, 1326, 1327
Hapi 5:609–610
  Hapi (Apis; Hepu; sacred bull) 1:93; 5:610
  Ptah and 9:1195
  Hapi (Hapy; Hepy; god of the Nile) 1:110–111; 3:349; 5:609–610; 7:979–981
  Hapi (son of Horus) 5:610
Harald War-tooth 8:1026, 1030–1031
Harappa 6:734
Hárbardsljód 8:1031; 10:1358
Hariti 10:1323
Harmonia 2:251, 253; 3:426; 8:1122
Harpies 1:31; 5:611–614; 6:779
Harsomtus 5:707
Hathor 4:462, 464, 466; 5:706, 707; 7:912, 997
  merger with Isis 6:767
hats, Phrygian 2:186; 7:891, 893
Hatshepsut 9:1210; 10:1332
Hattians 5:692–693
  influence on Hittite myths 5:694–695
Hattushash 5:699, 700; 10:1344
Haumea 8:1015
Hauptmann, Gerhart 6:743
Haurvatat 1:102; 6:747, 748

Hávamál 8:1029, 1030
Hawaii 9:1272
  creation myth 8:1013–1014
Hazzi 5:693
Head of Medusa, The (Caravaggio) 5:580
heads, severed, Celtic cult 2:281
hearth
  the Greeks and the 5:592, 683–684, 686; 10:1418
  the Romans and the 10:1412
Heart of Heaven 6:799, 841, 842, 845
Hebat 5:693, 699
Hebe 4:548; 5:615–616, 651
Hebe (Canova) 5:615
Hecate 3:349; 5:606, 617–620; 7:914, 931; 8:1128
  and Persephone 5:602, 618
Hecate (Blake) 5:620
Hecatoncheires (Hundred-Handed Ones) 4:564; 10:1395
  creation of 3:318, 334; 4:541; 10:1373
  war on Cronus and the Titans 3:335–336; 4:565; 10:1373, 1374, 1432
Hector 1:19; 5:621–625
  Achilles and the death of 1:17–18; 5:622–623; 8:1095; 9:1166
  battle against the Great Ajax 1:53
  cult of 5:625
  and Paris 8:1087
Hecuba 5:626–628; 9:1164
Hecuba Blinding Polymnestor (Crespi) 5:628
Heemskerck, Maerten van, painting of Ares and Aphrodite 2:150; 5:649
Hefring 1:26
Hegel, Georg Wilhelm Friedrich 1:106
Hegemone 5:582
Heh 1:93
Heimdall (Gullintanni) 1:34; 5:629–632; 8:1024
  horn (Gjallarhorn) 5:630, 631, 632
Heiss, Johann, painting of Pandora 8:1081
Heitsi-eibib 1:45

Hel 2:222; 3:377; 5:633, 633; 6:818; 8:1024, 1030
  Hermód and 5:677
Helen 3:394; 5:634–640; 6:813
  after the Trojan War 5:636, 637–638; 6:857, 858
  birth 5:634; 6:811–812
  as cause of the Trojan War 1:15, 49; 2:174; 4:490; 5:621, 636
  as a cloud image 8:1086
  Eros and 4:489–490
  and Deiphobos 5:637; 6:857, 858
  and dualism 4:445, 446
  in Egypt 5:638; 8:1086
  giving beauty to a young girl 1:118–119; 5:638
  as a goddess 5:638
  as an icon 5:638–640
  Homer and 5:637–638, 640
  marriage 6:856, 857
  Nemesis and 7:959, 960–961
  Pandora as a model for 8:1082
  Paris's abduction of 1:15, 118; 2:174; 5:621, 636; 8:1086–1087; 9:1165
  suitors 1:52; 5:713; 6:857; 8:1033, 1094, 1118
  Theseus's abduction of 2:275
  and tree worship 6:813
Helen (Euripides) 5:638; 8:1086
"Helen in Egypt" (Hilda Doolittle) 5:640
Helen on the Steps of Troy (Moreau) 5:638
Helenus 1:31; 5:627; 8:1118–1119
Helgi 9:1266
Heliades 8:1117
Helice 8:1144
Heliconians 4:440
Helicon, Mount, and the Muses 7:922, 923, 925
Heliopolis (Iunu)
  and Atum 2:188, 189; 4:501–502
  cult of Re 9:1206
  Ennead of 2:189; 9:1192, 1206
Helios 1:129; 5:641–644, 646–648; 8:1023; 10:1343–1344, 1345
  and the abduction of Persephone 5:602, 618

Helios (continued)
goblet (cup) **5**:642, 662–663
and Phaethon **5**:642;
8:*1115*–1116, 1117;
10:1344
and Poseidon **8**:1148
sacred sheep and cattle **5**:642;
8:1038; **10**:1372
similarity to Re **9**:1211
Helios in His Sun Wagon
(Chiari) **5**:*641*
Helle **5**:674, 678; **6**:776
Hellen **3**:398
Hemithea **1**:16
Hendrich, Hermann,
Rhinemaidens, The **10**:*1400*
Henryson, Robert, *Testament of*
Cresseid, The **10**:1390
Hephaestus **2**:151, 170;
5:**645–649**; **10**:1426–1427
and Athena **4**:486; **5**:649
birth and lameness
5:*645*–646, 651–652;
10:1435
creation of the first woman
5:584, 646; **8**:*1080, 1081*
cult of **5**:649
Dionysus and **3**:417
father of Erichthonius **4**:486;
5:649
as husband of Aphrodite
1:113–*114*; **5**:643, 646–648;
7:951
as husband of one of the
Graces **5**:584
link with Prometheus **9**:1182
Roman equivalent *see* Vulcan
Hepy *see* Hapi
Heqet **7**:912
Hera **5**:**650–657**
against Troy and the Trojans
1:31; **5**:655, 709–710
battle against Artemis **5**:652
birth **5**:650
the birth of Typhon **5**:652;
10:1394
and Dionysus **3**:413–414;
5:654
and Echo **4**:458; **7**:1001
and Hephaestus **5**:645–646,
651–652; **10**:1435
and Heracles **2**:172–173;
5:654–*655*, 659, 660; **6**:785;
7:1005
intervention in Zeus's love
affairs **5**:653–654

revenge on Callisto **2**:158,
262, 263; **5**:653–654;
7:1001
and Jason **5**:656–657; **6**:775
jealousy and injured pride
5:655–656
merger with Juno **6**:780–*781*
quarrel with Poseidon **5**:652;
8:1148
and Tiresias **10**:1371–1372
wife of Zeus **5**:650–*653*;
10:*1435*
see also Paris, Judgement of
Hera Barberini **5**:*652*
Heracles **5**:**658–665**
aided by Athena **2**:172–173
and Alcestis **1**:55; **5**:662
and the Amazons **1**:62; **5**:662,
687
and Atlas **2**:178–180;
5:*663*–665, 682
birth **5**:659
and the body of Icarus **5**:711
childhood and education
5:659–660
cult worship **5**:658–659;
7:925–926
death and immortality **5**:*664*,
665; **8**:1118
fight with Achelous **1**:13;
5:665
fight with Ares **8**:1122–1123
and the Gigantomachy
4:566–567
and Helios's goblet **5**:642,
662–663
and Hera (Juno) **2**:172–173;
5:654–*655*, 659, 660; **6**:785;
7:1005
killed the sons of Ares **2**:151;
8:1122–1123
Labors of **1**:62; **2**:173, 178;
3:425; **5**:655, 658, 659
apples of the Hesperides,
fetching of **2**:178; **3**:425;
5:*663*–665, 682; **7**:969–
970; **8**:1023; **9**:1181;
10:1387
Augean stables, cleaning of
5:662
belt of Hippolyte, fetching
of **1**:62; **5**:655, 662, 663,
687
birds of the Stymphalian
marshes, shooting of **5**:662
cattle of Geryon, capture of

4:568; **5**:642, 655,
662–663; **6**:772
Cerberus, capture of **5**:603,
607, 665
Cretan bull, capture of
5:662
Erymanthion boar, capture
of **5**:661–662, *663*
horses of Diomedes, capture
of **5**:*662*; **8**:1122
Hydra, killing of **5**:660–661
Nemean lion, killing of
5:*659*, 660, 663
stag of Ceryneia, capture of
5:661; **8**:1131
and Laomedon **6**:*805*, 806;
9:1164
marriage to Deianeira **5**:665
marriage to Hebe **5**:615–616,
665
and Minerva **7**:883
a mortal and a god **3**:*390*;
7:883
murder of his family **5**:660
and the Muses **7**:925–926
and Nereus **10**:1387
and the Olympic Games
4:514
rescue of Hesione **6**:*806*
rowing contest with Jason
6:777
and the Thespians **5**:660
wrestling match with Antaeus
4:568; **5**:*661*; **8**:1146
Heracles (Euripides) **10**:1355
Heracles on the Pyre (Reni)
5:*664*
Heraculaneum
bas-relief from **8**:*1050*
bust of a satyr from **9**:*1257*
Heraia (games for women)
5:657
Hercle **8**:1072
Herculaneum, mural showing
Galatea **4**:546
Hercules *see* Heracles
Hercules Killing the Dragon of the
Hesperides (dello Sciorina)
5:*682*
Hermanos **8**:1127
Hermaphroditus **5**:**666–669**,
674; **7**:1000; **9**:1169
Hermes **5**:**670–675**
and Aphrodite **5**:666
children **5**:674–675
as a fertility god **4**:502

god of boundaries **5**:670–*672*
guider of souls in the afterlife
5:605, 670
Hermes Psychopompos **5**:670
and herms **5**:*672*
Hestia and **5**:686
importance to brides
5:667–668, 672
link with Priapus **9**:1169
protector of children
5:673–674
Roman equivalent *see*
Mercury
a thief **5**:*672*–673, 674, *675*
tricks Apollo **5**:672–*673*
worship of **5**:675
Hermione **6**:856, 858; **8**:1053
Hermód **2**:221, 222; **5**:633,
676–677; **8**:1030
herms **5**:*619, 672*; **6**:859;
9:1169
Herm of a Vestal Virgin (Canova)
10:*1414*
Hero **5**:**678–680**
Herodotus **4**:466
and the Amazons **1**:60, 61
and Helen **5**:638
History **5**:638; **8**:1065
and the Iranians **6**:744–745
and rituals in honor of Ishtar
6:763
heroes *see* demigods and heroes
Hero Holding the Beacon for
Leander (de Morgan) **5**:*680*
Herophile **9**:1291
Hesat **7**:997
Hesiod
Catalogues of Women **8**:1052
Catalogue of Heroines **6**:742
and Elysium **3**:372
and the four winds **1**:77;
7:948
and the Graces **5**:582
and the Harpies **5**:611
and Hephaestus **5**:645–646
and heroes **3**:392
and the Hesperides **5**:681
and the Muses **7**:922, 923
and Poseidon **8**:1143
see also Theogony; Works and
Days
Hesione **6**:*805, 806*; **9**:1164
Hesperethusa **5**:681
Hesperides **5**:**681–682**; **8**:1130
Arethusa **1**:105; **7**:*1000*, 1002;
10:*1420*

golden apples of the **5**:*681*; **7**:*1004*

 Heracles' quest for **2**:178; **3**:425; **5**:663–665, 682; **7**:969–970; **8**:1023; **9**:1181; **10**:1387

Hestia **5**:**683–686**; **10**:1418

 birth **3**:335; **10**:1418

 Roman equivalent *see* Vesta

hierodules **2**:271

High God **7**:909

Hilaeira **2**:*276*

Hilaria festival **2**:187

Himinglaeva **1**:26

Himyarites **1**:137

Himyar **1**:138

Hina (Hine) **8**:1014, 1015, 1016, 1017, *1019*

Hinduism **6**:736–737

 apocalypse myth **1**:127

 and creation **3**:316, *319*, 320; **6**:736; **9**:*1268*

 deities **3**:382, *383*; **8**:1134, 1135, 1136

  animal-headed **1**:*80*

 dragons **3**:422

 fertility symbols **4**:502

 flood myth **4**:*522*, 523

 the *Mahabharata* **6**:737–738, 739

 monotheism **7**:908

 myth concerning the Pleiades **10**:1340

 polytheism **8**:1134, 1135

 pre-Aryan influences **6**:737

 the *Ramayana* **6**:738–739

 rebirth of the soul **3**:374; **9**:*1215*, 1216

 serpents **3**:*319*; **9**:*1268*

 in Southeast Asia **10**:1322

 and the tulsi plant **8**:1125–1126

 universe **3**:*322*

 and yoga **7**:*905*

Hine Ahu One **3**:323

Hine Hauk Ona **8**:1014

Hine Titama **3**:323; **8**:1014

hippocampus **9**:1273

Hippocoon the Usurper **5**:655

Hippocrates **2**:162

Hippocrene fountain **8**:1112

Hippodameia (Hippodamia) **2**:182, 183; **8**:1050, *1098–1099*, 1131

Hippolyte **5**:**687–688**

 Heracles and the girdle of

1:62; **2**:149; **5**:655, 662, 663, 687

 and Theseus **5**:*687–688*; **10**:1354

Hippolytus **3**:407–408; **5**:**689–690**; **10**:1420

 Artemis and **2**:159; **10**:1420

 Phaedra and **1**:*115*, 116–117; **2**:231; **8**:1149; **10**:1354, 1420, *1423*

Hippolytus (Euripides) **1**:117; **5**:689

Hippomenes **2**:168; **5**:682

hippopotamuses, Horus and Seth as **9**:1282

Hipta **5**:616

Hirpini **6**:835–836; **8**:1071

Hirsenti **8**:1071

Hisakitaimisi (Master of Breath) **7**:939

Hisham ibn al-Kalbi, *Kitab al-asnam* **1**:137

Historia de gentibus septentrionalibus (Magnus) **4**:*535*

Historia de los Indios (Duran) **9**:*1251*

Historia regum Britanniae (Geoffrey of Monmouth) **3**:427

History (Herodotus) **5**:638; **8**:1065

History of the Lombards (Paul the Deacon) **4**:535

History of Things in New Spain (de Sahagún) **9**:1201

Hittites **5**:**691–700**

 capital city **10**:*1344*

 gods and goddesses **5**:692–694

 of the sun **5**:695; **10**:1343, *1344*

 kingship **5**:697–699

 modern knowledge of **5**:699

 myths **5**:694–695, 696, 699

  the dragon Illuyankas **3**:422; **5**:694, 695

  the Kumarbi Cycle **5**:696–697

 religion **5**:697

 influence of **5**:699–700

 women in society **5**:*699*

Hjördis **10**:1300

Hlér *see* Aegir

Hlesey **1**:27

Höd **2**:220, *221*; **5**:633; **8**:1024; **9**:1260

Hoenir **7**:988–989; **10**:1404

Hogni **10**:1302

Holy Boy **1**:87

Holy Grail **4**:509–510

Holy Trinity **7**:906; **8**:1140

Homer **8**:1035

 and the elysian fields **3**:372

 and the four winds **1**:77

 and Helen **5**:637–638, 640

 and Hephaestus **5**:645

 and the Muses **7**:921–922

 and Poseidon **8**:1144

 and the underworld (Hades) **5**:607–608; **9**:1214

 see also *Iliad*; *Odyssey*

Homeric Hymns

 "Hymn to Aphrodite" **10**:1380

 "Hymn to Demeter" **5**:618; **8**:1106–1108

 "Hymn to Hermes" **5**:672, *673*; **7**:900

 "Hymn to Hestia" **5**:686

 "Hymn to Pan" **8**:1074

 "Hymn to Selene" **9**:1276

Homo Necans (Burkett) **9**:1245–1246

hope **8**:1081, 1082

Horace, *Odes*, and the Neptunalia **7**:968

Horae **1**:112; **10**:1435

Horn *see* Freya

horned gods **8**:*1075*

horses

 Boreas (north wind) as **10**:1313

 Diomedes eaten by horses **2**:*151*; **5**:662; **8**:1121–1122

 immortal horses of Achilles **1**:*18*, 85, *86*; **5**:612

 Odin's horse (Sleipnir) **5**:*676*, *677*; **6**:818; **8**:*1030*

 Pegasus **8**:*1112*

 Poseidon Hippion (god of horses) **8**:1149

 sacrificed **9**:*1248*

hortlaks **3**:297

Horus **1**:78, *83*; **4**:466, 467, 550; **5**:**701–708**; **8**:*1065*; **9**:1279

 eyes **5**:706–707, 708

 Horus the Elder **5**:701, 703; **9**:1210

 Horus of Nekhen **5**:*708*

Horus of Pe **5**:*708*

Horus the Younger (the Child) **5**:701, 703, 704–705; **9**:1210

 rivalry with Seth **5**:705–708; **6**:764; **9**:1208, 1281–1284

 sky god **10**:1312

Hou-I **3**:303, 308

household gods, Roman *see* Lares; Penates; Vesta

houses

 Roman, shrines to household gods **6**:808–*809*, *810*; **8**:1100, *1101*; **9**:*1224*

 Slavic tree spirits in **10**:*1319*

Howard, Henry, painting of the Pleiades **8**:*1131*

Hrönn **1**:26

Hrozny, Friedrich **5**:699

Hrungnir **10**:1360–1362

Hsi Wang Mu **3**:308

Hu **2**:235

Huang Ti **3**:305, 308

Huarab **3**:322

Hubal **1**:137

Hudhayl **1**:138

Huehueteotl **2**:205

Hugin **8**:*1025*, 1026

Huitzilopochtli **2**:203, *204*, 205, 207; **9**:1200; **10**:1346–1347

 battle against siblings **3**:338

 birth **2**:208, 209

huldra **1**:59

Huma Tikitiki **8**:1015

Hunahpu and Xbalanque **6**:844, 845

Hun Cam and Vucub Cam **6**:845, 846; **8**:1047

Hundred-Handed Ones *see* Hecatoncheires

Hun Hunahpu and Vucub Hunahpu **6**:846; **8**:1047

Hunland **10**:1300

Huns **3**:297

hunter-gatherers

 animal deities **3**:381

 and months of the year **3**:349–351

hunting

 honoring Dionysus **3**:415

 by the Inuit **7**:945

 by Native Americans **3**:350; **7**:*943*, *944*–945

 rituals involving sacrifice **1**:94

hunting (continued)
  rules of **3**:350
*Hunt of Meleager and Atalanta,
  The* (Rubens) **2**:168
Huracan **6**:841–842, 845;
  7:948–949
Hurrians **5**:693–694
  influence on Hittite myths
    5:694, 696
hurricanes **7**:948–949
Hushedar **6**:748
Hwanin **6**:*789*, 792, 793
Hwanung **6**:*789*, 793
Hyacinthus (Hyakinthos)
  1:133–134; **3**:395; **7**:936
Hyades **8**:1129
Hyakinthia festival **3**:395
Hybristika festival **5**:669
Hydra **5**:*660*–661; **6**:785
Hygieia **2**:161, *162*; **3**:*392*
Hyginus **10**:1334
  Astronomica **9**:1170
Hyksos, and Seth **3**:402; **9**:1284
Hylas **6**:777; **7**:999–1000
Hymen **8**:1058
Hymir **10**:1364
hymns, Homeric *see* Homeric
  Hymns
Hyndluljód **5**:631, 676
Hyokkose **6**:794, 795
Hyperes **8**:*1130*, 1131
Hyperion **4**:564
Hypnos **5**:584–585, **709–710**;
  7:1005
Hyrieus **8**:1131

Iambe **3**:387; **4**:506;
  8:1075–1076
Iapetus **2**:178; **4**:564
Iasion **8**:1132
Iaso **2**:161–162
Iasus **2**:168
Ibdju (Abydos) **7**:982;
  8:1067–1068
Iblis **1**:137, 138
Ibn Fadlan **9**:1264
Ibo peoples, creator deity **3**:314
Icarius **3**:415–416; **10**:1334
Icarus **3**:*358*–*360*; **5**:**711–712**;
  7:887, 888
Iceland **9**:*1259*; **10**:*1365*
  worship of Frey **4**:529
  worship of Thor **10**:1364
I Ching (Book of Changes)
  3:*305*
ichor **2**:236

Ida **3**:335
Idamantes **5**:714
Ida, Mount **3**:*324*, 326, 333;
  10:*1432*
Idas **2**:276; **6**:812–813
Idfu
  festival **5**:704
  temple **5**:*704*
idolatry **1**:138
Idomeneo, rè di Creta (Mozart)
  5:714
Idomeneus **3**:398; **5**:**713–714**
Idun **1**:36, 37; **7**:989–990;
  9:1260
Igigi, the *see* Annunaki
Ilia *see* Rhea Silvia
Iliad (Homer) **8**:1035
  Achilles **1**:18
  the Amazons **1**:61, 62, 63
  Ares **2**:149
  Bellerophon **2**:230
  Cassandra **2**:274
  the Furies **4**:538
  the Graces **5**:582
  the Great Ajax **1**:52–53
  Hebe **5**:615
  Hector **5**:621, 625
  Hecuba **5**:627
  Helen **5**:640
  Helen and Paris **5**:636–637
  Hypnos **7**:1005
  Idomeneus **5**:713
  the Lesser Ajax **1**:53
  Niobe **7**:986
  Paeon **8**:1069
  Paris **8**:1087
  Peleus **8**:1097
  Troilus **10**:1388
  the Trojan War **5**:595
Illapa **6**:727
Illuyankas **3**:422; **5**:694, 695
"Il Penseroso" (Milton) **7**:920
Ilus **6**:805
Imana **1**:40; **3**:323
Imbolc (Oimelg) festival **4**:513;
  6:758; **10**:1422
Imhotep **9**:1194
Imru' Al-qays Ibn Hujr **1**:138
Imset (Imsety) **1**:110, 111;
  5:610
Imy-uaf **2**:189
Inanna **1**:67; **4**:485; **5**:**715–718**;
  7:870
  changing roles **5**:715
  Dumuzi and **4**:449–450, 451,
    456–457; **5**:717

equivalent goddesses **6**:760
  Assyrian and Babylonian
    see Ishtar
  Phoenician *see* Astarte
  and the moon **3**:348
  parallels with Circe **3**:311
  sacred prostitutes of **5**:717
  in the underworld **3**:348,
    370–371; **5**:715–717
Inaras **5**:693, 694
Inari **4**:517
Inca **6**:**724–731**
  festivals **6**:*729*
  gods **6**:*726*–728
    sun god **6**:726;
      10:1347–1348
  Machu Picchu **6**:*725*, 726;
    10:1348
  myths **6**:729
    birth of the Inca Empire
      6:729–730
    creation myth **3**:322; **4**:523;
      6:729
    flood **4**:523; **6**:729
    the Quechua tradition **6**:731
  religion **6**:730–*731*
  sacrifice **6**:*728*
  the Spaniards and **6**:725–726
    chroniclers of Inca culture
      6:*730*
  worship of *huaca* **6**:728
incest **10**:1398, 1421
India **6**:**732–739**
  animal sacrifice **1**:94; **6**:737
  Aryans **6**:734–735
  battle between *ashuras* and
    devas **3**:338
  belief in reincarnation
    9:1215–1217
  Birhor **1**:103
  calendars **2**:257–258
  creation myth **3**:317
  death and the afterlife **5**:608;
    7:913
  Dravidian civilization **3**:364
  Indus Valley (Harappan)
    civilization **3**:*316*;
    6:732–*734*, 739
  myths **3**:317; **6**:737–738
  the Rig Veda **3**:422; **5**:672;
    6:735; **7**:892
  sacrifice of the original man
    9:1247
  shamans **9**:1285
  Stone Age civilizations **6**:732
  totemism **1**:103

Indonesia
  ancestor worship
    10:1328–1329
  belief in a soul **10**:1328
  Islam in **10**:1323
Indra **3**:364, 382, 422;
  4:504; **6**:735, *736*, 738;
  10:1312
  and the flood **4**:522
Indus Valley (Harappan)
  civilization **6**:732–*734*,
  737, *739*
  collapse **6**:734
  mother goddess **3**:*316*
Ing **4**:561
Ingres, Jean-Auguste-
  Dominique, painting of
  Zeus and Thetis **10**:*1356*
Ino **1**:116; **2**:253; **5**:654; **6**:776;
  8:1093
interpretatio Romana **6**:861
Inti **6**:726, 727, 728
Inti Illapa **6**:727
Inti Raimi festival **6**:*729*
Inua **7**:945
Inuit
  hunting by **7**:945
  moon and sun deities **7**:911;
    10:1346
  sea deities **9**:1271
  spirits **7**:945
Inutoto **8**:1014
Io (mistress of Zeus) **5**:653;
  6:*781*, 859; **8**:1076; **9**:1180;
  10:1435–1436
Io (Polynesian god) **8**:1016
Iobates **2**:230, 231
Iolaus **5**:616, 661
Iole **5**:665; **8**:1118
Ion **3**:398
Ionians **5**:593, 595
Ioskeha **7**:938, 939
Iphicles **5**:659; **10**:1436
Iphigeneia **2**:185; **3**:394;
  6:**740–743**
  Artemis and **2**:159, 160;
    3:408
  becomes Hecate **5**:619
  Orestes and **3**:408; **6**:742;
    8:1053
  sacrifice of **1**:16, 49; **2**:159,
    160; **3**:312, 408; **4**:470;
    6:740; **8**:1050, 1087
Iphigeneia (Ennius) **6**:743
Iphigeneia (Feuerbach) **6**:*740*
Iphigeneia (Goethe) **4**:497

Iphigeneia at Aulis (Euripides) **2**:159; **6**:740–742, 856

Iphigeneia in Aulis (Gluck) **6**:743

Iphigeneia in Brooklyn (Schickele) **6**:743

Iphigeneia in Tauris (Euripides) **3**:312; **4**:539; **6**:742

Iphigeneia in Tauris (Gluck) **6**:743

Iphigenie in Aulis (Hauptmann) **6**:743

Iphigenie in Delphi (Hauptmann) **6**:743

Iphimede **6**:742

Iphis, and Anaxarete **8**:1141–1142

Iqi Balam **6**:842

Iran **6**:744–749

apocalypse myth **1**:127

deities **1**:102; **6**:746–747, *748, 749*

painting of a giant **4**:*563*

Zoroastrianism **3**:402; **4**:443–444; **6**:744, 745–*749*

Iraq

and the earth mother **4**:*454*

ziggurats **1**:*66*

see also Mesopotamia

Ireland **6**:750–759

ancestor worship **1**:70–71

"boyhood deeds" stories **9**:*1226*–1227

carvings representing fertility **4**:506

Celts **6**:751

Christianity **6**:751–752, *759*

classes (cycles) of myths **6**:752–753

class system of the gods **6**:753

elves **1**:59

fertility of the land **4**:510

festivals **6**:757–759

gods and heroes **6**:757

horse sacrifice **9**:1248

measurement of time **6**:757

myths **6**:*753*, 754–757

name changes of the gods **6**:753–754

Neolithic tomb at Newgrange **6**:750, 751, *752*, 757; **9**:*1161*, 1163

the number three **6**:759

origin myths **6**:754–755

people of the Sidhe **8**:1133

tale types **6**:754

virgin goddess **10**:1422

Irenaeus, Saint **7**:906

Iris **10**:1313

Irmin **4**:561

Iryon **6**:790

Ished tree **2**:*190*

Ishkur **5**:693

Ishtar **4**:485; **6**:760–763; **7**:870

descent to the underworld **6**:762–763

equivalent goddesses **6**:760

Phoenician *see* Astarte

Sumerian *see* Inanna

and Gilgamesh **4**:571–572

and rainbows **10**:1313

sexual rituals in honor of **6**:763

symbols **6**:760

and Tammuz **1**:24; **6**:760–762

Ishtar Gate **6**:*760*, 763, *829*; **7**:*876*

Isia, the **6**:769

Isis **2**:188; **4**:466; **6**:764–769; **7**:*931*; **8**:*1065*

birth **4**:550

and the contest between Seth and Horus **5**:705–706; **6**:764; **9**:1282

cult of **6**:768; **9**:*1178*

as earth mother **4**:457

gain of power from Re **6**:764, 766; **9**:1210

Isis Pelagia (Isis of the Sea) **6**:767

link with Artemis **6**:768–769

link with Demeter **6**:768

merger with the goddess Hathor **6**:767

merger with the goddess Renenutet **6**:767

and the moon **6**:768–769

mysteries of **7**:931, 933

and Nepthys **7**:962, *964*

and Osiris **1**:109; **4**:457, 466–467, 503; **5**:704; **6**:764; **8**:1064, *1066*

roles **6**:766–767

Romans and **6**:768, *769*; **7**:933; **8**:*1138*; **9**:1238

and the seven scorpions **5**:703

Temple of Isis at Philae **6**:*767*

worship of **6**:767–769; **8**:*1138*

Iskur **4**:505

Islam

in Africa **1**:38–39

in Arabia **1**:*138*, 140

the black stone of Mecca **1**:*139*

circumcision **9**:1224

monotheism **7**:905–*907*, 908, 909, 910

in Southeast Asia **10**:1323

Ismene **1**:106; **8**:1042, 1045

Isthmian Games **8**:1144, 1149–1150; **10**:1307

Istros **8**:1022

Isturitz **9**:1159

Italy, cult of Isis **6**:768; **9**:1238

Itzá **6**:799

Itzamna **6**:842, 845; **10**:*1310*

see also Gucumàtz; Kukulkan; Quetzalcoatl

Ixchel (Ix Chel) **6**:844, 845; **7**:915

Ixion **5**:584, 652

Ixtab **6**:844–845

Iynx **5**:655; **8**:1076

Izanagi **3**:317–318; **9**:1267–1268

Izanami **3**:317–318; **9**:1267–1268

Iztaccíhuatl **7**:952

Jabiru and Emu, story of **2**:196, *197*

Jacomb-Hood, George Percy, illustration of Hermód and Balder **5**:677

Jacopo della Quercia, sculpture of Rhea Silvia **9**:*1220*

Jade Emperor *see* Yü Ti

Jaguar Baby **8**:1048

jaguar cult **8**:1048–1049

Jainism **9**:1217

Jambhala *see* Kubera

Jana **6**:773

Janus **6**:770–774, 780

Janus and Juno (Zelotti) **6**:*771*

Japan

Ainu **1**:94; **3**:381

ancestor worship **1**:72, 73

animal sacrifice **1**:94

animal worship **3**:381

constellations **10**:1337–1338, 1339, 1340

creation myth **3**:317–318; **9**:1267–1268

demons **3**:*406*

festivals **4**:517–*518*; **10**:1347

flag **10**:1347

imperial family **10**:*1347*

rites of passage **9**:*1227*

Shinto **3**:316, 317–318; **4**:517

weddings **9**:*1227*

jars, canopic **1**:110–111; **5**:*610*

Jason **6**:775–779

death **6**:779

voyage with the Argonauts **2**:149; **6**:775–779

and the Amazons **1**:62

and Atalanta **2**:167

and the Harpies **5**:*612*; **6**:779

and Hecate **5**:619

and Hera **5**:656–657; **6**:777–778

and Medea **2**:149, 236; **3**:310, 426; **4**:489; **5**:619; **6**:778, 779, *848–849*

and Orpheus **8**:1057

ship (the *Argo*) **8**:1126

and Talos **2**:236

and Triton **10**:1387

and Troy **6**:*805*

Jason Swearing Eternal Affection to Medea (de Troy) **6**:*849*

Java

deities **10**:1324

myth about volcanoes **10**:1327

Jayavarman II **10**:1322

Jayavarman VII **10**:1322, 1324

Jemshid *see* Yima

Jerash **6**:*808*

Jericho, Neolithic burials **9**:1162

Jesus Christ

and the apocalypse **1**:121

depicted as Orpheus **8**:1058

Norse mythology and Balder **2**:222, 223

Odin **8**:1029–1030; **9**:1265

Jeune Homme et la Mort, Le (Petit) **7**:*936*

Jews *see* Judaism

Jingo **9**:1270–1271

Jocasta **8**:1040, 1041, 1043, *1044*

Jordaens, Jacob, *Ulysses in the Cave of Polyphemus* **3**:*354*

Jordan

Jerash **6**:*808*

temple to Artemis **2**:*159*

Jörmungand **1**:126; **5**:633; **8**:1024, *1026*

Jörmungand (continued)
see also Midgard Serpent
Jötunheim **2**:234; **5**:631;
8:1027; **10**:1429
Jove see Jupiter
Joyce, James, Ulysses **8**:1039
Judaism
the afterlife **9**:1219
animal-headed figures **1**:81
circumcision **9**:1224
the devil and demons **3**:402
and monotheism **7**:905–907,
908, 910
Judgment of Paris (Bell) **8**:1089
Judgment of Paris (Rubens)
8:1089
Judgment of Paris, The
(Botticelli) **8**:1086
Judgment of Paris, The
(Feuerbach) **1**:118
Juksáhkká **9**:1266
Julia Domna **10**:1412, 1415
Juno **6**:780–782; **7**:931; **8**:1073;
9:1231
and the Milky Way **5**:659;
10:1338
and the pomegranate **8**:1109
and rainbows **10**:1313
wife of Jupiter **6**:783–785
Juno Showering Gifts on Venice
(Veronese) **6**:782
Jupiter (Jove) **3**:384; **4**:504;
6:783–788; **9**:1231
Greek counterpart see Zeus
interaction with mortals
6:785–786
Jupiter Dolicenus **6**:786
Jupiter Heliopolitanus **6**:786,
787
Jupiter-Mars-Quirinus triad
9:1233
love affairs **6**:785
many shapes **6**:785
temples to **6**:786–787; **9**:1234
Jupiter columns **6**:785, 788
Jupiter (planet), named **10**:1335
Jurakan **4**:447
Jurate **2**:227, 228
Juturna **6**:773

Kaang **1**:40–41, 43
Ka-aper **9**:1177
kachinas **1**:73
Kachin people
belief in the afterlife **10**:1329
and the soul **10**:1328

Kadaklan **10**:1326
Kadesh, battle of **5**:692
Kadmos see Cadmus
Kalaturru **5**:717
Kalb **1**:138
Kali **3**:402–403; **4**:447; **6**:732,
738
Kamala **3**:317
Kamrusepas **5**:693
Kanaloa (Tangaroa) **8**:1013,
1015
Kana'ti (Lucky Hunter) **7**:939,
942
Kane **8**:1014
Kapo **8**:1017
Kapoor, Anish, Marsyas **1**:135
Karma **1**:80; **6**:737
Karme see Carme
Karnak
statues of Sekhmet **9**:1194
Temple of Amun **9**:1177
Kashmir, shamans **9**:1285
Kassites **7**:872
Kastytis **2**:227–228
Kauai **9**:1272
Kauffmann, Angelica, The
Legend of Cupid and Psyche
9:1188
Kaupole **2**:228
Kazikamuntu **3**:323
Keats, John, Endymion **4**:475
Kedalion **8**:1055
Kelpie **3**:404
Keres (Destinies) **4**:493; **8**:1121
Ket people, and the south wind
10:1315
Khafre **9**:1206
pyramid **10**:1330
and the Sphinx **10**:1330,
1332
Khamba, and Thoibi
5:679–680
Khasekhemwy **9**:1279
Khasis **5**:711
Khaywan **1**:138
Khazraj **1**:138
Khepra **10**:1341–1342
Khepri **1**:78–79; **7**:962
Khmun (Khmun-Re; Khnum)
4:466; **5**:610; **7**:981; **9**:1206
Khoikhoi people **1**:45
Khong Lo **4**:570
Khonsu **4**:466; **7**:912
Khonvum **3**:314–316
Khors **10**:1318
Khufu, funerary boat **4**:463

Ki **1**:67; **3**:318; **6**:829
Kikuyu people **1**:44; **8**:1126
Kilyamama **6**:727
Kim Alji **6**:792
Kimberley **2**:201
Kim Pusik **6**:790
Kingu **3**:403; **6**:831
Kinich Ahau **6**:842
kinoly **1**:74
Kintu **1**:43
Kipling, Rudyard, Puck of
Pook's Hill **10**:1427
Kish **7**:869
Kishar **10**:1369
Kishelemukong **5**:588
Kitab al-asnan (Hisham ibn al-
Kalbi) **1**:137
Kitsune-Tsuki **3**:406
Klee, Paul, drawing of
Pandora's box **8**:1084
Kleitos **4**:483
Klinger, Max, sculpture of
Cassandra **2**:272
Klytaimestra see Clytemnestra
Koboka **2**:197
Koguryo **6**:789, 794
Köke Möngke Tengri
(Qormusta) **3**:295, 299
Kólga **1**:26
Koljada festival **10**:1320, 1321
Korea **6**:789–796
animism and magic
6:792–794
categories of myths
6:790–791
epics of the Three Kingdoms
6:794–795
kings of Silla **6**:794, 795–796
solhwa **6**:790, 795
Three Kingdoms **6**:789–790
Kos **2**:162; **5**:667
Kostroma **10**:1318
Kothar **2**:212, 214; **5**:711
Koyash **3**:296
Krafft, Johann Peter, Oedipus
and Antigone at Colonus
1:107
Kraken **9**:1273–1274
Kraken Wakes, The (Wyndham)
4:526
Kriemhild **7**:972–974; **10**:1304
Krishna **6**:738
death **1**:19
Krivichi, cremations **10**:1321
Krttika **10**:1340
Kruchina **10**:1318

Kshthathra Vairya (Khshathra
Vairya) **1**:102; **6**:747, 748
K'u **3**:308
Ku **3**:320; **8**:1013, 1015–1016
Kua **3**:319
Kuan Ti **8**:1140
Kubera (Vaisravana; Jambhala)
8:1139
Kud **6**:792
K'uei Hsing **3**:308–309
Ku-kapuna **8**:1019
Ku-kekoa **8**:1019
Kukulkan **6**:797–800, 842, 843,
845; **9**:1199
see also Quetzalcoatl
Kulla **4**:477, 505
Kullah **1**:66
Kuloskap **3**:321; **7**:939
Kumarbi **5**:693, 696, 697;
10:1398
Kunai people **2**:199
Kun Iun **3**:307
Kupalo festival **10**:1320
Kurdalagon **10**:1426
Kurgan, earthworks **10**:1321
Kurgaru **5**:717
Kurunta **5**:693
Kvasir **2**:235–236; **6**:801;
8:1028; **10**:1405
kykeon **3**:387, 389; **4**:508
Kyknos **8**:1122
Kyniska **3**:394

Labors of Heracles see
Heracles, Labors of
labyrinths (mazes) **3**:360–361
Minoans and **3**:330–331
and the Minotaur myth
3:358; **5**:595; **8**:1091;
10:1352
Lachesis **4**:493, 494, 496;
5:598, 599
Lada **10**:1318
Ladon (dragon of the
Hesperides) **3**:425; **5**:663,
681, 682
Lady Ashereh of the Sea
2:164–166
Lady of the Beasts **3**:409
Laestrygonians **4**:567; **8**:1036
Lagash **7**:869, 983
Lagrenee, Louis Jean François,
Education of Cupid, The
6:860
La Hire, Laurent de, painting
of Theseus **10**:1351

Lairesse, Gerard de
  painting by **2**:265
  painting of Dido and Aeneas
    1:*31*
Laius **8**:1040, 1041, *1042*;
  10:1331
Lake Nemi **3**:408, *410*
Lake Regillus, Battle of **2**:276
Lakshmi **3**:317, *319*; **4**:447;
  6:738; **9**:1268
lamba **1**:*74*
Lambton Worm **3**:422, *424*
Lamine, Peter Simon, statue of
  Faunus **4**:*499*
La Mojarra, Olmec inscriptions
  at **8**:1047–1048
Lampsacus **9**:1170
Landon, Charles-Paul, *Daedalus
  and Icarus* **5**:*712*
Laocoon **6**:**802–804**; **9**:1174
Laocoon (El Greco) **6**:*804*
Laocoon Group, The **6**:*802*
Laomedon **6**:**805–806**; **9**:1164
Laonytus **8**:1042
Laos
  creation myth **10**:1327
  flood myth **4**:521
Lara **6**:807, 861
Larentalia festival **4**:516; **9**:1205
Lares **6**:**807–810**, 861; **8**:*1101*;
  9:1224
  see also Penates; Vesta
Larsson, Carl, *Midwinter Sacrifice*
  4:530
La Salette, apparition at **1**:*124*
Lascaux, cave **9**:1160–1161
Last Judgment, The
  (Michelangelo) **3**:*419*
Lastman, Pieter, painting of
  Jupiter and Juno **6**:*781*
Lat, al- **1**:137–138
La Tène culture **2**:277–278
Latin League **9**:1234
Latinus **1**:32; **2**:265; **4**:498
Latinus Silvius **9**:1220
Latona and the Lycian Peasants
  (van Poelenburg) **6**:*815*
Laukamate **2**:228
laurel **3**:*365*, 367; **8**:1124–*1125*
La Venta **8**:*1046*, 1047, 1049
Lavinia **1**:*29*, 32–33; **9**:1232
Lavinium **1**:33; **8**:1101–1103
Leander, Hero and **5**:678–*679*,
  680
Lebanon, temple to Jupiter
  Heliopolitanus **6**:*787*

Leda **2**:275; **5**:634; **6**:**811–813**;
  10:1437
  children of **4**:445; **5**:634;
    6:811–813; **10**:1437
Leda and the Swan (Rubens)
  6:*811*
Ledberg Stone **6**:823
Legenda aurea (de Voragine)
  3:423
Legend of Cupid and Psyche, The
  (Kauffmann) **9**:*1188*
Lehmann, Karl, painting of
  Prometheus **9**:*1183*
Lehner, Mark **10**:1332
Leifthrasir *see* Líf and
  Leifthrasir
Leighton, Frederick
  paintings by
    of Electra **4**:*470*
    of Mnemosyne **7**:*900*
    of Persephone **3**:*388*
    of Perseus and Pegasus
      8:*1112*
Lelwani **5**:693
Lemnos **5**:646, 648, 649
  women of **1**:117–118; **6**:776
Lens, Cornelis Andries, *Zeus
  and Hera* **5**:*651*
Le Puy **1**:*98*
Leroux, Hector, *Vestal Virgins,
  The* **10**:*1414*
Lethe **5**:608
Leto **1**:128; **2**:157; **4**:543;
  5:653; **6**:**814–816**; **10**:1435
Letoon, and Leto **6**:816
Leuce **5**:603
Leucippe **6**:805
Leucippus, and Daphne
  3:365–367; **8**:1130
Leucothea **8**:1093
Leucothoe **7**:1002
Leucus **5**:714
Leuke **1**:64
Leukippos **4**:547
Leutze, Emanuel Gottlieb,
  *Amazons and Her Children,
  The* **1**:*61*
Leviathan **5**:695
Levi, Eliphas **4**:*443*
Liberia, myth about death **1**:47
Library, The (Apollodorus)
  2:251; **7**:986
"Lied vom hürnen Seyfrid,
  Das" (poem) **10**:1303–1304
Líf and Leifthrasir **1**:126–127;
  5:632; **6**:**817**

Limniads **1**:103; **7**:999
Limoniads **1**:103; **7**:999
Lincoln, Bruce **9**:1249
Lindow Man **2**:283; **9**:*1252*
lingams **6**:737
lingam symbol **4**:502
Linus **5**:659; **7**:925
Lir (Llyr) **9**:1186
Lisa **3**:319
Lithuania, flood myth **4**:521
Livy **9**:1175
  and the ritual of Fides
    9:1205
  story of Romulus and Remus
    9:1240
Ljosalfar (light elves) **1**:*57–58*
Llefelys **4**:510
Lleu Llaw Gyffes *see* Lugh
Lludd **4**:510
Llwyd **4**:510
Llyr (Lir) **9**:1186
Locrians, and Ajax **1**:54
Lodur **6**:818–820, 823
Lokasenna **1**:27; **6**:**822–823**;
  10:1361
Loki Bound (Winge) **6**:*822*
Loki (Loptr) **1**:27, 34–36;
  2:220–*221*, 222, 223;
  6:**818–823**; **9**:1260
  and the apocalypse
    (Ragnarok) **1**:126; **6**:822,
    823; **10**:1315
  blocks Balder's release from
    Hel **5**:677; **8**:1030
  and the Brising necklace
    (Brísingamen) **4**:533
  character **2**:220; **6**:820–823
  children **6**:818
  and the creation of the first
    humans **6**:818–820
  and the death of Balder
    1:34–36; **2**:220–*221*; **4**:536;
    6:822, *823*
    gods' revenge for **6**:801,
      822, 823
  and Idun **7**:990
  journey to Utgard **9**:1249
  name and images **6**:823
  punishment of **6**:*822*; **7**:948;
    10:*1406*
    the cause of earthquakes
      7:948
  shape-shifting **4**:534; **6**:801,
    818
  and Thor **6**:818; **10**:1361,
    1363

Thor's hammer **4**:568;
  6:818; **10**:1358–1360,
  1362, 1366
Lombards **4**:535
London, Gog and Magog
  4:*569*
Lone Man **5**:590
Longus, story of Pan and Echo
  4:459
Lono **8**:1017
Loptr *see* Loki
Lorrain, Claude, painting of
  Apollo and Hermes **5**:*673*
Lotus-eaters **8**:1034
Lovelock, James **1**:101; **4**:544;
  7:957
Love of Paris and Helen, The
  (David) **5**:*637*
Lucan **2**:281, 283
Lucifer **3**:410
Lucky Hunter (Kana'ti) **7**:939,
  942
Lucretius, *De rerum natura*
  6:743
Ludd *see* Nuada
Ludi Neptunales **7**:968
Ludi Romani (Roman games)
  6:787
Ludi Saeculares (Sacred Games)
  3:420
Lug *see* Lugh
Lugaid *see* Lugh
Lugal-e **7**:**983–984**
Lugh (Lug; Lleu Llaw Gyffes;
  Lugh Samildánach; Lugaid)
  2:279, 280, 281, 285; **6**:757,
  861
Lughnasadh, festival of **4**:513;
  6:758
Luna **3**:*344*; **7**:914
lunatics, the moon and **7**:914
Lupercalia festival **4**:*500*, 516
lycanthropy **7**:915
Lycaon (first king of Arcadia)
  2:262; **3**:397; **6**:**824–826**
Lycaon (son of Priam) **9**:1166
Lycaon, Mount **6**:824, 826
Lyceius **1**:130
Lycomedes **10**:1354
Lycorias **1**:105
Lycosoura festival **6**:824
Lycurgus **9**:1172
Lynceus **2**:276; **6**:812–813
Lyonesse **4**:524
Lysistrata (Aristophanes) **6**:743;
  7:902

Maat **4**:466, 469; **5**:608, 708; **7**:979; **9**:*1172*

maat, concept of **5**:708; **7**:979; **8**:1065

Mabinogi (*Mabinogion*) **1**:104; **2**:280, 286; **4**:510

Maboya **4**:447

Macha **2**:280, *282*; **6**:753–754, 757

Machu Picchu **6**:*725, 726*; **10**:1348

Mackennal, Edgar Bertram, sculpture of Circe **3**:*310*

Madagascar
  ancestor worship **1**:74
  creation myth **1**:46; **3**:323
  souls of ancestors **1**:45–46

Madrid Codex **6**:*843*

maenads (potniades; thyiades) **3**:*416*, 418; **6**:**827–828**; **7**:931
  and Orpheus **8**:1061
  see also Bacchants

Mae Thorani **4**:*452*

Maeve *see* Medb

magic
  in Korean mythology **6**:792
  sympathetic **9**:1160–1161

Magna Mater *see* Cybele

Magnus, Olaus, *Historia de gentibus septentrionalibus* **4**:*535*

Magog **4**:*569*

Magzor Gyalmo **1**:80

Mahabalipuram **4**:*525*

Mahabharata **6**:737–738, 739; **10**:1340

Mahatara **10**:1325, 1326

Mahishasura **4**:*448*

Mahrkusha **6**:749

Mahucutah **6**:842

Mahui-Ike **8**:1016

Maia **2**:178, 262; **8**:1131; **10**:1435

Malagasy people, ancestor worship **1**:74

Malaysia
  and the afterlife **10**:1329
  ancestor worship **1**:73
  myth about civilized behavior **10**:1325–1326

Malku *see* Melqart

Malory, Thomas **10**:1422

Malsum **3**:406; **4**:445; **7**:939, 940–941

Malta, terra-cotta goddess found in **4**:*502*

Mama Huaco **6**:730

Mamertines **6**:836

Mami Wata **1**:44

Manabozho **7**:940

Manah **1**:137, 138

Manannan Mac Lir **6**:757; **9**:1270, *1271*

Manat, al- **1**:137; **7**:909

Manco Capac **6**:727, 730

mandrake plant **8**:1126–*1127*

Manes **1**:70, *71*

Manetti, Rutilio, *Perseus and Andromeda* **8**:*1147*

Manetuwak **5**:588

Máni **10**:1405

manitous (great spirits) **7**:939–941

Manship, Paul, statue of Prometheus **9**:*1181*

Manu **4**:*522*, 523; **10**:1430

Maori
  apocalypse myths **1**:*123*, 125
  creation myths **3**:319, 320; **8**:1014–1015
  flutes **8**:*1014*
  trickster god **8**:1015–1016, *1018*

Mara **2**:228; **3**:402, *404*

Marathon, Battle of **8**:*1076*

Marcus Aurelius **8**:*1072*

Mardöll *see* Freya

Marduk **3**:317, 422; **5**:695; **6**:**829–833**; **7**:870, 873–874; **10**:1369
  battle with Tiamat **3**:317, 338, 403; **4**:480; **6**:829–*830*, 831–*833*; **10**:*1368*, 1369–1370, 1430
  and the constellations **10**:1370
  and the Murussu dragon **7**:*954*

Marena **10**:1318

Mariette, Auguste **9**:1195

Maris **8**:1072

Marmor Parium **3**:*399*

Mar'rallang **4**:446

marriage **9**:*1227*–1228; **10**:1416
  see also weddings

Mars **2**:152–153; **6**:**834–839**; **9**:1231
  birth **6**:781
  father of Romulus and

Remus **6**:835; **9**:1221, 1232, 1240; **10**:*1415*
  Greek equivalent *see* Ares
  Jupiter-Mars-Quirinus triad **9**:1233
  Mars Caecus (blind Mars) **6**:837
  Mars Ulltor **8**:1072
  and Minerva **7**:883
  paired with Neptune **7**:967
  rituals connected to **6**:835–*839*

Mars (planet) **10**:*1336*

Mars Disarmed by Venus and the Graces (David) **2**:150

Marshall Islands, female demons (mejenkwaar) **3**:406

Marsi **6**:836

Mars and Venus (Botticelli) **6**:*836*

Mars and Venus Caught in the Net (van Heemskerck) **2**:150

Marsyas **1**:89, 132, *135*; **7**:878–879, 923; **9**:1257, *1258*

Marsyas (Kapoor) **1**:135

Mary (Virgin Mary)
  apocalypse myths and **1**:*124*
  apparition at La Salette **1**:*124*

Masai people **1**:*42*, *43*–44; **9**:*1223*, 1224
  rain god **5**:614

Masewi and Oyoyewa **7**:939

Mashye and Mashyane **4**:444; **6**:749

masks
  of Anubis, and burial rituals **1**:110
  Aztec **2**:*206*
  Greek
    Agamemnon **1**:*48*, 49
    Demeter **3**:*386*
    Mycenaean burial mask **5**:*595*

Maslenica festival **10**:1320

Mass, as a sacrifice **9**:1249

Massacre of Niobe's Children, The (Dauphin) **7**:*986*

Master of Breath (Hisakitaimisi) **7**:939

Masters (Mistresses) of the Animals **9**:1287–1288

Math **1**:104

Math ap Mathonwy **10**:1422

Matronae (Dea Matres) **2**:279

Matronalia festival **6**:782

Matsya **1**:80; **4**:*522*

Máttaráhkka **9**:1266

Maui **8**:1015–1016, *1018*

Mawu **3**:319

Mawu-Lisa **1**:40; **3**:319

Maya **6**:**840–847**
  ball games **6**:*847*; **8**:1047
  beliefs about the earth **6**:842; **7**:947
  beliefs about the universe **6**:842
  calendar **2**:*259*–260
  creation myths **3**:322; **6**:797, 799, 841–842; **7**:948–949; **9**:1268
  deities **6**:841, *843*, 844, *845*; **9**:*1245*
  sky gods **10**:1310
  festivals **4**:517
  Great Cycles, and the apocalypse **1**:122
  human sacrifice **6**:797, 799–800, 845–847; **9**:*1245*
  bloodletting **6**:846; **8**:1049; **9**:1174–1175
  kings and queens **6**:844
  and the night sky **6**:846
    planet Venus **6**:843
  and the Olmecs **8**:1048
  periods of civilization **6**:840–841
  priests **9**:1173–*1175*
  pyramids **6**:*797, 800*, 840, *844*
  Spanish conquest of **6**:847
  and suicide **6**:844–845

maypole dancing **4**:513

Mayta Capac **6**:724–725

mazes *see* labyrinths

Mazzoni, Sebastiano, *The Three Fates* **4**:*496*

Mazzuoli, Giuseppe, *The Death of Adonis* **1**:*25*

me, concept of **1**:67

Mecca **1**:140
  black stone of **1**:*139*

Meda **5**:714

Medb (Maeve) **6**:752, 755, *757*

Medea **6**:**848–851**; **8**:1022, 1092
  and Hebe **5**:616
  and Jason **2**:149, 236; **3**:310, 426; **4**:489; **6**:*778*, 779, 848–849

murders committed by **6**:779, 849–*851*

and Theseus **6**:851; **10**:1351–1352

Medea (Euripides) **6**:779, 851

Medea (Sandys) **6**:*848*

Medes **6**:744

Medraut *see* Mordred

Medus **6**:851

Medusa
Athena and **8**:1113, 1144
Perseus and **3**:363; **5**:580–*581*, 674; **8**:1110–1112, 1113

Mefitis **10**:1410

Megaera **4**:540

Megalesia festival **9**:1237

megaliths (stone monuments) **9**:1163, 1228
at Carnac **9**:*1160*, 1163
Irish **6**:*750*, 752; **7**:916
Stonehenge **9**:*1162*

Megapenthes **6**:856, 858

Megara **5**:660

Mehen **9**:1208

Meilichios **8**:1132

meiligmata **8**:1132

mejenkwaar **3**:406

Melampus **1**:85

Melanion **2**:168; **5**:682

Melanippe **1**:62; **5**:687

Meleager **2**:167–*168*; **4**:495; **8**:1122

Meleager and Atalanta (Rubens) **2**:*168*

Meleboea (Chloris) **7**:986

Meles **4**:488

Melete **7**:900, 924

Meliads **4**:440; **10**:1397

Melissa **1**:105

Melpomene **7**:921, *922*

Melqart (Melkart; Melkarth; Malku) **2**:268, 270

Memnoides **6**:853

Memnon **3**:390; **4**:484; **6**:852–854; **10**:1380
death **6**:853; **10**:*1379*, 1380–1381

Memnon, Colossi of **6**:*854*

memory **7**:900–902

Memphis, and the god Ptah **9**:1192–1195

Menander **10**:1392

Mendelssohn, Felix, *Antigone* **1**:106

Menelaus **1**:15–16, 28, 49; **2**:174, 185; **5**:634; **6**:855–858; **8**:1086, 1087
in the afterlife **5**:638
in Egypt with Helen **5**:638; **6**:858
finds Helen after the Trojan War **5**:*636*, 637; **6**:*857*, *858*
and Proteus **6**:858; **7**:969–970; **9**:1186

Menerva (Menrva) **7**:882, 883 **8**:1072

menhirs **9**:*1160*, 1163

Menoeceus **8**:1043; **10**:1372

Menoetes **8**:1043

Men Shen **3**:309

menstrual cycles
first menstruation **9**:1224–1226
synchronization **7**:916

Menthe **1**:105; **5**:603

Menulis **2**:224, 228
Saule and **2**:*228–229*; **7**:914

Mercuralia festival **6**:861

Mercury **3**:*372*; **6**:859–862; **9**:1231
and the afterlife **6**:861–862
Greek equivalent *see* Hermes
as one of the Penates **8**:1100

Mercury (de Morgan) **5**:*670*

Mercury (planet) **10**:1335

Meriones **5**:713

Merlin **9**:1252

mermaids and mermen **1**:82; **9**:1271–1273

Mermerus **6**:851

Merope **8**:1054–1055, 1131; **10**:1307

Merovingians **4**:*560*

Mer-ur (Mnevis) **2**:189–191

Mesolithic Age
in India **6**:732, 750
time-reckoning **7**:916

Mesopotamia **7**:868–877
and the afterlife **3**:370–371
Akkadian Empire **7**:870–871
Amorites **7**:871
animal-headed gods **1**:79
Aramaean invasions **7**:872–873
Assyrians **7**:873–875
astrology **1**:68
astronomy **1**:68
Chaldeans **7**:874, 875
creation myth **4**:477–478, 480; **6**:832
and divination **1**:67–68

flood myth **3**:399; **4**:*480*, 519, *520*, 572; **7**:950–951; **10**:1313
gods **1**:102–103; **7**:868–869, 870, 877; **10**:1342–1343
Jews **7**:877
Kassites **7**:872
seals **7**:*874*
Third Dynasty of Ur **7**:871
trading contacts **7**:869
ziggurats **4**:*478*
see also Babylonia; Sumeria

Messene **6**:*826*

Metamorphoses (Ovid) *see* Ovid, *Metamorphoses*

Metamorphoses (The Golden Ass; Apuleius) **3**:341; **4**:490; **6**:769; **7**:931
and the Isis Mysteries **7**:931; **9**:1178
tale of Cupid and Psyche **3**:341–343; **9**:1187

Metaneira **3**:389; **4**:506; **8**:1106

metempsychosis *see* rebirth

metics **4**:488

Metis **2**:170; **5**:597; **8**:1022; **10**:1434

Metung **2**:199

Metztli **2**:205

Mexico, *see also* Aztecs; Maya; Olmecs

Mezamate **2**:228

Michabo **5**:588

Michelangelo
paintings
Sibyls **9**:*1171*, *1293*
Last Judgment, The **3**:*419*
Piabba del Campidoglio **2**:*275*
sculptures, *Bacchus* **2**:*216*, 218

Mictlantecuhtli **2**:205

Midas (Mita) **1**:132; **7**:878–880, 923
Silenus and **10**:1305–1306

Midgard **8**:1027

Midgard Serpent **5**:631, 632, 633; **6**:*817*, 818; **10**:*1362*, 1364
see also Jörmungand

Midir **6**:*755*, 757

Midsummer Night's Dream, A (Shakespeare) **3**:340; **5**:688; **10**:1355

Midwinter Sacrifice (Larsson) **4**:530

Mikelats **4**:446

Milda **2**:228

Miletus **7**:885

Milky Way **5**:659; **8**:1116; **10**:*1338*

Miltiades **1**:53

Milton, John
"Il Penseroso" **7**:920
and Pandora **8**:1083
Paradise Lost **2**:166; **7**:907

Milvian Bridge, Battle of **7**:897

Mimas **5**:646

mimih spirits **2**:197

Mímir **7**:988–989; **8**:1027–1028; **10**:1404–1405

Min **4**:466

Minaeans **1**:137

Minerva **6**:*809*; **7**:881–884; **9**:1231; **10**:1418–1419
Greek equivalent *see* Athena
Minerva Capta **7**:882

Minga, Andreo del, painting of Deucalion and Pyrrha **4**:*521*

Minoans **5**:712
art **7**:889
bronze **3**:324
cave and mountain sanctuaries **3**:333; **7**:886
cults **3**:331
bull **3**:*327*, *331*
deities **3**:332
adopted by the Greeks **2**:247–248
mother goddess **3**:321, 325
snake goddesses **3**:*329*, 330
double-ax symbols on pillars **3**:*326*, 330
earthquakes and volcanic eruptions **3**:325, 328; **7**:890, 951–952; **10**:1353
overthrown by the Myceneans **10**:1353
palaces **3**:330–331
Knossos **3**:*327*, *329–330*, 358; **7**:*885*, *886*, 889–890; **10**:*1353*
mazes **3**:330–331
religion **3**:325
see also Minotaur

Minos **3**:325; **4**:492; **7**:885–890
children **8**:1092
and Daedalus **3**:358–360
death **3**:360
and the death of Britomartis **2**:158, 247
judge of the dead **5**:606;

Minos (continued)
7:888–889, *890*
love affair with Procris
8:1093
and the Minotaur 3:327, 358;
7:887; 8:1092; 10:1352
Pasiphae's curse on
8:1092–1093
Poseidon and 7:886–887;
8:1090, 1149
ring retrieved by Theseus
10:1352
Minotaur 1:*78, 79*; 2:154, *155*,
189–191; 3:327–329, *332*;
7:*887*; 8:*1093*; 10:1352
birth of 3:358; 5:711; 7:887;
8:1149
children fed to 7:987;
10:1352
as a metaphor 7:888; 10:1353
Minotaur, The (Watts) 3:*332*
miscarriage, Japanese Buddhism
and 3:406
Misenus 10:1386
Mist-Calf 10:1360
mistletoe 4:*516*; 9:*1252*
Mistress of Animals 3:311, 332
Mita *see* Midas
Mithotyn 8:1029
mithraea 7:894, 895–896,
897–898, 933
Mithraism 6:747; 7:**891–898**,
933; 8:*1070*; 9:1238–1239
Mithras (Mithra) 2:*237*; 6:747;
7:*891–895*; 8:*1070*;
9:1238–1239
killing the cosmic bull 7:894,
898
Mitra 6:738
Mittani 5:691–692
Mixcoatl 2:205
Mjöllnir (Thor's hammer)
4:*568*; 6:818; 7:991; 9:*1264*;
10:1358–*1360, 1363*,
1366–1367
hammer images modeled on
10:*1360,* 1364–1365, *1367*
Mneme 7:900, 924
Mnemosyne 4:564; 7:**899–902**;
10:1435
Mnemosyne (Rossetti) 10:*1398*
Moabite people, and dualism
4:446
Mochica 1:*102*
modalism 7:906
Módgud 5:677

Mohenjo-Daro 6:732, *734*–735
Moirai *see* Fates
Molpadia 1:63
Momos 7:**903–904**
Momus (Alberti) 7:904
Mongolia 3:*293*
shamans 9:*1290*
Mongols 3:293–*294*
apocalypse myth 1:127
creation myths 3:297
demons 3:296–297
gods 3:295–296
Huns 3:297
life after death 3:299
Oghuzes 3:297
shamanism 3:294–*295*, 299
shrines 3:*299*
Uighurs 3:297
writing 3:293–294
monism 7:957
monotheism 3:380; 7:**905–910**;
8:1133, 1135
and devils 3:402
dualism as an element of
7:957–958
in Egypt 2:190; 7:907, *908*,
9:*1210*; 10:*1343*
ethical and intellectual 7:905
Monster Slayer and Child-of-
Water 7:939, 943
Montezuma II 9:*1203*
months 3:344, *351*
cycles 3:348
names 3:349–350
Monument Valley 10:*1316*
moon 7:**911–918**;
9:1275–1276, 1277
African myth 10:1348
creation of 7:915–916
cycles, effects of 7:916–917
deities 3:*344,* 348; 7:913;
8:1137
Aztec 3:*348*; 7:911
Baltic 2:228–229; 7:914
Chinese 3:*303*, 304
Egyptian 3:348; 7:*912*
Greek 3:348, *349*; 7:914;
9:*1275–1278*
Inca 6:727
Indian (Vedic) 7:913
Inuit 7:911; 10:1346
Mayan 7:915
Mesopotamian 7:870, 876;
8:1137; 3:348
Roman 3:407, 410; 7:914;
9:*1278*

Dyak myth (from Borneo)
10:1327
and lunacy 7:*914*
lunar cycles 3:345, 346–348
the man in the, Native
American myth 7:945–946
in prehistory 7:*916*
and the weather 7:917–918
worshiped by the Slavs
10:1319–1320
Mopsos 1:64; 5:656
morality, myths of 2:196, 197
Mordred (Medraut) 4:448
Moreau, Gustave
Helen on the Steps of Troy
5:*638*
painting of Diomedes 2:*151*
painting of Oedipus and the
Sphinx 8:*1043*
painting of Orpheus's head
8:*1062*
Morgause 4:448
morning star *see* Venus (planet)
Mo Rogrog 8:1017
Moros 5:709
Morpheus 5:710; 7:**919–920**
Morpheus and Iris (Guérin)
7:*920*
Morrigan 5:613; 6:757;
10:1401
Morris, William, tapestry of
Pomona 8:*1141*
Morte d'Arthur, Le (Malory)
10:1422
Moss Maidens 1:59
Mot 2:212, 214–215, 268
death 2:268–269
Mother of the Corn 7:931
mother goddesses 3:*316–317,*
381; 5:592, 597
Anatolian 3:*380*
in India 6:732
see also earth mother
Mother Shipton 1:124
mountains 10:1316
in China 3:*307*
Mount Shasta 5:*588,* 590
Mount T'aebaek 6:*789,* 793
Mount Zagros 6:*746*
Mourning Becomes Electra
(O'Neill) 3:313; 4:472
Moyang Kapir 10:1325–1326
Moyang Melur 10:1325, 1326
Moytura, Battle of 3:338
Mozart, Wolfgang Amadeus,
Idomeneo, rè di Creta 5:714

Muhammad 7:909
Muh'wäse 7:940
Muit *see* Mut
Muluku 1:40
Mulungu 1:40
mummification 1:88, *109*–110;
3:369, *371*
Anubis and 1:88, *109*; 3:*375*
Munin 8:*1025*, 1026
Muratos people, flood myth
4:523
Mursilis I 5:691
Mursilis II 5:698
Murussu dragon 6:*829*; 7:*954*
Musaeus 5:680; 7:*923*; 9:*1277*
Musdamma 4:505
Muses 7:**921–926**
birth of 7:899–900
and the Graces 5:582
and the Sirens 7:926; 9:1269
symbols 1:*128*
museums, Greek 7:925
Muspellsheim 4:568; 10:*1428*
Mussard, Pierre, engraving of
Laocoon 6:*803*
Mutilation of Uranus, The
(Vasari) 10:*1395*
Mut (Muit) 4:466; 5:610
Myanmar
belief in the afterlife
10:1329
belief in the soul 10:1328
nats (spirits) 10:*1323*–1324
and the origin of countries
10:1327
Mycenae
burial mask 5:*595*
graves 1:*50*; 3:*369*
overthrow of the Minoans
10:1353
Schliemann and 1:*49*
Treasury of Atreus 2:*184*
My Fair Lady (musical and
film) 1:115–116; 9:*1198*
Myrina 1:64
Myrmidons 7:**927–928**
myrrh 1:22, 25
Myrrha 1:22, 116; 5:690;
7:**929**; 8:1125
Myrtilus 2:182–183; 8:1050,
1099
mystery cults 7:**930–933**;
8:1137
of Mithras (Mithraism) 7:894,
895, 896–898, 933; 8:*1070*;
9:1239

Orphism and the Orphic Mysteries **4**:444; **7**:933, 1005; **8**:1061–1062; **9**:1214

and Villa of the Mysteries **7**:*932, 933*

see also Eleusinian Mysteries; rites of passage

Myth of Erra, The **7**:875, 877

Mythologiae (Natalis Comitis) **5**:*617*

"Myth of Sisyphus, The" (Camus) **10**:1308

"Myth of the Sun's Eye" **4**:464–465

Nabonidus **7**:876

Naevius, Gnaeus **10**:1409

Nagi Tanka **5**:588–589

Naglfar, and the apocalypse **1**:126

Naiads **1**:*103*; **7**:998, 999

and Hylas **7**:999–1000

Salmacis **1**:105; **5**:*666, 668, 674*; **7**:1000

see also Hesperides

Namhae **6**:795–796

Namma (Nammu; Ninmah) **1**:67; **4**:477

Namorrodo **2**:199

Nana **2**:186

Nanabozho (Glooskap) **4**:445

Nanak **7**:908–909

Nana Nu'u **8**:1019

Nanauatzin **2**:206; **9**:1200

Nanna (Mesopotamian) **4**:505; **7**:870

Nanna (Norse) **1**:37; **2**:221; **10**:1405–1407

Nanshe **4**:477, 505; **7**:984

Nantosuelta **2**:279

Napaea **7**:999

napea **1**:103

narcissi **7**:935, *936*

Narcissus **7**:**934–936**

Echo and **4**:*458, 459*; **7**:934

Narsinh **1**:80

Naru-Kami **7**:949

Nasr **1**:137, 138

Nataraja **7**:*956*

Native Americans **7**:**937–946**

Algonquians

hunters **7**:*944*

myth of Glooskap and Malsum **7**:940–941

supreme deity **7**:940

ancestor worship **1**:73

and animals **1**:92, 93

as healers **1**:87

apocalypse myths **1**:*122, 123*–124

Arapaho, creation myth **5**:586–587

Athabascan, hunting rules **3**:350

calendar **2**:*258*

Cherokee, myth of Kana'ti and Selu **7**:942

Choctaw, land of **7**:941

creation myths **3**:314, 321; **5**:586–587, 589–590; **7**:939, 941; **10**:1313

Crow, creation myth **5**:586

death and the afterlife **9**:*1218*

and devils **3**:406

Great Plains **7**:937, *943, 953*

Legend of the Buffalo Dance **7**:943–944

Great Spirit **5**:**586–590**; **7**:*909, 910*

Haida Indians, dual death god **4**:447

Hopi

ancestor worship **1**:73

apocalypse myth **1**:*122*, 124

fertility god **4**:*510*

hunters' concern for the hunted **7**:*943, 944*–945

Iroquois, spirit entities **7**:938–939

Kiowa

and the Great Spirit **5**:*586*, 587

Sun Dance **5**:*586*, 587

Leni Lenape (Delaware), manitous **7**:939

manitous (great spirits) **7**:939–941

monotheism **7**:*909, 910*

Navajo

calendar **3**:350–351

creation myth **10**:1313

day and night in legend **3**:344–346

Flint Chant **1**:87

healing animals in mythology **1**:87

hunting rule **3**:350

and Monument Valley **10**:*1316*

and the moon **3**:347

Mountain Way story **1**:97

rainbows **10**:1313

Rat Man and Rainboy ritual **1**:86

storm gods **10**:1311

and winds **10**:1313–1314

Yei deities **7**:*942*–943

Ojibwa

and the Great Spirit **5**:587–588

nocturnal spearfishing **7**:939–940

Onondaga, apocalypse myth **1**:123

and the origin of death **3**:376

Pawnee

stars and the seasons **10**:1339–1340

storm god **10**:*1315*

Pueblo Indians **7**:*940*

ancestor worship **1**:73

and healing animals **1**:87

religion in the modern world **7**:946

rituals **1**:86, 95; **7**:*946*

Blessing Way rites **7**:943

Sun Dance **5**:*586*, 587; **7**:*910*

sacred locations **7**:937–938

Seneca

apocalypse myth **1**:123

and sky people **10**:1315

Sioux **7**:*941*

the Great Spirit **5**:588–589, *590*; **7**:909

and healing animals **1**:87

White Buffalo Calf Woman **7**:941–942

and tornadoes **7**:949–950

totem poles **1**:*104*

Tuscaroras **7**:939

Zuni, Great Spirit and creation **5**:589–590

Native Cat **2**:199

nats **10**:*1323*–1324

Natseelit **10**:1313

natural forces **7**:**947–952**

nature religions **7**:**953–958**

see also animism

Naunet **2**:191

Nausicaa **2**:265; **7**:920; **8**:*1038*

Nausinoos **2**:265

Nausithous **2**:265

Nav **10**:1318

Neanderthals

burials **3**:381; **4**:454; **9**:*1156*, 1157–1158

and cave bears **9**:1158–1159

Nebuchadnezzar II **7**:876

Nechtan **7**:966, 967

Neck **1**:59

Nefertem **9**:1193, 1194

Nefertiti **6**:*765*

Neilos **8**:1022

Neith **4**:466

Neithon **7**:966

Nekhbet **4**:466; **5**:610, 701, 703

Neleus **7**:971, 986

Nemean Games **10**:1438

Nemesis (Retribution) **4**:493; **5**:598, 634; **7**:**959–961**

Nemesis's Triumph Over Sin (Veronese) **7**:*959*

Nenaunir **1**:44

Neolithic Age **9**:1161–*1163*

death and the afterlife **9**:1162

gods and goddesses **3**:383; **4**:*502*; **9**:1162

in Greece **5**:591–592

in India **6**:732

in Ireland **6**:*750*, 752

passage tomb at Newgrange **6**:*750*, 751, *752*, 757; **9**:*1161*, 1163

megaliths (stone monuments) **6**:*750*; **9**:1163

at Carnac **9**:*1160*, 1163

in Ireland **6**:*750*, 752

Stonehenge **9**:*1162*

Neoptolemus (Pyrrhus) **8**:1053, 1097, 1119; **9**:*1167*

Nephri **5**:610

Nepthys **2**:188; **4**:467; **7**:**962–964**; **8**:*1065*; **9**:*1284*

birth **4**:550

mother of Anubis **1**:108

Neptunalia festival **7**:967, 968

Neptune **7**:**965–968**; **9**:1231

Greek equivalent *see* Poseidon

Neptune (planet), named **10**:1336

Neptune Calming the Tempest (Rubens) **7**:*965*, 967

Nereids **1**:103; **7**:*969, 970, 998*, 999, 1000; **8**:*1022*; **10**:1356

see also Amphitrite; Galatea; Metis; Thetis

Nereus **5**:682; **7**:**969–970**; **8**:1020; **10**:1387

Nergal **7**:870

Nero **9**:1294

Nerthus **4**:529; **10**:1405

Nessus **5**:665

Nestor **7**:**971**

Nethuns **7**:966; **8**:1072; **9**:1269

Nethus **4**:561; **7**:991

Newgrange **6**:750, 751, *752*, 757; **9**:*1161*, 1163

New Zealand
  Maori
    apocalypse myths **1**:*123*, 125
    creation myths **3**:319, 320; **8**:1014–1015
    flutes **8**:*1014*
    trickster god **8**:1015–1016, *1018*

Ngai **1**:40, 43, 44; **5**:614

Ngalalbal **2**:197

Ngendi **8**:1015

Ngewo **1**:40

Niam **6**:*754*

Nias, ancestor worship **10**:1328–1329

Nibelungenlied ("Song of the Nibelungs") **4**:*562*; **7**:972, 974; **10**:1304

Nibelung I **7**:974

Nibelungs **7**:**972–974**

Nicostratus **5**:637; **6**:856

Nidaba (Nisaba) **4**:505; **7**:984

Nídud **10**:1424

nidughans **3**:*295*

Nietzsche, Friedrich, *Birth of Tragedy from the Spirit of Music, The* **1**:134

Niflheim **4**:568; **5**:633; **10**:1428, *1429*

Nigeria
  creator deity of the Ibo **3**:314–316
  creator deity of the Yoruba **1**:41

nightshade, deadly **8**:1128

Nijole **2**:228

Nike **7**:**975–977**
  Athena and **2**:175, *177*; **7**:975

Nike of Paionios **7**:977

Nile River **3**:349, *350*; **4**:*507*; **5**:609; **7**:**978–982**; **10**:1336
  Hapi as god of **5**:609–610; **7**:979–981
  Nilometers **7**:*980*
  Osiris and **7**:981–982; **8**:*1063*, 1064

Nimmug **4**:505

Nimrod, Mount, stone head of Tyche **10**:*1391*

Nineveh **7**:*874*

Ningirsu **7**:983
  sisters of **7**:984

Ninhursag (Ninhursaga; Ninmah; Belit) **4**:476, 478, 480; **7**:870, 983, 984

Ninigi **10**:1347

Ninisinna **4**:505

Ninlil **7**:870, 983–984
  see also Ninhursag

Ninmah **7**:870

Ninshubur **5**:717

Ninsun **4**:571, *574*

Ninurta **7**:870, **983–984**

Niobe **1**:13; **2**:160; **7**:**985–987**; **10**:1349

Niobe Poems, The (Daniels) **7**:987

Niobid Painter **7**:*985*, 987

Niobids, slaughter of **7**:985, *986*

Niobid of the Sallustian Gardens **7**:*987*

Nippur **4**:480, *482*; **7**:869

Nisaba *see* Nidaba

Niu **2**:191

Njörd **1**:34; **4**:570; **7**:**988–991**; **9**:1186; **10**:*1407*

Noah **3**:399; **4**:520–521

Nokomis (Grandmother) **7**:939

Nome, François de, painting of Persephone **8**:1109

Nomius **1**:130

Nonadieve **2**:228, 229

Nonnus, *Dionysiaca* **7**:970; **10**:1378

Norns **4**:497; **7**:**992–997**

Norse mythology
  Alfar (elves) **1**:**57–59**
  apocalypse myth (Ragnarok) **1**:*126*–127; **3**:323; **4**:535–536, 568, 570; **5**:*630*, 631–632; **6**:*817*, 818; **9**:1263, 1266
  Loki and **1**:126; **6**:822, 823; **10**:1315
  Midgard Serpent and **10**:1364
  the Norns and **7**:*992*
  Odin and **5**:631; **8**:1026
  Thor and **10**:1364
  blood in **2**:235–236
  creation myths **1**:36; **2**:233, 246, 249–*250*; **3**:320, *323*; **8**:1026–1027; **9**:1247, 1268; **10**:1429

deities **1**:26–27; **9**:1260, 1264
  the Aesir **1**:**34–37**; **4**:531, 554; **7**:988–989; **10**:1404–1405
  family tree **8**:*1135*
  household **9**:1266
  sky gods **10**:1311
  the Vanir **1**:34; **4**:531, 532–533; **7**:988–989; **10**:**1404–1407**

dragons **3**:425–426
  drinking the blood of **1**:85, *87*

Galdhopiggen **2**:*249*

giantesses, Skadi **4**:531, 570; **7**:989–*990*; **10**:*1406, 1407*

giants **4**:*568–570*
  Baugi **4**:568–569, *570*; **8**:1028–1029
  Bergelmir **2**:**233–234**
  Bor **2**:246, 250; **4**:568; **8**:1024; **10**:1428
  Geirröd **4**:570; **6**:822; **10**:1362
  Hrungnir **10**:1360–1362
  Skrymir **10**:*1363*
  Suttung **4**:569; **6**:801; **8**:1028, 1029
  Thor's encounters with **10**:1360–1362, *1363, 1430*
  Thrúdgelmir (Prudgelmir) **2**:233, 234, 246
  Thrym **4**:568; **7**:991; **10**:1362, **1366–1367**
  Utgard-Loki **10**:*1363*
  Ymir (Aurgelmir) **2**:233, 234, 246, *250*; **8**:1026–1027; **9**:1247, 1260, 1268; **10**:**1428–1430**

nature spirits **9**:1265

Norns (fates) **4**:497; **7**:**992–997**

sacrifice **1**:57

sea monster **9**:1273–1274

stave churches **2**:*222*

see also Scandinavia

northern lights **10**:1400, *1403*

Notus **1**:77; **4**:484; **7**:948; **10**:1314

Nü **3**:319

Nuada (Nudd; Ludd) **9**:1270

Nubia **4**:462

Nubilior, Marcus Fulvius **7**:925

Nubt **9**:1284

Nü Kua **3**:*314*, 319

Numa Pompilius **8**:1102; **9**:1205, 1233; **10**:1412

Numitor **6**:835; **9**:1221, 1231, 1240–1243

Nun **3**:349; **9**:1195, 1206

Nut **2**:188; **3**:*317*; **4**:550, *552*; **5**:703; **7**:**994–997**; **9**:1280
  and the calendar **2**:255
  in cow form **7**:996–997
  day, night, and **3**:*347*; **7**:994
  judge of the dead **7**:996
  personification of the sky **4**:*552*; **7**:994; **10**:*1312*, 1398–1399

Nux *see* Nyx

Nyama **1**:40; 42

Nyctimus **6**:824

Nymphae Infernae Paludis (the Avernales) **7**:999

nymphaeums **7**:998

nymphs **1**:103, 105; **2**:158; **7**:**998–1002**
  see also Dryads; Naiads; Nereids; Oceanids

Nyx (Nux) **3**:352; **4**:493; **5**:709; **7**:**1003–1006**

Nzame **1**:40

obelisks, Egyptian **4**:469

Oceania **8**:**1012–1019**

Oceanids **1**:103; **7**:999, 1000; **8**:1020, 1022; **9**:*1183*

Oceanus **3**:352; **8**:**1020–1023**; **9**:1269

October Horse sacrifice **6**:839

Ocypete **5**:611, 614

Od **4**:534

Odes (Horace) **7**:968

Odin (Wotan) **1**:27, 34, *36*; **2**:*246*; **4**:528, 535; **8**:**1024–1031**, 1133–1135; **9**:1260
  and the apocalypse **1**:*126*
  and Balder **2**:220
  and Baugi **4**:568–569
  and Bergelmir **2**:234
  and the Brising necklace (Brísingamen) **4**:533
  and creation **2**:234; **8**:1026–1027
  cult of **9**:1264
  divine possessions **8**:1026
    hall (Valhalla) **3**:377; **4**:534; **5**:676; **8**:1026, *1030*
    horse (Sleipnir) **5**:*676, 677*; **6**:818; **8**:*1030*

magic ring 4:555
ravens 8:*1025*, 1026
and Freya 4:533, 534
and Frigga 4:535, 536, *537*
god of battle 8:1027
house of 9:*1265*
limits of his power
8:1030–1031
and Mímir 10:1405
personality 10:1311
quest for wisdom
8:1027–1029
and the mead of poetry
4:568–569; 6:801;
8:1028–1029
suffering and 6:801;
8:1029–1030; 9:1265
and Ragnarok 5:631; 8:1026
sacrifices to 9:1264
and Thor 8:1031; 10:1365
Odosha 10:1316
Odqan Ghalaqan (Odqan
Ghalaqan Eke) 3:295–296
Od Tengri 3:296
Oduduwa 1:41
Odur 4:534
Odysseus (Ulysses)
8:**1032–1039**; 10:1307
Athena and 2:172
childhood 8:1032
comparison with Aeneas 1:30
death 3:310; 8:1038
and Helen 5:637, 638; 6:*858*;
8:1033
and Penelope 8:1033, 1038,
1104–*1105*
tomb 8:1036
travels after the Trojan War
(the Odyssey)
and Aeolus 8:1035–1036
and Calypso 2:*264–265*;
7:*999*; 8:1038
and the Ciconians 8:1034
and Circe 3:310, 311;
8:1036; 10:1372
and the Dodona oak 8:1126
and Helios's cattle 5:642;
8:1038; 10:1372
and the Laestrygonians
4:567; 8:1036
and the Lotus eaters 8:1034
and Nausicaa 7:920; 8:*1038*
and Polyphemus
3:*354–355, 356*;
4:*567–568*; 8:1034–*1035*,
1147–1148

Poseidon and 8:1038, *1146,*
1147–1148
sailing between Charybdis
and Scylla 8:1037,
1146–1147
and the Sirens 3:*393*;
8:*1037*; 9:1269
spirits of Hades,
consultation of 2:238;
8:*1036*; 10:*1371*, 1372
sees Tantalus in the
underworld 10:1350
and the Trojan War 1:50;
8:1033–1034
discovery of Achilles 1:16;
3:*412*
partnership with Diomedes
3:411–*412*; 8:1033
receives Achilles' armor
1:53, *54*
stealing the Palladium
3:*412*; 8:1033
tricking the hermit
Philoctetes 3:411–*412*;
8:1119
Odyssey (Homer) 8:1035
Achilles' spirit in the
underworld 1:18
Calypso 2:264, *265*
the Cyclopes 3:354–355
description of Crete 3:325
the Harpies 5:614
Helen 5:637–638
Helios's cattle, eating of 5:642
Heracles 5:658
the oracle of Dodona 8:1126
Orestes 8:1052
Penelope 8:1104, 1105, 1108
Tantalus 10:1350
Oeax 3:412
Oedipus 8:**1040–1045**;
10:1372, 1398
and Antigone 1:106, *107*
death 3:393
and the Theban Sphinx
6:772; 8:1042, *1043*;
10:1331
Oedipus and Antigone at Colonus
(Krafft) 1:*107*
Oedipus at Colonus (Sophocles)
1:106; 3:*393*; 8:1040;
10:1355
Oedipus complex 8:1044
Oedipus the King (Sophocles)
1:106; 8:1040, 1042
Oeneus 2:167; 8:1096

Oengus 6:751, 755, 757
Oenomaus 2:182; 4:514;
8:*1050*, 1098–1099, 1130,
1131
Oenone 1:105; 8:*1085*, 1088
Oenopion 8:1054–1055
Ogdoad 1:*93*, 94–95; 3:344;
9:1192
Oghuzes 3:297
Oghuznama 3:294
Ogygia 2:264
Oholiab 5:711–712
Oimelg (Imbolc) festival 4:513;
6:758; 10:1422
Oinoe 5:656
Oisín 6:*754*
Oizus 5:709
Okolnir 2:234
Olaf, *king of Sweden* 2:223
Olaf Tryggvason 10:1364
Old Clootie (Old Cloots)
3:404
Old Man (the Great Spirit)
5:586
olive oil, Athens and 2:175
Olmecs 8:**1046–1049**
worship of Tlaloc 10:1385
Olofat 8:1015
Olorun (Olodumare) 1:40, 44
Olympia, Temple of Zeus
2:181; 8:1099; 10:*1438*
Olympian gods 5:598; 10:1374
war with the Titans
(Titanomachy;
Titanomachia) 2:178;
3:335–336; 4:542–*543*, 565;
6:*785*; 10:*1374*–1378, 1432
Olympic Games 4:473, 475,
513, 514–515; 9:1249;
10:*1437*, 1438
Olympus (de' Gianuzzi) 6:*785*
Olympus, Mount 5:*591*, 593,
646; 10:1316, 1375, 1417
Ometeotl 2:205, 206
omophagia 3:*415*; 6:827
Omphale 5:665
omphalos 3:294
O'Neill, Eugene 2:160
Mourning Becomes Electra
3:313; 4:472
Oneiroi, the 5:709
Oneness, concept of 7:906
On the Gallic Wars (De Bello
Gallico) (Julius Caesar)
4:436, 438
oni 3:*406*

onions 8:1127–1128
Onjo 6:794
Opeconsivia festival 9:1254
Opening of the Mouth
ceremony 9:1195
Ophion 10:1313
Ops 9:1231, 1236, 1253, 1254,
1255
oracle bones 3:302
oracles 7:920; 9:1176–1177;
10:1421
at Delphi (Pythian Sibyl)
1:128–129, *130*; 7:924;
9:*1171*, 1177, *1291*,
1293–*1294*; 10:1421
oracle of Dodona 8:1126
oracle of Trophonius 7:*902*
Temple of Amphiaurus 3:*395*
see also Sibyl
Orchomenus 5:585, 660
Orcus 3:419
Oreads 1:103; 4:440; 7:999
Oreithyia 8:1122
Oresteia 8:1052
see also Aeschylus, *Oresteia*
trilogy; Euripides, *Oresteia*
Orestes 2:185; 8:**1050–1053**
cult of 3:393
and Electra 4:*471–472*;
8:1051, *1053*
the Furies and 4:*539*; 8:1051,
1053
and Iphigeneia 3:408; 6:742;
8:1053
in literature 1:51; 6:742
murder of Clytemnestra and
Aegisthus 1:50; 2:172
Orestes (Euripides) 5:640
orgia see Bacchanalia
Origen
and Mithraism 7:897
and Pandora 8:1083
and rebirth 9:1217
Origin of the Milky Way, The
(Tintoretto) 10:*1338*
Orion 8:**1054–1056**
and Artemis 2:157; 5:690;
8:1055
birth 8:1054
a constellation 8:*1054*,
1055–*1056*, 1065;
10:1338–1339, *1340*
Eos and 4:483; 8:1055
and the Pleiades 8:1129
Orisa 1:*38*, 44
Ormazd *see* Ahura Mazda

ornithomancy **1**:138; **8**:1071
Oro **8**:1015
Orochey people, and animal
    mothers **1**:96
Orpheus **5**:605, 607; **7**:923,
    936; **8**:**1057–1062**; **9**:1190
  Orphism and the Orphic
    Mysteries **4**:444; **7**:933,
    1005; **8**:1061–1062
Orphica, the **8**:1061
Orphism and the Orphic
    Mysteries **4**:444; **7**:933,
    1005; **8**:1061–1062; **9**:1214
Orseis **3**:398
Orthus (Orthrus) **5**:663; **6**:772
Orunmila **1**:41
Oschophoria festival **7**:987
Oseberg ship **7**:*991*
Osiris **2**:188; **4**:466; **5**:703, *706*;
    8:**1063–1068**
  birth **4**:550; **5**:703; **8**:1063
  and the concept of *maat*
    8:1065
  the dead and **1**:108–109;
    2:242–243; **3**:372–373;
    4:552; **5**:608; **8**:1065
  death of **4**:466–467, 503;
    5:704; **8**:1064; **9**:1281
    body embalmed **1**:109, *110*
    and the moon **7**:912
  in the heavens **8**:1065–1066
  identified with Re **9**:1209,
    1242
  images of **8**:1066
  Isis and **1**:109; **4**:457,
    466–467, 503; **5**:704; **6**:764;
    8:1064, *1066*
  and the Nile River
    7:981–982; **8**:*1063*, 1064
  Osiris Khenty-amentiu
    8:1066
  Osiris Wenen-Nefer **8**:1066
  rituals involving **4**:*506*;
    8:1067
  and Seth **5**:703–704; **7**:982;
    8:1064; **9**:1281
Osorkon II **5**:*706*
Ossetes **6**:745
Ostara **4**:513, 561
Ostia, *mithraea* **7**:895–896
Ostrogoths **4**:558
otherworld, Celtic **2**:283, 284
Othrys, Mount **10**:1375
Otr **3**:425, 426; **10**:1303
Otus **2**:150; **4**:567
Ouende **4**:522

Ovid
  Art of Love, The **1**:56; **3**:341
  and Cupid **3**:341
  and Daphne **3**:367
  and Echo **4**:458
  Fasti **6**:861; **9**:1170
  and the Lares **6**:807, 809
  and Memnon **6**:853
  Metamorphoses **1**:104; **3**:341,
    356, *415*; **4**:441
    Actaeon **1**:20
    Arachne **1**:91, 141
    Aurora **4**:485
    Caenis **8**:1144
    flood myth **4**:*519*
    Hermaphroditus **5**:666
    Icarus **5**:712
    Juno **6**:781
    Morpheus **7**:919–920
    Myrrha **7**:929
    Narcissus **7**:934
    Niobe **7**:987
    Orpheus **8**:1059
    Pan and Syrinx **8**:1076
    Phaethon **8**:1116
    Pomona **8**:1141
    Poseidon **8**:1144
    Proteus **9**:1185
    Pygmalion **1**:114–115
  the Muses **7**:923
  Perseus **2**:180
Owuo **1**:46–47
Oya **7**:949

Pachacamac **6**:727
Pachamama **6**:727
Padikhonsu **1**:64
Padma **3**:317
Paekche **6**:789, 794
Paeon **8**:**1069**
  Paeon (a Trojan) **8**:1069
  Paeon (god of healing) **1**:129;
    8:1069
  Paeon (son of Endymion)
    4:473, 475; **8**:1069
Paestum
  Temple of Neptune **7**:*968*
  temple to Hera **5**:*657*
paganism **8**:**1070–1073**
Pagan Way **8**:1073
Paidia **5**:582
paintings, rock *see* rock
    paintings
Pajou, Augustin, *Psyche
    Abandoned* **9**:*1187*
Pak **6**:795

Palaemonius **5**:649
Palaikastro, worship of Zeus
    10:1432
Palamedes **8**:1033, 1034
Paleolithic Age **9**:1157–1161
  horned god **8**:1075
  time-reckoning **7**:*916*
  see also Neanderthals; Venuses
Palestrina (Praeneste), engraved
    mirror found in
    10:1408–1409
palingenesis *see* rebirth
Palinurus **5**:710
Palk **6**:792
Pallas **1**:*33*
Pallas Athena *see* Athena
Palmyra (*now* Tadmur), temple
    to Baal **2**:*210*
Pan **2**:217; **5**:*669*, 674;
    8:**1074–1078**
  and the Battle of Marathon
    8:*1076*
  and Echo **4**:459; **8**:1075–1076
  mistaken for a satyr
    9:1257–1258
  musical contest with Apollo
    1:132; **7**:*879*; **8**:1078
  and panic **8**:1075, *1076*
  panpipes **7**:1001; **8**:*1074*,
    1076, *1078*
  and Pitys **8**:1075
  and Psyche **8**:*1077*, 1078
  Roman equivalent *see* Faunus
  and Selene **8**:1075; **9**:1276
  and Syrinx **7**:1001; **8**:1076
Panacea **2**:162
Panathenaea festival **4**:513–514;
    10:1353, 1376
Panchen Lama **3**:375
Pandaisia **5**:582
Pandareos **5**:613; **10**:1350
Pandia **9**:1277
Pandora **3**:318; **8**:**1079–1084**;
    9:1180; **10**:1437–1438
  creation of **5**:584, 646;
    8:*1080, 1081, 1083*; **9**:1180
  Pandora's Box (film) **8**:1084
  Pandora's Box (Panofsky) **8**:1083
Panhellenic Games **3**:395
Panku **3**:302–303, 308,
    319–320; **4**:570
Pannykhis **5**:582
Panofsky, Irwin and Dora,
    Pandora's Box **8**:1083
Pan and Psyche (Burne-Jones)
    8:*1077*, 1078

pantheism **3**:380
Papa **1**:*123*, 125
Papatuanuku **8**:1014, 1015,
    1017
Paphian Aphrodite **7**:931
Paphos, worship of Aphrodite
    1:119
Parabrahm **3**:382
Paradise Lost (Milton) **2**:166;
    7:907
Pararo **8**:1014
Parcae *see* Fates
Parilia festival **4**:*515*
Parion Marble **3**:*399*
Paris **5**:*622*; **8**:**1085–1089**
  abandoned as a baby **5**:621,
    627; **8**:1085; **9**:1164
  Cassandra and **2**:272–273;
    8:1085
  and Helen
    abduction **1**:15, 49; **2**:174;
      4:489–490; **5**:621, 634–
      636; **6**:856; **8**:1086–*1087*
    relationship with **5**:*636–637*
  Judgment of **1**:14, *118*;
    2:*173*–174, 272; **5**:634–636,
    657, 682; **8**:1085–1086,
    1088–1089, 1097
  and Oenone **8**:*1085*,
    1088
  and the Trojan War
    8:1087–1088
  death **6**:857
  the death of Achilles **1**:18,
    133; **6**:853; **8**:1088;
    10:1357
  dual with Menelaus
    2:236; **6**:856–857; **8**:1087
Paritegi **6**:793
Parthenios, Mount **8**:1078
Parthenon **2**:175–176, *177*
  Elgin Marbles **5**:*684*
  statue of Athena in **7**:975;
    10:1376
Parthians **6**:744
Parvati **1**:80; **4**:447; **6**:*738*
Pasiphae **3**:*358*; **5**:711; **7**:887;
    8:**1090–1093**, 1149
Pasithea **5**:582, 584, 710
Patinir, Joachim de, painting of
    Charon **8**:*1022*
Patrick, Saint **2**:*285*; **9**:1271
Patrimpas **2**:228
Patroclus **1**:14, 16, *17*;
    8:**1094–1095**
  and Achilles' horses **1**:85

death **1**:133; **5**:622–623;
  8:*1095*; **10**:1357
Paul the Deacon, *History of
  the Lombards* **4**:535
Paul, Saint **10**:*1317*
Pausanias **2**:159–160, 231,
  251–253; **4**:475; **6**:812
  and Cleomedes of Astypalaea
    3:392
  and the Cumaaean Sibyl
    9:1292
  and Daphne **3**:365–367
  and Euthymus **3**:390
  and griffins **1**:88
  Guide to Greece **7**:961; **8**:1149
  and Hecate **5**:620
  and Idomeneus **5**:713
  and Iphigeneia **5**:619
  and the Memnoides **6**:853
  and Mnemosyne **7**:902
  and the Muses **7**:900, 902,
    924
  and Narcissus **7**:934–935
  and Niobe **7**:986
  and Pan **8**:1078
  and Pasiphae **8**:1093
Pazuzu **3**:404
peacocks
  attitudes toward **1**:86
  tail **10**:*1436*
Pegasus **2**:*230*, 231, 232; **5**:*581*;
  8:*1112, 1149*
Peirithous **5**:603, 665; **10**:1354
Pelasgians **5**:592, 650; **10**:1311
Pele **7**:*952*; **8**:1015
Peleus **7**:928; **8**:**1096–1097**;
  10:1357
  marriage to Thetis **1**:14;
    7:1000; **8**:1097; **9**:1181,
    1186; **10**:1356
Pelias **1**:55, 56; **5**:656; **6**:775
  death **6**:779, 849–851
Pelopia **2**:184, 185
Peloponnese Peninsula **2**:*182*,
  183; **8**:*1099*
Pelops **6**:855; **8**:**1098–1099**
  chariot race with Oenomaus
    2:182–183; **8**:1050,
    1098–1099, 1131
  cooked in a stew **3**:337;
    6:855; **8**:1098;
    10:1349–1350
  Hephaestus and **5**:646
Pemphredo **8**:1110
Penates **8**:**1100–1103**; **9**:1224
  see also Lares; Vesta

Penelope **5**:638; **8**:1033,
  1104–1105
Penrose, J. Doyle, painting of
  Loki **10**:*1406*
Penthesileia **1**:63–64; **5**:688
Pentheus, *king of Thebes* **2**:216;
  3:416–417; **6**:828
Perdix **3**:358
Pere **9**:1271
Pergumum, Altar of Zeus
  4:497; **5**:620; **10**:1378
Periboea **8**:1040
Peribsen **9**:1279
Pericles **2**:175
Periphetes **5**:649; **10**:1351
Perkunas (Perkons) **2**:228, 229
Perrier, François
  *Aeneas and His Companions
    Fighting the Harpies* **5**:*613*
  painting of Acis and Galatea
    3:*357*
Perse **7**:1000
Persephone (Proserpina)
  8:**1106–1109**
  abduction of **3**:386, *388*, 389,
    420; **5**:*602–603*; **8**:1106,
    1108
  and Adonis **1**:22, 116
  Eleusinian Mysteries and
    7:931; **8**:1106; **9**:*1229*
  and Psyche **3**:342
  queen of the underworld
    5:*601, 602, 604, 618*;
    8:*1108, 1109*
  and the seasons **3**:349, 420;
    4:504–506; **5**:717
  showing cycles of fertility
    and death **4**:506
Perseus **3**:*364*; **8**:**1110–1114**
  and Andromeda **1**:75–76;
    3:424–425, *429*; **5**:581;
    8:*1110, 1112*–1113, *1147*
  and Atlas **2**:180; **8**:1112
  cap of invisibility **7**:*891*
  conception and birth **3**:362;
    6:*788*; **8**:1110; **10**:*1437*
  and the Gorgon Medusa
    3:363; **5**:580–*581*, 674;
    8:1110–1112, *1113*
  and Pegasus **8**:*1112*
  Perseus and Andromeda (Manetti)
    8:*1147*
  Perseus Frees Andromeda
    (Wtewael) **1**:*75*
  Perseus Releases Andromeda
    (Rubens) **8**:1114

Persians **6**:744
  Mithraism **7**:892–893
Perun **4**:504; **10**:1318
Perun's Day **10**:1320
Perusa **9**:1247
Peruzzi, Baldassare, *Dance of
  Apollo and the Muses*
  7:*921*
Pessinuntica **7**:931
Petit, Roland, *Le Jeune Homme
  et la Mort* **7**:936
Petronias **9**:1292
Peyron, Jean Francois Pierre,
  painting of Alcestis **1**:*56*
Phaeacians **3**:354
Phaedra **1**:63, *115*, 116–117;
  2:231; **5**:687, *689*; **8**:1092,
  1149; **10**:1354, 1420, *1423*
Phaedrus (Plato) **7**:900
Phaenna **5**:582
Phaethon **1**:122; **4**:484; **5**:642;
  8:**1115–1117**; **10**:1344
Phaethon (Euripides) **5**:643
Phanes **7**:1005
Phantasos **5**:710; **7**:919
pharaohs **2**:189; **4**:461, 465;
  9:1284
  association with the gods
    9:1174, 1206, 1279, 1283
  as heirs of Geb **4**:550
  priesthood **9**:1174
  royal titles **5**:701; **9**:1206,
    1279, 1284
  as sphinxes **10**:1330, 1332
  tombs **7**:995–996
Pharos **9**:*1185*, 1186
Pheidippides **8**:1076
Pheres **6**:851
Phersipnai **8**:1072
Phidias (Pheidias) **2**:175, *177*
  bust of Zeus **8**:*1133*
  statue of Athena **7**:975;
    10:1376
  statue of Nemesis **7**:960, 961
  statue of Zeus **10**:1438
Philae, Temple of Isis **6**:*767*
Philemon, and Baucis
  6:785–786; **8**:1125
Philip II of Macedonia **7**:923
Philoctetes **3**:411–412; **5**:665;
  6:857; **8**:**1118–1120**
Philoctetes (Sophocles) **8**:1120
Philonectes **5**:648
Philonoe **2**:231, *232*; **6**:812
Philyra **3**:339
Phineus **5**:611–*612*; **6**:779

Phlegethon **5**:606
Phlegyas **2**:151
Phlios **5**:616
Phobetor **5**:710; **7**:919
phobias **8**:1123
Phobos **1**:116; **2**:149;
  8:**1121–1123**
Phocus **7**:928
Phoebe **2**:*276*; **6**:812
Phoebus **3**:341; **5**:643
Phoebus Apollo **1**:129;
  10:1344, 1396
Phoenicia *see* Canaan and
  Phoenicia
Phoenicians **2**:212–213
phoenix **1**:88
Phoenix, *king of the Dolopians*
  1:14
Phorcides **5**:674
Phorcys **5**:619
Phra In **10**:1324–1325, 1326
Phra Sao **10**:1325, 1326
Phrastor **8**:1042
Phrixus **5**:674; **6**:776
Phyllis **3**:394
phyllomancy **4**:442
Picart, Bernard
  engravings
    of Eos and Tithonus
      10:*1381*
    of Lycaon **6**:*824*
    of Phineus and the Harpies
      5:*612*
    of Tantalus **10**:*1350*
  illustration of Myrrha **7**:*929*
  print of Cassandra **2**:*273*
Picasso, Pablo **10**:1355
Piceni **8**:1071
Picentes **6**:836
Picus **1**:91; **4**:498; **6**:773
Pierre, André, *Le Banquet des
  Guédés* **3**:*374*
Pierus **7**:900, 924
Pietas, shrine **9**:1236
Pikuolis **2**:228
pillars
  depicting Hecate **5**:*619*
  Germanic religious artifacts
    4:560–561
  herms **5**:*619, 672*; **6**:859;
    9:1169
  phallus-like **4**:502
Pindar **2**:231
  and Elysium **3**:372
  and the Graces **5**:584
  and Hecuba **5**:627

Pindar (continued)
  and the Muses **7**:902
  Pythian Odes **3**:365
  and Tyche **10**:1391–1392
pine trees **8**:1075
Pinturicchio, fresco of
  Penelope **8**:*1105*
Piryu **6**:794
Pittheus **10**:1351
Pittoni, Giovanni Battista,
  painting by **2**:*156*
Pitys **1**:105; **8**:1075
Pizarro, Francisco **6**:725–726
Placia **6**:805
planets **10**:*1337*
  named **10**:1334–1336, 1396
plants **8**:**1124–1128**,
  1138–1139
  used by shamans **9**:*1286*,
  1289
  see also trees
Plath, Sylvia **4**:472
Plato
  and apocalyptic beliefs **1**:123
  and Atlantis **2**:181; **4**:524;
  7:951
  a demigod **3**:390
  and the overthrow of Uranus
  10:1397
  Phaedrus **7**:900
  Republic
    and the Fates **4**:496
    and the soul **9**:1215
    and the underworld **5**:608
  and sacrificial rituals **6**:824
  Symposium **1**:56
  and Tyche **10**:1392
Platzer, Ignác, *Battling Titans*
  10:*1377*
Plautus, and the Lares **6**:807
Plautus, Titus Maccius **10**:1409
Pleiades **2**:178; **7**:999, 1000;
  8:**1129–1131**
  constellation **6**:846; **8**:1055,
  1129, 1130; **10**:*1335*, 1340
  names **8**:1130
Pleisthenes **2**:185
Plexippus **2**:167
Pliny the Elder, and Neptune
  7:967
Pliny the Younger, ghost stories
  3:373
Plutarch **2**:271; **4**:466
  Amatoriae Narrationes **4**:539
  and Cronus **3**:335–336
  and moonlight **9**:1276

and Nut's womb **5**:703
and Phobos **8**:1122
and Saturn **6**:783
story of Seth's killing of
  Osiris **9**:1281
Pluto *see* Hades
Pluto (planet), named **10**:1336
Pluton *see* Hades
Plutus (Aristophanes) **8**:1132
Plutus (Ploutos) **3**:420; **8**:**1132**
Po **8**:1013
Podarces *see* Priam
Podarge **5**:611, 612, 614;
  10:1315
Poeas **8**:1119
Poelenburg, Cornelis van,
  *Latona and the Lycian
  Peasants* **6**:*815*
Poetic Edda (Elder Edda) **2**:220,
  233, *234*; **4**:554; **10**:1403,
  1425
  and Aegir's feast **1**:27
  and Frey **4**:527
  and Gerd **4**:555
  and Hoenir **1**:36
  "Lokasenna" **4**:554
  and Thrym **10**:1366
  Thrymskvida **10**:1366
  and Tyr **1**:*37*
  Völuspá **2**:246; **3**:320; **5**:631;
  6:817, 818–820; **10**:1315,
  1430
poetry
  blood as inspiration for
  2:235–236
  Greek **5**:640; **7**:902
  in Norse mythology **6**:801;
  10:1405
Pokoh **5**:588
Polemos **7**:977
Poliporthes **8**:1032
polis **5**:598
Pollainolo, Antonio, painting of
  Heracles and Antaeus **5**:*661*
Polybius **10**:1392
Polybus **8**:1041
Polyclitus, statue of Diomedes
  3:*411*
Polydectes **3**:363; **5**:580, 581;
  8:1110, 1113
Polydegmon *see* Hades
Polydeuces *see* Castor and
  Pollux
Polydora **8**:1097
Polydorus **1**:116; **5**:626–628
  sculpture of Odysseus **8**:*1033*

Polygnotus, painting of
  Memnon **6**:854
Polymede **6**:775
Polymestor **5**:626, 628
Polymnia **7**:921, *924*
Polyneices **1**:106; **8**:1042,
  1043–1045
Polynesia **8**:1012, 1013–1014,
  1140
  creation myths **3**:*320*, 323;
  8:1013–1015, *1016*; **9**:1271
  land-of-long-ago **9**:1272
  Mount Kilauea **7**:*952*
  myths about volcanoes
  7:952
  sea gods **9**:1271
  sea monsters **9**:1274
  see also New Zealand
Polyphemus **3**:*352*
  Galatea and **3**:356, *357*;
  4:*545–546*
  Odysseus and **3**:*354–355,
  356*; **4**:*567–568*;
  8:1034–*1035*, 1147–1148
Polytechnos **5**:653
polytheism **3**:380; **8**:**1133–1140**
  and devils **3**:402–403,
  404–406
  supreme deity **8**:*1133*–1135
Polyxena **1**:16; **5**:628
Poma de Ayala, Guaman **6**:730
pomegranates **8**:*1106*, 1108,
  1109
pomerium **6**:837–838
Pomona **7**:999; **8**:**1141–1142**
Pompeii
  frescoes
    of Aphrodite and Ares
    8:*1121*
    of Bacchus **2**:*218*
    of a banquet scene **9**:*1204*
    of Cassandra **10**:*1418*
    of Eros **4**:*491*
    of Galatea **4**:*546*
    of Pasiphae **8**:*1093*
    of Priam, Menelaus, Helen
    and Deiphobos **6**:*857*
  and Priapus **9**:*1168*, 1170
Pompey the Great
  and the Amazons **1**:65
  temple to Venus **10**:1411
pontifex maximus **9**:1235,
  1236
  and the vestal virgins
  10:1412, 1414
Pontus **8**:1020; **9**:1268–1269

Popoca **7**:952
Popocatepetl **2**:205
Popul Vuh **6**:797, 841, 846,
  847; **9**:1268
Porphyrion **4**:489, 566–567;
  5:652
Poseidon **8**:**1143–1150**
  and Amphitrite **9**:1269
  and Aphrodite **7**:951
  and Athena **8**:1148
  birth **8**:1143
  and Caenis (Caeneus) **5**:669;
  8:1144
  and Cassiopeia **1**:75; **3**:*424*;
  8:1147
  children **8**:1144–1147
  and Demeter **8**:1144
  and Erechtheus **8**:1146
  and Helios **8**:1148
  Hera's quarrel with **5**:652;
  8:1148
  and Hippolytus **5**:689
  and Laocoon **6**:803–804
  and Laomedon **6**:805–806
  and Minos **7**:886–887;
  8:1090, 1149
  Poseidon Heliconius
  8:1143
  Poseidon Hippion (god of
  horses) **8**:1149
  power over natural forces
  7:948, 965–966; **8**:1144
  "courtship" tidal wave
  7:951
  Roman equivalent *see*
  Neptune
  and Thetis **1**:14; **10**:1356
  worship of **8**:1149–*1150*
Posidonius **4**:436
Po Tlen **10**:1326, 1329
potniades *see* maenads
Potter, Harry **4**:448
Poussin, Nicolas
  paintings
    of Aurora **4**:485
    Bacchanal Before a Temple
    4:*512*
    of Echo and Narcissus
    4:*459*
    of Endymion **4**:*473*
    of Galatea and Acis **4**:547
    *Triumph of Neptune and
    Amphitrite, The* **7**:967
    of Zeus and the goat
    Amaltheia **10**:*1433*
Praamzius *see* Dievas

Praeneste (Palestrina), engraved
   mirror found in
   10:1408–1409
Prakurimas *see* Dievas
Pramzimas **4**:521
Praxiteles, sculpture of Hermes
   and Dionysus **5**:*674*, 675
predetermination **7**:993
prehistoric man *see* hunter-
   gatherers; Mesolithic Age;
   Neolithic Age; Paleolithic
   Age
prehistoric religion
   9:**1156–1163**
   cave paintings **1**:92; **3**:*381*;
      8:1075; **9**:1156, *1159–1161*
   at Altamira **9**:*1158*, 1160
   and the earth mother
      4:454–455
   Neanderthal burials **3**:381;
      4:454; **9**:*1156*, 1157–1158
Priam (*formerly* Podarces)
   3:*394*; **5**:*640*; **6**:805, 806,
      857; **7**:986; **9**:**1164–1167**
   abandonment of Paris **5**:621,
      627; **9**:1164
   and Aeneas **1**:30
   chief wife *see* Hecuba
   death of **9**:*1166–1167*
   meeting with Achilles **9**:*1166*
Priapus **5**:655, 685;
   9:**1168–1170**; **10**:1412
priests and priestesses
   9:**1171–1178**
   Aztec **2**:203–204, *239*;
      9:*1173*
   Egyptian **9**:*1177–1178*, 1195
   Galli **2**:187; **9**:1237
   in Greek myth **9**:*1174*
   Mayan **9**:1173–*1175*
   Roman **9**:1175, 1235
      emperors as priests **9**:1172,
         1236
      flamens (flamines)
         9:1204–1205
      Galli **2**:187; **9**:1237
      vestal virgins **9**:1176;
         10:1412–1415, 1420–1421
   virgin priestesses **10**:1421
   see also druids; oracles
Primitive Culture (Tylor) **1**:100
Proclus, and Philoctetes **8**:1120
Procris **4**:483; **8**:1093
Procrustes **3**:327; **10**:1351
Proetus (Proitus), *king of Argos*
   2:230

Prometheus Bound (Aeschylus)
   7:*926*; **8**:1023, 1135; **9**:1180
Prometheus Misbound (Gide)
   9:1184
Prometheus **2**:170; **3**:396;
   9:**1179–1184**
   chained to a rock **9**:1180,
      1182, 1183, 1246; **10**:1437
   and Cheiron **1**:16
   creations of, judged by
      Momos **7**:904
   and fire **8**:1080; **9**:1180, 1182,
      1246
   and Heracles **2**:178; **5**:663;
      9:1181
   and Pandora **3**:318; **8**:1080
   parallel with Loki **6**:822
Prometheus Unbound (Shelley)
   9:1184
Prose Edda (Snorri Sturluson)
   2:220, 233, 234, 249, 250;
      10:1403, 1405
   Aegir **1**:27
   the afterlife **3**:377
   Frey **4**:529
   Freya **4**:533
   Frigga **4**:535, 537
   Gerd **4**:555
   "Gylfaginning" chapter, and
      Gefjon **4**:553
   Heimdall **5**:629
   Hermód **5**:676, 677
   Loki **6**:818
   Njörd and Skadi **7**:990
   Thor **10**:1358
   Ymir **10**:1430
Proserpina *see* Persephone
Proserpina (Rossetti) **5**:*602*
Proteus **6**:858; **7**:969–970;
   9:**1185–1186**
Prthivi **4**:446–447
Prudgelmir *see* Thrùdgelmir
prytaneion **5**:686
Psyche **9**:**1187–1191**
   Cupid (Eros) and **3**:341–343;
      4:*490–491*; **8**:1078;
      9:*1187–1191*
   Pan and **8**:1077, 1078
   punished by the Furies **4**:*540*
   tasks of **4**:491
Psyche Abandoned (Pajou)
   9:*1187*
Ptah **2**:191; **4**:466;
   9:**1192–1195**, 1210;
      10:1426
Ptah-Sokar **9**:1192

Ptah-Sokar-Osiris **9**:1192
Ptah-Tatenen **9**:1195
Puck of Pook's Hill (Kipling)
   10:1427
Punishment of Eros (fresco)
   4:*491*
Purification of Mercury, The **6**:*862*
"Pursuit of Diarmuid and
   Grainne, The" **6**:755
Purusa **10**:1430
Pusat Tasik **9**:1274
Pushan **5**:672
Puzzuoli, cave of the Cumaean
   Sibyl **9**:*1292*
Pygmalion **1**:114–116;
   9:**1196–1198**
Pygmalion (Shaw) **1**:115; **9**:*1198*
Pygmalion and Galatea
   (Gérôme) **9**:*1196*
Pylades **4**:471–472;
   8:1051–*1053*
pyramids
   Egyptian **4**:*462*
   Mayan **6**:797, *800*, 840, 844
   see also ziggurats
Pyramid Texts **1**:108; **2**:242,
   243; **6**:764; **7**:994; **8**:1064
   and the eyes of Horus **5**:707
   and Seth **9**:1281, 1284
Pyramus, and Thisbe **5**:679
Pyrrha
   Deucalion and **3**:*397–399*;
      4:*521*; **6**:824; **9**:1179
Pyrrhus (Neoptolemus)
   8:1053, 1097, 1119; **9**:*1167*
Pyrrhus of Epirus **1**:28
Pythagoras and Pythagoreans,
   and transmigration of souls
   (rebirth) **3**:374; **7**:924, 931;
      9:1214–1215, *1217*
Pythia **1**:129, *130*; **3**:424
Pythian Games **1**:129; **3**:*365*;
   4:514
Pythian Odes **3**:365
Pythian Sibyl *see* Sibyl, oracle
   at Delphi
Python **1**:128, 129, *131*;
   3:422–424

Qadashu *see* Astarte
Qat **8**:1015
Qebehsenef (Qebhsenuef)
   1:110, 111; **5**:610
Qormusta *see* Köke Möngke
   Tengri
Quechua **6**:731

Quellinus, Erasmus, painting of
   Odysseus and Diomedes
   3:*412*
Quetzalcoatl **2**:203, 205, 209;
   6:797; **8**:1049;
   9:**1199–1203**;
      10:1382–1384
   a creator god **3**:322; **9**:1200;
      10:1385
   a twin **4**:445
   wind god **7**:949; **9**:1202
   see also Kukulkan
Quiché tribe **6**:797, 841
Quincy, Quatremère de, shield
   8:*1023*
Quinquatrus festival **7**:884
Quintus Ennius **7**:882
Quintus Smyrnaeus **6**:803
quipus **6**:724
Quirinalia festival (Feast of
   Fools) **9**:1205
Quirinus **4**:446; **9**:**1204–1205**,
   1231, 1232, *1233*
   Jupiter-Mars-Quirinus triad
   9:1233
Quraysh **1**:138

Ra *see* Re
Rackham, Arthur
   illustrations of
      Alberich and Hagen **7**:*972*
      Brynhild **10**:*1401*
      Freya **1**:*36*
      Fricka **4**:*537*
      Loki and the Rhine
         maidens **6**:*818*
      Midas **7**:*878*
      the Norns **7**:*992*
      Odin **1**:*36*
      Pandora **8**:*1082*
      Siegfried and Brunhild
         4:*562*
      Sigurd drinking dragon's
         blood **1**:*87*
      Thor **10**:*1358*
Radunica festival **10**:1320
Ragana **2**:228
Ragnarok **1**:*126–127*; **3**:323;
   4:535–536, 568, 570; **5**:*630*,
      631–632; **6**:*817*, 818;
      9:1263, 1266
   Loki and **1**:126; **6**:822, 823;
      10:1315
   Midgard Serpent and **10**:1364
   the Norns and **7**:*992*
   Odin and **5**:631; **8**:1026

Ragnarok (continued)
   role of winds in
      10:1314–1315
   Thor and **10**:1364
Raiju **3**:406
rainbows **10**:*1313*
Rainbow Serpents **2**:196, *198*;
      4:523; **5**:614
Rainboy **1**:86
Raja Naga **9**:1274
Rama **6**:738, 739
Ramayana **6**:738–739; **10**:1324
Ramses II **9**:1192
   funerary temple **9**:*1172*
Ramses III **6**:*768*; **7**:873, *963*
Ramses VI, tomb **3**:*347*
Rán **1**:26; **9**:1269–1270
Rangda **10**:1324, *1326*
Rangi **1**:*123*, 125; **8**:1014,
      1015
Ranitokona **8**:1015
Rape of Europa, The (de Vos)
      3:*333*
Rape of Proserpina, The (Bernini)
      5:*603*
Raphael
   painting of Galatea **4**:*547*
   painting of Saint George
      3:*423*
Rasa **2**:228
rats, attitudes toward **1**:85–86
Rat Woman **1**:86
Ravana **6**:738; **8**:1139
Raven Banner **10**:1401
Re (Ra) **1**:78, 86; **2**:189; **4**:466;
      5:644, 695; **9**:**1206–1211**
   and creation **3**:320; **4**:550,
      552
   Isis gains power from **6**:764,
      766; **9**:1210
   Re-Amun **2**:190; **7**:994;
      9:1206, 1209; **10**:*1342*
   Re-Atum (Atum-Re) **2**:188,
      191; **9**:1209
   revenge on humankind
      9:1211
   Seth and **9**:1208, 1282
Realm of Hypnos, The (Carpioni)
      5:*710*
Rea Silvia *see* Rhea Silvia
rebirth (reincarnation;
      transmigration of souls)
      2:285; **3**:374–375, *376*;
      9:**1212–1219**
   Buddhism and **3**:374–375,
      376; **9**:*1212*

Greeks and **10**:1313
   Orphism **8**:1062; **9**:1214
   Pythagorus/Pythagoreans
      3:374; **7**:924, 931;
      9:1214–1215, *1217*
Hinduism and **6**:737
Romans and **5**:608; **10**:1313
Redon, Odilon, painting of
      Polyphemus and Galatea
      4:*546*
Reformed Druids of North
      America **8**:1073
Regin **3**:425, 426; **10**:1300,
      1302, 1303
Regino von Prüm, *De
      Ecclesiasticis Disciplinus*
      8:1073
"Reginsmál" (poem) **10**:1303
Regnault, Jean-Baptiste
   paintings
      of Theseus and Ariadne
         2:*155*
      of Xanthus and Balius **1**:*86*
Re-horakhty (Re-"Horus-of-
      the-Two-Horizons") **5**:703,
      705, 706; **7**:994; **10**:*1342*
religion, evolution of **7**:954,
      956–957
Religion Romaine de Vénus, La
      (Schilling) **10**:1409
Rembrandt
   paintings
      of Actaeon and Callisto
         1:21
      of Athena **2**:*171*
      of Diana **2**:160
Renenutet, merger with Isis
      6:767
Reni, Guido
   Heracles on the Pyre **5**:*664*
   paintings by **2**:168; **4**:485
Renoir, Pierre-Auguste,
      painting of Diana and
      Actaeon **3**:*409*
Republic see Plato, *Republic*
Resheph **2**:268, 270
resurrection **9**:1212, 1219
revenge killings **1**:50–51
Rex Nemorensis **3**:409
Rhadamanthys **4**:492; **5**:606;
      7:885; **10**:1435
   a judge in the underworld
      7:888
Rhamnous, temple of Nemesis
      7:*961*
Rhamnubia **7**:931

Rhea **3**:326, 414; **4**:441, 442;
      5:594; **10**:1311
   birth of the gods **3**:335;
      5:601; **6**:783; **10**:1374,
      1431–1432
   Roman equivalent *see* Cybele
Rhea Silvia (Rea Silvia; Ilia)
      6:835; **9**:**1220–1221**, 1232,
      1240; **10**:1414–1415
Rhesus **8**:1033
Rhiannon **2**:279–280
Rhinegold and the Valkyrie, The
      (Rackham) **4**:*534*
Rhinemaidens **6**:*818*; **10**:*1400*
Rhinemaidens, The (Hendrich)
      10:*1400*
Rhine River **10**:*1304*
Rhodes
   Colossus of **5**:642
   cult of Helios **5**:642
Rhodope **1**:105
Rhome **9**:1240
Rhomulos and Rhomus
      9:1240
Rig **5**:631
Rígsthula **5**:631
Rig Veda **3**:422; **5**:672; **6**:735;
      7:892
Rind **10**:1425
Ring des Nibelungen, Der
      (Wagner) **1**:127; **4**:537, 562;
      7:972
rites of passage **7**:930;
      9:**1222–1229**
   Aborigines, blood-drinking
      2:239
   Greek, and the Lares **6**:808
   initiation of shamans **9**:1287,
      1289
   into mystery cults **7**:930
   Masai **1**:*42*; **9**:*1223*, 1224
   Roman, before and after war
      6:836–837
   see also mystery cults
rituals and ceremonies
   of the Aborigines **2**:*195*, 200,
      201
      blood-drinking **2**:239
   African **1**:41–43
   ancestor worship **1**:70–71, 72,
      73
   Babylonian, sexual ritual
      6:763
   of the Balts **2**:226
   childbirth ritual **9**:1222–1223
   Egyptian, for the dead **9**:1195

French, Return of the
      Gleaners **7**:*917*
   funeral **3**:371–372
      Egyptian **1**:110; **4**:552
      Slavic **10**:1321
   Greek
      for Adonis **1**:25
      Bacchanalia (*orgia*) **2**:217;
         3:385, 418
      at Deucalion's grave **3**:399
      sport as a religious ritual
         9:1249
      Thesmophoria festival
         3:386, 389; **5**:585
      weddings and marriage
         rituals **5**:667–668, 672;
         7:976; **10**:1416
      see also Eleusinian Mysteries
   Korean **6**:*791*
   Native American **1**:86, 95;
      7:*946*
      Blessing Way rites **7**:943
      Sun Dance **5**:*586*, 587;
         7:*910*
   Roman
      ritual of Fides **9**:1205
      Ver Sacrum rite **6**:835–836
   shamanic rituals **9**:1289–1290
   Sumerian **4**:479; **5**:717–718
   Umbrian **8**:1072
   see also festivals; mystery cults;
      rites of passage; sacrifice
River-Earl **6**:795
Robigalia festival **9**:1205
rock carvings, Scandinavian
      9:*1260*, 1261
rock paintings, Aborigine
      2:*196, 197, 199*
Rodriguez, Diego, painting of
      the forge of Vulcan **8**:*1080*
Rök Stone **9**:*1263*
Roman Antiquities (Dionysius of
      Helicarnassus) **8**:1100–1101
Roman de Troie (de Sainte-
      Maure) **10**:*1390*
Romano, Giulio
   painting of the Trojan Horse
      8:*1034*
   *Vulcan Forging the Arms of
      Achilles* **5**:*646*
Rome **9**:**1230–1239**
   the afterlife **5**:*605*
      Elysium **3**:372; **5**:608
      the Last Judgment **3**:420
      Lethe **5**:608
   ancestor worship **1**:70, *71*

augurs **9**:1175

Augustan Altar of Peace (Ara
  Pacis Augustae) **8**:*1103*

Bacchanalia scandal **2**:217

calendars **2**:*260*, 261; **6**:770;
  9:1233

Campus Martius **7**:967, 968

and the Celts **2**:278, 279

  druids **4**:*438*–439

and Christianity **8**:1070, 1071

Colosseum **9**:*1230*

deities **9**:1231, 1236

  three-group system **9**:1233

  two names **8**:1072

emperors

  divine **9**:1238

  as priests **9**:1172, *1236*

empire **9**:1236–1237

festivals *see* festivals, Roman

first kings **9**:1220,
  1232–1233, *1234*

Forum **9**:*1237*

Forum gates **6**:774

foundation myths **4**:446;
  6:835; **9**:1231–1232, *1233*,
  1242–1244

Golden Age **9**:1253–1254,
  1255

gods, characters of **6**:780

household gods

  shrines to **6**:808–*809*, *810*;
    8:1100, *1101*; **9**:*1224*

  see also Lares; Penates; Vesta

House of the Vestal Virgins
  10:*1415*

invasion of the British Isles
  4:438–439

Latin League **9**:1234

Mithraism **6**:747; **7**:894–898;
  9:1238–1239

mother goddess **4**:*455*, 457

paganism **8**:1071

patricians **9**:1235

priests and priestesses **9**:1175,
  1235

  emperors as priests **9**:1172,
    1236

  flamens (flamines)
    9:1204–1205

  Galli **2**:187; **9**:1237

and the rape of the Sabine
  women **9**:1232

Regia (royal palace) **6**:838,
  839

and reincarnation **5**:608;
  10:1313

religion **7**:931

the Remoria **9**:1243

a republic **9**:1234–1235

ritual of Fides **9**:1205

and sacrifice **1**:*94*; **2**:237;
  9:*1251*

  to Mars **6**:834, *839*

Santa Constanza **2**:219

senate **9**:1172–1173

temple, the Lares **6**:810

temples to

  Apollo **1**:*133*

  Diana **3**:410

  Heracles **7**:925–926

  Janus **6**:836

  Juno **6**:782

  Jupiter **6**:786–787; **9**:1234

  Mars **6**:*835*, 837

  Minerva **7**:882, 884

  Mithras **7**:*895*

  Quirinus **9**:1205

  on Tiber Island **4**:498

  Venus **10**:*1410–1411*

  Vesta **10**:1412, *1421*

Trajan's forum **9**:*1205*

vestal virgins **9**:1176;
  10:1412–1415, 1420–1421

weddings and marriage
    10:1416, *1417*

  and household gods **9**:1224

Romulus and Remus **4**:446;
  9:*1220*, 1221, **1240–1244**;
  10:1415

and the founding of Rome
  4:446; **6**:835; **9**:1231–1232,
  1233, 1242–*1244*, 1251

Romulus taken to heaven
  10:1310

Rongala **8**:1017

Rongo **8**:1017

Ronsard, Pierre **8**:1083

Rosmerta **10**:1423

Rossetti, Dante Gabriel
  Mnemosyne **10**:*1398*

  painting of Pandora **8**:*1084*

  Proserpina **5**:*602*

Rowling, J. K. **4**:448

Royal Commentaries of the Inca
  (Garcilasco de Vega) **6**:730

Rubens, Peter Paul
  paintings **3**:339

    of Achilles **7**:*928*

    of Aeneas **1**:*32*

    of Bellona **2**:*152*

    of Castor and Pollux
      2:*276*

of earth mother Cybele
  4:*453*

of Erichthonius **4**:487

Fall of the Titans **10**:*1375*

of Ganymede **4**:*549*

of Hippolytus **5**:*690*

Judgment of Paris **8**:1089

Leda and the Swan **6**:*811*

of Meleager and Atalanta
  2:*168*

of Midas, Apollo, and Pan
  7:*879*

of Neptune **7**:*965*, 967

of Persephone **8**:1109

Perseus Releases Andromeda
  8:*1114*

of Saturn (Cronus) **3**:*334*,
  339

of Thetis and Achilles **1**:*15*

Rübezahl **1**:*58*, 59

rune stones, Viking **10**:*1405*

Running Antelope **7**:939,
  945–946

Rusalki **10**:1320

Rusal'naia Week **10**:1320

Russia, the moon and weather
  lore **7**:917, 918

Rustic Vinalia festival **10**:1410

Ryugu **9**:1270

Ryujin (Luminous Being)
  7:952; **9**:1270–1271

Sabaeans **1**:136–137

Sabatelli, Francesco, painting
  Ajax **1**:*52*

Sabines, attack on Rome **6**:772

Sabine women, rape of the
  9:1232

Sabrina **2**:279

sacrifice **2**:237–238;
  9:**1245–1252**

  animal **1**:*94*; **9**:1246–1247

    and cracked bones **9**:1249

    horses **9**:*1248*

  Egyptians and **4**:469

  foundation offerings
    9:1251–1252

  Greeks and **2**:*235*, 237; **3**:337;
    9:1245–*1247*, 1249

  in Greek mythology **2**:238

  human sacrifice **3**:337

  to Artemis **2**:159–160

  to Zeus **6**:824–826

  human **2**:237

    in Africa **1**:47

    Aztecs and **2**:204–206, *208*,

238–239; **3**:*385*; **9**:1200,
  1249, *1251*; **10**:1347, 1384

Balts and **2**:227

Carthaginians and **2**:*271*

Celts and **2**:239, 281, *283*;
  9:1249–1251

druids and **2**:239; **4**:439

Greeks and **3**:337

Incas and **6**:728

Indus Valley civilization
  6:732

Lindow Man **9**:1252

Mayans and **6**:797,
  799–800, 845–847;
  9:*1174–1175*

Minoan **3**:331

Phoenicians and **2**:271

in Scandinavia **4**:529;
  9:*1262*, 1264

Slavic **10**:1320

Tollund Man **9**:1262

Turks, Mongols and **3**:299

Incas and **6**:728

in India **1**:*94*; **6**:737; **9**:1247

Norse **1**:57; **4**:532–533;
  9:1264

in the Roman Empire **1**:*94*;
  2:237; **9**:*1251*

  to Mars **6**:834, *839*

self-sacrifice **9**:1251

to dead ancestors **2**:238

Sacrifice of Iphigeneia, The
  (Tiepolo) **6**:*742*

Sacrifice to Priapus (de' Barbari)
  9:*1170*

Saga **10**:1407

Sagagún, Bernadino de **2**:207

*Saga of the Volsungs see Völsunga
  Saga*

Sahagún, Bernardino de **2**:208,
  209

  History of Things in New Spain
    9:1201

St. Egorij Day **10**:1320

Saint Elmo's fire **2**:276; **6**:813

Sainte-Maure, Benoît de,
  Roman de Troie **10**:1390

Saivism **8**:1134

Sakai people, and the afterlife
  10:1329

Salacia **7**:967

Salamis, Battle of **1**:53; **7**:976

Salmacis **1**:105; **5**:666, *668*,
  674; **7**:1000

Salmacis and Hermaphroditus
  (Spranger) **5**:*668*

Salmoneus **10**:1307

Salus, shrine **9**:1236

Salvi, Niccoló, Trevi Fountain **7**:*966*; **8**:1150

Salviati, Cecchino, painting of the Fates **5**:*599*

Samas *see* Utu

Sama Veda **6**:735

Samguk Sagi **6**:790

Samguk Yusa **6**:790

Samhain **1**:70–71; **4**:512; **6**:758–759

Sami **9**:1259–1260, 1265, 1266
shamans **9**:1249
thunder god images **10**:1362

Samothrace **1**:64

samsara **3**:*376*

Sandys, Frederick, *Medea* **6**:*848*

San Giovanni, Giovanni de
fresco of Hebe and
Ganymede **5**:*616*
painting of Eos **4**:*485*

Sango **1**:44

San Lorenzo **8**:1046, 1047, 1049

San people
myths **1**:40–*41*
about the moon **7**:911–912

Santorini (Thera) **3**:325, *328*, *330*; **7**:890, 951; **10**:1387

Saoshyant **6**:748

Sapa Inca **6**:730

Saphon, Mount **2**:*212*, 213, 215

Sappho **8**:1061
and Helen **5**:638
poem to Aphrodite **1**:114

Saraceni, Carlo, *Fall of Icarus, The* **3**:*360*

Sáráhkka **9**:1266

Saramama **6**:727

sarcophaguses *see* coffins and sarcophaguses

Sargon **7**:870–871

Sarpedon **4**:492; **5**:709; **7**:885; **10**:1435

Sassanian Empire **6**:744, *745*, 746

Satis **7**:981

Sat Nam **7**:908

Satres **8**:1072

Saturn **9**:1230, 1231, **1253–1255**
devouring his children **6**:783
Greek equivalent *see* Cronus
and Janus **6**:770–772

Saturn (planet) **9**:*1254*
moons **10**:1378
named **10**:1335

Saturnalia festival **4**:515, 516; **6**:770–772; **9**:*1254–1255*

Saturn Devouring One of His Children (Goya) **3**:*335*, 338–339

Saturn Devouring a Son (Rubens) **3**:*334*

Satvaras *see* Dievas

Satyavan **6**:739

satyr plays **9**:1258

satyrs **1**:82, 89; **2**:216–217; **3**:*413*; **4**:*447*; **9**:**1256–1258**; **10**:*1305*
see also Faunus; Marsyas; Pan; Silenus

Saule **2**:224, *225*, *228*
and Menulis **2**:*228–229*; **7**:914

Saules Meita **7**:914

Saules meitas **2**:228

Savitri **6**:735, 739

Saxo Grammaticus **4**:529; **8**:1026, 1029; **9**:1265; **10**:1365, 1407

Saxons **4**:557, 558

Scaiaro, Giovanni, painting of Paris and Helen **8**:*1087*

Scamander **8**:1022

Scandinavia **9**:**1259–1266**
Christianity **2**:*222–223*; **9**:*1264–1265*; **10**:*1360*, 1364
family tree of deities **8**:*1135*
human sacrifice **4**:529; **9**:*1262*, 1264
Rök Stone **9**:*1263*
ships **7**:*988*, 989
worship of Frey **4**:529

scapulimancy **3**:302

Scenes from the Trojan War (de' Gianuzzi) **5**:*626*, 628

Schiavonetti, Luigi, engraving of Idomeneus **5**:*713*

Schickele, Peter **6**:743

Schilling, Robert, *Religion Romaine de Vénus, La* **10**:*1409*

Schliemann, Heinrich **1**:*49*

Schoeneus **2**:168

Schram, Alois, *Vestal Virgin, The* **10**:*1412*

Schubert, Franz **6**:743

Schütz, Sebastian, picture of Apollo and Python **1**:*131*

Schwind, Moritz von, painting of Psyche **4**:*540*

Sciorina, Lorenzo della, painting of Heracles **5**:*682*

Sciron **10**:1351

scorpions **1**:85

Scotland
Blue Men of the Muir **9**:1273
devils **3**:*404*
good spirits **1**:59

Scott, Stephen, "The Tears of Niobe" **7**:987

Scylla **5**:619; **8**:1037, *1092*, 1146, 1147; **9**:*1270*, 1274

Scythia, Amazons **1**:60

sea **9**:**1267–1274**
Blue Men of the Muir **9**:1273
Celtic gods **9**:1270, *1271*
Greek gods of **9**:1268–1269
Glaucus **8**:*1092*; **9**:1274
Nereus **7**:**969–970**
Nethuns **9**:1269
Oceanus **8**:**1020–1023**; **9**:1269
Phorcys **5**:619
Pontus **9**:1268–1269
Poseidon **8**:**1143–1150**; **9**:1269
Proteus **6**:858; **7**:969–970; **9**:**1185–1186**
Triton **7**:884; **8**:1144; **10**:**1386–1387**
Greek sea nymphs
Nereids **1**:103; **7**:*969*, 970, *998*, 999, 1000; **8**:1022
Sirens **3**:*393*; **8**:1037; **9**:*1269*
Japanese gods of, Ryujin **7**:952; **9**:1270–1271
mermaids and mermen **1**:82; **9**:1271–1273
Norse gods of
Aegir **1**:26–27; **9**:1269
Njörd **7**:989; **10**:1407
Polynesian gods **9**:1271
Roman gods of, **7**:**965–968**
sea monsters **8**:*1092*; **9**:*1273–1274*
Charybdis **8**:1037, *1146*
Scylla **5**:619; **8**:1037, *1092*, *1146*, 1147; **9**:*1270*, 1274

sea serpents **3**:430; **5**:695; **9**:1274

sea witches **9**:1273

seals, Mesopotamian **7**:*874*

Sea Peoples **2**:213

seasons **3**:348–349
Baal and **2**:215
Greek myths
Adonis **5**:717
Persephone **3**:389, 420; **4**:504–506; **8**:1106–1108
modern **3**:351
Sumerian mythology, Dumuzi and **5**:717

Sebek-Re **9**:1206

Secret History of the Mongols, The **3**:*294*

"Secret Name of Re, The" **6**:764, 766

Sed festival **4**:*514*; **5**:708

Sedna **9**:1271

Sedna (planet or planetoid), named **10**:1336, 1396

Sekhmet **1**:78, 108; **4**:463–465, 466; **9**:1193, 1194, *1211*

Selene **4**:*474*, 475; **7**:914; **8**:1075; **9**:**1275–1278**

Seleucids **6**:744

Selinunte **10**:*1435*

Selket **1**:85

Selu (Corn) **7**:939, 942

Selvans **8**:1072

Semara **10**:1324, 1326

Semargl **10**:1318

Semele **1**:21, 116; **2**:253; **3**:*413*; **4**:444; **5**:654; **10**:*1436*, 1437

Semik festival **10**:1321

Semnai Theai *see* Furies

senate, Roman **9**:1172–1173

Sennacherib **7**:875

Sequana **2**:279

Serapis **6**:788; **8**:1067

Serbs, and the moon **10**:1319

serpents (snakes) **3**:*422*, 430; **8**:1139
Aboriginal Rainbow Serpents **2**:196, *198*; **4**:523; **5**:614
in apocalypse myths **1**:126, 127
in Babylonian mythology **5**:695
in the Biblical Old Testament **5**:695; **8**:1139
in creation mythology **3**:*314*, *319*, 321; **5**:695
earth mother as **4**:456

eating **1**:85
in Egyptian mythology **5**:*695*
see also Apophis
in Greek mythology
biting Philoctetes **8**:1118,
1119, 1120
symbolism **4**:486
as healers **1**:86–87
Hindu
cosmic serpent **9**:*1268*
serpent of eternity **3**:*319*
in Hittite mythology **5**:694
Hopi Snake Dancers **1**:*89*
Minoan snake goddesses
3:*329*, 330
and Mithraism **7**:*897*
in Norse mythology **1**:126;
5:631, 632, 633; **6**:*817*, 818;
8:1024, *1026*; **10**:*1362*,
1364
the punishment of Loki
6:*822*; **7**:948; **10**:*1406*
Olmec deity **8**:*1049*
sea serpents **3**:430; **5**:695;
9:1274
Serpot **1**:64
Sertürner, Friedrich W.A. **7**:920
Servius Tullius **9**:1233, 1234
Sesha **1**:127
Seshanaga **9**:*1268*
Sesostris (Senusret) I, *king of*
Egypt **2**:*188*
Sessrúmnir **4**:534
Setesuyara **10**:1324, 1326
Seth **2**:188; **3**:402; **4**:457, 466,
467, 503; **9**:**1279–1284**
animal representations of
9:1280, *1282*
birth **4**:550; **9**:1280
and the desert **8**:1064
and lightning **7**:950
and Osiris **5**:703–704; **7**:982;
8:1064; **9**:1281
and Re **9**:1208, 1282
rivalry with Horus the
Younger **5**:705–708; **6**:764;
9:1208, 1281–1284
Sethlans **8**:1072
Seti I **8**:1068; **10**:1332
temple of **9**:*1281*
tomb **10**:*1336*
Seven Against Thebes **1**:106;
8:1045
Seven Against Thebes, The
(Aeschylus) **8**:1040
Shabaka Stone **9**:1192–1193

Shabbat Hamalka **4**:448
Shachihoko **9**:1274
Shakespeare, William
and Falstaff **10**:1306
A Midsummer Night's Dream
3:340; **5**:688; **10**:1355
Troilus and Cressida **10**:1390
Shakti (Kamala; Padma;
Lakshmi) **3**:317
Shalmaneser III **7**:875
Shaman, The (Vitebsky) **9**:1289
shamans **3**:381–382;
9:1171–1172, *1274*,
1285–1290
in Africa **1**:40, 41–43, 45
and animals **1**:91
and the "otherworld" **3**:370
in Siberia **1**:*96*
the first shamans **1**:99
Turks, Mongols, and
3:294–*295*, 299
see also priests and
priestesses
Shamash see Utu
Shang-Ti **3**:302, 308
Shan Hai Ching **3**:428
Shan people, and earthquakes
7:947–948
Shao Hao **3**:308
Shapash **2**:268; **10**:1343
shape-shifting **1**:45, 105
Loki **4**:534; **6**:801, 818
Nereus **7**:969–970
Proteus **7**:969–970; **9**:*1186*
Thetis **9**:1185–1186
Sharruma **5**:693, 698
shawabtis (shabtis) **2**:244
Sheela-na-gig **4**:506
Shekhina **4**:448
Shelley, Mary Wollstonecraft,
Frankenstein **9**:1184
Shelley, Percy Bysshe,
Prometheus Unbound **9**:1184
Shen Nong **3**:305, 308
Shen Yi **9**:1211
Sheol **9**:1219
Shepherd, George, painting of
Gog and Magog **4**:*569*
Shield, The (Menander) **10**:1392
shinhwa **6**:790–791, 792–796
Shinto
creation myth **3**:317–318
festivals **4**:517
supreme deity **3**:316
ships
Broighter **9**:*1271*

Scandinavian **7**:*988*, 989, *991*
see also boats
Shoki, spirit of **3**:406
Shou-Hsing **3**:*308*, 309
Shu **2**:188; **4**:463; **7**:995;
9:*1207*; **10**:1310, 1312, 1399
Shun **3**:306, 308
Sia **2**:235
Siberia
animal worship **1**:95–99
creation myth **3**:403–404
elk mother **1**:88, 95, 96
Evenki people **1**:96, 99
Ket people **10**:1315
Orochey people **1**:96
shamanism **1**:*96*
Sibil **10**:1358
Sibyl **9**:**1291–1294**
oracle at Delphi (Pythian
Sibyl) **1**:128–129, *130*;
7:924; **9**:*1171*, 1177, *1291*,
1293–*1294*; **10**:1421
Persian **9**:1291–1292, *1293*
Sibyl of Cumae **1**:133;
9:1291, *1292*
Sibylla **9**:1291
Sibylline Books **9**:1234
Sibzianna **8**:1056
Sidhe, people of the **8**:1133
Siduri **4**:572
Siegfried see Sigurd
Siegfried (Wagner) **10**:*1300*
Sierra Leone, creation myth
1:40
Sif **10**:1358
Siggeir **1**:34; **7**:974
Sigmund **7**:974; **8**:1030;
10:1300, 1304
Sigurd (Siegfried) **1**:34, 85, *87*;
3:426; **4**:562; **7**:972; **8**:1030;
10:**1300–1304**, 1402
and the ring **10**:1303,
1402–1403
Sigyn **1**:37; **6**:818, *822*; **7**:948
Sikhism
and monotheism **7**:908
and reincarnation **9**:1217
Sila (Silap Inua) **7**:939, 945
sileni **10**:1305
Silenus **9**:1257; **10**:**1305–1306**
Silk Road **3**:*293*
Silla **6**:789, 794–*795*
Silvius **9**:1220
Simhamukha **1**:80
Simonides, and Hippolyte
5:687

Sin **3**:347; **7**:870, 876; **8**:1137
Sumerian equivalent see
Nanna
Sinai, Saint Katarina monastery
7:907
Sinfjötli **1**:34
Sinis **10**:1351
Sinon **6**:802–803, 804
Sinope **1**:133
Siqiniq **7**:911
Sirens **3**:*393*; **8**:*1037*; **9**:*1269*
and the Muses **7**:926; **9**:1269
Sisyphus **2**:149; **5**:608; **8**:1131;
10:**1307–1308**
Sisyphus (Titian) **10**:*1307*
Sita **6**:738
Sitowa festival **6**:729
Siva **3**:316; **6**:736, 737, 738
cult of (Saivism) **8**:1134
as Nataraja, lord of the dance
7:*956*
and Parvati **1**:80
rulers as incarnations of
10:1322
Siyamek **6**:749
Sjaelland **4**:554
Skadi (Goddess of Snowshoes;
Ski Goddess) **4**:531, 570;
7:989–*990*; **10**:*1407*
and the torture of Loki
10:*1406*, 1407
Skáldskaparmál (Snorri
Sturluson) **6**:801
Skallagrímsson, Egill **2**:250
Skanda **10**:1340
Skíðbladnir **4**:529–530
Ski Goddess see Skadi
Skírnir **4**:527, 555
skogsra **1**:59
Skookums **7**:939, 945
Skrymir **10**:*1363*
Skuld **4**:497; **7**:*992*
sky **10**:**1309–1316**
gods
of the Ashanti people **3**:383
10:1310
Canaanite **10**:1312–1313
Chinese **10**:*1311*
Egyptian **10**:*1312*,
1398–1399
Greek **10**:1310, 1311
Indo-European
10:1311–1312
Mayan **10**:*1310*
Mesopotamian **10**:1313
of the Navajo **10**:1311

sky (continued)
    Norse **10**:1311
    paradise in the **10**:1310
    sky people **10**:1315–1316
Skywalker, Luke **4**:448
Slagfid **10**:1424
Slavs **10**:**1317–1321**
    apocalypse myth **1**:127
    creation myths **10**:1318–1319
    deities **10**:1318–1319
    festivals **10**:1320, 1321
    moon worship **10**:1319–1320
    rituals for the dead **10**:1321
    sacrifices made by **10**:1320
    shrines **10**:1320
    and the unclean dead
        10:1321
    and vampires **10**:1321
Sleipnir **5**:*676, 677*; **6**:818;
    8:*1030*
snakes *see* serpents
Snorri Sturluson **8**:1029;
    9:1265
    and the Aesir **1**:34
    and funeral pyres **9**:1264
    and the Norns **7**:992
    and Odin **8**:1024
    Skáldskaparmál **6**:801
    and Ymir **10**:1429
    Ynglinga Saga **4**:529, 536, 553,
        555
    see also Prose Edda
Snowshoes, Goddess of *see*
    Skadi
Sobek **5**:610; **7**:981, *982*
social Darwinism **1**:100
Sockburn hogback **6**:823
Socrates, link with Silenus
    10:1306
Sokchonje **6**:*791*
Soko **1**:40
solhwa **6**:790, 795
Sol Invictus **5**:644; **7**:933
Solon **1**:123
    laws of **5**:598
Solymi, the **2**:231
Soma **3**:347, 382; **6**:735, 738;
    7:913
Somnus **5**:710
Sonchis **1**:123
"Song of the Lord" ("Bhagavad
    Gita") **6**:738 ·
"Song of the Nibelungs" *see*
    Nibelungenlied
"Song of Noble Siegfried,
    The" **10**:1303–1304

"Songs of Isis and Nephthys,
    The" **7**:964
Songs of the Kings, The
    (Unsworth) **6**:743
Sopdet **8**:1066
Sopdu **8**:1066
Sophocles **5**:598; **6**:803
    Ajax **1**:53
    Antigone **1**:106–107
    Electra **3**:313; **4**:472;
        8:1052
    Oedipus at Colonus **1**:106;
        3:393; **8**:1040; **10**:1355
    Oedipus the King **1**:106;
        8:1040
    and Philoctetes **8**:1120
Soranus **3**:419
Sorli **10**:1403
Sothis **5**:610
soul
    belief in a **3**:369–370
    Southeast Asian belief in
        10:1328
    transmigration of the *see*
        rebirth
Sounion, temple of Poseidon
    8:1149, *1150*
Southeast Asia **10**:**1322–1329**
    and the afterlife **10**:1329
    ancestor worship
        10:1328–1329
    creation myths **10**:*1326–1327*
    deities **10**:*1324–1326*
    religions **10**:1322–1323
    rice myths **10**:*1327–1328*
    and the soul **10**:1328
Spagnolo, Lo *see* Crespi,
    Giuseppe Maria
sparagmos **3**:415; **6**:827
Sparta **5**:598
    Carneia festival **9**:1275
    Hyakinthia festival **3**:395
    marriage ritual **5**:667
    and the Muses **7**:923
    tree worship **6**:813
Sparta, League of **8**:1053
Spartoi **2**:253
Spell of the Twelve Gates, The
    2:244–245
Spenser, Edmund, *Faerie
    Queene, The* **5**:585, 640
Spenta Armaiti **1**:102; **6**:747,
    748
Spenta Mainyu **6**:747, 748
sphinxes **1**:82–83; **5**:*611*;
    10:**1330–1332**

Great Sphinx at Giza **1**:*82,
    83*; **10**:*1330*–1332
    Theban Sphinx **7**:926;
        8:1041, *1043*
    riddle **6**:772; **8**:1042;
        9:1288–1289; **10**:1331
Spider People **1**:87
spirits
    in Aboriginal mythologies
        2:196–197, *199*
    manitous (great spirits)
        7:939–941
    Norse
        guardian spirits **9**:1266
        nature spirits **9**:1265
    see also devas; devils
Spranger, Bartholomeus
    painting of Glaucus and
        Scylla **8**:*1092*
    Salmacis and Hermaphroditus
        5:*668*
standing stones, in Ireland
    6:*750*
Stanhope, John Roddam
    Spencer
    Charon and Psyche **9**:*1191*
    Cupid and Psyche **3**:*342*
stars **10**:**1333–1340**
    Arcturus **2**:263; **6**:826
    Capella **3**:*338*
    evening star *see* Venus (planet)
    Milky Way **5**:659; **8**:1116;
        10:*1338*
    morning star *see* Venus
        (planet)
    Sirius (Dog Star)
        Egyptians and **2**:255; **6**:766;
            8:1065–1066; **10**:1336
        Greeks and **6**:772
    see also constellations
Star Trek: Voyager (TV series)
    8:1039
Star Wars (film) **4**:448
Statius, *Achilleid* **1**:19
stelae **8**:*1065, 1067*; **9**:*1195,
    1279*; **10**:*1312*
Stephens, John Lloyd **6**:841
Stepterion **1**:129
Stepterion festival **1**:129
Sterope **8**:1130
Steropes **3**:352; **10**:1395, 1396
Sterrett, Virginia Frances,
    Tanglewood Tales **2**:*252*
Stesichorus **5**:634, 638; **8**:1052
Stheno **5**:580
Stoics, and Tyche **10**:1392

Stoker, Bram, *Dracula* **10**:1321
Stone Age
    Middle *see* Mesolithic Age
    New *see* Neolithic Age
    Old *see* Paleolithic Age
Stonehenge **9**:*1162*
Strabo, and priestesses to
    Aphrodite **1**:119
Stratton, Helen, illustration
    of Freya **10**:*1366*
Strauss, Richard **3**:313; **4**:472
Stribog **10**:1318
Strinennia festival **10**:1320
Strophius **8**:1051
Strymo **6**:805
Stuck, Franz von
    painting of Athena, Hera, and
        Aphrodite **5**:*656*
    painting of Helen **5**:*634*
    Wounded Amazon **1**:*65*
Stygian Proserpine **7**:931
Styrbjörn **8**:1027
Styx River **3**:369, *370*; **5**:*605*,
    606; **7**:991; **8**:*1022*; **9**:*1191*
    Achilles dipped in **10**:*1357*
Subleyras, Pierre, painting
    of Charon **3**:*370*
subordinationism **7**:906
Sucellus **2**:278–279, *279*
suicide, Mayans and **6**:844–845
Sulawesi
    Bada people **10**:1323
    burials **10**:*1329*
    care for the ancestors **10**:1329
    rice myth **10**:1328
Sülde **3**:296
Suleyman (Sulieman) **1**:138
Sulis **2**:279
    Sulis Minerva **2**:279; **8**:1073
Sulla, Lucius Cornelius **9**:1294;
    10:1411
Sumatra, myth about Batara
    Guru **10**:1324
Sumeria **6**:829
    belief in the underworld
        5:606–607
    calendars **4**:479
    cities **7**:869
    creation myths **3**:318–319;
        4:477–478
    demons **3**:404
    flood myths **3**:399;
        4:478–479, 519–520
    gods **4**:478; **6**:829
    rituals and ceremonies **4**:479;
        5:717–718

urban and fertility deities ·
4:503, 505
writing 4:476; 7:869–870
sun 10:1341–1348
African myth 10:1348
Chinese mythology 3:303
deities 8:1137
Aztec 10:1346–1347
Baltic 2:228, 229
Chinese 9:1211
Egyptian 2:189, 190, 242;
5:644, 703; 7:907, 908;
9:1206–1208, 1209;
10:1341–1342
Greek 5:641–644;
10:1343–1344, 1345
Hindu 5:644
Hittite 5:695; 10:1343,
1344
Inca 6:726; 10:1347–1348
Inuit 7:911; 10:1346
Japanese 3:316;
10:1345–1346
Mayan 6:842; 9:1211
Mesopotamian (Sumerian
and Babylonian) 4:450;
9:1211; 10:1342–1343
Native American 10:1346
Syrian 1:140; 5:644
of Ugarit 10:1343
eclipses, and Baltic mythology
2:228–229
Greek mythology and
Apollo 5:600
Phaethon 5:642;
8:1115–1116
Mayans and 6:842
Norse mythology and
9:1261–1262
Roman mythology 5:644
Sun Chariot 7:989
Sun Dance ritual 5:586, 587;
7:910
sunflowers 7:1002
"Sun's Eye, Myth of the"
4:464–465
Suovetaurilia ceremony
6:834
Supay 6:727
superstitions
and the fall of Troy 6:803
Roman 6:803
Suppliant Women (Euripides)
10:1355
surfboard, the first 8:1019
Surt 1:126; 9:1260, 1266

Surya 3:382; 5:644; 6:738
Suryavarman II 10:1322, 1324
Susanowo 10:1345
Sutasoma (Tantular) 10:1323
Suttung 4:569; 6:801; 8:1028,
1029
Suwa 1:137, 138
Svaha 10:1340
Svartálfar (black elves) 1:58–59
Svear people 4:557, 558
Symplegades 6:777
Symposium (Plato) 1:56
syncretism 2:165; 9:1209–1210,
1278
Syria
sun god 1:140
wall painting of Gaia 4:542
Syrinx 1:105; 7:1001; 8:1076

Taakura 8:1018–1019
Ta'aroa 8:1019
Tabriz, painting of a giant
4:563
Tabu Eriki 8:1017
Tacitus 4:559, 560; 8:1027
Germania 4:529, 559; 9:1263;
10:1405
Tagliolini, sculpture of Jupiter
4:504
Tahmuras 6:749
T'ai Ho see Fu Hsi
Tailtiu 6:758
"Táin, The" ("The Cooley
Cattle Raid") 6:755
Tai Shan (mountain) 3:307
Tajin 10:1385
Taklimakan Desert 3:292
Taku Skanskan 5:589
Taliesin 1:105; 6:801
Talos 2:236; 6:849
Tammuz 1:24; 6:760–762
Sumerian equivalent see
Dumuzi
Tane 3:323; 8:1017
Tane Mahuta 8:1014–1015
Tangaroa (Kanaloa) 8:1015,
1016, 1017; 9:1271
Tanglewood Tales (Sterrett)
2:252
Tango-no-Sekku 4:518
Tan'gun, Legend of 6:792–794
Tanit (Tinith; Tinnit; Tint)
2:214, 268, 269
Tantalus 10:1349–1350
Tantalus (son of Thyestes)
2:185

Tantalus (son of Zeus)
cooks Pelops in a stew
3:337; 6:855; 8:1098;
10:1349–1350
eternally punished 5:608;
10:1349, 1350
Tantular, Sutasoma 10:1323
Tanum, rock carvings 9:1260
Taoism 3:303
gods 3:307–309
Taqqiq 7:911
Taranis 2:281
T'arhae 6:795–796
Tarhuhiawahku 7:938–939
tarot cards 3:401
Tarquinia, Tomb of the Bulls
10:1389
Tarquinius Priscus, Lucius
9:1233
Tarquinius Superbus (Tarquin
the Proud) 9:1233, 1292
Tarsus, worship of Mithras
7:893
Tartarus 3:337; 5:608; 7:1005;
10:1373
Tantalus punished in 10:1350
Taru 5:691, 693, 694, 695
Tatenen 9:1195
Taurobolium 2:237; 9:1218
Taweret 4:466; 5:613
Tawiskara 3:406
Ta'xet 4:447
Taygete 8:1131
Ta Yü 3:306, 308
Tears of Andromache (David)
5:625
"Tears of Niobe, The" (Scott)
7:987
Tecciztecatl 2:206
Tefen 5:703
Tefnut 1:83; 2:188; 3:320;
7:995
Tegeans 8:1053
Tegnér, Esias 4:556
Telamon 6:806; 7:928
Telegonus 2:265; 3:310–311;
8:1038, 1104
Telemachus 3:311; 8:1032,
1038
Telephassa 2:251
Telephus 1:16
Telepinu 5:693, 695
Telesto 1:105; 7:1000
Tellus 9:1231, 1238; 10:1399
Greek equivalent see Gaia
Temesa 3:390–392

temples
Anglo-Saxon 4:561
Baltic 2:226
Egyptian 4:467–469; 5:704;
9:1177–1178
Greek
on the Acropolis
2:175–177; 5:596; 7:975,
976
Temple of Amphiaurus
3:395
to Hera 5:657
Mayan 6:797, 800, 843, 847
Phoenician 2:269, 270, 271
Roman, to Diana 3:408, 410
Tenes 1:16
Tengri 3:295, 296, 299
Tennyson, Alfred, Lord,
"Tithonus" 10:1381
Tenochtitlán 2:202, 203, 204
Teocalli temple 10:1384
Teotihuacán
Temple of Quetzalcoatl
9:1200, 1202
and Tlaloc 10:1382, 1385
Teotihuacános 8:1048, 1049
Tepeu 6:799, 841
Terminalia festival 4:511
Terpsichore 7:921
Teseida (Boccaccio) 5:688
Teshub 5:693, 696, 697;
10:1398
Testament of Cresseid, The
(Henryson) 10:1390
Tethys 2:263
Teucer 6:805
Teutates 2:279, 281
Tezcatlipoca 2:203, 205; 4:445;
6:799; 9:1201; 10:1382,
1385
Thailand
creation myth 10:1327
deities 10:1324–1325
flood myth 4:521
rice myth 10:1327–1328
Thalestris 1:65
Thalia 1:134; 5:582; 7:921
Thaltybios 3:312
Thamus 7:900
Thamyris 7:926
Thanatos 2:149; 5:709;
10:1308
Thasus 2:251
Thebes (Egypt)
litany featuring Re 9:1208
sarcophagus lid from 4:552

Thebes (Greece)
founding of **2**:149, 251–253;
3:426
statues of Amenhotep III
6:853–*854*
temple of Heracles **5**:659
Tiresias and **10**:1372
Theias **1**:22, 116; **7**:929
Themis **7**:959, 960–961;
10:*1376*
as mother of the Fates **4**:493;
10:1435
as mother of the Horae
10:1435
prophesies concerning
Achilles **1**:14
Thens, the **10**:1325, 1326, 1327
Theocritus
and Pan **8**:1074
story of Polyphemus and
Galatea **4**:545–546
Theodosius I **9**:1294
Theogony (Hesiod) **1**:77; **3**:352;
4:488, 501, 564; **5**:641;
7:1005
and creation **8**:1020; **10**:1373
and the Fates **4**:493; **5**:598
and Hecate **5**:617
Hittite influence on **5**:697
and Nemesis **7**:959
and Nereus **7**:969
and Nike **7**:975
and Pandora **8**:1079–1081
Theophrastus
Characters **5**:667
and mandrake collectors
8:1127
theosophy **9**:1217
Thera (Santorini) **3**:325, *328,
330*; **7**:890, 951; **10**:1387
Thersites **1**:64
Theseus **10**:**1351–1355**
abduction of Helen **2**:275;
10:1354
and the Amazons **1**:62–63;
5:*687–688*; **8**:*1122*;
10:*1354*
and Ariadne **2**:154–*155*;
3:329, 358; **8**:1092;
10:*1352*–1353
cult of **3**:393
death **10**:1354
escape from the underworld
5:603, 665; **10**:1354
grave discovered **10**:1355
and Hippolytus **1**:116; **5**:689

as king of Athens **10**:1353
and Medea **6**:851;
10:1351–1352
and the Minotaur **1**:*78*;
2:154, *155*, **3**:327–329,
358; **5**:594–595; **7**:*887*;
10:1352–1353, *1355*
a metaphor **7**:*888*; **10**:1353
and Periphetes **10**:1351
and Phaedra **1**:116; **10**:1354
and Procrustes **3**:327;
10:1351
retrieves Minos's ring
10:1352
and Sciron **10**:1351
and Sinis **10**:1351
sword and sandals **10**:*1351,*
1352
Thesmophoria festival **3**:386,
389; **5**:585
Thespians **5**:660; **7**:923
Thespius **5**:660
Thetis **1**:*53*; **10**:**1356–1357**
and Achilles **1**:14, *15*, 17;
6:853; **7**:1000;
10:1356–*1357*
marriage to Peleus **1**:14;
7:1000; **8**:1097; **9**:1181,
1186; **10**:1356
rescue of Hephaestus
5:645–646; **10**:1357
shape-shifting **9**:1185–1186
Theuth **7**:900
Thisbe, Pyramus and **5**:679
Thjazi **7**:989, 990; **10**:1407
Thoibi, Khamba and
5:679–680
Thökk, Loki disguised as
2:222; **5**:677; **6**:818, 822
tholos **2**:162
Thompson, Bob **8**:1089
Thong, Prince **10**:1327
Thor **1**:34; **4**:504, *528, 535*;
9:1260; **10**:**1358–1365**
children **10**:1358
and Christianity **10**:1364
death **10**:1364
and Geirröd **4**:570; **6**:822;
10:1362
and Hrungnir **10**:1360–1362
journey to Utgard **9**:1249
and lightning **7**:950
and Loki **6**:818;
10:1358–1360, 1361, 1363
and the Midgard Serpent
10:*1362*, 1364

and Odin **8**:1031; **10**:1365
parallel gods **10**:1360
Jupiter **6**:788
people and places named for
10:1365
personality and attributes
10:1311, 1358
possessions
hall (Bilskírnir) **10**:1358
hammer (Mjöllnir) **4**:*568*;
6:818; **7**:991; **9**:*1264*;
10:1358–*1360*, 1362,
1363, 1364–1365,
1366–*1367*
and Skrymir **10**:*1363*
and Thrym **4**:568; **10**:1362
and Utgard-Loki **10**:1363
worship of **10**:1364–1365
Thórdarson, Sighvat **1**:57
Thoth **1**:*79*, 93; **3**:348; **4**:466;
5:608; **7**:*912*, 996
and the calendar **2**:255;
4:550
Thrace **2**:152
Amazons **1**:60
Three Fates, The (Mazzoni)
4:*496*
*Three Goddesses: Athena, Hera,
and Aphrodite* (von Stuck)
5:*656*
Three Graces (Canova) **5**:*585*
Thrúdgelmir (Prudgelmir)
2:233, 234, 246
Thrym **4**:568; **7**:991; **10**:1362,
1366–1367
Thrymskvida **10**:1362
Thucydides **1**:53
Thugga **3**:*353*
Thunderbird **10**:*1315*
thunder and thunderstorms
7:949
Thuringians **4**:557, *558*
Thutmose I **9**:1210
Thutmose IV **10**:1332
Thyestes **1**:48; **2**:182, 183–185;
6:855
thyiades *see* maenads
thyrsos **3**:414, 415, 418
Tia **4**:447
Tiamat **6**:*831*; **10**:**1368–1370**
battle with Marduk **3**:317,
338, 403; **4**:480; **6**:829–*830,
831*–*833*; **10**:*1368*,
1369–1370, 1430
creation myth involving
3:316–317, 422; **4**:480;

5:695; **6**:830, 833;
10:1368–1370, 1430
Tibaldi, Pellegrino, paintings of
Polyphemus **3**:354, *356*;
4:*567*
Tibet
apocalypse myth **1**:127
book of the dead **3**:373
reincarnation belief
3:374–375; **9**:1212
Tibullus, and household gods
6:808
tidal waves **7**:951–952
Tien-Mu **7**:949
Tiepolo, Giovanni Battista
Apollo and Daphne **3**:*367*
Diana and Actaeon **1**:*20*
painting of the Trojan Horse
8:*1089*
The Sacrifice of Iphigeneia
6:*742*
Venus Receives Mars **5**:*648*
Tifata, Mount **3**:410
Tiglath-pileser III **7**:875
Tigris River **7**:*868*, 983;
10:*1370*
Tikal **6**:*844*
tiles, monster-mask, Korean
6:*792*
Tilo **1**:40
Timaeus **8**:1103
Timaeus (Plato) **2**:180
Timagoras **4**:488
Timandra **6**:812
Timer Kazyk **3**:296
Tin (Tinia) **8**:1072
Tinaicaboga **8**:1018
Tinith *see* Tanit
Tinnit *see* Tanit
Tint *see* Tanit
Tintoretto
paintings
of Arachne **1**:*141*
Origin of the Milky Way, The
10:*1338*
*Vulcan Surprises Venus and
Mars* **1**:*114*
Tiresias **5**:607, 652–653, 669;
7:934; **8**:*1036*, 1043;
10:**1371–1372**
Tisamenus **6**:858; **8**:1053
Tischbein, Johann Heinrich,
painting by **2**:*169*
Tisiphone **4**:540
Tisna Wati **10**:1324, 1326
Titan (Algardi) **10**:*1373*

Titanomachy (Titanomachia; Olympians' war with Titans) 2:178; 3:335–336; 4:542–*543*, 565; 6:*785*; 7:*1003*; 10:*1374*–1378, 1432

Titans 4:564; **10:1373–1378**
  children of 10:1376
  derivation of the name *Titan* 10:1378
  formation 2:235; 3:318, 334; 10:1373
  war with the Olympians (Titanomachy; Titanomachia) 2:178; 3:335–336; 4:542–*543*, 565; 6:*785*; 7:*1003*; 10:*1374*–1378, 1432
  Zagreus and 4:444; 10:1378

Titan Struck by Lightning (Dumont) 10:*1374*

Tithonus 6:805, 806; **10:1379–1381**
  Eos and 4:484, *485*; 10:1379–1380, *1381*

"Tithonus" (Tennyson) 10:1381

Titian
  paintings by 2:160, 218–219
  Bacchus and Ariadne 3:*414*
  Danae 3:*363*
  Diana and Callisto 2:262, *263*
  Flaying of Marsyas, The 1:*135*
  of Venus and Adonis 1:*24*
  Venus Blindfolding Cupid 3:*343*
  Sisyphus 10:*1307*

Tityus 4:543; 6:815–816

Tiwanaku civilization 6:*726*–727

Tiwaz (Tiw) 2:261; 4:561; 9:1263
  see also Tyr

tjets 6:764

Tlaloc 2:203, 205, 209; **10:1382–1385**

Tlalocan 10:1382, 1385

Tlaloques 10:1382, 1384–1385

Tlaltecuhtli 9:1200; 10:1385, 1430

Tlingit people, sea monster 9:1274

Tmolus 8:1078

toga virilis 6:808

To Kabinana 8:1015

Tolland Man 9:*1262*

Toltecs
  myths, Kukulkan 6:843
  and Quetzalcoatl 8:1049; 9:*1201, 1202*

Tomam 10:1315

Tomo 3:347–348

Tonacacihuatl 2:206

Tonacatecuhtli 2:206

Tonatiuh 2:203, 205, 206, *209*; 7:*948*; 9:1200

tornadoes 7:*947*, 949–950

totemism 1:103–105
  Aborigines and 1:92; 2:194–*196*
  totem animals 1:103
  Central Asian 3:297, *298*

totem poles 1:*104*

Toxeus 2:167

trees
  banyan 8:1126
  baobab 8:*1126*
  Christmas 4:559
  cypress 8:1125
  Dryads and 4:440–442
  Hamadryads and 7:998
  laurel 3:367; 7:*1002*; 8:*1124*–*1125*
  myrrh 8:1125
  mythological
    Ished Tree 2:*190*
    of the Kikuyu people 8:1126
    World Tree 3:321–322, *323*; 5:631; 6:817; 7:*992*; 8:1029, 1126; 9:*1265*, 1286
    Yggdrasil 3:321–322, *323*; 5:631; 6:817; 8:1126
  oak 3:*407*, 409; 4:441, *442*, 560; 8:1125
    at Dodona 4:442; 8:1126; 9:1177; 10:1433
  pine 8:1075
  poplar 8:1117
  spirits 10:*1319*
  sycamore 7:*996*, 997

Trevi Fountain 7:*966*; 8:1150

Trickster gods 6:861
  Aboriginal 2:197
  African 1:44
  Greek, Hermes 5:672–*673*
  Maori 8:1015–1016, *1018*
  Native American 6:861
    Coyote 3:376, 404; 5:587; 7:*939*, 945

in Norse mythology 2:220; 6:821
  Roman, Mercury 6:861, 862

Trinity (Holy Trinity) 7:906; 8:1140

"tripartite ideology" 9:1233

Triple Goddess 4:455

Triptolemus 3:386, *387*; 4:506; 8:1020–1023; 9:*1229*

Tritogeneia *see* Athena

Triton 7:884; 8:1144; **10:1386–1387**

tritons 10:1387

Triumph of Neptune and Amphitrite, The (Poussin) 7:967

Troezen 8:*1130*, 1131

Troilus **10:1388–1390**
  and Cressida (Criseyde) 3:412; 10:*1388*–*1390*
  death 9:1166

Troilus and Cressida (Shakespeare) 10:1390

Troilus and Criseyde (Chaucer) 10:1388–1390

Trois Frères, Les, cave painting at 9:*1159*, 1161

Trojan Horse 1:50; 2:174, 273; 8:*1034, 1089*
  Helen and 5:637–638; 8:1034
  Laocoon and 6:802–804; 9:1174

Trojan War 5:595, *714*
  Achilles and 1:15–16, 50; 6:853
    the death of Hector 1:17–*18*; 5:622–*623*; 8:1095; 9:1166
    the death of Lycaon 9:1166
    the death of Memnon 6:853; 10:1380–1381
    the death of the sons of Priam 9:1164–*1166*
    the death of Troilus 9:1166; 10:1388
    dispute with Agamemnon 1:17, 19; 2:*169*, 174; 7:971; 8:1094–1095
    friendship with Patroclus 1:133; 5:622, 623; 8:1094, 1095; 10:1357
  Aeneas and 1:28–30
  Agamemnon and 1:49–50; 7:920
  Amazons and 1:63–64
  Apollo and 1:132–133; 5:622

Ares' involvement in 2:151–152; 3:411; 5:615, 655

Cassandra and 2:*273*; 10:*1418*

causes of 1:15, 49; 2:174; 4:490; 5:621, 636
  Momos and 7:903–904
  Zeus and 7:903–904, 960–961

death of Priam 9:1166–*1167*

Diomedes and 3:411–412

Greeks' conditions for winning the 8:1118–1119

Hector and 1:17–*18*; 5:621–625

Hecuba and 5:627

Hera's involvement in 5:709–710

Idomeneus and 5:713–714

Menelaus and 6:856–857

Nestor and 7:971

Odysseus and 1:50

Philoctetes and 8:1119–1120

Trojan Horse and the fall of Troy 1:50; 2:174, *273*; 5:637–638; 6:802–804; 8:*1034, 1089*; 9:1174

Trojans' wanderings after 1:31–33

Trojan Women (Euripides) 5:625
  and Ganymede 4:549
  and Hecuba 5:627, 628
  and Helen 5:640; 6:858; 8:1088

Trophonius, oracle of 7:*902*

Tros 4:548

Troy 1:28
  excavation of 1:49
  fall of 2:174, *273*; 5:626; 6:804
  Hector as the symbol of 5:623–624
  Laomedon and 6:*805*, 806

Troy (movie) 1:19

Troyan 10:1318

Troyens, Les (Berlioz) 6:804

Troy, Jean-François de, painting of Jason and Medea 6:*849*

Ts'ai Shen 3:308, 309

Tsao Shen 3:308, 309

Tsuki-Yomi 4:446

Tuatha De Danann 1:125, 126; 3:338, 364; 6:752, 754–755

Tuat 9:1206, 1208

Tubilustrium, festival of the 6:838

Tuby, Jean-Baptiste **6**:*814*

Tuccia **10**:1421

Tucumbalam **6**:842

Tula **9**:*1201*

Tulasi **8**:1125

Tuli **8**:1017

Tullus Hostilius **8**:1102; **9**:1233, *1234*

Tulúm, temple at **7**:*913*

Tu Matauenga **8**:1014, 1015

Tungus **6**:789

Tunisia, Sbeitla **7**:*881*

Turkey
  Aphrodisias **1**:*119*
  Midas's tomb **7**:880

Turks **3**:293–294
  creation myth **3**:297
  demons **3**:296–297
  gods **3**:295–296
  and life after death **3**:299
  shamanism **3**:294, 299
  writing **3**:293–294

Turms **8**:1072

Turner, J.M.W., painting of Lake Nemi **3**:*410*

Turnus **1**:*29*, 33

Tutankhamen **2**:190; **4**:*467*; **9**:1210
  treasures from tomb of **2**:*244*; **9**:*1194*
    canopic jars **1**:110–111
    funeral mask **4**:*460*

T'u-ti **3**:308

Tvashtri **10**:1426

twins **4**:*445–446*

Two Ladies **5**:703

Tyche **7**:961; **10**:1334, **1391–1392**

Tydeus **3**:411

Tylor, Edward Burnett **1**:69, 100–*101*; **7**:954

Tyndareos **3**:312; **5**:634, 655; **6**:811, 857; **8**:1033

Tyno Helig **4**:524

Typhon **3**:422; **7**:948; **10**:**1393–1394**
  birth **5**:651, 652
  defeat of **2**:171; **4**:495, 543; **10**:1393–1394, 1432–1433

typhoons **7**:949

Tyr **1**:36–*37*; **4**:*561*; **8**:1024; **9**:1260, 1261
  see also Tiwaz

Tyre
  and Astarte **2**:*164*
  and Melqart **2**:270

Tyro **10**:1307

Tzahui **10**:1385

Tzununiha **6**:842

Ubangui people **1**:45

Uga-no-Mitama **4**:517

Ugarit (*now* Ras Shamra) **2**:164, 210, *213*
  fertility goddess **4**:*501*
  sun god **10**:1343

Uighurs **3**:297

Uixtocihuatl **10**:1384

Uksáhkká **9**:1266

Uku Pacha **6**:728

Ulgan **3**:403–404

Ull **1**:*37*; **7**:990

Ullikummi **5**:697

Ulysses *see* Odysseus

Ulysses (Joyce) **8**:*1039*

Ulysses and Calypso (Giordano) **2**:*265*

Ulysses in the Cave of Polyphemus (Jordaens) **3**:*354*

Ulysses and the Cyclops (Tibaldi) **3**:*356*

Umay **3**:295, 296

Umbrians
  foundation myth **8**:1071
  religious rituals **8**:1072

Una **4**:456

Unas **9**:*1280*

"undead, the" **2**:238

underworld (land of the dead) **5**:606–607, 608
  Egyptian **2**:242, 244; **5**:608
  Greek (Hades) **5**:605, 606, *607*–608; **7**:991
    Cerberus and **5**:*601*, *607*
    Orpheus in **8**:*1058*–*1060*
  Inanna's descent to the **3**:348, 370–371; **5**:715–717
  Ishtar's descent to **6**:762–763
  Norse **2**:221–222; **5**:633, *676*–677; **7**:989

Uni **8**:1072

unicorns **1**:88, *91*

Union of Water with Earth, The (Rubens) **4**:*453*

Unkulunkulu **1**:40

Unn (Ud) **1**:26

Unsworth, Barry **6**:743

Upanishads **7**:*913*; **9**:1216

Uppsala **4**:529, 530

Ur **7**:869
  ancient flood **4**:*524*

Standard of **7**:*984*
  ziggurats **1**:66–67; **4**:*478*

Urania **7**:921

Uranus **10**:**1395–1399**
  and creation **3**:318, 334; **4**:501, 541–542; **10**:1396
  giving birth to Aphrodite **1**:112; **10**:1397
  overthrow and castration by Cronus **3**:334, *336*; **4**:565; **10**:1373–1374, *1395*, 1397
  in Roman mythology **10**:1399

Uranus (planet) **10**:1336, *1396*

Urash **1**:67; **7**:983

Urcaguary **6**:727

Urd **7**:*992*

Ureia **9**:*1273*

Urker **3**:296

Urshanabi **4**:572

Uruk **7**:869, *871*
  temple to Anu **1**:68
  temple to Inanna **5**:*718*

Usas **4**:484

ushabtis **2**:*244*

Usins **2**:228

Ustrecha **10**:1318

Utagawa Kunisada, painting of Amaterasu **10**:*1346*

Utgard **4**:568

Utgard-Loki **10**:1363

Utixo **1**:40

Utnapishtim **3**:371, 399; **4**:480, 519, 572

Uttu **4**:505

Utu (Shamash; Samas) **4**:*450*, 505; **7**:*870*; **9**:1211; **10**:1313, 1342–1343

Uxmal **6**:*840*
  Palace of the Governor **6**:843

'Uzza, al- **1**:137–138; **7**:909

Vafthrúdnir **2**:234

"Vafthrúdnismál" (poem) **10**:1430

Vainamoinen **4**:566

Vaishnavism **8**:1134

Vaisravana *see* Kubera

Vaitarami River **5**:608

Vakarine **2**:224, 226

Valhalla **3**:377; **4**:534; **5**:676; **8**:1026, *1030*
  the Valkyries in **10**:1400

Váli **1**:37

Valkyries **5**:613; **8**:1026; **10**:**1400–1403**

Raven Banner **10**:1401
  see also Brynhild

vampires **2**:*238*; **3**:371; **10**:1321

Vanaheim **4**:531; **10**:1404

Van Dyck, Anthony, painting of Marsyas **9**:*1258*

Vanir, the **1**:34; **4**:531; **10**:**1404–1407**
  gods included in **10**:1404
  gold sacrificed to **4**:532–533
  war with the Aesir **4**:531; **7**:988–989; **10**:1404–1405

Vanth **3**:401, *403*

Varah **1**:80

Varro, Marcus Terentius **7**:882

Varuna **6**:735, 738; **7**:*892*; **10**:1312

Vasari, Giorgio, *Mutilation of Uranus, The* **10**:*1395*

Vaya **6**:738

Vé **2**:234, 246; **8**:1026–1027

Vedas, the **6**:735, *737*
  Rig Veda **3**:422; **5**:672; **6**:735; **7**:892; **10**:1430
  and Yama **5**:608

Vedism **6**:735–736

Vejamate **2**:228

Velàzquez, Diego, paintings of Arachne **1**:*142*

Velde, Adriaen van de, *Vertumnus and Pomona* **8**:*1142*

Velnias **2**:228

Venezuela, Yekuhana people **10**:1315–1316

Venus **9**:1231, 1236; **10**:**1408–1411**
  and Adonis **10**:1409
  affair with Anchises **10**:1408
  affair with Mars **1**:*114*
  and Cupid **3**:340, *343*
  goddess of gardens **10**:1409
  Greek equivalent *see* Aphrodite
  the name of **10**:1409
  as one of the Penates **8**:1100
  and Psyche **3**:341, 342; **4**:*540*; **9**:1188, 1189–1190
  and purification **10**:1410
  temples to **10**:1409–*1411*
  Venus Erycina **10**:1410
  Venus Genetrix **10**:1411
  Venus of Mount Eryx, cult of **10**:1410
  Venus Obsequens **10**:1410

Venus Verticordia
10:1410–1411

Venus Victrix **10**:1411

Venus (planet) **10**:*1335*, 1336,
1410

Astarte and **2**:163

Maya and **6**:843

Quetzalcoatl and **9**:1201,
1202, 1203

Venus Blindfolding Cupid
(Titian) **3**:*343*

Venus de Milo **1**:*117*

Venuses (prehistoric figurines)
4:454–455, 502; **9**:1157,
1159

Venus of Laussel **3**:346;
4:455, 502, 503; **7**:*919*;
9:1228

Venus of Lespugue **4**:502;
9:*1157*

Venus of Willendorf **4**:455,
502, *503*; **9**:1157

*Venus and Mars, Victory and
Cupid* (Bordone) **2**:*149*

Venus Receives Mars (Tiepolo)
5:*648*

Verdandi **4**:497; **7**:*992*

Veronese, Paolo

Nemesis's Triumph Over Sin
7:*959*

painting of Juno **6**:*782*

Ver Sacrum rite **6**:835–836

Ver Sacrum ("Sacred Spring")
8:1071

Vertumnus **7**:999; **8**:1141,
1142

Vertumnus and Pomona (van de
Velde) **8**:*1142*

Vesta **10**:**1412–1415**

cult of **9**:1176, 1231

Greek equivalent *see* Hestia

vestal virgins and **9**:*1176*;
10:1412–1415

see also Lares; Penates

Vestalia festival **10**:1412

Vestal Virgin, The (Schram)
10:*1412*

vestal virgins **9**:*1176*;
10:1412–1415, 1420–1421

Vestal Virgins, The (Leroux)
10:*1414*

Vetis **8**:1072

Viani, Antonio Maria, painting
of Apollo **5**:*600*

Vichama **6**:727

Victoria **7**:977; **9**:1236

Victoria, *queen of Great Britain*
9:*1228*

Vídar **1**:37; **5**:632; **8**:1024

Vienna Codex **9**:1202

Vietnam

Confucianism **10**:1323

creation myth **4**:570

dragons **3**:*421*, 428

Vígríd **1**:126

Viking Brotherhood **8**:1073

Vikings **9**:1264

burial **3**:*377*

rune stones **10**:*1405*

shield bosses **10**:*1404*

see also Norse mythology;
Scandinavia

Vili **2**:234, 246; **8**:1026–1027

Villa of the Mysteries **7**:*932,
933*

Villca Umu **6**:731

Vilnius, Tale of the Castle of
2:226

Viracocha **3**:322; **6**:726–727,
728, 729

Virbius **3**:407–408; **5**:690;
10:1420

Virgil

and Charon **5**:605

and Elysium **3**:372; **5**:608

Georgics, and Orpheus **8**:1059

and Hephaestus **5**:646

see also Aeneid

virginity **10**:**1416–1423**

Daphne's wish for **3**:367

in Norse mythology, Gefjon
4:554

Virgins of the Sun (Allca
Cuna) **6**:*731*

Virgo Vestalis Maxima **10**:1412

Vishnu **6**:738

and creation **3**:316, 317, *319*;
6:736; **9**:*1268*

cult of (Vaishnavism) **8**:1134

and the flood **4**:*522*

many incarnations (avatars)
1:80, 93; **3**:316

and the tulsi plant **8**:1125

Visigoths **4**:557–558

Vitebsky, Piers, *The Shaman*
9:1289

Vogel, Hermann **6**:*810*

Vohu Mano (or Manah) **6**:747,
748

volcanoes **7**:*952*

Javan myth about **10**:1327

Voldemort **4**:448

Völsung **1**:34; **7**:974

Völsunga Saga **4**:537; **8**:1026;
10:1303, 1304

and Brynhild **10**:1401–1402

Völsungs, the **1**:34; **7**:974

"Volundarkvida" **10**:1425

Voluptas **4**:491

Völuspá (poem) **2**:246; **3**:320;
5:631; **6**:817, 818–820;
10:1315, 1430

Völuspá in skamma **6**:818

voodoo religion

evil devils **3**:404

souls **3**:370

Vortigern **9**:1252

Vos, Maerten de, *Rape of
Europa, The* **3**:*333*

Vrinda **8**:1125

Vritra **3**:422; **6**:736

Vrta **3**:364

Vulcan **7**:952; **9**:1231; **10**:*1425*

creation of the first woman
8:*1080*, *1081*

Germanic equivalent *see*
Wayland

Greek equivalent *see*
Hephaestus

Vulcanalia festival **4**:516

*Vulcan Forging the Arms of
Achilles* (Romano) **5**:*646*

Vulcan Surprises Venus and Mars
(Tintoretto) **1**:*114*

Wachilt **10**:1425

Wadd **1**:137, 138

Wadjet **4**:466; **5**:701, 703

Wagner, Richard

Der Ring des Nibelungen
1:127; **4**:537, 562; **7**:972

Siegfried **10**:*1300*

Wakan Tanka **5**:589; **7**:909, 939

Wakonda **5**:588

"Waldere" (poem) **10**:1425

Wales

dragon **3**:*427*

elves **1**:59

fertility of the land **4**:510

story of Arianrhod
10:1421–1422

Wanadi **10**:1315–1316

Wanadi II **10**:1316

Wanadi III **10**:1316

Wandjina **2**:*199*; **4**:523

Wang Mu **3**:308

Warka vase **5**:*715*

Warpalaurus **5**:*691*

Warrior's Husband, The **5**:688

wars, cosmic **3**:337–338

wasteland, story of the
4:508–510

Watts, George Frederic,
Minotaur, The **3**:*332*

Wayland **10**:**1424–1427**

Weber, Max **9**:1171–1172

weddings

in Greece **5**:667–668, 672;
7:976

Roman **10**:1416, *1417*

and household gods **9**:1224

see also marriage

weeks, days of the, Norse
2:260; **4**:537

Wen Ti (Wen Ch'ang) **3**:308,
309

Wepwawet **1**:111

werewolves **1**:104; **7**:*915*

Wheel of Life, Buddhist **3**:*404*;
9:*1212*

whetstone, in Norse myths
10:1362

White Buffalo Calf Woman
7:939, 941–942

Wicar, Jean Baptiste Joseph

paintings

of Electra **4**:*471*

of Jupiter **3**:*384*

Wildenmannlisloch **9**:1159

Willow-Flower **6**:795

Winaboozhoo **7**:939–940

Windigo **3**:406

winds

beliefs about **1**:77;
7:*948–950*; **10**:1313–1315

Greek and Roman *see*
Anemoi

Winged Victory of Samothrace, The
7:*977*

Winge, M.E., *Loki Bound*
6:*822*

Winter Thunder **1**:87; **10**:1311

Wise Crow (Ga-gaah) **7**:939

witches **1**:104; **7**:949; **9**:*1277*,
1288

Wodan (Woden; Wotan) **4**:561

and Mercury **6**:861

see also Odin

women

and the earth mother
4:452–454

in Greek society **5**:584, 668;
8:1091

Woolley, Leonard **4**:*524*

Works and Days (Hesiod)
  and the end of the world
    1:123
  and Nemesis **7**:959
  and Pandora **8**:1079,
    1081–1082
  and the Pleiades **8**:1130
Wounded Amazon (van Stuck)
  1:*65*
Wrathful Jupiter, The (Wicar)
  3:*384*
writing
  Canaanite **2**:266
  Egyptian **4**:467
  Mongol **3**:293–294
  Sumerian **4**:*476*; **7**:869–870
  Turks **3**:293–294
  types
    cuneiform **4**:*476*; **7**:870,
      877
    demotic **4**:467
    hieratic **2**:243; **4**:467
  see also alphabets
Wtewael, Joachim, *Perseus Frees*
  Andromeda **1**:*75*
Wuali **10**:1323, 1326, 1328
Wulfstan, *archbishop* **5**:632
Wurunkatte **5**:693
Wyndham, John, *Kraken Wakes,*
  The **4**:526
Wyrd **4**:497

Xanthikos **3**:*321*
Xanthus **1**:14, *18*, 85, *86*;
  4:538; **5**:612; **10**:1314
Xbalanque *see* Hunahpu and
  Xbalanque
Xecotcovach **6**:841–842
xenia **8**:1086
Xenodamus **6**:856
Xerxes I **3**:367; **6**:746
Xib Chac **6**:844, *845*, 846, 847;
  9:*1175*
Xipe Totec **2**:203, 205
Xisuthrus *see* Ziusudra
Xiuhtecuhtli **2**:205
Xochicalco, Temple of the
  Feathered Serpent **9**:*1199*
Xochipilli **2**:*205*
Xolotl, a twin **4**:*445*
Xquic **6**:845
Xuthus **3**:398

Yaghuth **1**:137, 138
Yajur Veda **6**:735
yaksas **8**:1139

Yakumama **6**:727
Yam **2**:166, 212, 268
  conflict with Baal **2**:213–214,
    267
Yama **4**:445; **5**:608; **6**:735, 738,
  739; **9**:*1216*; **10**:1310
Yami **4**:445; **5**:608
Yao **3**:305–306, 308
Ya'uq **1**:137, 138
Yazilikaya, Hittite carving
  5:*694*
years **3**:344
  cycles **3**:348
Yei deities **7**:*942*–943
yeks **3**:297
Yekuhana, sky people and
  creation **10**:1315–1316
Yen Ti **3**:305
Yer-Sub **3**:296
Yggdrasil **3**:321–322, *323*;
  5:631; **6**:817; **8**:1126; **9**:1286
  the Norns and **7**:992
  Odin and **8**:1029; **9**:1265
Yima (Jam; Jemshid) **6**:749
yin and yang **3**:302, *304, 421*
Ylvunda Kotta **1**:96
Ymir (Aurgelmir) **2**:234;
  9:1260; **10**:**1428–1430**
  creation myth concerning
    2:233, 246, 249, *250*; **4**:568;
    8:1026–1027; **9**:1247, 1268;
    10:1429
Ynglinga Saga (Snorri
  Sturluson) **4**:529, 536, 553,
  555
yoga **6**:737, *739*; **7**:*905*
Yolkai Estsan **4**:445
Yol Tengri **3**:296
Yoruba people **1**:41, *44*–45
  ancestor-worship **1**:*69*
Yuan Xiao **2**:*257*
Yum Kaax **6**:845
Yuri **6**:794
Yü Ti (Yü Huang Shang Ti)
  3:307–308

Zagreus **4**:444; **10**:1378
Zákinthos **2**:*182*
Zalmoxis **2**:269
Zaltys **2**:228
Zapotec, ball court **8**:*1047*
Zelotti, Giambattista, *Janus and*
  Juno **6**:*771*
Zelus **7**:975
Zeme **2**:224, 228
Zemi **4**:447

Zephyrus **1**:77; **3**:341; **4**:484;
  7:948; **9**:1188, *1189*;
  10:1314, 1315
Zetes **5**:*612*; **6**:779
Zeus **4**:504; **8**:*1133*;
  10:**1431–1438**
  aegis **10**:1433
  and Ares **2**:149; **5**:655
  and Asclepius **2**:161; **10**:1438
  battle against the Giants
    10:1432–1433
  birth **3**:326, 333, 335; **4**:542;
    10:1432
  and the birth of Athena
    2:170–171; **3**:*378*;
    10:1434–1435
  and the birth of Dionysus
    3:390, 413
  character **5**:594
  creations of, judged by
    Momos **7**:904
  and Cronus **3**:326, 335–336,
    337; **4**:565; **5**:601–602, 684;
    10:1374, 1431–1432
  defeat of Typhon **2**:171;
    4:495, 543; **5**:652;
    10:1393–1394, 1433
  early life **3**:*338*
    and Crete **3**:*324*, 326, 333
  and the flood **4**:*519*, 521
  and Hestia **5**:685
  and Hypnos **5**:709–710
  love affairs **5**:655;
    10:1433–1434
    Aegina **5**:654; **7**:927
    Alcmene **5**:654, 659, 709;
      10:1436
    Aphrodite **5**:655
    Callisto **1**:21; **2**:158, 262,
      263; **5**:653–654; **6**:826;
      7:1001
    Danae **3**:362, *363*; **8**:1110;
      10:1436–1437
    Electra **8**:1131
    Europa **2**:251; **3**:*333*; **4**:*492*;
      7:885; **8**:*1091*; **10**:1435
    Eurymedusa **7**:927
    Eurynome **10**:1435
    Ganymede **4**:548–549
    Io **5**:653; **6**:*781*; **8**:1076;
      9:1180; **10**:1435–1436
    Iynx **5**:655
    Leda **2**:275; **5**:634; **6**:*811,*
      812; **10**:1437
    Leto **5**:653; **6**:814–815;
      10:1435

Maia **8**:1131
  Mnemosyne **7**:899; **10**:1435
  Nemesis **7**:961
  Semele **3**:413; **5**:654;
    10:*1436*, 1437
  Taygete **8**:1131
  Themis **10**:1435
and Lycaon **6**:824
Nemean Games and **10**:1438
Olympic Games and
  10:*1437*, 1438
and Pegasus **8**:1112
and Prometheus
  9:1179–1181, 1182, *1183*,
  1246; **10**:1437
roles **10**:1433
  as god of guests **10**:1434
Roman counterpart *see*
  Jupiter
a sky god **10**:1310, 1311,
  1312
and Thetis **1**:14; **9**:1181,
  1186; **10**:*1356*
thunderbolts **3**:352, *353*
and Tiresias **10**:1371–1372
wife (Hera) **5**:650–*653*;
  10:*1435*
Zeus-Chthonios **5**:605
Zeus Horkios **8**:1137
Zeus Xenios **10**:1434
Zeus and Hera (Lens) **5**:*651*
Zhiva **10**:1318
ziggurats **1**:*66*–67; **4**:*478*
Zipacna **6**:846
Ziusudra (Xisuthrus) **3**:399;
  4:519, 520
zodiac **3**:348; **10**:*1339*
  Aries **1**:94, *95*
  Taurus **1**:94
Zoroaster **6**:745–746, 748
Zoroastrianism **6**:744, 745–749
  the afterlife **6**:748–749
  creation myths **3**:314;
    4:443–444; **6**:747, *749*;
    9:1268
  and dualism **4**:443–444
  evil spirits **3**:402; **4**:443; **6**:747
  monotheism **7**:908
Zuccari, Federico and Taddeo,
  Apollo and Daphne **1**:*105*
Zulu people **1**:45
Zurvan Akarana **6**:746–747,
  748